D0099162

FLIGHT 232

For my dear belongs
Helen Buck
Bartlett

FLIGHT

232

xoxo

A STORY OF DISASTER AND SURVIVAL

L. Gonzales

Laurence Gonzales

W. W. NORTON & COMPANY

NEW YORK   LONDON

Copyright © 2014 by Laurence Gonzales

All photos courtesy of the
Iowa Department of Public Safety
unless otherwise noted.

All rights reserved
Printed in the United States of America
First Edition

For information about permission to reproduce
selections from this book,
write to Permissions, W. W. Norton & Company, Inc.,
500 Fifth Avenue, New York, NY 10110

For information about special discounts for bulk purchases,
please contact W. W. Norton Special Sales at
specialsales@wwnorton.com or 800-233-4830

Manufacturing by Courier Westford
Book design by Daniel Lagin
Production manager: Devon Zahn

ISBN 978-0-393-24002-3

W. W. Norton & Company, Inc.
500 Fifth Avenue, New York, N.Y. 10110
www.wwnorton.com

W. W. Norton & Company Ltd.
Castle House, 75/76 Wells Street, London W1T 3QT

1 2 3 4 5 6 7 8 9 0

To My Son Jonas

CONTENTS

LIST OF ILLUSTRATIONS

FLIGHT 232

PROLOGUE

Gregory S. Clapper drove into the hills overlooking Sioux City, Iowa. He had taken the afternoon off to see a movie with his wife Jody and their two daughters, Laura, seven, and Jenna, five. Not only would he enjoy the warm nostalgia of seeing the original Walt Disney version of *Peter Pan*—"You can fly! You can fly! You can fly!"—but he and his family could escape the heat. Although the temperature on that Wednesday in July was only 80 degrees, a storm two days earlier had left the humidity steaming off the fields of corn and soybeans and made the day feel much hotter.

Tall and lanky, a youthful thirty-seven, Clapper, who taught theology, had an aspect both serious and gentle. That put people at ease and made him more effective as a college professor. It also helped him in his role as the chaplain for the 185th Tactical Fighter Group of the Iowa Air National Guard, which had its headquarters at the Sioux City airport. Clapper parked the car and stepped out with his wife and daughters. As the family crossed the hot paving toward the theater at the Southern Hills Mall, a sudden roaring whine turned Clapper's gaze skyward. Silhouetted against a bright sky, the dark form of a jumbo jet, low and tremendous, surged over the bluffs, its engines moaning in an odd uneven fashion. It appeared to be heading for the Sioux Gateway Airport. Clapper thought, "Jumbo jets don't land at Sioux City." As he watched, stilled, with one of his little girls' hands in each of his, the plane crossed Highway 20 and Morningside Avenue and flew over Sertoma Park. It then sank out of sight. His family was waiting, but for some reason Clapper continued to watch. They stood that way, this tableau of people beneath the sun, for what seemed a long time but was in reality only seconds. Then a reef of black smoke rose and coiled from beyond the industrial buildings, and a low, almost imperceptible, rumbling vibration shook the pavement. Clapper felt his face go clammy.

He led his family back to the car. His children may have been asking what was going on, but it was as if he'd gone deaf. He opened the car and put the key in the ignition. He turned on the radio. Music, static, voices. Then an announcer, with grim solemnity, said that he had received an unconfirmed report that a plane had crashed. Clapper felt "a crushing sensation" in his chest. He started the car.

"Jody, Laura, Jenna, get in the car," he said. His wife buckled the girls in, and Clapper fled the mall for the nearby entrance to Interstate 29. He drove south toward the airfield. Perhaps five minutes had elapsed since he saw the smoke, yet already a state trooper was blocking the exit to the field. Clapper pulled up, wondering how the police had arrived so soon. He rolled down his window and showed the officer his military ID. "I am a chaplain and need to be at the crash scene," he said.

"I don't care," the officer said. "No one is getting off here."

Seeing that arguing would not work, Clapper pulled the car another hundred feet down the highway and put it in park. "Jody," he told his wife, "take the kids back to the theater. There's nothing you can do here. I'll get my own ride back home." Then Clapper started running down the highway toward the column of grimy smoke that rose into the clear blue sky.

CHAPTER ONE

Martha Conant traveled regularly for her job with Hewlett-Packard in Denver. On that Wednesday, she was on her way to Philadelphia to work with a client. She didn't even look at her ticket until she was at the airport. She had been assigned a seat in the last row. She checked the display boards and saw that she could wait a couple of hours for a nonstop flight instead of this one, which was making a stop in Chicago. After thinking it over, she decided that she could get some work done on the plane. She kept her reservation for United Flight 232. The date was July 19, 1989.

Conant took the second seat in from the port* aisle in the center section at the back of the plane. She wore a black skirt and a pink sweater. She carried a briefcase and a purse. Conant anticipated people milling around the bathrooms behind her as flight attendants bustled about with their carts in the galley. She resigned herself to a few unpleasant hours and decided to lose herself in her work. Martha Conant opened her briefcase.

She didn't pay much attention to the preparations for departure and the takeoff: a routine flight among many routine flights. She glanced up once or twice at the in-flight movie, a documentary

---

* Looking forward from the back of the aircraft, *port* refers to the left side and *starboard* refers to the right.

about the Kentucky Derby or the Triple Crown—something about horseracing narrated by a sportscaster named Jim McKay. The in-flight meal was a "picnic" lunch, as United Airlines called it that summer: a plastic basket with a red-and-white-checked napkin in which were nestled greasy chicken fingers, a package of Oreo cookies, and a paper cup with a few cherries in it. Conant had just eaten one of the chicken fingers when an explosion shook her from her reverie. Her first thought was that a bomb had gone off, and her heart went into her throat. Susan White, the young flight attendant in the port aisle, went to her knees with an armload of drinks as the plane slewed to the right. Conant felt the tail drop out from under her as the plane began climbing.

At forty-six, Conant had curly auburn hair, brown eyes, and an endearing smile. She had hoped to have a good portion of her life ahead of her as well, yet she realized that she was likely going to die that day. Fear contracted within her torso like a black spider. After a minute, though, a steady male voice came over the loudspeakers and explained that they had lost the number two engine, the one that ran through the tail above and behind Conant's head. But, said the voice, the plane had two other engines, one on each wing. They could proceed to Chicago at a slower speed, a lower altitude.

Conant tried to think. She tried to convince herself of the reassuring story Dudley Dvorak, the second officer, or flight engineer, had broadcast throughout the cabin. Shortly after the explosion, the four flight attendants in her part of the plane disappeared into the galley to whisper among themselves. Now they emerged again with their carts and resumed serving drinks. Five rows ahead of Conant, Paul Olivier, a businessman who was also the mayor of Palmer Lake, Colorado, was surprised that the flight attendants continued serving. He would later recall Susan White, who would turn twenty-six that October but looked like a teenager. "She was just shaking," said Olivier, "visibly shaking." She asked if he wanted something to drink, and he ordered a vodka. White opened the liquor drawer on her cart. It was neatly lined with mini liquor bottles, all arranged by type. She selected a vodka, placed it on his table with a glass of ice, and closed the drawer. "Make it a double," said Olivier. When White pulled out the service drawer the second time, her shaking hand seemed to have a mind of its own, and the little liquor bottles scattered all over the floor. On her hands and knees, she gathered up the bottles as they rolled around on the carpet. Once she collected herself and her bottles, she stuffed them into the drawer any way they'd fit and slammed it shut. Observing her rattled state, Olivier told White, "It really looks like *you* need one of these."

Embarrassed, White hurried to the galley and started straightening up. She raised her eyes from her work and saw the head flight attendant, Jan Brown, coming toward her. From Brown's face, White knew that the situation was much worse than her friend Dvorak had let on in his announcement.

"Pick everything up," Brown said sharply.

In an attempt at levity, White said, "No second coffees?"

At forty-nine, Brown was a seasoned flight attendant, having been on deck a dozen years. At the age of twenty-one, she had been hired as the flight attendant on John F. Kennedy's family airplane, *The Caroline*. To Brown, Susan White seemed as eager and good-natured as a puppy. "Susan always half-laughed, half-cried," Brown said many years later. But Brown, who had been frightened out of her wits by something—White did not yet know what—was in no mood for joking. "No, no second coffees." White could see that she was dead serious and felt a knot form in her stomach. Brown, though technically her boss, liked to joke around. And they always served second coffees. White quickly began securing the galley, as Jan Brown briefed the three flight attendants and then hurried back up the aisle to attend to her duties.

From the way the flight attendants were moving, Conant knew something bad was happening. They looked pale and drawn. She had no idea that three of them were now holding hands and praying in the galley behind her. Conant's emotional system had come to full alert. She began taking more notice of her surroundings. A man sat on her left, a couple in their fifties or sixties on her right. She observed the last row of two seats against the window on her left. She saw a handsome young boy in a Chicago Cubs baseball cap seated in the window seat with a woman next to him. Conant was looking at Dave Randa, nine, and his mother Susan, forty. The rows were staggered, so mother and son were ahead of Conant with nothing behind them but White's jump seat, which faced the lavatories. A few rows forward on her right, Conant noticed that she could sometimes see the ground where she expected to see only sky.

Her thoughts went to her family. She had a husband and three children. Rich, twenty-one, was her eldest. He was living at home and working at a job. Her middle son, Rob, had graduated from high school a month earlier. At the age of eighteen, he had taken a trip out to California. Patrick, sixteen, was at home on his summer vacation.

"I was thinking about what a not-very-good mother I was," Conant recalled. "And what a not-very-good wife I was. And I found myself bargaining with God." She had become preoccupied with her job, "and my values had gotten screwed up." She felt that she had put a distance between herself and her family. "I was not as connected with my family as I could have been. And in those moments when I was contemplating not returning to my family, it became crystal clear to me that I needed to make some changes." She was not a religious person. She belonged to no church. God had meant nothing to her before. Yet she said, "It felt like a time of reckoning." She had earned degrees in both chemistry and computer science. She was smart and attractive and worked for one of the great high-tech companies. She thought she had it all, as she sat there with the realization gnawing at her that the plane she had boarded was likely going to crash. She desperately longed to be back on the ground, to feel her feet touching the soil. To see the green earth and feel the heat of summer. To hug her children, her husband.

The aft cabin around her remained quiet during those seemingly endless minutes. With the engine in the tail silenced now, she could barely hear the other two engines squalling on the wings so far away. The air seemed to be whispering over the skin of the plane. The man on her left was silent, within himself. Conant didn't know him. His name was John Hatch. He was forty-six years old. He later said that he went through "a lot of self reflection" in those moments. He thought of his family, his wife Sandra, and his three children, Sheila, twenty, Mark, fifteen, and ten-year-old Ryan. "I made a lot of promises that I probably haven't totally kept," Hatch said. He traveled extensively and worked hard. He silently promised to be a better husband, a better family man, to spend more time with his kids. "I knew we were in serious trouble." A man who liked control in his life, he was abruptly and utterly without it.

The man and woman to Conant's right were quietly whispering to each other. *What's going on? What do you think will happen?* And like Hatch, Conant went into what she called "this state of review," a kind of melancholy reverie in which she envisioned the life she would lead if she survived, a life in which she was devoted to her husband and children. Perhaps a life that included God in a more meaningful way. Her view of her life opened up to include her parents and her sisters, and she realized that she was mentally saying good-bye to each person she loved. She believed that her feet would never touch the earth again. And she was deeply saddened by what she felt was her imminent and final departure from this sweet old world. She said in her mind, "God, if you let me out of this alive, I'll clean up my act."

"Being in the last row of this massive tin can that didn't seem to be under control," she later said, "I was pretty convinced that I was not going to make it out of there."

About twenty minutes had passed since the explosion, and now the passengers could see a mesmerizing mist spraying out from the wings as the crew dumped fuel in what Conant now understood was a last desperate bid for salvation.

Far ahead of Martha Conant and nine-year-old Dave Randa, nearly two hundred feet away on the flight deck, William Roy Records, the first officer, was flying the Denver-to-Chicago leg of the trip in this McDonnell Douglas DC-10, with Captain Alfred Clair Haynes in the left seat acting as his copilot. Behind Records, Dudley Joseph Dvorak was manning the gauges and monitoring all systems. Jerry Lee Kennedy, thirty-six, a deadheading pilot, recently hired by

United Airlines, had been visiting the cockpit to observe the operations. One of the flight attendants came up to ask if he wanted to eat
his lunch in the cockpit or in his first class seat.

"You're welcome to stay up here," Captain Haynes told him.

"Thanks," Kennedy said. "But I'm tired of eating off my lap." He
said his good-byes to the crew, thanked the captain, and returned
to seat 1-A. In the row behind Kennedy, Walter Sperks, eighty-one,
and his wife Marie, eighty, were returning from a trip to the Colorado Rockies, where they had spent their honeymoon fifty-two years
earlier. Mass would be said for them a week later at 10:30 Wednesday morning in St. James Catholic Church on Fullerton Avenue in
Chicago.

On the flight deck, the crew ate lunch in their seats, as usual.
They were a bit more than an hour into the flight. The plane was on
autopilot. The trays had been cleared away, and Haynes was nursing
a cup of coffee. The crew had few tasks to perform until the time
came to descend into Chicago. "Everything was fine," Haynes said
many years later. "And there was this loud bang like an explosion. It
was so loud, I thought it was a bomb." He had no recollection of the
plane shaking or jerking, but he said he spilled his coffee "all over."

Records lurched forward and took the control wheel (called
the yoke), saying, "I have the airplane." The plane slewed hard to
the right. It shuddered and shook violently and almost immediately
climbed three hundred feet, as the tail dropped sharply.

Dudley Dvorak radioed the Minneapolis Air Route Traffic
Control Center in Farmington, Minnesota, saying, "We just lost
number two engine, like to lower our altitude, please."

While Records struggled with the controls, Haynes called for
the checklist for shutting down the failed engine. He asked Dvorak
to read it to him. The first item on the list said to close the throttle,
but "this throttle would not go back," Haynes said later. "That was
the first indication that we had something more than a simple
engine failure." The second item on the list said to turn off the fuel
supply to that engine. "The fuel lever would not move. It was bind-
ing." Haynes realized that the number two engine, the one that was

Aircraft N1819U on final approach. Note the daylight coming through the hole in the leading edge of the horizontal portion of the tail (near the tip). What appears to be a small white spot is actually a foot-long hole. Because no slats or flaps were deployed on the leading and trailing edges of the wings, the crew was forced to attempt a landing at twice the normal speed. *From the collection of Carolyn (Zellmer) Ellwanger*

mounted through the tail, must have suffered some sort of physical damage. The crew as yet had no idea what had happened, but Haynes felt a deep wave of concern surge through him. He knew that he was facing something far more serious than the loss of power to an engine. Events unfolded at lightning speed. Only a minute or so had elapsed since the explosion when Records said, "Al, I can't control the airplane."

The DC-10 had stopped its climb and had begun descending and rolling to the right. Records was using the control wheel to try to steer, but the aircraft wasn't responding. He was commanding the aircraft to turn left and to bring its nose up. The aircraft was doing the exact opposite. Haynes saw this dissonant image. It didn't take a pilot to know that something was dreadfully wrong. Moreover, the pilot can't wrench the controls to the stops in high-speed cruising flight. Doing so would cause the airplane to break apart. Records later recalled the startled look on Haynes's face: "I think the picture was worth a thousand words when he looked over at me and saw what was going on."

As the plane continued its roll, Haynes said, "I've got it," taking hold of his own control wheel. Both Records and Haynes now struggled with the failing steering, while Dvorak watched his instrument panel. Something bizarre was happening. The gauges were showing the pressure and quantity of hydraulic fluid falling lower and lower.

"As the aircraft reached about 38 degrees of bank on its way toward rolling over on its back," Haynes later explained, "we slammed the number one [left] throttle closed and firewalled the number three [right] throttle."

Dudley Dvorak recalled the moment: "I looked forward, and we're rolling to the right. I just said, 'We're rolling!' And Al, in one quick movement, took his right hand off the yoke and swatted the number one engine back, and on the way back up, pushed the other engine up and was back on the yoke in just a matter of seconds."

If Haynes had not decided—somehow, reflexively—to steer the plane with the throttles, the crippled DC-10 would have rolled all the way over and spiraled into the ground, killing all on board. After a few agonizing seconds, "the right wing slowly came back up," Haynes said. He had no idea what made him use the throttles. Nothing in his training would have suggested it. The DC-10 manual does briefly mention "the use of asymmetric thrust," but Haynes had no memory of having read that entry. He responded automatically, as a reflex that has remained a mystery to him ever since that day. Now as Dvorak watched his instruments, he was horrified to see the pressure and quantity of fluid in all three hydraulic systems fall to zero.

Before takeoff from Denver, Jan Brown stepped out of the galley amidships, between the forward and aft coach cabins, to check on the unaccompanied minors. She always worried about the children. Reviewing her manifest, she noted that a number of younger children would have no seats. Each would have to ride in someone's lap. As the chief flight attendant, Brown constantly worried about safety. She wore the white shirt and tie of her uniform, as always, but she chose the navy slacks over a skirt because she knew that the natural materials, cotton and wool, offered protection from fire. Anyway, skirts in an emergency would be disastrous. She was amazed that United even allowed the flight attendants to wear them and had told her superiors as much. Her sandy-colored hair was done in a bob, framing her face at the jawline. When a fireball came through the exit door beside her jump seat about two hours later, it would turn that hair into "a complete frizz job," as she would put it. But that hair would also save the smooth tan skin beneath, while her wool and cotton clothing would protect her body.

The flight had arrived in Denver from Philadelphia on the last leg of a four-day trip. The pilots had departed and a fresh crew came on board: Haynes, Records, and Dvorak. Brown planned to go up to the cockpit to introduce herself, but Haynes came back to the galley and beat her to it. The fact that he bothered to brief her had reassured Brown. Haynes said that he expected a smooth ride, maybe a few bumps on the descent into O'Hare International Airport. Brown decided to speed up the lunch service at the beginning of the trip in case the flight attendants had to strap in toward the end.

Brown liked everything to be perfect on her flights and lost no opportunity to make it so. If she was serving passengers in first class, she would write a personal note to each one and tuck it inside the white linen napkin on the service tray. She always called her work "the service," a nearly religious experience, as it must be: after all, she was about to be lofted among the clouds, miles over the earth, even as her congregation sipped coffee and broke bread, virtually in heaven itself.

In fact, Brown had become something of a legend among DC-10 cabin crews. In what she called "the old days," an elevator would take flight attendants down to a lower galley and into a splendid kitchen with convection ovens. Brown said that flights from Chicago to Boston were often so empty in those days that she'd bring her muffin tin and all the ingredients and bake for the crew down there, in what they called "the Pit."

"They're still talking about it to this day," she said, "about my blueberry muffins and my apple pancake." In addition, she said, flight attendants liked to go down to the Pit to smoke.

On July 19, 1989, Brown made the preflight safety announcement. She first carefully checked what she called her "demo card," the safety instructions found in the pocket on the back of every seat. She checked it because one time a fellow flight attendant had taped a piece of paper to her card. In big block letters, it said, "I NEED A DATE!" Satisfied that no one had tampered with her card, she told her passengers that she was well aware that many of them were seasoned travelers and had heard this briefing dozens of times. She asked those adults to set a good example for all the first-time fliers—and especially all the children—and to please pay attention. It was the bane of a flight attendant's existence: no one paid attention. Brown, however, took the possibility of a crash seriously. "I was really so concerned, because when we'd have to stand at our demo position, looking at our area of responsibility, I'd just look at people and think: I can tell who are the survivors, because they're the ones who are watching this. We know how to get out of the aircraft in sixty to ninety seconds, but you won't if you're in the dark."

Once the plane was airborne, Brown served the port side in the forward coach cabin, known as B-Zone, rows 9 through 20, while Rene Louise Le Beau worked the starboard aisle across the five-seat center section from her. Then Brown and Le Beau quickly began picking up the service trays so that everything would be put away early. As busy as she was, Brown couldn't help noticing Le Beau, thin, petite, and striking. Her hair was such a brilliant red, it always attracted attention. That day she wore a large navy-blue bow in it for a startling contrast. Both Brown and Le Beau lived in Schaumberg, Illinois. Le Beau, twenty-three, had not been scheduled for this flight. She was put on at the last minute because the plane was so crowded.

Brown had rehearsed how to react in any kind of emergency. She was acutely aware that a United Airlines 747 had lost a cargo door five months earlier. As the door had ripped away, it had taken a large piece of the cabin wall with it, and nine people were sucked out over the Pacific Ocean and never seen again. When Brown heard the explosion on this flight to Chicago, she went to the floor and held onto the nearest armrest, fearing that the cabin might lose pressure and suck someone out.

"I held on until we stabilized." Brown was about two-thirds of the way down her aisle. "And since I was facing aft, I could see Sylvia Tsao holding Evan." At thirty, Sylvia had her twenty-three-month-old son in her lap. "She was working up into panic, and I was like: 'No, I don't have panic on my airplanes. We're all calm. No matter what, we're all calm.'" For just as Haynes was captain of the ship, Brown was the captain of her cabins.

When she felt that the plane was stable, she stood up and went to Sylvia Tsao. In a low and gentle voice she said, "We're going to be okay." She explained about the plane still having two good engines. As she spoke, Dvorak announced the same thing: they would descend to a lower altitude and fly more slowly to Chicago. Jerry Schemmel, twenty-nine, sat in the next row back, across the aisle from Sylvia. He was the deputy commissioner for the Continental Basketball Association, which oversaw the teams that fed new players into the National Basketball Association. Schemmel watched Brown and Sylvia and baby Evan Jeffrey. He thought about how he would respond once the plane was on the ground: he would help them get out.

Brown crossed the aisle from Sylvia and Evan and reassured another woman "who looked petrified," in Jan Brown's words. Then the chime rang at her station, indicating that someone was calling on the interphone. From where she stood at the 3-Left door between B-Zone and C-Zone (rows 21 through 38), she could see most of her crew and knew that the call was not coming from any of them. From long experience, she knew that if the captain was calling her at this point in the flight, it could be nothing but bad news. She picked up the handset, and Dvorak's voice confirmed her fear. He told her to report to the cockpit. She hung up and walked deliberately up the port aisle, trying to look calm, "knowing that passengers were still watching, that they were very concerned. So I gave my best casual walk." As she passed into B-Zone, she walked by the Osenberg family, Bruce and Dina and Ruth Anne, holding hands with Tom Postle, a lay minister who had his thick old Bible out. The couple and the man with the Bible appeared to be in their forties or fifties. The girl Dina was college age. They were all praying together, heads bowed. The Wernick family, Pete and Joan with their six-year-old son Will, watched Brown go forward. Brown passed Joseph Trombello and Gitte Skaanes; Margo Crain, Rod Vetter, and Ron Sheldon in row 19; and Aki Muto in the next row back, a tall Japanese girl in a white blouse and light-blue skirt, college age, with jet-black hair, alabaster skin, and big dark eyes, like a doll's.

"I knocked on the door like we're trained to do," Brown said. "And they opened the door. And the whole world changed just in that instant when that door opened." She saw no panic, she said. "I just took it all in, but it was what was in the air. It was so palpable. I remember thinking: 'This isn't an emergency, this is a goddamned crisis.' And I don't usually talk that way."

As Brown spoke to me about this in her brightly lit modern kitchen over coffee and chocolate chip cookies, which she had taken out of the oven moments before, her face contorted in the agony of her remembered horror, and I could see the goose flesh rise on her forearms. Her face mobilized into anguished expressions, and at times as she recounted what she had gone through, her sad winter-brown eyes rolled heavenward as if she had reached the exasperating edge of all experience.

Dvorak sat at a console facing the starboard side of the aircraft. On his right was the cockpit door, which he had opened for Brown, and beyond that, the bathrooms, the first class galley, and then the first class cabin, A-Zone. As Brown stepped into the cockpit, holding onto the back of Dvorak's chair, she watched Haynes and Records each wrenching his control wheel back and to the left, as the plane tipped more and more steeply to the right. The two pilots were not only trying to steer with the yoke, they were each manipulating one of the throttles, as the plane repeatedly tried to roll over on its back.

"I could just feel the strength that was being put into that motion from both of them."

The words that were exchanged between Haynes and Brown have been lost to history. The Sundstrand model AV557B cockpit voice recorder operated on a thirty-minute loop, and after the explosion, forty-four minutes elapsed before the plane crashed. The first ten minutes and thirty-six seconds of the recording were overwritten during the last minutes of the flight. Nevertheless, as reported by both Brown and her captain, Haynes said, "We've lost all hydraulics."

As Brown explained to me, "I don't know what that means, but I do know that we are banking to the right and I am looking out Bill's window, and I'm guessing we're at thirty-seven thousand feet. And I think this situation means we could go straight down." Brown was not the sort to panic. But "I have not found the appropriate word that can describe the pure terror of an airplane that was always my friend, that I knew in the dark. If the lights went out and I was working in the Pit, people would lift the hatch and call down, 'Are you okay?' Oh, yeah. I could still keep working, because I could see in the dark. But now it's a metal tube, and it holds my fate. And there's nowhere to go. There's nowhere to hide."

She stepped out of the cockpit and shut the door behind her. She stood in the septic smell of the lavatories, "and I prayed, 'Oh, please, God, let me be someplace else.'"

Jan Brown and I sat on stools at her kitchen counter. At the age of seventy-one, she was trim and neatly dressed. She smiled wryly and said, "Oh, wow. Quick answer. Okay, one foot in front of the other."

She went on: "I told myself, 'Jan, you've got to be tough, you've got to be calm, and we can't let the passengers know.'"

She walked down the aisle, pale and shaken and almost in a stupor of fear and grief. She felt grief, she later said, for all the people, the children. "I couldn't look at anybody," she said. "It's like I just withdrew into myself, because I was working a plan, and I didn't want anybody to read the absolute terror in my eyes. I remember thinking as I came out of the cockpit and was walking through first class that the video was still running. So it gave the appearance of normalcy."

Brad Griffin could see her from his first class seat, 2-E. When Brown came out of the cockpit, he saw how ashen and defeated she looked. All her faith cast out, she'd been gutted. Griffin didn't know what he was seeing. He didn't realize that her captain had told her in no uncertain terms that the plane was going to crash. But he knew that her expression and demeanor signaled something dire.

As she passed through first class, she decided she could not call the crew together for a briefing. It would be too obvious to the passengers. She would talk to her flight attendants quickly and quietly wherever they happened to be. In the forward galley she caught Virginia Jane "Jan" Murray and Barbara Gillaspie, the two first class flight attendants, and began telling them what Haynes had said. Rene Le Beau came forward and caught part of what Brown was saying, and Le Beau's pale and childlike face took on a stricken look beneath her bright red hair. Then Brown added, "And I don't know how this is going to turn out, so be prepared." Then she squared her shoulders, forced herself into an attitude of professionalism, and began walking down the aisle, trying to figure out how to protect all those babies that people were holding in their laps. She proceeded to the aft galley and told Susan White, "Pick everything up."

And White responded, "No second coffees?"

At around the time Dudley Dvorak declared that November 1819 Uniform* had an emergency, Mark Zielezinski, thirty-six, the supervisor in the control tower at Sioux Gateway Airport, was attending a meeting in an office down in the bowels of the building that housed both the tower and the terminal. John Bates, an air traffic controller, was downstairs in the break room eating his lunch. In the tower cab—a fishbowl of glass atop the terminal building with a 360-degree view of the field and the surrounding land—the phone

---

* Like ships, all airplanes have to be registered somewhere. Those from the United States have a registration number (a "tail number") beginning with the letter *N*— hence, *November* in the International Phonetic Alphabet used in aviation. The tail number of the DC-10 flying as United Flight 232 that day was 1819U, so that plane was uniquely known as November 1819 Uniform.

had rung a minute or two earlier, and a controller from Minneapolis Center had alerted Sioux City to the fact that the crippled plane was coming. Bates heard someone holler down the stairwell that an emergency was on its way. He didn't think much of it. "An emergency at Sioux City was a daily thing," he said, because the airport was an Air National Guard base. The pilots of the A-7 Corsair II fighter-bombers were taught to treat most anomalies as emergencies to be on the safe side. In fact, two emergencies had already been declared that day. Bates packed up his lunch and went trudging up the stairs anyway. As he arrived, Kevin Bachman, the approach controller, heard a voice from Minneapolis Center come over his headphones.

"Sioux City, got a 'mergency for ya."

"Aw-right," Bachman replied in his native Virginia drawl. At twenty-seven, he was a fairly new air traffic controller, having joined the Federal Aviation Administration (FAA) at the end of 1985 and having been rated as a controller for Sioux City in May of 1989. Bachman listened to the breathless, speedy voice of the controller trying to bark out the information that had clearly scared him out of his wits. "I gotta, let's see, United aircraft coming in lost number two engine having a hard time controlling the aircraft right now he's outta twenty-nine thousand right now on descent into Sioux City right now he's—he's east of your VOR* but he wants the equipment standing by right now."

Bachman could see United Flight 232 on his radar screen, a bright phosphorescent target with the plane's altitude and an identifying transponder code beneath. "Radar contact," he said.

Zielezinski picked up the phone and called downstairs to Terry Dobson, the manager of the tower. Dobson hustled upstairs. Once he understood the situation, he reported the emergency to the regional office of the FAA in Kansas City. Kansas City in turn notified FAA headquarters at 800 Independence Avenue in Washington, D.C., across the street from the Smithsonian Institution and the National Mall. Then someone at the tenth floor command center

---

* VOR is a radio navigational aid. The initials stand for VHF omnidirectional range.

at FAA headquarters telephoned Terry Armentrout, the director of the Office of Aviation Safety at the National Transportation Safety Board (NTSB), located two floors below in the same building. The NTSB is responsible for investigating all air crashes, and from the sound of it, this emergency would soon fall into that class of events.

As Bachman listened for word from United Flight 232, the voice of the Minneapolis controller came on the air again sounding more rattled than before. "He's havin' a hard time controllin' the airplane right now and tryin' to slow down and get to Sioux City on a heading right now, as soon as I get comfortable, I'll ship him over to you, and he'll be your control."

"Awright," said Bachman.

Then Al Haynes said, "Sioux City Approach, United Two Thirty-Two heavy,* we're out of twenty-six, heading right now is two nine oh, and we got about a five-hundred-foot rate of descent." He meant that the plane was passing through twenty-six thousand feet, traveling roughly west, and losing five hundred feet of altitude every minute. The handoff from Minneapolis Center was complete.

Bachman gave 1819 Uniform the standard briefing, including weather, barometric pressure, and a compass heading to fly to reach the airport. He told Haynes that he could expect to land on Runway 31.†

Haynes responded, "So you know, we have almost—no controllability. Very little elevator, and almost no ailerons, we're controlling the turns by power. I don't think we can turn right, I think we can only make left turns." Then he paused and corrected himself. "We can only turn right, we can't turn left."

Bachman said, "United Two Thirty-Two Heavy, understand, sir, you can only make right turns?"

---

* The word *heavy* reminds pilots of smaller aircraft that they can be upset by the wake of larger planes.

† Runways are named for the cardinal direction they face. If a pilot is landing on Runway 31, his compass will say 310 (North being 360). If a pilot is landing in the opposite direction on the same runway, the compass will read 130, so it would then be called Runway 13, even though it's the same stretch of concrete.

"That's affirmative."

An airplane is a submarine of the air. Like a boat, it is steered by rudders, but since it moves in three dimensions, it has rudders for moving left and right (yaw), rudders (called elevators) for moving the nose up and down (pitch), and even rudders (called ailerons) to roll the airplane into a bank when it turns. On small planes all of those movable surfaces can be controlled by cables, a direct physical connection between the pilot's hands and the controls. On jumbo jets, the control surfaces are so large and the airstream produces forces so great that the power of human muscle cannot overcome them. Hydraulic power is needed to move those surfaces.

If the driver of a forklift wants to lift a thousand-pound pallet, he moves a lever and the object rises off the ground. But the lever isn't moving the pallet. The lever turns on the hydraulic power. The same is true of the DC-10. When the pilot moves the yoke, he is moving cables that move switches that turn on the hydraulic power to move the rudder or elevators or ailerons. Hydraulic fluid, not fuel, is what keeps the plane flying in a controllable fashion. If the plane runs out of fuel, the crew can deploy a wind-driven generator into the airstream to power the hydraulic system and then continue to fly as a glider. Without fluid in the hydraulic lines, Captain Haynes and crew were unable to steer with the precision needed to land safely. They had no way to extend flaps or slats to slow the airplane for landing. And even if they managed to get the craft on the ground, they had no brakes. Although most of the passengers did not yet know it, the great ship known as November 1819 Uniform was going to crash.

Bachman could see that on its present track, the plane would wind up eight miles north of the airport. It would also fly over the most populated part of Siouxland, as the locals call the neighborhoods at the confluence of the Missouri River, the Floyd River, and the Big Sioux River. Siouxland encompasses parts of Iowa, South Dakota, and Nebraska, and its spirited and capable people are used to responding to emergencies. Because the rivers flood with grim predictability, because farming involves chemicals and chemical plants explode, and because calamity has always seemed bent on routinely visiting Siouxland in one form or another, the people there pride themselves on being able to face adversity. It was as if Siouxland comprised a cargo cult of sorts and had been planning for the arrival of United Flight 232 for years. The Woodbury County Disaster and Emergency Services (WCDES) had actually simulated the crash of a jumbo jet during training.

As Bachman watched, he could see that the DC-10, rather than heading for Sioux City, was now heading back around into the airspace controlled by Minneapolis Center. He picked up the phone and called the controller out in Farmington.

"Yeah," Bachman said, "that United, he can only make right turns. I'll have to jockey him back around to the right into your airspace, too—"

"Yeah, you've got him for anything you need."

As Bachman watched the radar track, he decided to adjust the heading and told Haynes, "United Two Thirty-Two Heavy, fly heading two-four-zero, and say your souls on board."

"Say again," Haynes said.

"Souls on board, United Two Thirty-Two Heavy." Bachman was asking how many lives were at risk.

"We're gettin' that right now," Haynes said.

A little less than a minute later, Bachman asked again. "United Two Thirty-Two Heavy, say souls on board and fuel remaining."

"We have thirty-seven six fuel," Haynes said, "and we're countin' the souls, sir." He meant that the plane had 37,600 pounds of fuel in its tanks. (Fuel on planes is measured in pounds, not gallons or liters.)

Dvorak heard a knock on the door and opened it to find a first class flight attendant, Jan Murray, standing there. Her eyes grew wide as she saw the state of affairs on the flight deck. Without entering, she called out that a United DC-10 flight instructor was on board and had offered to help.

Haynes said, "Okay, let him come up." Murray backed away fast, shaking from the shock of what she'd seen.

Addressing Bachman on the radio, Haynes began, clipped, staccato, breathless, "We have no hydraulic fluid, which means we have no elevator control, almost none, and very little aileron control. I have serious doubts about making the airport. Have you got some place near there that we might be able to ditch? Unless we get control of this airplane, we're going to put it down wherever it happens to be." In fact, as the flight data recorder would later show, in the first seconds after the explosion, the autopilot tried to correct the upward pitch of the aircraft with the elevator, and the controls responded. As the plane rolled right, either Records or the autopilot moved the yoke to the left to lift the left aileron and stop the roll as well. About twelve seconds after the explosion, though, the horizontal stabilizer started to move down and then froze. One minute and five seconds after the explosion, the nose pitched up again, and in response Records moved the elevator for the last time. The left inboard elevator went from –3.94 degrees to –1.55 degrees and then remained there for the rest of the trip. The crew was then completely disconnected from all flight controls.

The airplane, Bachman realized, was going to crash. He had no idea how to respond. He said, "United Two Thirty-Two Heavy, roger, uh, stand by one."

In the control tower, John Bates was still watching from the sidelines, waiting to see if his services would be needed. When he heard Al Haynes's last transmission, he thought, as he said later, "Wow, this is an honest-to-goodness real emergency instead of what we considered to be play emergencies with the [Air] National Guard." And now with the hair rising on the back of his neck, Mark Zielezinski rearranged the duties of his air traffic controllers to meet the demands of the situation. Dale Mleynek worked ground control, directing traffic on the surface of the airport. Charles Owings controlled aircraft in the local area, for 1819 Uniform was not the only airplane in the sky around Sioux City that day. And Zielezinski put John Bates on flight data, which is a catchall position for such tasks as delivering clearances to pilots and updating the recorded broadcast of the weather. The ground controller can normally handle flight data, but because of the emergency, Zielezinski wanted the two jobs separated. As the person on flight data, it would fall to Bates to determine what level of emergency response to request from the agencies in the area, such as fire departments and ambulance services.

The airport was already on Alert Two status, as it had been since word first arrived that the crippled plane was on its way. Now with Captain Haynes announcing that he might ditch, Bates immediately turned to Bill Hoppe, the new tower supervisor, a fifteen-year veteran as an air traffic controller. Bates trusted his judgment. "Alert Two or Alert Three?" he asked Hoppe. "There's nothin' in the books for this one. They say they're going to put the plane down wherever they can."

"I don't know," Hoppe said. "What do you think?"

Alert Two means that emergency equipment will be put on the field, but that might be for any sort of emergency. The plane itself might not be in trouble. Instead, someone on board the flight might be having a heart attack. Alert Two does not anticipate a mass casualty. Alert Three means that a plane has crashed or is about to crash. Because Woodbury County, home of Sioux City, had a disaster plan that involved an emergency response from all the surrounding communities of Siouxland, the two controllers reasoned that declaring Alert Three was the most expedient way of rapidly calling as much emergency equipment as possible to the field. Bates was in a real bind because he had to make the call. If he allowed Alert Two to remain in effect and people survived the crash, there might not be enough rescuers and equipment to take care of all the injured. Lives could be lost. If, on the other hand, he elevated the status to Alert Three and the flight landed uneventfully, the 270 organizations that responded would have wasted time and money for nothing. "I would have been in real hot water," Bates said.

But at this, the moment of truth, Hoppe and Bates looked at each other and blurted it out in unison: "Alert Three!"

"We broke a rule was what we did," Bates told me later. "The call was made simply because the plane was out of control. It was going down. We just didn't know where."

From the time Haynes told Bachman the condition of his plane to the moment Bates and Hoppe made the decision to call Alert Three, only fifteen or twenty seconds had passed. Then Bates used the special phone line to the fire department dispatch center in downtown Sioux City to explain the situation. Those dispatchers, in turn, notified other emergency agencies. In addition, Gary Brown (no relation to Jan), director of WCDES and an emergency medical technician by training, "escalated it above the normal Alert Three," as he later said, requesting even more equipment than the emergency plan called for. Sirens took up a wailing chorus all across the corn-green countryside, as eighty pieces of emergency equipment from forty communities began converging on the Sioux City airport.

Since the field was an Air National Guard base, its equipment and the airport fire and rescue vehicles were the first to move. All of the emergency services involved in disaster planning had been assigned positions where they would wait in case of an emergency on the airfield, and the heavy equipment now went roaring across the field to those locations, blowing diesel smoke. Mleynek coordinated the movement of the vehicles on the ground. The Air National Guard fire-fighting equipment used no sirens or lights. As the base fire chief, James Hathaway, put it, "There is no one out there, just jack rabbits and us."

At about 3:40 the emergency dispatcher had called the Marian Air Care helicopter, known as MAC, that was on standby on the pad at Marian Health Center. He had alerted the crew to go to the pad immediately and then ordered the helicopter to take off and fly to the home of Dr. David Greco, land there, and pick him up. Chuck Owings, the local controller up in the tower, called MAC, too, and asked its pilot to stand off about three miles from the field when he returned and wait in loitering flight for the crippled plane to come in. By that time, emergency vehicles from the nearest communities had begun to arrive and line up at the main airport gate. Gary Brown drove his truck full of emergency medical equipment and technicians out onto the field. Bates could see Gary's big white Ford trucks from above, as Mleynek cleared them into position. They parked on the ramp* with immediate access to the runways. They would be among the first to respond if the plane made it to the airport. As Bates looked out the window of the tower, he felt an acute sense of alarm. The landscape below, normally vacant and dead quiet at this time on a summer day, steadily filled with emergency equipment.

In the meantime, across the sunlit room, Jimmy Weifenbach was bringing in six Air National Guard A-7s that had been out on maneuvers over Kansas. When Zielezinski split the radar coverage in two, he gave Kevin Bachman his own scope for handling only United Flight 232. The approach controller would normally handle all traffic out to about forty miles, but that day, everything but United Flight 232, including the A-7s, went to Weifenbach, who would hand them off to Owings for the last minute or two of flight.

Also, the supervisor of flying for the Air National Guard, Dennis Nielsen, was talking to the pilots of the A-7s and listening to the transmissions from the tower. Although he couldn't hear what Captain Haynes was saying, because his military radio operated on a different frequency, he realized that an emergency was under way and had directed the A-7s to return to base.

The first two A-7s landed to the northwest on Runway 31. They taxied into the de-arm area at the end. Dale Mleynek called Al Smith, the lead A-7 pilot, and said, "Bat† Three-One, Sioux City Ground. After de-arming, hold short runway three-five at Lima." (Taxiway Lima is the one labeled with the letter *L*.) Smith and his wingman Romaine "Ben" Bendixen began to realize that they were in a bad place, indeed. Mleynek transmitted the same words again about forty-five seconds later, and Smith responded, "Three-One, Wilco."

Within two minutes, Mleynek ordered the fire equipment to be shuttled off to the northwest side of the field, since the DC-10 had

---

* The words *ramp* and *apron* are used interchangeably to refer to the paved areas at an airport that are neither runways nor taxiways.
† According to Colonel Lawrence Harrington (retired), a lieutenant colonel named Gordy Young gave the 185th Tactical Fighter Group the call sign "Bats."

no brakes. As the trucks moved off, Smith called Mleynek and said, "Ground, Bat Three-One, we're ready to taxi back now."

Mleynek gave them permission to taxi and added, "Bat Three-One use caution for two emergency vehicles just off the right side of Taxiway Lima."

The fire-fighting equipment pulled off the taxiway onto the grass to wait. As other emergency vehicles came onto the field, Mleynek directed them toward their staging positions. Smith called to make sure that he was cleared to cross Runway 17-35, and then proceeded to the ramp, where the two fighter-bombers passed Gary Brown's white truck and the KTIV Channel 4 News cameraman, Dave Boxum, who was setting up his equipment outside the fence.

Al Smith and Ben Bendixen climbed down from their cockpits and began crossing the Air National Guard ramp. "I was walking northbound slowly with my head down somewhat," Bendixen recalled, "not anticipating that United 232 was going to land as soon as it did." He thought that it would approach from the south and land on Runway 31. He couldn't see the northern part of the field because his view was blocked by the National Guard buildings and a group of old World War II hangars. He walked along in the heat, carrying his helmet, heading for the room they called maintenance control, where they would shed their flight gear. Then he heard—and almost felt—a sound that he would never mistake for anything else, and he turned to see the rising smoke and fire.

CHAPTER TWO

During boarding in Denver, Jan Murray had been in A-Zone, first class, helping people to their seats and hanging up coats. She had noticed Rene Le Beau, the newest hire, who was helping out in first class. Murray would always remember Le Beau. "I remember how pretty she was, and I remember her hair in particular. It was strawberry blonde and very curly and beautiful." Once the flight had taken off and the lunch service was under way, Murray, a former registered nurse who was thirty-four at the time and had eleven years of seniority as a flight attendant, chatted with the younger woman. Le Beau was excited because she was going to be with her boyfriend that weekend and they were talking about getting married. The two women laughed together, enjoying the flight.

Indeed, they sensed a festive atmosphere in first class that day. Murray, a thin, youthful woman with bleached silver hair, had stopped to talk with William Edward and Rose Marie Coletta Prato and Gerald Harlon "Gerry" Dobson and his wife Joann from Pittsgrove Township, New Jersey. All four were dressed in Hawaiian clothes, laughing and enjoying the first class luncheon, the perfect ending to their trip to Hawaii. "They stay on my mind," Murray said more than two decades later. "They were so having a good time." The ladies were dressed in muumuus and their husbands wore Hawaiian shirts. "It was obvious they'd had a wonderful vacation. They were just very pleasant people. I think about them all the time."

After lunch, Murray was cleaning up, standing in the galley between first class and coach, bending down to put a tray into the cart, when the engine exploded. Murray went to the floor reflexively. "It just was so loud that there's no way to describe how loud it was. The plane was shaking pretty fiercely," she recalled. "The plane was making sounds that I had never heard before." When I asked Murray to describe those sounds, she made a noise like a siren wailing. She was hearing the hydraulic motors pumping all the fluid out of the system and overboard, as Dvorak, up in the cockpit, watched his gauges fall to zero. "It was very obvious that something was very, very seriously wrong."

With her heart sinking, Murray continued cleaning up after lunch. When Jan Brown emerged from the cockpit and told her and Barbara Gillaspie and Rene Le Beau that they had lost all hydraulics, it merely strengthened her conviction that she was going to die. Murray had been serving lunch to two deadheading United pilots in the last row of first class on the starboard side. Peter Allen was in uniform. Dennis Fitch, by the window, wore civilian clothes. Murray had learned that Fitch was a DC-10 instructor at the United training facility in Denver. He was on his way home for the weekend. Fitch had first noticed Murray when she served his lunch. He had heard her lilting southern accent as the three chatted pleasantly.

Fitch was the oldest of eight siblings, and as such he had developed what he called "people radar." He could spot a distressed person at a hundred yards, as he liked to say. Now he saw that Murray looked grave and worried as she rushed past. Fitch reached out, touched her arm, and stopped her. Murray leaned down. "Don't worry about this," he told her. "This thing flies fine on two engines. We just simply need to get to a lower altitude, and we're gonna be fine."

She leaned in closer and fixed him with a penetrating gaze. According to Fitch's account, she said, "Oh, no, Denny." She spoke softly so as not to be overheard. "Both the pilots are trying to fly the airplane, and the captain has told us that we have lost all our hydraulics."

Fitch stared at her for a moment. He knew that wasn't possible, but as he later put it, "A flight attendant is not a pilot." She could not be expected to know anything about airplanes. "DC-10s *must* have hydraulics to fly them. Period."

"Oh, that's impossible," Fitch told Murray. "It can't happen."

"Well, that's what we're being told," Murray said.

"Well, there's a backup system."

"We're being told that that's gone too."

Fitch thought about that for a moment and said, "Well . . . I don't think that's possible, but . . . would you go back to the cockpit. Tell the captain there's a DC-10 Training Check Airman back here. If there's anything that I can do to assist, I'd be happy to do so."

Fitch watched Murray go forward as quickly as she could without alarming passengers. Fitch had been on full alert for a while now, and this new development was baffling and more than a little alarming. When the explosion occurred, he had finished his lunch and was having that second coffee that Susan White, tongue in cheek, had asked a nonplussed Jan Brown about far in the back of the plane. "The whole fuselage went very sharply to the right," Fitch recalled. "That coffee cup is now empty. Its contents are in the saucer, and it's all over the table linen. And my rear end, which is sitting in the middle of a leather seat, is now up against the arm rest to the left. It was abrupt and violent."

As a Training Check Airman, or TCA, Fitch had conducted five days of training with a group of DC-10 pilots in Denver during the past week. When the engine exploded, he turned to Peter Allen and said, while mopping up coffee, "It looks like we lost one." Fitch then felt the plane begin making a series of strange excursions across the sky, first up, then down and to the right in long, loopy spirals, and up and down again and again, like a boat on uneasy seas. With one engine out, they were supposed to be going down, not up. The right turns made it seem to him as if the number three engine on the right wing had failed, causing drag on that side. But the announcement said that number two quit. As a TCA, Fitch was exposed to every conceivable emergency, week in and week out, yet nothing he saw or heard made sense.

More than twenty years after Fitch had sent Jan Murray to the cockpit to offer his services, she described her experience there. "I went to the cockpit, knocked on the door. It flew open." As she tried to describe the horrifying scene in there, she stuttered and stammered with the pain of remembering. "Th-th-the pilots were struggling so, it was just, it was incredible, the struggle that they were—just the visual of it was just—*so frightening*. It was like they were struggling to hang onto the controls. So I just hollered in there, I said, 'You have a Training Check Airman back here if you need him.'"

Haynes didn't turn around. He called out, "Okay, let him come up."

"Immediately I closed the door, and trying to be as calm as possible, I walked back through the first class cabin and I leaned down to Denny and I told him, 'They want you up there.'"

Fitch reached the cockpit, still thinking that the flight attendant didn't understand the situation. But as the door opened, he recalled, "the scene to me as a pilot was unbelievable. Both the pilots were in short-sleeved shirts, the tendons being raised in their forearms, their knuckles were white." As he closed the door behind him, Fitch's eyes flicked over all the instruments and switches on Dvorak's panel. He clearly saw that the motor pumps and rudder standby power were both armed. No rudder standby light. No bus ties (similar to circuit breakers) were open, the navigational instruments were working normally, and the plane had electrical power. Someone had already deployed a generator driven by air that was meant to pump hydraulic fluid in the event that the regular engine-driven pumps weren't working. But the hydraulic gauges read zero and the low-pressure lights were on.

The plane was porpoising in a slow cycle, up and down, hundreds of feet every minute, even while both Haynes and Records fought the yoke to no effect. On the radio, Dvorak was pleading for help from the United Airlines maintenance base in San Francisco, while

Records, breathing hard from his effort, used his knee to help force the yoke forward during one of the aircraft's uncontrollable climbs.

Fitch later said, "The first thing that strikes your mind is, Dear God, I'm going to die this afternoon. The only question that remains is how long is it going to take Iowa to hit me? That's a very compelling moment in your life. Life was good. And here I am forty-six years old and I'm going to die. My wife was my high school sweetheart, loved her dearly, and I had three beautiful children." The last thing his wife had said to him was, "I love you, hurry home. I love you." Fitch turned away from Dvorak's gauges and saw that Records didn't even have his shoulder harness fastened. Fitch leaned over him and fastened it.

Haynes had hoped that Fitch would know some secret trick to bring the plane back under control, perhaps a hidden button that only flight instructors get to know about that would make everything all right. Dvorak was telling United Airlines Systems Aircraft Maintenance in San Francisco, known as SAM, that they needed assistance and needed it quickly. When Fitch entered the cockpit and saw the hydraulic gauges reading zero, his reaction was similar to that of the United engineers at SAM, who were telling Dvorak that what he had reported was impossible. Having hydraulic fluid in the lines is a necessary condition of flight in a DC-10. After a complete loss of hydraulic power, the plane would have no steering. It would roll over and accelerate toward the earth, reaching speeds high enough to tear off the wings and tail before the fuselage plowed into the ground. Or it might enter into an uncontrollable flutter, falling like a leaf all the way to the earth, to pancake in and burst into flames. Under no circumstances would it continue to fly in any controllable fashion. To an expert pilot's eye, what Fitch saw was like watching someone walk on water. Haynes later said that Fitch "took one look at the instrument panel and that was it, that was the end of his knowledge."

Haynes told Fitch, "See what you can see back there, will ya?"

Records said, "Go back and look out [at] the wing and see what we've got."

"Okay," Fitch said, and he left the cockpit. As he hurried down the aisle, he brushed past Gerry and Joann Dobson in their Hawaiian clothes. He passed Brad Griffin in 2-E, who had been thrilled to make this trip to play in a golf tournament with his brother. Fitch passed Paul Burnham, whose body, at first unidentified, would be labeled with nothing more than the number 43. Fitch left first class and entered the coach cabin, standing by the exit door behind his own seat and Peter Allen's. Allen would eventually escape from the wrecked aircraft by the seemingly impossible maneuver of going through a broken passenger window. In fact, he wasn't the only one who attempted that. In the immediate aftermath of the crash, a young police officer named Pat McCann, who happened to be training at the airport that day, saw a man who had managed to get the upper half of his body through his window before the lower half was incinerated inside the plane.

Fitch passed down the aisle into B-Zone. What he saw through the window only deepened his dread. He crossed to the port side and looked out at the left wing to confirm what he suspected. He rushed back through A-Zone, passing row 9, where Upton Rehnberg, who wrote technical manuals for the aerospace giant Sundstrand, sat in the window seat. Helen Young Hayes, an investment analyst from Denver, sat next to Rehnberg, on the aisle. A young woman with Chinese features, Hayes was fashionably dressed in a miniskirt and blouse. Across the aisle from her sat John Transue, forty. Rehnberg and Hayes would soon share adjacent rooms in the burn unit at St. Luke's Hospital. Transue would save Jan Brown's life. Fitch reached the cockpit door and knocked. No one answered.

On the other side of the door, Haynes was saying, "We're not gonna make the runway, fellas. We're gonna have to ditch this son of a bitch and hope for the best." Fitch knocked again, louder, and Haynes shouted, "Unlock that fuckin' door!"

"Unlock it!" echoed Records.

Dvorak opened the door, and Fitch stepped into the cockpit. He'd been gone less than two minutes. He said, "Okay, both inboard ailerons are sticking up. That's as far as I can tell. I don't know."

The extreme stress was still affecting Haynes's thinking. He responded, "That's because we're steering—we're turning maximum turn right now." Ailerons always move in opposite directions, up on one wing and down on the other. Both of them can't be up at the same time unless they're floating from lack of hydraulic power.

"Tell me what you want," Fitch said, "and I'll help you."

Haynes said, "Right throttle. Close one, put two up." He was under so much stress that he had simply misspoken. In reality, he was trying to tell Fitch to reduce power on the left engine (one) and increase it on the right (three, not two, which had obviously quit). "What we need," Haynes said, "is elevator control, and I don't know how to get it."

Fitch was confused but willing. "Okay, ah . . . ," he said. He stood between the two pilots, took the handles in his hands, and began to move them in accordance with instructions from Haynes and Records, surfing this 185-ton whale five miles in the sky at 83 percent of the speed of sound.

Dudley Dvorak was known as an unflappable guy. He had started his career in the Air Force as a navigator and flew back seat in F-4 Phantoms in Vietnam. He had been a flight instructor and examiner in numerous aircraft during his military career. Dvorak retired from the Air Force in 1985 and joined United with two decades of experience. Haynes could not have asked for a more competent pilot. Despite that, as Dvorak talked to SAM in San Francisco, he was under so much stress that he was having trouble saying what he meant to say. "Roger, we need any help we can get from SAM as far as what to do with this, we don't have anything, we don't—what to do, we're having a hard time controllin' it, we're descending, we're down to seventeen thousand feet we have . . . ah, hardly any control whatsoever."

In the meantime, Haynes suggested to Fitch that they try the autopilot, and Fitch said, "It won't work." Then Haynes began coaching Fitch concerning how to steer against the constant and uncommanded climbing and descending. "Start it down," he said. Then, "No, no, no, no, no, not yet . . . wait a minute till it levels off . . . Now go!"

Immediately after the explosion, the plane made one big slow right turn about twenty to thirty miles in diameter. Then the plane proceeded to make several more spirals of five to ten miles each, downward and to the right. Robert Benzon, an investigator for the NTSB, would say later, "The flyers in the cockpit became instant test pilots when the center engine let loose. They were line pilots," meaning workaday guys, "with no training on a total hydraulic failure situation. Period. They are heroes in every sense of the word." In fact, the pilots who later attempted landings in a simulator that was configured to fly as the damaged DC-10 flew, found that the aircraft eventually crashed, despite their best efforts.

Haynes and Records continued to try to fly the plane using the yoke, even though the controls were dead. Haynes later said that after forty years of flying, it was difficult to get it into his head that he was flying a plane unless he was holding onto something. Fitch said

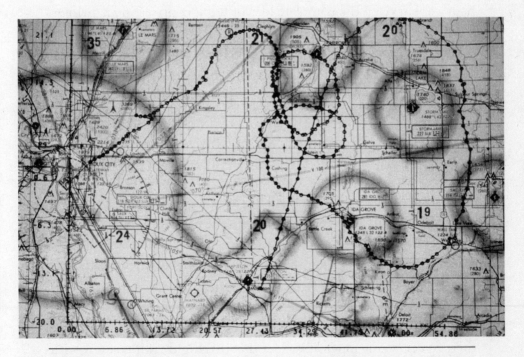

This radar track shows the path of Flight 232. The plane was traveling northeast at thirty-seven thousand feet. Just east of the Cherokee airport, the fan on the number two engine blew apart, cutting hydraulic lines and disabling flight controls. *From NTSB Docket 437*

the same thing: they reacted reflexively. And he later dared any aviator under those circumstances, "*You* let go of it if you're the pilot." Haynes also said that he and the crew really had no idea what had gone wrong with their beautiful ship.

As Fitch acquired a feel for steering with the throttles, Haynes asked, "How are they doing on the evacuation?"

"They're putting things away," Fitch said, "but they're not in any big hurry."

"Well, they better hurry," said Haynes. "We're going to have to ditch, I think." Then, after a moment, "I don't think we're going to make the airport."

Fitch's response was, "Get this thing down, we're in trouble!"

Many years later, Haynes laughed at that, saying that it seemed like a pretty profound case of stating the obvious. But as a TCA, Fitch knew that in the twenty-five years prior to this event, no one had ever survived the complete loss of flight controls in an airliner. They were merely buying time.

As Fitch nursed the throttles, Dvorak continued talking to SAM. Someone in San Francisco said, "We'll get you expedited handling into Chicago. . . . Put you on the ground as soon as we can."

Exasperated at the preposterous remark, Dvorak said, "Well, we can't make Chicago. We're gonna have to land somewhere out here, probably in a field." Whoever was on the line at SAM was so shocked that the frequency went dead for more than a minute before anyone spoke again. And then all he had to say was, in effect, Tell us where you're going to crash.

Even at this late stage, the gathered engineers on the ground at SAM were still scratching their heads in disbelief, and the cockpit was awash in confusion from the extreme stress that was making it difficult for the crew to think straight. Haynes denies that they were afraid, but from the mistakes they were making and the sound of their voices on the tapes, it is clear that this highly skilled crew with its long experience was not functioning normally. Fitch was later frank about how afraid he was. Records asked Haynes if he wanted to put out the flaps, but the flaps are hydraulically operated, so that was not possible. (Slats and flaps are extensions on the front and back of the wings, respectively. When deployed, they allow the plane to fly at slower speeds for takeoff and landing.) Haynes responded, "What the hell. Let's do it. We can't get any worse than we are and spin in."

Records went so far as to pull the slat handle and report, "Slats are out."

The wings aren't visible from the cockpit, so the pilots were unable to see whether pulling that handle had any effect. But Fitch said, "No, you don't have any slats."

Haynes realized his mistake at last, saying, "We don't have any hydraulics, so we're not going to get anything."

Moreover, at that point, they didn't even know where they were. "Get on [frequency] number one," Fitch said, "and ask them what the—where the hell we are."

Haynes radioed the Sioux City tower, "Where's the airport now, ah, for Two Thirty-Two as we're turning around in circles?"

Bachman said, "United Two Thirty-Two Heavy, ah, say again."

Haynes said, "Where's the airport to us now as we come spinning down here?"

"United Two Thirty-Two, ah, Heavy, Sioux City airport's about twelve o'clock and three-six miles."

"Okay," Haynes said, "we're tryin' to go straight, we're not havin' much luck."

Indeed, in their uncontrollable series of right turns, they would drift farther away from the airport instead of closer to it. And yet that would put them at an altitude from which they might actually reach the runway.

Bruce Osenberg and his wife Ruth Anne were sitting in the center section of row 21 with their twenty-year-old daughter Dina between them. Tom Postle, forty-six, sat on Ruth Anne's right. "We had just eaten our lunch," Ruth Anne said more than twenty-three years later, "and I had just put a package of Oreo cookies from the lunch into my purse. And then we heard this loud explosion at the back of the plane."

Dina, who had recently finished her sophomore year in college, turned to her father and said, "Daddy, I don't want to die."

"Dina," he said, "we're okay. Just be patient. Things'll work out here." He looked to his left to check the door over the wing. Beyond the bulkhead, Sylvia Tsao held her squirming toddler, Evan. Bruce decided that he was taking his family out that door as soon as they were on the ground. All three of the Osenbergs noticed that the plane had begun to perform a number of strange maneuvers. The first was its tendency to roll over on its back, which they noticed because they could see the earth out the starboard windows. That would not ordinarily be possible from their center seats. The plane had also begun a long series of excursions up and down. First the plane would descend, rapidly gaining speed. The increased speed would produce more lift on the wings, causing the plane to reverse direction and climb. As the plane climbed, it lost speed the way a ball does when it's thrown in the air. As the speed bled off, the plane lost lift and resumed its descent. And so it went, with each oscillation taking a minute or so. The plane always wound up at a lower altitude. They were going to return to earth no matter what.

Bruce later said, "It felt like we were in a boat in rough waters rocking back and forth." Sometimes the plane went into a bank as steep as 38 degrees. To the passengers the plane appeared to stand on its wingtip in knife-edge flight.

Immediately after the engine exploded, the man next to Ruth Anne, Tom Postle, brought out his old Bible. He had been reading it through much of the flight. Now as the Osenbergs talked among themselves, Postle glanced over and asked, "Are you praying people?" Ruth Anne said that indeed they were—they had been praying since the explosion. Now they all held hands and began to pray together.

In the cockpit, grunting with effort against the yoke, Haynes told his crew, "If we have to set this thing down in dirt, we set it in the dirt." Haynes maintained his sense of humor throughout this grim interval. At one point he laughed and said, "We didn't do this thing on my last [check ride]." Yet at the same time, the cockpit voice recorder picked up swearing, sighing, and groans of despair as the crew fought a losing battle.

As the plane approached Sioux City, Ruth Anne finished her last prayer with Postle and Bruce and Dina. She felt no fear. The praying had put her into a serene state of otherness. "I felt God's presence," she would say later, but she still had one concern that was gnawing at her in those moments before the great calamity of her life over-took her. "I had on a fairly new outfit that day, and in those days, very full skirts were in style." In the middle of a hot July, she imagined that she could get away without wearing pantyhose. And wouldn't you know it, she was about to be in a plane crash. "And my fear was that we were going to have to go down the chute and that my skirt was going to fly up, and whoever was on the ground to catch me was going to see that I didn't have on pantyhose."

Dvorak continued to plead with SAM. Haynes described this facil-ity as "maintenance experts sitting in San Francisco for each type of [aircraft] that United flies. They have all the computers . . . all the history of the aircraft, all the other information that they can draw on to help a crew that has a problem."

Fitch later said, "They know this airplane cold, they know all the systems, they have all the technical manuals, they have everything at their disposal, and if there's a backdoor way of pulling a circuit breaker or something to do, they can see this backdoor way of help-ing you out."

The first difficulty Dvorak encountered was that the engineers at SAM didn't believe him when he said that the plane had no fluid in any of its three hydraulic systems.

"We blew number two engine and we've lost all hydraulics," Dvorak said in his first transmission to SAM around 3:30 in the afternoon over Iowa, about eleven minutes after the engine exploded.

The engineer on the line at SAM said, "Your, ah, system one and system three? Are they operating normally?"

"Negative. All hydraulics are lost. All hydraulic systems are lost."

"United Two Thirty-Two, is all hydraulic quantity gone?"

"Yes! All hydraulic quantity is gone!" Dvorak answered in frustration.

In his stuttering disbelief, the engineer at SAM asked, "Okay, United, ah, Two Thirty-Two, ah, what-what-what-what's, ah, where you gonna set down?" In other words, Where can we find the wreckage?

Dvorak was practically begging by then, saying, "We need some assistance right now! We can't, ah, we're havin' a hard time controllin' it."

When the engineer at SAM ran out of ideas, he said, "I'll pull out your flight manual." SAM had wasted two precious minutes getting to that point. The engineers at SAM thought that the crew had to be mistaken in its diagnosis. And in fact, later that evening, the chief training officer for the DC-10 at United in Denver, Mike Downs, would tell Roger O'Neil, a reporter for NBC television, that he had been listening in on the conversation between Dvorak and SAM. To begin with, Downs claimed that Dvorak never said that the plane had lost all hydraulics. (In fact, as Dvorak told me, "I repeat[ed] it over and over again to them.") Downs further told O'Neil that he didn't believe United 232 had suffered a complete hydraulic failure, because if it had, the plane would not have been able to fly at all.

But in the cockpit that afternoon, Dvorak opened his flight manual to compare notes with the engineer at SAM. Both men were realizing at about the same time that no procedure existed for what they were facing. In fact, during the investigation of the accident, a SAM engineer was heard to comment that they had no idea what to say to the crew, because they felt that they were talking to four dead men.

SAM replied to Dvorak, "United Two Thirty-Two, ah, in the flight manual, page 60 . . ." The engineer from SAM went to call other engineers, but no one had even a suggestion of what the crew might try.

"With all those computers, with all the knowledge at their fingertips . . . ," Haynes said years later, "there's absolutely nothing they could do to help a crew."

Fitch later said that as he flew the plane with the throttles, he was wondering if "the aircraft was going to be a smoking hole in Iowa."

Several minutes into the conversation with Dvorak, SAM was still asking him to confirm that he had lost all three hydraulic systems. Haynes was getting really angry, as Dvorak responded, "That is affirmative! We have lost all three hydraulic systems! We have no quantity and no pressure on any hydraulic system!"

CHAPTER THREE

Jan Brown had begun to realize that the crisis was even worse than she had imagined. Because of a United Airlines promotion, more than fifty children had come on board. Some people were holding infants in their laps. They had no seats, no restraints. Sylvia Tsao, for example, was trying to hold squirming Evan. Now rather helplessly, Brown made the decision to tell mothers to place those lap children on the floor, because that was how she had been trained. And for the first time, the idiocy of this idea struck her with its full force. She understood at last: There is no provision for protecting babies on airliners. None at all. She watched with her heart sinking as her flight attendants went up and down the aisles, telling people to take off their eyeglasses and remove items such as pens and combs from their pockets. They passed seventy-six-year-old Linda Ellen Couleur. She had a titanium shoulder. They passed Walter Williams. He had perfect teeth. He had never needed a filling in all his twenty-eight years. He wore a mustache and a tie tack with a *W* on it.

As the flight attendants moved down the aisle, they heard mothers ask, "What should I do with my baby?" Brown was sickeningly aware that in all likelihood, in a few minutes, some of these children were going to die.

None of the flight attendants remembered who helped Sylvia Tsao change her seat. She should not have been in an exit row with a baby, and no one was sure how she came to be there. Neverthe-less Jerry Schemmel recalls that a female flight attendant led Sylvia and Evan to another seat. Schemmel had been the last person to board the flight. He and his boss and best friend Jay Ramsdell had waited all morning as flight after flight took off without them. All the planes had been full. Ramsdell had been given a seat assignment on an earlier flight, but there had been no room for Schemmel. Since Ramsdell was the commissioner of the Continental Basketball Asso-ciation, it seemed more important for him to get to Columbus first. And although Schemmel urged him to go, Ramsdell said, "Hey, we're in this thing together, we'll fly together." It seemed a trivial decision at the time. Allowed at last onto Flight 232, Schemmel and Ramsdell were greeted at the gate by Susan White. "How are you fellas doing today?" she asked cheerfully. Schemmel told her that they weren't doing all that great. She took their tickets and joined them for the walk down the Jetway, as Schemmel and Ramsdell complained to Susan about how they'd been at the airport all morning trying to find a flight to Columbus, Ohio.

"Hey!" Susan said. "I'm from Ohio!" Schemmel and Ramsdell good-naturedly grumbled a bit more, and Susan advised them, "I hope you're not planning on getting any sleep on this flight, because we have a lot of kids on board today." Ramsdell sat seven rows behind Schemmel in the starboard window seat, craning his neck to see his friend.

Whoever reseated Sylvia spoke to Charles Kenneth Bosscher, thirty-seven, who willingly gave up his seat in the center section for the mother and child. He took the aisle seat by the 3-Left exit. He would arrive home in Grand Rapids, Michigan, many days later in a Batesville casket that had been delivered to Sioux City from Bates-ville, Indiana.

Jan Brown helped Sylvia place Evan on the floor at her feet and gave her pillows to pad him. As Sylvia tried to arrange Evan on the floor, the toddler squirmed and struggled into his mother's lap. Then he stood and grinned at Schemmel from over the back of Sylvia's seat.

"I never would forget that face," Schemmel later wrote in a

memoir. As he prepared for the crash, planning his own survival, he resolved that he would help Sylvia and Evan as soon as the plane stopped. He told himself to stay calm, to avoid panic, and above all to help others. He noted the emergency exit, 3-Right, two rows ahead of him. As he looked back down the aisle, he saw Ramsdell smile and give him a thumbs up. Schemmel returned the signal. Two rows behind Ramsdell, fourteen-year-old Tony Feeney, a skinny kid with big glasses, watched the two men signal each other. They looked so competent and confident in their business suits. Feeney wondered if they had a secret plan. He wondered if they thought they were going to die. The teenager was traveling alone to Chicago to attend Michael Jordan's basketball camp. Now he thought that if those two business guys had a plan, he was going to follow them out of this mess.

After her first visit to the cockpit, Jan Brown quickly briefed Barbara Gillaspie, Jan Murray, and Rene Le Beau. Brown then hurried to the aft galley to let Susan White, Donna McGrady, and Tim Owens know what was going on.

Before takeoff, Jan Brown had noticed Janice-Long Brown and her eleven-year-old daughter Kimberly Allison on board. She had made a point of going back to greet them. Janice had been a flight attendant with United. "Out of this packed airplane, I spotted her. They always got us mixed up. Our mailboxes were together." About a year after she started flying, Jan Brown met Janice Brown, and the more senior woman helped Jan Brown to get flights that were more convenient so that she could spend extra time with her children. Janice had married a successful businessman and didn't really need to fly anymore. She now wore a Piaget watch. Kimberly had a single pierced ear. As Jan Brown hurried back to brief her flight attendants in the aft galley, she passed down the port aisle and her eyes met Janice's. "It was like this nonverbal conversation we had. She looked at me like: *How bad is it?* And I looked at her like, *It's as bad as it could possibly be.*" Jan Brown desperately wanted to ask Janice for help, "but I couldn't because she was traveling with her daughter." Jan Brown later berated herself for not moving them up to the two empty seats in row 9. Everyone in that row survived. Of course, she could not have known that beforehand. Still, many people would feel undeserved guilt long after the crash.

Jan Brown hurried down the aisle past Karin Elizabeth Sass, thirty-two, who was pregnant with her second child. Brown encountered Tim Owens and whispered that they were going to deliver a "quick and dirty" briefing to the passengers. Owens followed her aft. They joined Susan White and Donna McGrady in the rear galley. "Okay," Jan said. "We have no hydraulics. We have no way to steer and we can't brake. Be prepared for fire. Also, be prepared to ditch, because there's a river near there. Just be prepared, because I don't know how this is going to turn out." Then she added, "Don't bother reconciling the liquor."

At twenty-seven, Tim Owens was the only male flight attendant on board. He had joined United Airlines a month before. As soon as Brown explained the situation, she returned to the forward cabin. The others watched her go. Then Donna took the hands of Owens and White and led them in a prayer right there in the galley behind Martha Conant's back. "It wasn't the longest prayer," Owens later said, "because we were kind of busy at the time, but it was powerful and succinct."

As she passed up the starboard aisle, Jan Brown knew that she had to keep a tight grip on herself. Earlier, she had seen her own hand shake. She knew that she would have to stand before the congregation in this doomed cathedral and lift a microphone to her lips and speak the words of preparation. And she would not be able to if she was palsied with fear. She had no desire to try to evacuate a plane full of panicked people. She passed near Lena Ann Blaha, sixty-five, who sat beside James Matthew Bohn. The boy had celebrated his twelfth birthday in May. Blaha reached out to Jan Brown. She told Brown to look out the starboard window at the tail. Already deeply afraid, Brown leaned over the woman and the boy and craned her neck to see toward the rear. And now she understood that the situation was so much worse than she had imagined. She saw a piece of torn metal sticking up from the tail "like you'd peeled a pop-top tab off." The hole was a foot wide. As she raced from C-Zone to B-Zone, Wilbur and Vincenta Eley, both in their seventies, waved at her. "I think I'm having a heart attack," the woman said.

Brown later mused with a laugh, "I can't believe I said, 'I'll get back to you.' I was walking away through B-Zone going, 'Jan, was that you that said that?' I mean that is so totally contrary to who I am." As she passed into the forward galley, she said to Jan Murray, who had been a nurse, "The woman in 22-F thinks she's having a heart attack." Then she continued on toward the cockpit. She knocked on the door for the second time that day. She received no response.

Behind the door, after almost twenty minutes of working together at the edge of human tolerance, Haynes had introduced himself to Denny Fitch, reaching his left hand over his right shoulder to shake Fitch's hand without looking.

"I'll tell you what," Fitch said, "we'll have a beer when this is all done."

Haynes said, "Well, I don't drink, but I'll sure as hell have one."

Brown waited half a minute—an eternity—and knocked again. She didn't know that the plane had been approaching a towering cumulus cloud. If the crew allowed the plane to enter it, they would have to fly not only blind but also in the turbulence usually found inside those incipient summer thunderheads. So the crew was trying to steer the plane clear of the cloud. Oblivious of this close call, Brown waited a quarter of a minute and knocked again—three distinct raps. She was thinking, as she later recalled, "The tail? No one said anything about the tail." And "I have to tell the captain." Another three-quarters of a minute passed before the door opened at last.

When Brown entered the cockpit, before she could get a word out, Haynes launched into his explanation of the situation. "We almost have no control of the airplane," he began, as she stared in shock and horror, her mind frozen. "We have no hydraulics at all." He was so keyed up with adrenaline and with the effort he was exerting on the yoke that his ability to make sense was deteriorating. "We can't go to Sioux City, and we're gonna try to put it into Sioux City, Iowa," he said, a clear contradiction.

All Brown could say was, "Yeah . . ."

"It's gonna be tough," Haynes said as he struggled with the useless controls. "Gonna be rough."

"So we're gonna evacuate?" Brown asked.

"We—yeah. Well, we're gonna have the gear down."

"Yeah . . ."

"And if we can keep the airplane on the ground and stop standing up, give us a second or two before you evacuate," Haynes said. "Brace—the brace will be the signal. It'll be over the PA system: 'Brace, Brace, Brace.'"

Brown was confused too when she asked, "And that will be to evacuate?" She later said that all she could think about was evacuating because she just wanted to be out of that plane.

"No," Haynes said. "That'll be to, ah, to, ah, brace for landing."

Brown was practically speechless at that point. She said, "Uh-huh."

"And then, if we have to evacuate, you'll get the command signal to evacuate, but I think—really have my doubts you'll see us . . . standing up, Honey." Haynes paused and then said, "Good luck, Sweetheart."

"Thanks," Brown said, her eyes clouding with tears. "You too."

As she left the cockpit and started down the aisle, his words rang in her head. *I doubt you'll see us standing up.* Her mind was racing ahead, trying to cover her plans. She desperately wanted to reach that point of evacuating and be done with it. And she suddenly realized that she had been in such a state of shock from his declaration and from her focus on making a plan that she had neglected to tell him about the tail.

Brown spun on her heel and rushed back to knock on the door again. This time Dvorak opened it immediately, and she bent to whisper to him. She quickly closed the door and left, still thinking that she had done something wrong. In her terror, she'd been unable to remember the term *horizontal stabilizer* or even *elevator*, so she told Dvorak that she had seen damage on "the rear wing." And indeed, the stabilizer was larger than many wings, it being more than seventy-one feet across, twenty-seven hundred square feet, "a good bit larger than the average ranch house," as Dale Warren, a vice president at Douglas Aircraft, later put it.

Now Dvorak announced to the cockpit crew, "She says there appears to be some damage on that one wing. Do you want me to go back and take a look?"

"No," Fitch said. "We don't have time."

"Ain't got time for it, no," Haynes agreed. Then he thought better of it and changed his mind. "Okay, go ahead. Go ahead, see what you can see. Not that it'll do any good."

Dvorak unlatched his harness and left the cockpit.

Roughly twenty-five minutes had passed since the explosion. "So here I am," said Martha Conant, recalling what seemed an eternity in the last row, "bargaining with God and reviewing my life, and all of a sudden, I had this vision of myself in the palm of God's hand. And it was unexpected. It was intense. And it was immensely reassuring." She had been looking for a miracle. Now she felt that she might get one. She could not imagine what it would look like.

Conant watched Dave Randa, the boy in the Chicago Cubs baseball cap, who sat by the window across the aisle and just ahead of her. Beside Conant, John Hatch had tried to reassure Dave, making something up to explain the fluid streaming across the windows, the white mist streaming back from the wings, and in the quiet of the failed engine, everyone nearby could hear his explanation: steam. The mist they saw was fuel that the crew was dumping. The fluid flowing across the windows was condensation from the cold aircraft descending into warmer air. But Hatch said it was steam. Conant saw Dave nodding while he listened to Hatch. Then Susan White said something to the mother and child, and Dave bent over and clutched his ankles. It was too early for bracing, but Dave was afraid. Terribly afraid. And his mother's heart was breaking, as she placed her left hand on his back and whispered something to him. She told him that he didn't need to brace yet, but the child would remain bent over, clenched tight, all the way to the ground.

Dave and his mother Susan, a librarian, had left Denver that Wednesday for vacation, expecting that Dave's father Jim would follow on Friday. They would attend the Cubs-Giants baseball game on Saturday afternoon at Wrigley Field and then drive to South Haven, Michigan, for a few days at the beach. As Hatch reassured her son, Susan Randa looked over and their eyes met. "I know in my heart that he would have taken care of Dave if something happened," she later said. "He was looking at me and looking at Dave, and I knew he'd do it. I knew it."

Across the aisle to her right, Conant could see a young boy wearing a yarmulke seated next to a businessman with a mustache. They occupied the two seats by the starboard window. Yisroel Brownstein, nine, sat on the aisle. Donna McGrady came down the aisle and asked the boy to trade places with the businessman, Richard Howard Sudlow, thirty-six, because she might need the man's help in opening the exit door that was immediately behind them. The boy looked terrified, his eyes darting all over, his posture rigid with fear. When the engine exploded, Yisroel had gone into a relentless state of terror. For Yisroel, it lasted in some forms into his adult life. The sensation that the plane was falling and rolling over only added to his panic, which was so deep-seated that he was struck deaf. Later in life, he would remember no noise, only the sensation of falling and rolling as the tail dropped.

Now Conant saw the tense and nervous pilot who came hurrying down the starboard aisle to look out the windows. After Jan Brown had talked with her flight attendants in the galley behind Conant, she had gone forward up the right aisle. Conant had seen the woman seated next to a young boy reach out and stop Brown and show her something out the window. Brown had hurried away toward the cockpit. Now Conant watched Dvorak, grim and drawn, look out the same window, his face ashen, his eyes walled like those of a horse in a fire.

As Dvorak recalled it, "I went down the aisle on the right side of the airplane, and these guys pointed out, showed me, and you could see pieces of metal sticking up on the tail."

White was watching him too. "Dudley and I had known each other for three years," she said later. They had lived in an apartment building designed for commuting airline employees. "And every time I'd see Dudley, he was joking and happy and funny. And now Dudley comes walking to the back of the plane, and I see him white as a ghost."

Dvorak recalled that when he saw the tail, "basically I knew that the engine had destroyed itself. That was pretty obvious." But he "didn't have the time to sit there and think what could have caused the engine failure. All we knew is the engine failed." And "if you're doing your job, you don't have time to analyze. I kept going back to the thing I was thinking: Have I missed something?"

"Dudley," White said to him, "I need to show you something this pilot just showed me." After Jan Brown had seen the damaged tail, a deadheading Eastern Airlines pilot had pulled his ID out of his boot and showed it to White. He offered to help the cockpit crew. She explained that a check pilot was already up there, and the man showed her the damage on the other side of the tail. Now she showed Dvorak. He peered out the window on the port side and then turned a grim countenance on her.

"Are you doin' okay?" he asked evenly.

Although it was far from the truth, she said, "I'm okay. Are you okay?"

Dvorak watched her eyes for a moment. He later said, "Susan was really shaken up." He told her, "You're going to be okay." Then he put his hand on her arm and said, "Good luck."

"Good luck to you too," White said, and she watched him hurry up the port aisle, past forty-one-year-old Jasumati J. Patel, whose jewelry would be photographed as part of her identification: the beaded necklace held together with two safety pins, its pendant shaped like a teardrop, and strands of her hair still tangled in it, and her two rings and her earrings and two braided bracelets and her keys on a key ring.

Susan White felt overwhelmed. She felt that at any moment she would burst into tears and make matters worse. The day before, she and Tim Owens had enjoyed some poppy-seed crackers left over from the first class luncheon service and joked about the headlines they would make if the plane crashed and their toxicology reports showed opiates in their blood from the poppy seeds. And now it appeared that they might make those headlines. She could feel her eyes watering and her nose stuffing up. She could see people going to the bathroom and others taking the cordless Airphones out of their cradles to make calls.

"I knew we had to be in front of everyone and I had to be together," she would say later.

She saw someone emerge from one of the toilets and took the opportunity to duck inside. She blew her nose and straightened herself up as best she could. She looked in the mirror. She saw the young flight attendant in uniform, not ready to die. Especially not ready for all these others to die. "I finally had my dream job," she later said, "and it's turning into the nightmare of my life. You think you're going to have this great job and this is what we all train for, but we hope that it never happens." They had been less than an hour from Chicago. Now the captain was saying they were turning back west to make an emergency landing at Sioux City. She asked herself, "Where the heck is Sioux City?" She turned away from the mirror, closed her eyes, and then she prayed. She prayed and prayed. And when she emerged from the bathroom, she felt strong and ready to face whatever was coming. As she closed the door to the lavatory, she heard Jan Brown announce, "Demo positions," so she strode forward to exit 3-Left, where she could stand before her congregation and demonstrate what needed to be done.

As Martha Conant watched White recede up the aisle, she thought, "Why won't they tell us what's going on?" Then again, Conant thought, perhaps she didn't really want to know. Perhaps it would be quick and painless. She noticed a young woman ahead of her. Conant watched the woman—a girl, really, about college age—jump up, snatch an Airphone, and rush back to her seat. As Conant eavesdropped, twenty-one-year-old Kari Milford called her boy-friend, Kyle Persinger, the man she hoped would one day marry her. The cabin had fallen so quiet that Conant could hear everything Kari said. "Yeah, we're going to be a little late, we're having some kind of problem," she said. "I'll let you know."

More than twenty-three years later, Susan Randa remembered nearly the same words: "We've had a problem with the flight. We're going to be late coming into Chicago. So I'll give you a call when we're closer."

Susan Randa realized that Kari was sitting with two children. She was traveling with her brother Jerry, thirty-eight, and his sons, David, seven, and Tom, nine.

"I've always remembered that," Conant recalled, "because she was so matter-of-fact."

And Susan Randa thought, as she later said, "Late coming into Chicago! You are so dreaming. Your reality is so much different from my reality."

But she and Conant misunderstood what they were hearing. Kari had wanted to call her boyfriend to keep him from leaving for the air-port, but he had already left. She reached his grandmother instead. Kari was trying not to upset her, even though she could feel her heart collapsing in her chest at the thought that she might never see Kyle again, might never marry or have children such as these two little boys traveling with her. And now she had missed her last chance to say good-bye.

At about nineteen minutes to four in the afternoon, as Jan Brown left the cockpit to prepare the cabin, the pilots were trying without success to point the plane toward Sioux City, as the rudderless ship continued its right-hand spirals. In addition, the pilots were still struggling with the oscillations that were carrying the nose slowly up and down from a few hundred to more than a thousand feet each minute in an irregular undulating wave. The DC-10 was flying the way a paper airplane would fly if thrown from a height—first nose down, then nose up, then nose down, then nose up. That motion is called a phugoid oscillation, and the crew well understood that they could not possibly land the plane safely without putting an end to it. So they had been trying to get ahead of the plane and to control how much the right wing dropped and how much the ship pitched up and down during each phugoid cycle. They tried to anticipate the behavior of the craft, and in fact, they were gradually "getting in tune with the airplane," as Fitch later put it.

Records said, "While Denny was in fact controlling the throttles, it was not without a lot of input from both Al and me. As he was not on headphones or microphone, he several times asked, Where do you want to go?"

In a documentary film by Errol Morris, Fitch said, "It just became like the airplane was an extension of me. And I could feel these stimuli coming at me before I actually felt them or saw them." He said that at one point, "it struck me like a thunderclap. Dear God, I have 296 lives literally in my two hands."

Dvorak recalled that as the plane approached Sioux City, "Al told me to run the throttles." Dvorak's seat swung around in tracks so that the second officer could operate the throttles on takeoff. Fitch relinquished the throttles to him for a time and sat in the jump seat behind Haynes. "I was all in the seat, strapped in and running the throttles," Dvorak said, "and Denny was over my shoulder saying, Do this, do that, and I finally decided that he's been doing it and he knows what it takes, it's not the right time for me to learn what the differences are." Haynes, Records, Dvorak, and Fitch all had 296 lives in their hands at one point or another during the flight, but Fitch handled the throttles longer than anyone else. He brought the plane in as safely as anyone considered possible, given the dire circumstances. Yet the crew wound up resenting his outgoing public persona.

Rosa Fitch, Denny's widow, said, "My husband was a hero, not only in what he did on July 19, 1989, but in the way he lived his life every day."

Tammy Randa, Dave Randa's wife, said this about Fitch: "The first time Dave mentioned Denny Fitch to me he [referred to] him as the 'man who saved my life.' We also attended his memorial service in May of 2012, and when Dave introduced himself to Denny's daughter, she immediately started to cry. I could tell that her childhood was also deeply affected by the crash. I also spoke to Denny a couple of times . . . and got the impression that he was very friendly and thoughtful. Sounds like some may have felt he was a little arrogant, but nonetheless, I have a wonderful husband (and in-laws) and two amazing children thanks to him and the other pilots that day."

Brad Griffin had shoulder-length hair and a handlebar mustache. He wore jeans and—apart from the sandals—looked as if he would be at home among the cowboys in Colorado where he lived. Now he watched Dudley Dvorak "sprint" back through the cabin. He later said, "I mean, he's *running* to the back of the plane."

"I wasn't running," Dvorak countered. "I might have walked fast. You don't do anything like that on an airplane, because that can cause panic." On the other hand, numerous passengers told of being alarmed at how fast the flight engineer was moving down the aisle.

Griffin was on his way to Battle Creek, Michigan, to play golf with his brother. "I've got my golf clubs," he recounted. "I'm excited. My brother and I are best friends. This'll be the first time I've done this with him. I'm looking forward to seeing my family, which is from Michigan."

In the boarding lounge in Denver, Griffin had given his ticket to Susan White. He boarded the plane and was greeted by Jan Murray in first class. After takeoff and lunch, he decided to get up from his aisle seat in the second row on the starboard side. He wanted to stretch his legs and look out the window. He was traveling in a luxury craft on the Nile of the sky. Life didn't get much better. "I'm standing looking out the emergency exit window, and then all of a sudden, the plane just shook and I was knocked to my knees." He hurried to his seat and fastened his seat belt. Over the next few minutes, he and Michael Kielbassa, thirty-eight, beside him in the window seat, discussed the fact that the plane wasn't flying right. "Now there's starting to be tension with the crew, and my thought comes and goes: you know, you can die on this plane." He decided that he had better start meditating, a practice that he had undertaken in 1972 and had continued daily for seventeen years.

"So, the dialogue before I go into meditation on the plane went like this," he recalled. "In a conversation with myself: You can die on this plane. I would like to see my children grow up." He had heard people talk about praying to Jesus, and he thought, "*You* had better pray to Jesus. I am with Maharaji this lifetime. *You* had better pray. I have something better than prayer. And then I go into meditation."

He told me, "Within every human being—every human being—there is a place inside where there is no fear. And so I touched that place." He closed his eyes and went into a meditative trance. When he came out of it a few minutes later, "There's no fear for me. You hear what's going on, you understand what's going on," he said. All the passengers in first class were adults, but from the coach cabin, Griffin could hear young mothers wailing, "What should I do with my baby?"

"It was the worst part of the flight," he said. "And the answer is: Put them between your feet. Because you can't hang onto them. And you feel that you can't do anything to help them. That's a terrible feeling. But at the same time, there's no anxiety for me. There's no adrenaline for me. But I was very aware of what was going on. And I knew I could die on that plane."

When Griffin saw Dvorak rush past him, he turned and watched him go. He lost sight of him as the pilot faded down the aisle into B-Zone. Dvorak passed Garry Priest, who was trying to comfort Linda Pierce across the aisle. When the engine blew, the plane had not only lost a third of its thrust but also produced an instant wind brake from the drag of the dead engine. That's why the tail dropped so sharply. And that's why Priest, whose seat belt was loose, "ended up almost tucked under the seat in front of me where your carry-on little bag is supposed to go. Seat belt up around my armpits as I slid forward in my seat."

Dvorak passed Sister Mary Viannea Karpinski, the Felician nun who had been brought aboard in a wheelchair ahead of the other passengers. She was feeding her red rosary beads through her fingers, praying rapidly, softly, in both English and Polish. He passed Clif Marshall, production manager for a company in the livestock industry. With the help of Ron Sheldon, two seats to his left, Marshall would save eight lives: Terri Hardman and her two teenagers, Sheli and Ryan; Gitte Skaanes, an exchange student on her way home to Norway; Lawrence Hjermstad and his two children, Alisa, eight, and Eric, eleven; and Aki Muto, nineteen, the tall Japanese girl with the pale and beautiful features of a doll.

Dvorak rushed away into C-Zone past Jerry Schemmel and an ex-Navy fighter pilot named Charles Martz, who sat with an eighty-year-old ex-Navy nurse, Luella Neubacher. Dvorak passed Jay Ramsdell on his left and Tony Feeney on his right, then a handsome young man in his twenties, who would require an electroencephalogram to determine if he was dead or alive, and twenty-two-year-old Elaine Asay. Her tattoo of a bunny would assist the forensic team in identifying her.

Dvorak came into view of Yisroel Brownstein and Richard Howard Sudlow and stopped short of the 4-Right exit, the last door in the tail of the plane. For years afterward, he would have dreams in which all those people around him would rise up before him. In his dreams, they were all his friends. Dvorak looked outside. He "had to hold onto the seats . . . to steady himself against the movements of the aircraft," according to testimony by an investigator. He saw the damage to the elevator and the horizontal stabilizer. Susan White saw him and called to him and pointed out the damage on the other side. Dvorak took her arm, pulled her close, and looked deep into her eyes. She felt that he was saying his last good-bye. Then he hurried back to the cockpit.

CHAPTER FOUR

General Electric made the engines for the DC-10. They were known as Model CF6-6 high-bypass turbofans. If you go out to the airport and look at one, you will see a metal fan more than seven feet in diameter at the front. Behind that number one fan are a stage two fan, compressor wheels, a combustion chamber, and turbine wheels. All of those rotating parts make the airplane go.

The words *ejaculate* and *jet* derive from the Latin verb *jacere*, meaning to throw. A flying machine must throw a fluid—usually air—in order to move itself in accordance with Newton's laws, one of which says that any action results in an equal and opposite reaction. A wing produces lift only when it's moving through the air. To achieve that forward motion, the machine has to push a mass of fluid in the opposite direction. (To an engineer, air is a fluid because it flows.) In the CF6 engines the so-called working fluid is 99 percent air, with a little exhaust mixed in from the fuel that the engine burns.

Each of the CF6 engines that powered November 1819 Uniform on that July day in 1989 was capable of producing on the order of thirty-nine thousand pounds of thrust. GE makes an engine today that produces more than a hundred thousand pounds of thrust. Either way, such engines produce a great deal of energy, and those who make and use them want to be careful where all that energy goes. For example, the number one fan on the CF6-6 engine has

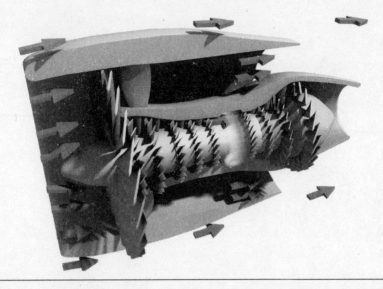

A generic turbofan engine is pictured here. Arrows show the path of the air. Direction of travel of the aircraft is to the left. The fan and compressor blades blow air backward, compressing it before directing it into the combustion chamber, where it is mixed with fuel. The exhaust from the burning fuel turns the turbine blades at the rear, thus creating the power that rotates concentric driveshafts, which in turn spin the fans and compressors at the front. *Courtesy Richard Wheeler*

thirty-eight fan blades, each of which is twenty-eight inches long and weighs ten pounds. Those blades are mounted in dovetail slots in the rim of a wheel known as the number one fan disk. Without the blades, the fan disk weighs 370 pounds and has a diameter of thirty-two inches. Spinning at about thirty-five hundred revolutions a minute in cruise flight, the centrifugal force that those blades exert on the fan disk amounts to nearly four million pounds.

Turbofan engines perform their work based on principles that say, in effect, that temperature, pressure, and volume are all interrelated and interdependent. If you force a gas into a smaller space (reducing volume), you will increase temperature and pressure. If you increase the temperature of a gas in a fixed space, you increase the pressure (but not the volume). Conversely, if you increase the volume of a flowing gas, the pressure goes down and the gas moves faster. A gas turbine engine such as the CF6 does all of those things at various points in its operating sequence. The number one fan on the front pushes a large volume of air backward, about thirteen hundred pounds of it every second. That air takes two paths. The innermost path leads to the compressor wheels. The combustion chamber receives the compressed air, accounting for a small amount of the total. The greatest share of the air flows around the whole working assembly, providing thrust while cooling and quieting the engine.

The compressor is a series of fans that alternate with sets of stationary fins. The fans are wheels that are fitted with blades. They work much the way propeller blades work, pushing air backward. The stationary fins, called stator vanes, redirect the air to keep it moving in a nearly longitudinal direction. Each set of compressor blades and stator vanes increases the pressure and temperature of the air while reducing its volume. The air goes through four low-pressure stages, then through sixteen high-pressure stages, until the air achieves an incandescent heat. All this takes place before the air has combined with any fuel.*

We think we know air, but most of us really don't. Unless you've been in a hurricane or a tornado, you know only one possible state of air, the gentle and forgiving state we find all around us for most of our lives. I once went to an Air Force base to watch the testing of a jet engine for a fighter plane. I was with a group of engineers and pilots in a concrete underground bunker about the size of a small motel room. The engine was on a stand and was being run by a man behind a glass wall that appeared to be two feet thick. We each wore several layers of protection for our ears, lest we emerge stone deaf, so we had trouble communicating. One of the engineers wanted to warn me not to walk in front of the bleed air. This was not the jet of working fluid that propelled a plane. Bleed air was air that had to escape while the engine was spooling up to speed, so that the compressor blades didn't choke and shatter from being fed too much air all at once. He put his hand into the column of bleed air to show me: *don't walk here.*

---

* Take a spray can of anything that's pressurized and spray it for a while. The can will get cold. If you keep spraying, it will get so cold that ice will form. That's the opposite of what happens in the compressor section of a jet engine. Compress a gas and it gets hotter.

I put my hand into the column of air, and it felt as if someone had thrown a broomstick end-on into my hand. By virtue of its speed alone, its mass and momentum, the air had set like concrete. It was a startling revelation, and I never again wondered how a tornado could drive a soda straw through an oak tree. If I had inadvertently stepped into the exhaust of that engine, it would have slammed me into the concrete flume that led up to the surface of the earth to dissipate the exhaust, and it might well have killed me. All this force came from those blades, delicate as tuning forks, spinning at thousands of revolutions a minute. Some of the blades have needle-fine holes drilled in them so that air can pass through and cool them as they spin. In some cases, the tips of the blades break the sound barrier.

As the compressor pushes the air back and back into smaller and smaller spaces, building the pressure and heat, it eventually must meet fuel in the combustion chamber, where that air will be given the extra kick it needs to make the whole operation go. The fuel will require a flame in order to burn. And flame cannot live in a wind. The air is moving at hundreds of miles an hour when it reaches the combustor. This does not sound like a recipe for success. That a turbine engine works at all seems something of a miracle. The highest speeds that the plane can achieve require the lowest speeds of the air flowing through the engine. In the middle of this immense, dynamic mass of whirling parts, the air has to come to a near standstill.

The combustion chamber is a hollow torus of metal, a shape like a doughnut. In cross section, it isn't round as a doughnut is. It is elongated. That cross section measures seven and a half inches by a bit more than three inches. It has numerous small holes in it forming complex patterns. The highly compressed air is forced through the holes all around the circumference, even as fuel is sprayed into the swirling air inside that hollow shape. The purpose of the shape of the combustion chamber is to keep the flame away from the driveshafts that run lengthwise through the center of the engine, connecting all the wheels. As jet fuel (a type of kerosene) enters the combustion chamber, it mixes with the compressed air, ignites, and blows exhaust gas back through turbine wheels, giving them their power. By way of two concentric driveshafts, one spinning inside the other, those turbine wheels transmit their power to the fans and compressors at the front of the engine.

If the airflow over one small section of a single blade is interrupted for any reason, it can create a turbulence that cascades down across the other blades, one after another, forming a blockage that makes it seem as if the air had turned to stone. It's called a compressor surge or a compressor stall. When it happens, all the energy of those spinning wheels reverberates upon itself at once. Sometimes parts break. Thus could the air itself betray us. Modern turbine technology is a high-energy high-wire act in which any slight upset can bring the whole house of cards down with a bang. Yet this is what makes our system of air travel possible: working close to the limits of catastrophe. Most people never fully realize what sort of daredevils pioneered airline travel and still run it to this day.

When Boeing was about to introduce the 707, the company arranged a demonstration of the prototype. It took place at Seafair on Lake Washington in Seattle. The Gold Cup hydroplane race was the big attraction at Seafair, but the Blue Angels also flew. In 1955, the International Air Transport Association, including every airline company, along with the Society of Aeronautical Engineers, held their annual meetings in Seattle during Seafair week. As it happened, Boeing's factory and headquarters were close by.

With no customers on board, no orders for the craft, Bill Allen, the president of Boeing, had spent the equivalent of $137 million in 2013 dollars to develop the prototype of the 707. Designated 367-80, the plane was affectionately known as the Dash 80. When the time came for the flyby on that perfect summer day in August, the test pilot, Alvin M. "Tex" Johnston, with Jim Gannet as copilot and Bell Whitehead as engineer, rolled the plane as it passed over the Gold Cup course with two hundred thousand people watching. The big 707 was not inverted for long, but the effect was stunning.

Allen called Johnston to his office the next day and asked, "What did you think you were doing yesterday?"

Tex replied, "Selling the airplane." He explained to his boss, "The airplane does not recognize attitude, providing a maneuver is conducted at one G."

"You know that," Allen said. "Now we know that. Don't do it anymore."

That evening Tex was summoned to Allen's house for dinner, and when he arrived, a guest jumped up from his seat on the patio and "grabbed my Stetson by the brim with both hands, and jerked it down over my ears, saying, 'You slow rollin' S.O.B. Why didn't you let me know? I would have been ridin' the jump seat.'" The guest was Eddie Rickenbacker, the most successful fighter ace of World War I.

The founders of airlines, along with the airframe and engine manufacturers, had to be risk takers in part because of the expense of building and flying jet transport planes. In the industry they say that when a manufacturer sets out to design a new engine or a new airplane, the leaders are betting the company. By the time United Flight 232 crashed, only two jet airliners were known with any certainty to have made a profit: Boeing's first offering, the 707, and its 727. The DC-10 would lose $2.5 billion (about twice that much in 2013 dollars) before McDonnell Douglas canceled production not long after the crash of 1819 Uniform.

Even so, the CF6-6 proved to be a reliable and successful engine. It began powering commercial flights in 1971, and some parts that were manufactured that year wound up on the number two engine that was mounted on 1819 Uniform as Dudley Dvorak looked out on the damaged tail. Technology takes time to mature, to become fine and smooth. Because a company must make money, mechanical inventions are often introduced before they have achieved that state of grace. United Flight 232 crashed because of a complex sequence of events, but that sequence began with a beautifully designed engine that was not quite ready to carry people around in the sky for quite as long as the manufacturer had promised it would.

And yet the CF6 in its many forms went on to become one of the best commercial aircraft engines ever made. Based on an engine that GE had developed for the military, the CF6 was chosen by both United and American Airlines in 1968 to power their brand new DC-10 aircraft. Since then, GE claims, that engine has put in more hours of service than any other gas turbine, "the equivalent of one engine running 24 hours a day, 365 days a year for more than 26,000 years." By 1985, the CF6-6 had evolved into the CF6-80C2. That new version of the design was chosen to hang on the wings of *Air Force One*. Unfortunately, that development was of no help to the lovely old ship known as 1819 Uniform.

Now as United Flight 232 made its wandering way toward Sioux City, the crew may have wondered about all the things that could have gone wrong in that number two engine. The ship itself was fifteen years old. How many times had it taken off and landed? Many thousands of times, to be sure. And then there was the engine itself, known by the serial number 451-243: How long had it been on this plane? How often had it flown? Surely it had been installed on other airplanes. The mechanics swapped engines freely in the United Airlines maintenance base in San Francisco. You never knew where one might end up, half a world away one day and right behind your head the next. The situation was even more complicated than that, because whenever mechanics tore down one of those engines to service it, they switched parts with other engines. One of those spinning wheels may have been on half-a-dozen other engines at one time or another. Meticulous records of all the parts and pieces were meant to be kept. Where were those records now?

In fact, engine 451-243 was a collection of spare parts flying in close formation. And since June 23, 1972, when that engine was first installed on the right wing of a DC-10, it had been all over the place. Its internal parts had been changed and changed again. In reality, then, the engine itself, 451-243, had no unique identity. However, the components, once cast and forged and machined, were given serial numbers and did retain unique identities. You never knew for sure what atoms made up a given engine, but you knew that the atoms of a component remained an integral part of its personality. So to understand the engine that failed—to grasp how its beautiful workings could go so hideously wrong—we will ultimately have to understand those component parts.

Dvorak had been away from the cockpit for less than two minutes when he came back through first class, past Jerry Kennedy, the newly hired United pilot, and stood banging urgently on the door. As Brad Griffin watched, the door remained shut. Haynes was saying, "I wish they'd unlock that fuckin' door. Pull the circuit breaker on that door and just unlock it, will ya?"

Fitch was at last able to open it, and Dvorak entered, pale and drawn, to announce, "Damage on the tail."

"On the tail," Haynes said. "That's what I thought."

Records asked, "You see it?"

"It's not the wing," Dvorak said, correcting Jan Brown's slip of the tongue. "It's the tail. Yeah, you can see it."

Dvorak sat at his engineer's console once again and buckled in at nearly a quarter to four in the afternoon. He keyed the microphone and told SAM, "Alright, I walked to the back and we got, ah, a lot of damage to the tail section that we could see through the window."

The engineer on the line said, "Okay, ya, United Two Thirty-Two, ah, you have, ah, you have a lot of damage to the tail section."

"Ah, the leading edge of the elevator is, ah, damaged, ah, it's not . . ." And here he heaved a weary sigh. "I mean, ah, there's damage there that I can see. I don't know how much is . . . that I cannot see. I can see it on the leading edge. On the outer part."

The man on the line said that other engineers were now listening in. Dvorak gave them a lengthy summary of what had happened so far, even as Haynes addressed the passengers, explaining that they would attempt an emergency landing at Sioux City and that his signal, before they met with the earth, would be the word *brace*, repeated three times.

At fourteen minutes to the hour, Fitch began the only left turn that the disabled plane was to make. While the crew had been unable to make left turns until then, he'd had twenty minutes of practice at steering the plane with the throttles, and this was his finest performance, his swan song. This crucial maneuver put 1819 Uniform on a southwesterly course direct to Sioux City at nearly the correct altitude to make the runway. It happened to be the wrong runway, though, one with a large number of fire engines parked on it and a big yellow *X* painted across the approach end to let pilots know that it was permanently closed.

As Brad Griffin listened to the captain's announcement, he heard a roar of anxiety and despair rise from the coach cabin, like that from a crowd in a theater when the projector breaks in the middle of the movie. Rene Le Beau was coming up the starboard aisle, first through B-Zone, past Ruth Pearlstein in her bright-green dress, taking care of five-year-old Devon McKelvey beside her, then past the little girl's brother Ryan, seven, sitting beside his mother Debbie. Debbie and Ruth were tennis partners. Le Beau passed on into first class. Brad Griffin noticed her because of her bright-red hair with the big blue bow in it, her startling youth. "I remember her walking backwards, telling people about the crash position. And her hands were shaking" as she held the briefing card. "She was so brave. And so scared."

Now up in the cockpit, as the plane descended below nine thousand feet, Haynes asked Dvorak, "What did SAM say? 'Good luck'?"

"He hasn't said anything," Dvorak responded.

"Okay, well, forget them," Haynes said. "Tell 'em you're leaving the air and you're gonna come back up here and help us. And screw 'em."

SAM called again, saying, "United Two Thirty-Two, one more time: No hydraulic quantity, is that correct?"

Dvorak said in frustration, "Affirmative-affirmative-affirmative!" More than twenty minutes had elapsed since he first reported that the craft had lost all hydraulic fluid.

After giving the passengers a ten-minute warning, Haynes discussed with the crew how to put the wheels down without hydraulics. They decided that the simplest procedure was to open the doors and let the landing gear fall out. Once that was done, Haynes said, "Okay, lock up and put everything away." Then he said to himself, "Well, Mama, we'll make those baseball games after all."

When Haynes's two sons were young, they played on Little League baseball teams. One day a friend of his who was the umpire for the local teams was unable to attend the games. Haynes found himself hastily learning the rules so that he could officiate. "I had a lot of fun and they were short on umpires, so I said I'd do the next one, and pretty soon I'm in it full time. I've been in it now for thirty years." Now, in the grip of the emergency, he was expressing hope. The crew might land the plane safely and make it to those weekend games that were coming up at the height of the Little League season.

Records keyed his mike and asked the Sioux City tower, "Where's the airport for Two Thirty-Two?"

"United Two Thirty-Two," said Bachman, "the airport's currently twelve o'clock and, ah, two-one miles."

Bachman was unsure. Should he let the DC-10 wander at will, even over the city where it might kill people on the ground? Should he direct the craft to turn away from the city and risk upsetting the plane and causing it to crash before it reached the airport? Even if a turn didn't compromise the plane's stability, the crew had to steer past several electronics towers, some of them more than two thousand feet tall. If 1819 Uniform hit one of those towers while attempting a turn, the wreckage would fall all over Siouxland. Bachman turned to Zielezinski and said, "Make the call."

Mark Zielezinski well knew that if anything went wrong, the responsibility would fall on him. "Kevin was a good controller for his experience level," Zielezinski later said. "But it was the team work of all the controllers that pitched in to make Kevin's job just a little bit easier. Kevin's only real task was responding to the crew [of 1819 Uniform] and passing along information that they requested. There were no other aircraft he was dealing with. Those aircraft were being worked by my other radar controller, Jim Weifenbach, who was responsible for separating them from [1819 Uniform]." Weifenbach was bringing in the A-7s. "Sitting between and monitoring

both positions," Zielezinski went on, "I was able to feed Jim information on what was going on with the emergency aircraft. He was
able to vector aircraft away from the emergency. When the one time
came that actually required Kevin to make a decision, he turned to
me and said 'Make the call.' If something would have happened, he
could have easily said, 'Mark told me to do it.'"

Zielezinski told Bachman to instruct United Flight 232 to turn.
"After the fact," Zielezinski recalled, "when I thought about it, it
scared the crap out of me, because if they didn't turn tight enough
or [weren't] able to stay above the towers, the wreckage would have
been up in that area instead of the airport. Would I make that call
again? Not sure. It was a call from my gut and experience as a pilot,
but sitting on the ground, I had no assurance the turn would be tight
enough."

Bachman keyed his mike and said, "United Two Thirty-Two
Heavy, you're gonna have to widen out just slightly to your left,
sir, ah, to make the turn to final, and also it'll take you away from
the city."

Haynes was quick to respond, "Whatever you do, keep us away
from the city."

Fitch continued to work the throttles as Haynes coached him
with remarks such as, "Back! Back!" and "Level, baby, level-level."

Bachman told Haynes, "You're currently, oh, one-seven miles
northeast of the airport. You're doing good."

Dvorak offered Fitch his seat. Fitch had been standing the whole
time, but he would not have any hope of surviving if he stood during
the landing. Fitch took the engineer's seat to run the throttles for the
final minutes of the flight. Dvorak strapped himself into the jump
seat behind Haynes.

At seven minutes before 4:00, Bachman said, "United Two
Thirty-Two Heavy, been advised there is a four-lane highway, ah, up
in that area, sir, if you can pick that up."

"Okay," Haynes said, "we'll see what we can do here. We've
already put the gear down, and ah, we're gonna have to be puttin' on
something solid if we can." Half a minute passed in static incoher-

ence and then Bachman said, "United Two Thirty-Two Heavy, if you can hold that altitude, sir, the right turn to one-eighty, ah, would put you on about, oh, ten miles east of the airport."

"That's what we're tryin' to do," Haynes said.

Dale Mleynek received a call from one of the flights of A-7 Corsairs that had not yet landed. The pilot said, "If that DC-10 needs an escort, Bat Eight-One could help him. . . . I thought with our BMDS* map we could help him find the airport."

"I don't think his problem is finding the airport," Mleynek said. "It's just gettin' here."

"Okay," said the A-7 pilot.

"Thanks anyway," said Mleynek.

"All right, thanks."

"You bet," Mleynek said.

Fifteen seconds later a woman called Mleynek and asked, "Are you guys taking any media calls?"

"Uh, no," Mleynek answered. "Not really."

Another flight of A-7s had landed, and Mleynek heard, "Bat Forty-One, a flight of two Alpha-Sevens, de-armed to the Guard ramp."

"Bat Four-One, Sioux City Ground. Taxi to the Guard ramp." A minute later another flight of two, Bat Eight-One, called, and Mleynek gave the pilots permission to follow Bat Four-One.

In the cockpit, Fitch asked Haynes, "Now where do you want to go?"

"Want to keep turning right," Haynes said. "Want to go to the airport."

"You want to go to the airport?"

"I want to get as close to the airport as we can."

"Okay," Fitch said.

Dvorak announced to the passengers, "We have four minutes to touchdown, four minutes to touchdown."

---

* Ballistic Missile Defense System.

Records looked out and saw the airfield sweep into the frame of his windscreen.

"United Two Thirty-Two Heavy," Bachman said, "the airport is, ah, oh, about, ah, eighteen miles southeast of your position about two-twenty on the heading. But we're gonna need you southbound away from the city first, if you can hold one-eighty heading."

Records responded, "We're tryin'. Tryin' to get to it right now." The reason that they were farther from the airport than they had been about three minutes earlier was that the plane made an unexpected tight right turn, and that turn took them about three miles back to the northeast, away from the field. As it happened, that was another crucial maneuver. The plane had now descended to an altitude that would allow it to reach the end of the runway.

"United Two Thirty-Two Heavy," said Bachman, "advise if you can pick up a road or anything where you can, ah, possibly land it on that."

Haynes replied, "Okay, we're, ah, we're a hundred-eighty degree heading. Now what do you want?"

"United Two Thirty-Two, if you can hold the altitude, the one-eighty heading will work fine for about, oh, seven miles."

"Okay," Haynes said. "We're tryin' to turn back." Then Haynes said to Fitch, "Back. Back-back-back. Forward-forward-forward! Won't this be a fun landing?"

"United Two Thirty-Two Heavy, can you hold that heading, sir?"

Haynes had begun his announcement to the passengers, so Records responded, "Yeah, we're on it now for a little while."

"United Two Thirty-Two Heavy, roger," Bachman said. "That heading will put you, oh, ah, currently fifteen miles northeast of the airport. If you can hold that, it'll put you on about a three-mile final."

"Okay, we're givin' it heck."

Half a minute later, Bachman said, "United Two Thirty-Two Heavy, the airport's currently twelve o'clock and one-three miles."

"Okay," Records said, "we're lookin' for it."

I asked Records why he had seen the airport before and now had to look for it again. He said, "We were at a very low altitude at eighteen miles out, and the airport looked much different than normal, especially since it was also shorter and narrower than the usual picture seen from a DC-10. When told we were at thirteen miles, we were preoccupied with vertical speed and heading problems, and it took a few seconds to relocate it." Ordinarily, they could have easily located the airport with a radio navigational aid called a VOR. But the facility was out of service for maintenance that day.

"We're startin' down a little bit now," Haynes told Bachman. "We got a little better control of the elevator. It's not full, but a little bit."

"United Two Thirty-Two Heavy, roger," said Bachman. "Ah, the airport's currently at your one o'clock position one-zero miles."

Out on Taxiway Lima, the pilots of the last four Corsairs to arrive began to move toward the ramp.

Haynes looked out on a sea of green. The crash was 144 seconds away, but he still could not see the slim runway in the vastness of the American heartland.

Then Fitch said, "I got the runway if you don't."

"I don't," Haynes admitted. Then to Fitch, "Come back–come back."

"It's off to the right. Over there."

Records said, "Right there."

The compass showed a southwesterly course. Haynes, for one, had been convinced that they would never make it to any runway. Yet here they were, pointing right at the Sioux City airport and a usable stretch of cracked and weedy 1940s concrete.

Dvorak recalled, "We're coming down final. I was more afraid at that time that we were going to go off the end of the runway and be in a ball of fire."

Bachman now said, "United Two Thirty-Two Heavy, if you can't make the airport, sir, there is an interstate that runs, ah, north to south to the east side of the airport, ah, it's a four-lane interstate."

Haynes said, "We're just passin' it now, we're going to try for the airp—" He cut the word *airport* in half by releasing the microphone button on the yoke too soon. He peered out into the bright sunlight and asked, "Is that the runway right there?"

"Right."

Elated, he told Bachman, "We have the runway in sight!"

"Two Heavy, roger."

Haynes was so excited, in fact, that he transmitted on top of Bachman and obscured whatever the controller said next. "We have the runway in sight!" Haynes said again as if he couldn't believe it himself. Bachman and Haynes transmitted over each other for a few seconds. Then Haynes said it a third time: "We have the runway in sight! We'll be with you very shortly. Thanks a *lot* for your help." You can hear the relief in Haynes's voice. They had rolled wings level, and all at once Haynes saw the sight that for decades had represented for him the accomplishment of the ultimate goal of any aviator: To return safely. To bring your people home.

The control tower fell eerily silent. The controllers had brought the flight in, and now they could almost hear the applause. Bates and Zielezinski and Bachman all looked out the window and saw the festive red and white and blue and yellow lights sparkling across the field and still streaming down the highways from all directions, as if the whole green world had decided that Christmas should come in July. All they needed now was a snowstorm.

Dvorak announced to the passengers that two minutes remained before touchdown. Nearly two hundred feet behind him, his friend Susan White was wondering how on earth she was going to protect all her passengers, that boy in the Chicago Cubs hat behind her jump seat with his mother, and a few rows ahead of them, pretty thirteen-year-old Cinnamon Angelina Martinez. Cinnamon was traveling alone. At the beginning of the flight, she had talked to White about her ambition to become a flight attendant. White had pinned plastic United Airlines wings to her shirt. After the engine exploded, White had asked the man sitting next to Cinnamon to make sure that she escaped. He promised that he would.

A hundred and twelve seconds remained in the flight when

Bachman said, "United Two Thirty-Two Heavy, the wind's currently three-six-zero at one-one. Three-sixty at eleven. You're cleared to land on any runway."

Haynes laughed and asked, "You want to be particular and make it a runway, huh?" In the control tower, some of the men chuckled, their tension dissipating. Everyone knew that November 1819 Uniform had made it. Maybe it would roll off the end of the runway into the corn. The crew would deploy the evacuation slides. The fire engines would respond. But in that moment of levity, they were convinced that the crippled McDonnell Douglas DC-10 was going to land safely.

Bates recalled of those moments, "We were just waiting to see the aircraft lift up over the bluffs." Bates and the other controllers listened quietly as Bachman talked to Haynes in those final seconds. In his jubilation at seeing a runway, Haynes was so excited that he had to ask for the wind speed and direction three times. The wind was at his back, not ideal.

A few seconds later, the aircraft lifted up over the bluffs, into a blue sky now populated by an afternoon buildup of cumulus clouds that had appeared like great white schooners as the sun baked the rain off the land. At that moment, the Air National Guard chaplain, Gregory Clapper, stood in the parking lot of the Southern Hills Mall, holding the hands of his little girls and watching the great ship pass overhead.

Zielezinski later said, "Quite honestly, we had very high hopes, because the aircraft looked fairly stable on the final [approach]."

Gary Brown stood beside his white Woodbury County rescue truck on the airport ramp and raised a pair of binoculars to his eyes. The press later reported that he could see Haynes's face through the windshield, his eyes, his whole countenance, as he wrestled with the controls. The *Sioux City Journal* even quoted Brown as saying, "Probably the toughest thing was when I had eye contact with the pilot. . . . He didn't see me, of course, but I could see his face through my binoculars. His face looked busy."

Two decades later, Brown said, "That was not true. I could see that there was a crew in there, but I was looking at the plane, really, just to see what I could tell about the damage."

On the Air National Guard ramp, Al Smith and his wingman Ben Bendixen had climbed down from their cockpits, drenched in sweat, and were crossing toward the maintenance control room to get out of their flight equipment. Although they couldn't see 1819 Uniform, the air traffic controllers high above them could. As they watched, the aircraft seemed to be screaming toward them. "The speed was extremely high," Bates said. "There was a very small amount of vapor coming off the wingtips, which could have been condensation, could have been fuel." Otherwise, he said, "It looked like a normal landing. It started settling down."

Bachman stood up from his position and yelled, "He's gonna make it!"

CHAPTER FIVE

It had rained a bit earlier in Washington, D.C., barely enough drizzle to raise the humidity. Cloud cover had begun moving in as a fresh breeze picked up from the south. Robert MacIntosh, in his early fifties, sat in his office across the street from the Smithsonian Institution, and worked on a report in his role as a major aircraft accident investigator for the National Transportation Safety Board. At about 4:30 in the afternoon, the director of the Bureau of Accident Investigation at the NTSB, Terry Armentrout, rang MacIntosh's phone and said, "You'd better come in here."

MacIntosh went down the hall to Armentrout's office. "Bob, it looks like we've got a DC-10 in trouble," Armentrout said, nodding at the speakerphone in the center of a conference table. A disembodied voice explained that Minneapolis Center had the plane and was about to pass it off to the Sioux City Approach Control. As the two men listened, people began entering the room and taking chairs. The voice described the situation that was developing. As MacIntosh listened and more and more people arrived in Armentrout's office, it became clear that the person speaking was upstairs in the tenth-floor Command Center. Someone up there was summarizing what was being said by an air traffic controller and a pilot on board the aircraft. They learned that the plane had lost all its hydraulic power. The crew was having trouble with directional control and could make only right turns. Everyone in the room was expert enough in matters of aviation to know that this spelled disaster. Indeed, they knew that in 1985 a Japan Airlines 747 had lost all of its hydraulic systems. The crew was able to steer with the throttles for a while, but the plane eventually crashed into Mount Ogura, killing more than five hundred people.

MacIntosh later described the eight or so people in Armentrout's office as "a kind of war room setup." Then, as word spread, people began converging on the director's office from all over the building. "It got real crowded," as MacIntosh put it. The more they heard, the darker the collective mood grew. Everyone had the same thought: Somebody's going to die. Maybe everybody. They listened as long as they could stand it, before Armentrout turned to MacIntosh and said, "Bob, this is a big one. Do you think you can handle it?"

"I sure can," MacIntosh said.

"We'll send as many people as you need," Armentrout said, "but you're gonna take it." Then he turned to Robert Benzon, another major investigator, and said, "Bob, you've just done a big one out in Denver. Why don't you go with Bob and we'll put both Bobs on it."

Then, as MacIntosh described it, "We were headed out the door."

He had been at the NTSB for about fourteen months, and this was his first major crash for "the Board," as the people there called that organization. From 1966 to 1978, MacIntosh had been flight safety officer and accident investigator for the Air Force. He had then joined Beech Aircraft and conducted sixty accident investigations in three years for that company. In addition, as Benzon put it, MacIntosh "flew RF-101 Voodoos over North Vietnam for at least one tour. Very fast flying, but very low, and unarmed. No way to shoot back . . . no way. Very scary stuff." So MacIntosh brought considerable experience to the job as he drove home to suburban Virginia to get packed for the Go Team.

NTSB Go Teams have become burdened with a good deal of mythology over the years. It is said, for example, that each member of the Go Team keeps a packed suitcase under his desk to make a quick getaway any time a plane crashes. However, as members of the Go Team that responded to United Flight 232 later explained, that would be impractical, since you never knew if you were going to Alaska in January or to Iowa in the middle of summer. Ted Lopat-kiewicz, who was the public affairs officer for the NTSB during the investigation, said, "The rule is you need to be able to leave town in two hours. That's a little exaggerated. I don't know when we've actu-ally left in two hours." The NTSB issues a schedule each Monday at 5:00 p.m. designating the Board member, public affairs officer, and the technical specialists who will be on the Go Team in the event of a crash. Every Go Team includes one of the five members of the Board.

As MacIntosh made his way home, the administrative staff at NTSB headquarters flew into action. It was up to them to arrange for an aircraft to take the Go Team to Sioux City. They also set about securing the resources that the Go Team would need on the ground once they arrived. The staffers were acutely aware of the potential hazards of moving more than a dozen highly technical investigators across the country and establishing them effectively in the midst of a wrecked 185-ton aircraft and its contents. Foremost in the minds of administrative staff members was securing hotel rooms and rental cars. They knew that members of the press, even in those crucial first moments, were descending on the town and snapping up all lodging and transportation. Network TV stations and CNN would buy off blocks of rooms. As it happened, by the time the NTSB staff mem-bers called Sioux City, the only lodging left was a run-down motel called the Flamingo. Across the river in South Sioux City, Nebraska, it would quickly become known among Go Team members as "the Flamin' O."

Susan White stood at her demonstration position waiting for Jan Brown to give the final briefing to the passengers. Looking aft from exit 3-Left, she noticed a blonde woman in a window seat a few aisles back. Cynthia Louise Muncey, twenty-five, was on her way back from vacation in Hawaii, as were many passengers on flight 232 that day.

Muncey was dressed in bright summer yellow. She had sent a post-card to her little sister Pam before boarding a flight to Denver. "Hello All!" read the card from the Outrigger West Hotel in Honolulu. "I made it!! You wouldn't believe it here!! Lots of really big motels! You would love it here, Pam! Even better than Florida! Call you if I ever go home! Ha! Ha!"

Now Cindy "was crying hysterically," White later said. She thought, "I should go comfort her before this starts spreading." White left her position and hurried down the aisle. She stood before Cindy's row. The dark-haired man sitting next to her, Efram Upshaw, twenty-three, looked imploringly into White's eyes. She could see that he was both frightened and at a loss for how to help the weeping woman. Upshaw would be severely injured, the last of all the survi-vors to be released from the hospital, but he would live. White said, "Excuse me," and leaned across him to hug Cindy. "She was sweaty from crying. I just wanted to cry right there with her," White said, "and I just prayed for the will, the strength not to cry."

Cindy began keening, "Are we gonna die? Are we gonna die? I feel like we're gonna die! I can't die, I have three small children. They're waiting for me to come home. They need me! I can't die!"

Years later, White said, "I honestly felt we were going to die when she asked me, that's how afraid I was inside. But I had willed myself not to cry and I somehow remained composed."

Cindy's three little girls—seven-year-old Kayce; Amber, who was about to turn five; and Audra, who had recently celebrated her second birthday—were waiting for her at home, along with Pam, twenty-one. Pam adored her sister and was especially eager to reunite with Cindy. "My first memory of our special sister bond," Pam recalled, "is a day that we were running late for school. I was in first grade and she was in fifth." As the two girls came out the front door, they saw the school bus pulling away. Cindy ran down the street to catch the bus, but little Pam was too slow. Pam was seized with the fear that Cindy was going to leave her forever. She screamed, "Wait for me!"

Cindy turned around to look at her little sister. She could hear the panic in her voice. She returned to Pam and said, "I wasn't going to let the bus leave you. I was going to have it wait for you."

"At that moment," said Pam, "I knew she would always have my back."

When Pam was five years old, she had a crush on a boy named Rick. Cindy, along with Rick's sister, contrived to marry them behind a bush outside the church they all attended. Rick slipped a pop top from a soda can onto Pam's finger, and Cindy pronounced them married for life. Later, when they were older, Pam confided in Cindy that she was in love with that same boy, Rick McDowell, but it seemed unlikely that they would ever get together.

"Others thought I was nuts and that I should move on," Pam said. Pam and Rick had stayed in touch by phone and through letters. But "he was on one coast, and I was on the other. It seemed impossible." She was living on Carolina Beach where her family ran a motel, and Rick was in San Diego in the Marines. "I mean, you couldn't get farther away."

But Cindy assured her, "I believe in fairy tale endings, Pam."

Rick proposed over the phone. They were apart during the entire year of their engagement. In fact, Rick was swept up in the Gulf War and was out on a ship for six months. Pam had wanted her sister to be her maid of honor, but the wedding didn't take place until two and a half years after the crash. Pam had saved the pop top from her wedding ceremony at the age of five. She wore it around her neck at the real wedding on December 14, 1991. "I married that boy and have been happily married for over twenty-one years," Pam said when we spoke the day before her anniversary. After the wedding, they had the pop top embedded in an acrylic cube and made into a nightlight that burns in their bedroom.

As White held Cindy in her arms, wondering what to tell her, Captain Haynes announced, "This is gonna be the roughest landing you've ever had." And White was thinking, as she later put it, "Oh, my goodness. For a DC-10 captain to say that, you know it's gonna be bad." White said, "I couldn't lie to her and tell her that we're going to be okay, because in my heart at that moment, I did not feel we were going to be okay." White held Cindy tighter and said, "We need to pray." She took a breath and explained, "We need to be prepared for the roughest landing, like the captain just said. And we need to pray."

"Okay," Cindy said, gulping air in hard shuddering sighs.

White returned to her exit. As she glanced to her left, she saw Bruce and Dina and Ruth Anne Osenberg holding hands with one another and praying with Tom Postle. Postle had his Bible in his lap. Their heads were bowed. White felt a rush of emotion and confidence that what she had told Cindy was right. She looked up and saw that Cindy "still had tears, but she had calmed down." White later said, "She made such an imprint on my heart. I will never forget her, and we only shared a brief moment." Later, while testifying about Cindy in court, White burst into tears and ran out of the courtroom.

When Jan Brown finished briefing the passengers, White started down the aisle, helping people practice bracing. She came across thirty-one-year-old William Phillip McNulty III across the aisle from Janice-Long Brown and her daughter Kimberly. Three-year-old Annabelle Lee McNulty sat in her father's lap with a blanket over her. White lifted the blanket and saw that McNulty had belted Annabelle into his own seat belt, which would almost certainly have killed the child on impact. White explained to him that he was supposed to put the baby on the floor cushioned with pillows and blankets. "I'll go get some pillows," White told the young father.

Janice and Kimberly overheard the conversation and passed their pillows and blankets across the aisle. "And so we wrapped his baby in pillows and blankets and he put the baby on the floor." White paused and sighed wearily as she spoke about it. "And then I learned that he and the baby both died."

White proceeded down the aisle, looking around her at the surreal scene. A man in a Hawaiian shirt comforted his wife. People wrote notes as last testaments. "I saw a few women put their [driver's] license down their shirts." She felt as if she were in a movie. Nothing seemed real any longer. When she reached the rear of the plane, she assessed how she would respond to the emergency evacuation. She decided that Dave Randa and his mother could not help. Dave was still folded completely in half, clutching his legs, his mother's left hand draped across his back. He still wore his favorite Chicago Cubs hat. White turned to John Hatch beside Conant and asked him to help with the door.

White strapped herself into the jump seat, facing aft, back to back with Susan Randa. "We got a four-minute warning, and it just seemed like it was . . . *forever*," White recalled. "And I looked up at the Airphone and I wanted to call home. And I thought, Oh, no, I can't call home, because that'll just make them sad." Her mind was racing, crazy, jumping all around. She remembered Jan Brown telling her to watch out for fire when they landed. She remembered that her United Airlines coed softball team was playing that night. They played every Wednesday night in Chicago, and she had promised to be there. She leaned forward in her jump seat to look around the magazine rack with the *Newsweeks* and *Times* and *Wall Street Journals*. She called in a stage whisper to Donna McGrady, the flight attendant who had switched the seats of Yisroel Brownstein and Richard Howard Sudlow.

"Donna! Donna! Do you think they'll know why I'm not at my game tonight?"

"I think they'll know," McGrady replied.

"Okay," White said. She sat for a while, letting her thoughts churn and fidgeting in her seat. Then she leaned forward again and called out, "Donna! Donna! Do you think they're going to release me for tomorrow?" She had two more days of reserve when the airline could call her for any flight, but after this experience, she didn't want to work.

"Yes!" McGrady said. "I think you'll be released."

As White leaned forward, looking across the galley, she saw that McGrady had taken out her earrings. She liked big earrings. "I thought, Gosh, I need to take my earrings out too. Here we went through and told everybody take off their eyeglasses and pens out of their pockets, and here I had my earrings on." She unfastened her harness and stood up.

"What are you doing?" McGrady called in alarm.

"I'm taking my earrings off!" she said. The passengers—Conant and Hatch and Dave and Susan Randa—could hear the two flight attendants, and must have been wondering what on earth they were thinking. White opened the cubby behind her seat—they called it the doghouse—and hauled out her tote bag. She took off her earrings and put them in the bag. Then she stowed it once again. She sat down, fastened her harness, and "about every five seconds, I kept tightening my seat belt. I couldn't get it tight enough."

She checked her door again, rehearsing in her mind how she would open it. She recited all her commands and reviewed how she would notify the cockpit, while at the same time recalling her whole life and wondering how her parents were going to survive losing a child. "I have five sisters, and I thought about my sisters, and they were going to wear my jewelry and my clothes after I died, and I just kept thinking of all these horrible sad, sad thoughts. And I thought, 'My goodness, I wish I'd never gotten this job.' I got this job to see the world, and I'd only been to Jamaica, and I started feeling sorry for myself. I just remembered everything in detail. I could picture my pastor up at the pulpit announcing my death in the church I grew up in, and how my mother was going to be so sad. And then I would go back to, No, we're going to evacuate and we're going to be fine. And then I kept going back to more thoughts. How are they going to get my car keys? How are they going to get my car out of the employee parking lot? All my bills are paid. Everything is in order."

She craned her neck around toward the front and saw a man with his arm around his wife, comforting her, Forrest and Sandra Mixon, in their fifties, from Chapel Hill. White wished for someone to comfort her. Then she began focusing on a movie she had seen about people who had died and then come back to tell their stories. "I started focusing on that thought of going to heaven, a much better, peaceful place." And White's experience of all those thoughts and memories took a mere two minutes, for now she heard Dvorak call out the two-minute warning from the flight deck.

Conant watched White and the boy in the baseball cap and his mother. She saw White glance around at her passengers with a drawn and ashen expression. Conant now lowered her head and tried to make herself small. But then as the landing approached, she began to panic. "I just started to lose it," she said. "It felt like I was just churning, like I had no center and no control over my limbs, my arms, my legs, and I was so frightened that I couldn't think."

A DC-10 is nearly two hundred feet long, and she was in the last row. The initial point of impact was about a hundred feet ahead of her. In fact, as she tried to control her panic, the impact had already begun.

When the plane rolled out lined up with Runway 22, Fitch understood that they had 369,000 pounds of flesh and metal going nearly 250 miles an hour with no way to stop it. "But," he later said, "the beautiful thing was at the end of the runway was a wide open field that was laced in corn." The Sioux City airport leased about a thousand acres of its land to the Sioux Land Farm Agency, which planted corn and soybeans in the fields and in return provided the airport with about 15 percent of its operating revenue. This meant that 1819 Uniform would be landing, in effect, on a rich, green, wet, midsummer farm. "And I thought, Perfect," Fitch said later. He had envisioned all that plant matter gently slowing the plane, cushioning the blow. It would be like dropping a ceramic vessel into a pile of newly mown hay. It would not even crack. Then the eight doors would open, the yellow slides would blossom, and all the passengers would emerge from the cathedral in a jubilant procession. "And we're going to the nearest saloon," said Fitch, "and I'm buying."

In the final seconds of the flight, at an altitude of about four hundred feet, Haynes saw their excessive speed and was concerned that the tires would explode on contact. The plane would normally land at about half its present speed. Haynes told Fitch to take the power off. Records, too, told Fitch to cut the power. But Fitch was on his own, Records said. Fitch later said that he had planned to close the throttles as the plane touched down, "but then I looked over to see the incredibly high sink rate, eighteen hundred feet per minute toward the ground, three times in excess of the structural capability of the landing gear. So I firewalled both the engines." He stretched his arms forward as far as he could reach, straining against his harness as he sat in Dvorak's seat.

The left engine spooled up to almost 96 percent power, while the right reached only 66 percent at first. It's possible that Fitch pushed both throttles the same amount and the engines happened to respond that way. The relationship between the position of the throttle and the thrust that an engine produces is not linear. The second possibility is that Fitch made a mistake. While he thought that he was pushing the throttles evenly, he may not have done so. A third possibility is that the plane, which had been trying to turn right for more than forty minutes, turned right once more on its own. Whatever the case, the right wing went from about 2 degrees of bank to more than 20. This happened less than a hundred feet above the ground, and it happened fast. Once the right wing began to drop, it took but a fraction of a second for it to tear into the runway at roughly the same time that the right landing gear gouged a trench through the concrete.

Records believes that whatever caused the difference in thrust, "had we made a real nice touchdown, we probably would have gone off the end of the runway at 150 knots with no brakes, no nose-wheel steering, no spoilers, speed brakes. Who knows what could have happened? As it turns out, maybe we were fortunate." He believes that the difference in power was not a blunder on Fitch's part but was nothing more than the difference in the time the engines took to spool up.

Tim Owens was strapped into his jump seat at 3-Left looking at all the seats on his side of C-Zone, all the heads down, all the way back to Dave and Susan Randa, with Owens's dear friend Susan White in her jump seat right behind them. Along with the other flight attendants, he was shouting, "Brace! Brace! Brace!" over and over again. At the same time, he kept glancing out the small window in his exit door.

"I could see how excessively fast we were going," he said later. And he could no longer shout "brace" with quite the same conviction, because he knew that the plane was going to crash and considered it likely that everyone would die. "Right before we hit the ground, I took one last look out the window and everything was just a blur." He braced himself as hard as he could, gritted his teeth, put his head back, and then felt himself slam into the ground. He felt the plane bounce and tip and then pole-vault up onto its nose. He vividly recalled looking down his aisle toward Susan White. He couldn't see her, but he knew where she was, sixteen rows away. He could see her elbow as she crossed her arms and tried to brace in her jump seat facing the toilets. And then to Owens's amazement, the entire tail of the airplane broke off and departed. As the plane rolled up onto its nose, the great aperture that had opened where the tail had been now angled across an arc of intense blue sky, and then—shockingly—it pointed directly at the high summer sun. "And I was blinded by the sunlight," Owens said. That shaft of pure sun streamed down the aisles, supersaturating all the colors and giving the scene a surreal cast. The celestial light flooded the cabin, illuminating a sight that Owens would never forget, as people who were still strapped into their seats were torn free and sent tumbling out onto the runway. Some of the banks of seats were thrown high into the air, far above the fuselage in great parabolas, shot there as if from a cannon by the centrifugal force as the aft end of the fuselage swung in its majestic, flaming arc. What must it have been like to take that ride, alive, aloft, alone, aware, unhurt as yet and looking down on the green earth? Then as the plane continued its balletic progress, the breached fuselage swept past the sun, and the cabin went dim once more.

"It all happened so fast," Owens said. "The plane was breaking apart, things were coming apart around me, people were screaming." Soon his view of those people who were being cast out was obscured as Owens was buried by debris. And once again he became certain that this was how his life would end.

Far away in the departed tail, Martha Conant could not yet tell what was happening. All she knew was that the plane was shaking and shuddering and vibrating and wrenching so violently that she couldn't keep her hands on the seat in front of her. Conant's left hand flew free, as if of its own accord, and she involuntarily took hold of John Hatch's necktie.

"And then this voice in my head said, 'If you panic, you're not going to be able to get out.'" She withdrew her hand and put it back on the seat in front of her and tried to steady herself. Only seconds had passed, but it seemed much longer.

"Then there was this huge rush of air and dirt and grit." She involuntarily closed her eyes. She felt as if she had blacked out. When her memory trace picked up again, she was still in motion with a hot torrent of air and sharp grit, like shattered glass, lashing her face. She had barely enough time to think, as she reported, "Oh, I'm still alive." Then her memory was again wiped clean. It seemed to her that she blacked out again. When her consciousness resumed, all motion had stopped.

Conant opened her eyes and saw the earth, a scabby field of grass and weeds, hot and moist from recent rains. "There was nothing in front of me," she said, still incredulous after more than two decades. She could not see the seat in front of her, now tilted to the right, torn almost free of its mounts. John Hatch to her left, the couple to her right—if they were there, she could not see them either, nor Susan White in her jump seat nor Dave Randa and his mother. To Conant's right, nine-year-old Yisroel Brownstein and Richard Howard Sudlow were buried in debris. The entire plane was gone, that much was true. And in Conant's perception, only the hurtful beauty of the green earth remained, the place she had so dearly longed to be beneath the vast, impossibly blue sky. Some colossal force had set her gently on this soil and had opened a passage the size of the entire circumference of the ship through which to escape. Nothing else existed. If she'd been looking for a miracle, it appeared that she had found one.

She took a breath and paused for a moment to let this astonishing sight sink in. From somewhere far off, the cicada sound of a red-winged blackbird reached that section of seats. Killdeer raced past the opening into the corn. "I unbuckled my seat belt. The seat was tilted forward, and I dropped probably two or three feet to the ground." The drop was closer to eight or ten feet. She landed in torn and twisted metal, but noticed nothing, felt nothing, not even as she walked out, cutting her ankles on the twisted shards. It seemed as easy as stepping out of a car. She stood on the warm earth in the smell of the corn, the moist heat of the day. In her view now, as she looked around, she saw no fire, no airplane, no debris. "I was the only person out there, and I kind of looked to see—where should I go?" She turned and turned and turned, peering, searching. Then she saw something in the distance that she thought might be people or vehicles, and at last her emotional system let her go. She ran flat out with her heart jammed up in her throat. Airports are big. The way seemed endless. A man appeared as if out of nowhere, and said, "Where did you come from? How did you get here?"

"Off that plane," she said, pointing to the foul cloud of black kerosene smoke that she could now see crawling across the green world, the blue sky. "And I am scared to death."

CHAPTER SIX

The seven-foot fan on the front of the CF6-6 engine is made of an alloy of titanium. So are some of the compressor wheels behind it. As you move back through the engine, where the combustion of fuel must take place, the temperature will grow so hot that titanium cannot withstand it. The combustion chamber, therefore, is made of one of the so-called nickel superalloys designed to hold together in the extreme heat. The turbine wheels at the back, which drive the engine, are also made of nickel superalloys.

Miners in medieval Saxony were after copper and silver, but they sometimes had their wares contaminated by niccolite, a bedeviling alloy of arsenic and nickel. They called it *kupfernickel*, a reference to Old Nick, Satan himself. When Axel Fredrik Cronstedt, a Swedish chemist, isolated that metal in 1751, the name stuck. This hard white metal certainly could have been the culprit in the explosion. It's more than three times as dense as titanium (and hence weighs considerably more). When it spins, the stresses on it are great indeed. And superalloy wheels had been known to break before.

But nickel was elsewhere in the plane too. The hydraulic lines were made of stainless steel, which is part nickel. When Dvorak had watched the hydraulic pressure fall from three thousand pounds per square inch to zero, when he assessed the damage to the tail, he most likely knew that something had gone wrong with those stainless-steel lines. Nickel may have been the culprit, but nickel was the victim too. No one yet knew. The trouble may have been elsewhere.

For titanium is a strange and temperamental material. Perhaps it should have been named for Old Nick, because it certainly could pass for the work of a diabolical intelligence. It seems almost as if it were put on earth specifically to tempt us into this clever trick of spinning wheels and launching ourselves into flight. For one thing, titanium is found everywhere—in sand, rock, clay, soil, coal, water, oil, plants of all sorts, and in the flesh of animals. We find titanium in lava from volcanoes, in the bottom of the ocean, and in the meteorites that fall from the sky. We can find it in our own bones. Moreover, there are plenty of places where titanium is highly concentrated in a form that is easily mined. Titanium dioxide is a common ingredient in paint. It makes it white. If the paint is colored, titanium gives it opacity. Titanium dioxide makes great sunscreen. And it's not poisonous.

An Englishman named William Gregor originally described titanium in 1791. In 1795 a German pharmacist named Martin Heinrich Klaproth named it for the mythical Titans because of its strength. But titanium was unusable because of its strong affinity for oxygen and nitrogen. Whenever one chemist or another tried to isolate titanium, he wound up with metal that was contaminated with those other elements. It wasn't until 1910 that an American chemist named Matthew Arnold Hunter managed to combine titanium with chlorine, making titanium tetrachloride and revealing yet another confounding mystery about that metal.

Titanium tetrachloride is a clear liquid, what's known as a "rare transition metal halide." *Transition* means that titanium is always on the way to becoming something else. It does not want to be itself, because one of its shells of electrons, the sub-shell designated by the letter d, is not completely filled, so titanium constantly longs to mate with a material that can fill that shell. Nitrogen and oxygen will suffice, but chlorine can strip those electrons away to form titanium tetrachloride.

In the business of making this elusive metal, titanium tetrachloride became known as "Tickle," based on its chemical formula: $TiCl_4$.

Tickle must be kept in a vacuum or in a vessel that contains an inert gas, such as helium or argon. If Tickle is exposed to air, it combines with moisture and bursts into view as a cloud of corrosive white smoke that is made up of tiny droplets of hydrochloric acid. Titanium is full of tricks. It will burn in chlorine gas and will explode in red fuming nitric acid. Melt it with nitrogen, and it turns into a ceramic material that looks like gold and is suitable for coating everything from knife blades to prosthetic hips. By varying the thickness and the voltage used in anodizing titanium, it can be made pink, green, purple, blue, brown, and any number of colors in between. The trouble with those materials is that they are so brittle they crack except when used as a thin coating.

Darrell F. Socie, professor of mechanical science and engineering at the University of Illinois and an expert in metal fatigue, said of such materials, "They're intermetallic compounds, but they're really a ceramic. They are very hard, very brittle, very strong and have no ductility." That means they won't bend or stretch. They break.

Titanium is a paradox, a thing that both can and can't exist. James Wildey, a metallurgist, was thirty-seven years old when he helped investigate the crash of United Flight 232 for the NTSB. He said, "Under some conditions, titanium can be soft and weak. When soft, it can stretch without breaking. Under other conditions, it can be hard and brittle like crystal. When mixed with small amounts of other elements, it can retain much of its hardness, but unlike crystal it is very tough." It is so tough that about half a million square feet of it, just a third of a millimeter thick, was used to build the retractable roof of the Fukuoka Dome arena in Japan.

Like meat, titanium has grain. It can flex and flow like muscle. When titanium gets hot, it can smear like peanut butter. But within that muscle of metal we find crystals. The engineers themselves may sometimes think of their metals as living things. In public testimony during the investigation of the crash, one of the designers of the CF6-6 engine from General Electric, Christopher Glynn, was trying to explain how these engines can break. He said, "You have to ask the material, 'How do you feel about having a crack in you, and how fast is it going to grow?'" He described the tests in his lab this way: "It's letting the material tell you how it feels about that."

It is preferable that the crystal structure of titanium be perfect. However, minute imperfections, small impurities, can creep into the process of making those fans and compressors and turbines. Impurities can sometimes cause the metal to fail under the tremendous strain of spinning.

Titanium can also burn. Sometimes the spinning titanium wheels catch fire, and the flame passes from wheel to wheel and destroys the engine. That provided yet another possibility for what might have happened to the number two engine on 1819 Uniform.

As Kevin Bachman watched the DC-10 approach Sioux Gateway Airport, he was convinced that it would land safely. Hundreds of others were watching too—Zielezinski and Weifenbach, Mleynek, Bates, Charles Owings, Terry Dobson, and all the other controllers who had joined them in the tower, as well as the A-7 pilots waiting on Taxiway Lima, along with scores of fire fighters, police, and Air National Guard men and women, and Gary Brown with his binoculars raised to his eyes—they all watched as the jumbo jet unfolded against the sky into a great winged shape. As the controllers gazed out the wraparound windows of the tower cab, they saw that the plane wasn't floating the way airliners ordinarily seem to, that deceptive illusion of slow motion. Rather this plane was howling down the glide slope, dropping like a stone under the high summer sun in a sky full of majestic cumulus clouds.

In the cockpit, Haynes was still trying to hear the wind speed and direction. "Okay," he said to Bachman, "we're all three talkin' at once. Say it again one more time."

"Ah, zero-one-zero at one-one and there is a runway, ah, that's closed, sir, that could, ah . . . probably work to the southwest. It runs, ah, northeast to southwest."

Haynes wasn't sure what runway he was aiming for, but he said, "We're pretty well lined up on this one here . . . think we will be."

As the jumbo jet blossomed in Bachman's field of vision, he realized that Haynes was going to attempt to land on the old runway where the fire engines waited. Haynes could detect the urgency in Bachman's voice when he spoke. "United Two Thirty-Two Heavy, ah, roger, sir, tha-that's a closed runway, sir, that'll work, sir, we're gettin' the equipment *off* the runway. They'll line up for that one."

Zielezinski turned to Mleynek and called for him to clear Runway 22. Mleynek keyed his mike and said, "Bat Four-One, hold your position there. Bat Eight-One, hold your position." A moment later, Mleynek called the fire trucks, which had assembled on the old closed World War II runway, and said, "Red Dog One and Red Dog Three, exit Runway, ah, Four-Two-Two. That DC-10 will be landing Four-Two-Two."

One of the fire fighters responded, "We'll exit and get outta here."

Mleynek's voice shot up then, as he said, "Red Dog One and Red Dog Three and Red Dog Six, exit Four-Two-Two immediately!" And in another few seconds, he said, "Red Dog Two and Red Dog Four, that DC-10 is three, uh, two mile final Runway Four-Two-Two!"

Five seconds later, Mleynek said, "All emergency equipment, remain to the right of runway Four-Two-Two. That DC-10 is on one-and-a-half mile final."

Dave Hutton, the assistant fire chief who drove Jim Hathaway, the base fire chief, in a Jeep truck, said many years later, "We were at the southwest end of Runway Two-Two-Four. We were looking toward Runway Three-One-One-Three, waiting for the plane to land on that. About a minute before it came in, they said, 'All crash equipment, get off that runway, because the plane's comin' in.'"

Off to the side of the command vehicle that Hutton was driving, the Corsair pilots sat watching through their open canopies as the jumbo jet appeared as a white shark shape with a red stripe, trembling in heat waves against the blue July sky, even as the fire trucks began to blow black diesel smoke and roll forward, and the mammoth ship settled in and dove toward the field.

"How long is it?" Haynes asked.

"Sixty-six hundred feet," Bachman said, his voice rising. "Six thousand six hundred feet, and the equipment is coming off."

As the plane neared the field, a number of fire fighters on the ground radioed, "We got him in sight over here!"

After twelve seconds of radio silence, Bachman added, "At the end of the runway, it's just a wide open field so, sir, so the winds won't be a problem." The plane was landing with the wind on its tail, so it carried even more speed than it would have otherwise. Even if the plane reached the runway, it was going to go off the end.

Haynes said, "Okay." The time was 3:59 and 34 seconds. Less than a minute remained in the life of 1819 Uniform.

The first of several alarms went off, the Ground Proximity Warning System meant to tell a pilot when the plane was descending too rapidly while too close to the ground. Haynes groaned audibly as the whooping klaxon sounded and a lazy mechanical voice insisted, "Pull up. Pull up. Pull up."

Of that moment, Records would later say, "We discussed it on short final about pulling the power off, but Denny [Fitch] said, 'No, that's what's controlling us.' And we were rapidly running out of time to discuss it any further."

As the right wing dropped, Records was saying, "Left throttle. Left, left, left, left, left, left left. Left, left . . ."

One second before impact, someone said the word *God*.

Many years later, I met Dave Randa in Geneva, Illinois, a sleepy historic river town west of Chicago. We ate lunch at an airy bar and grill called Fox Fire, because of the Fox River and the flames the chef had kindled to sear burgers and chicken and fish. The room, with its bare brick walls and curving vaulted ceiling of nineteenth-century rough-hewn pine beams, looked like a refurbished factory. Dave commented that the ceiling resembled the interior of a DC-10 after the decorative walls and ceiling had been ripped away. He was right. I had seen many of those unbuilt frames at the Douglas factory in Long Beach, California, and Dave had seen one from the inside, even as it was torn asunder around him.

Dave was tall and athletic, thirty-one years old by then, with black hair and dark eyes. In his role as vice president of a bank, he wore a business suit and tie. He looked sharp. He sat next to me at a table for four, and he was trying to remember what Captain Al Haynes had said over the loudspeakers as the plane approached Sioux City for the attempt at landing. He could not recall the word that had been meant to prepare him and his mother Susan for the worst. Dave had banished it from his memory, kept it out of his conscious mind all these years because the word had been paired with a rush of black fear, dread, and even sorrow. But I knew. I knew the word he was searching for.

I waited as he struggled against himself, his sense that he was better off not knowing, better off not remembering, and then I said the word.

"Brace."

I watched Dave go into a flashback. I had no idea that this would happen. I had never seen such a thing before. His face changed into a mask of horror, of sorrow, and his eyes went into a strange neutral mode, as if he were looking far into the misty distance. A thousand-yard stare. It lasted only a second, a flicker, but he was rendered incoherent as he tried to speak, because, as he later said, the whole scene was there before him again, the sight of looking over the seats ahead of him, the wobbling heads of people who in moments would be torn apart between the shearing of metal and the disjointed slabs of concrete runway, the sharp and toxic smells of the crash, the sensations, the unfamiliar violent forces, wrenching, jerking, tearing at him. His clothes and his mother's splashed with the blood of the people two rows ahead, most likely Roland Stig Larson, forty-nine, and Marilyn Fay Garcia, thirty-five. (Larson suffered a fractured skull so severe that most of his brain was missing when he was found. He was torn limb from limb.) And then the flashback was over, and Dave was back in the restaurant with me. More than twenty years after the crash, the memory lay dormant like a snake, raw and alive within his emotional system. He picked himself up and went on with his breathless narration.

"Then we're going down. You could feel we're good. And then we got wobbly." As he tried to tell me about this moment, his eyes grew red and teary, and he became intense and struggled with his words. Perhaps I saw anger, perhaps a deep sadness. He could not tell it as if it had happened to him. He told it as if it had happened to someone else—that boy, that vanished boy, so long ago. This is how he said it: "And then there's three big . . . We hit. And you could feel the dirt and the impact and glass and things fly by your face and head and everything. I mean, the dirt and smell of mangled metal and dirt and kind of that rustic—is very vivid. You know, I can still, if you're near a manufacturing plant or something, you still have that feel and taste and smell. So I still have that."

The "glass" Dave felt was sharp bits of concrete ground up from the runway by the metal frame of the airplane. The loamy smell of the earth came from the tail tearing up the tall weeds that grew between the abandoned concrete slabs and from plowing up the summer earth off the side of the concrete, flinging the soil into his face. And to this day the smell of summer earth hurtles him back into the lethal mayhem he survived. That's what he meant when he said, "So I still have that." He means that he possesses it within him. It will never go away.

As he continued his story, he became that nine-year-old boy again. Little things could always bring back the boy. In a sense, the boy died in the crash, and his spirit went on to inhabit Dave Randa the man. Most of the time these days, the man protects the boy. But sometimes the boy surfaces, interrupts the attention of the grown man, and rattles him to his core.

As we sat together in that restaurant, he had trouble speaking. He squared his shoulders and went bravely on, reverting to an almost primitive-sounding cadence of words as he groped for clarity and at last found the first person in that boy. "So we're going down, and you hit. And then we kind of flipped, and you hit. And I think we broke off on the first or second hit. I didn't know it until we stopped, because my head is down and my eyes are closed. And then some people were screaming. I stayed down and just said, 'Stay low, stay low,' you know what I mean? Not said, but I just, just said, 'Okay, I'm still going. We're still good. We're bouncing.' I don't know that we're on fire. I don't know that we're dislodged from the main cabin." And as he said those words, he laughed in disbelief as if to refute it all.

"As we pancaked onto the runway," Records recalled, "the number two engine came out of the mount. So with no weight on the tail, the left wing comes up, and we're essentially pirouetting on our nose, touching down about three or four times, finally ending up scuffing the cockpit clear off the airplane." He was awake and alert through most of the sequence. The windows burst, and "I could feel the debris coming into the cockpit." He momentarily lost consciousness or suffered retrograde amnesia, "and the next thing I know, I'm lying in a bean* field with my left ear sideways by my right thigh." Records's seat had collapsed, crushing him and trapping him inside its metal frame. "I realized at that time that we had crashed and I was alive. I didn't know whether my limbs were attached or what condition I was in. I could see a fireman in one of those big aluminum-colored suits coming across the field. So I mentioned to someone in the pile of debris who was moaning, 'Just try to relax. I see help coming.'" He may have been seeing Larry Niehus, who crossed the field in a so-called proximity suit not long after the crash. But the fire fighter Records saw walked right past the cockpit.

Dvorak said that he didn't remember anything about the crash itself but woke to the quiet that followed. "I'm in the wreckage and I could tell I'm basically upside down. Everything's closed in around me. And I tried to kick some material that was above me out of the way, and that's when I realized my right [ankle] was broken. I could hear Denny Fitch. I didn't know who it was at first, but, uh, he was in shock. He was just saying, 'Help me, save me, get it off me, help me, save me,' just over and over again. And then I heard Bill Records. Al [Haynes] was just moaning. Bill and I had a little bit of a conversation. He asked me what I could see and I said I could see a little bit out. There's something burning in the distance and there's people over

---

* The airport property was planted in both soybeans and corn, and the cockpit had come to rest in the beans.

there that I could see and stuff like that. And then Al quit moaning, and I said, 'I think we lost Al.' "

Records said, "Yeah, I think so."

Records and Dvorak tried to talk to Fitch, but he just kept saying, "Help me, save me, get it off me, help me, save me . . ."

"And then Al came to and he was very lucid," Dvorak said. "He was completely aware of everything."

"Where are you?" Haynes asked Dvorak.

"I'm right on top of you," Dvorak told him.

"You're gonna have to lose some weight," Haynes said. "You're too heavy."

Dvorak broke a piece of plastic off of Haynes's seat and stuck his handkerchief out on the end of it, "but the wind was blowing so fast I think that it blew the handkerchief away." Still no one came.

Haynes had been knocked unconscious on impact and was able to remember only bits and pieces of the rescue. He remembered wailing, "Oh, I killed people!" Haynes was bruised and cut up. One of his ears was nearly severed. He received ninety-two stitches in the hospital. But he had broken no bones and suffered no internal injuries. Records broke his pelvis, both hips, his sacrum, and numerous ribs. He suffered compression fractures of his spine and internal injuries, as well as a variety of bruises and contusions. Fitch suffered facial lacerations, a compound fracture of his right arm, and compression fractures in his spine, among other injuries. The tendon that controlled the use of his thumb was severed. Dvorak sustained a broken ankle and burns on his arm, probably from electrical wires when they were pulled apart and shorted out as the cockpit was torn away from the plane. As the pilots came to their senses, trapped in the wreckage, they could not understand why rescue workers were passing them by.

And yet that crew had done something considered impossible by all the engineers that McDonnell Douglas and United Airlines could assemble: they had brought a plane home without using any of the conventional flight controls. If you're a seasoned pilot, you are one with the aircraft. Your nerves grow out into the wings and tail and your brain connects up with all the control surfaces. You can tell when you're slowing or falling or climbing. You can tell with your eyes closed. Haynes and his crew had that deep sense of the airplane. They were in the zone. According to his wife Rosa, Fitch later commented that "he had never felt more alive as when he stepped into the cockpit that day." But long before Fitch entered the cockpit, if Haynes had not reached over and closed the left throttle and advanced the right one as the plane rolled to the right, everyone would have been killed.

No one yet had any idea what had happened to that plane to cause this accident. There was a loud noise, an engine quit, and the hydraulics failed, leaving the plane uncontrollable. As Robert Mac-Intosh, the lead investigator for the NTSB, drove toward his home in Virginia, he wondered how that could happen. Seven miles beneath the aircraft at a company called Mellowdent Hybrids in Storm Lake, Iowa, workers heard the explosion when the engine blew. Like distant thunder, the sound took about half a minute to reach them. Then they turned toward the source above their rich summer fields. They looked up at the white jet and saw something amazing: great pieces of the craft spinning and falling in a hail of metal, and one big piece so large that Chuck Eddy, the sheriff of Buena Vista County, would later stand inside of it. Another piece that looked like half of a giant steel ring, said Eddy, was "whirling as it came down, sounding like a helicopter." One of the farmers felt the ground shudder as a heavy piece of metal hit. But in the green sea of corn and soybeans, it was impossible to say where it might have fallen.

Even as Kevin Bachman shouted, "He's gonna make it!" the air traffic controllers saw the left wing come up. The buildings between the tower and the runway hid the right wing, but Bates said, "You could see the jolt in the aircraft when apparently it hit the ground." As the DC-10 shuddered and began grinding off its own right wing, fracturing the main spar, it emerged from behind the buildings already on fire. Then the fireball and smoke rose, obscuring the middle portion of the plane from view, as banks of seats began vaulting and somersaulting high above the flames.

Bates heard Zielezinski say, "Oh, my God, oh, my God, oh, my God."

"It was so dead silent in the tower cab," Bates recalled, "and he said it softly, but it was almost like it was an extremely loud break of the silence." In fact, at the moment of the crash, a scream or yell can be heard on the tape recording of Dale Mleynek's position as he transmitted, "All emergency equipment, proceed."

When the plane burst into flames, Zielezinski said, "three of us at the same time said, 'My God, nobody could live through that.'"

"At the point that the fireball came on up," Bates continued, "the tail snapped off, hit the ground, tumbled once, and then went straight on the taxiway and *stopped*. Just *bam!* I was terrified at that point, because I remembered the A-7s were on that taxiway." As the A-7 pilots watched, the tail came to a stop about two hundred yards from the first aircraft in line, by Bates's estimate. And inside that tail sat Richard Howard Sudlow, his body now draped over nine-year-old Yisroel Brownstein in an effort to protect him. After the tail snapped off, the rest of the plane began to rise up onto its nose as the left wing started its rotation. "I saw it *bounce*," Bates said. "It was amazing. I never could believe that an aircraft could bounce, but it bounced on its nose . . . and then it landed on its back."

Fitch said, "We hit so hard that my hands flew off the throttles." As he described it, "a giant hand was behind my head, and it slammed my face down into the radio below me." Then he "bounced back up like a Jack-in-the-box. And for some reason—why I don't know—I looked left through a veil of blood, because blood was running over my eyes." He saw "the captain's profile—corn stalks going by."

Fitch described the impact. "There was this terrible sound, tearing of metal, G-loads, there was yaw to the right. And simultaneous with that change of direction was this sensation that something was like drop-kicking your backside. You feel yourself coming up and over, head over heels. The windshield went completely green and brown. Split second. Cold air blowing on my left shoulder."

When the right wing ruptured, more than ten thousand pounds of kerosene sprayed out and turned to an aerosol. The right landing gear tore an eighteen-inch deep gash in that World War II concrete. The right engine, number three, was ripped off the wing and demolished when it hit the runway as the landing gear collapsed. As Tim Owens watched the eerie mix of sunlight and firelight flood the cabin, the seats between rows 29 and 36 began ripping free and arching high in the air or else tumbling down the runway, including those carrying the Mixons, Cinnamon Martinez, Lena Ann Blaha, who had pointed out the damage on the tail to Jan Brown, and the boy beside her, James Matthew Bohn. Gene Chimura, sixty-three, in the starboard aisle seat in row 28, suffered minor injuries. In the rows behind him, except for a few children, who, owing to their short stature, were protected by the backs of their seats, nearly everyone else was killed. Brenda Ann Feyh's scalp was ripped off, her head crushed, as she breathed in a spray of her own blood. Her son, Jason, eight, beside her, survived. He suffered brain damage and was in a coma for nineteen days. Likewise, in 32-A, six-year-old Lauren Marsh survived, while her mother, beside her in 32-B, died when her neck and spinal cord were snapped. The pattern continued with a few exceptions back through the rows, until all but one person died in each of rows 34 through 36. Rows 37 and 38—the last two rows—remained attached within the tail, and all but two of the people seated there survived.

As Richard Howard Sudlow and Elenore E. Gabbe, sixty-three, were dying in the last row, the single remaining engine, mounted on the left wing, was still running full throttle, because Fitch's hands had been knocked from the controls and he was unable to shut it down. "Like a pinwheel, it's just causing the airplane to rotate, because the engine's pushing it around," Fitch said. "When the tail broke off, the airplane is much heavier forward, so the airplane is now coming up in the air like a seesaw that somebody got off. And the cockpit is getting pointed straight to the earth, and we skip like a pogo stick. The first skip, when I saw the windshield go dark brown and green and I still felt the air-conditioning, we were still integral to the aircraft." But on the second skip, "the stress caused the cockpit to break off like a pencil tip." As that was happening, the lift on the left wing, as well as some thrust, perhaps, from the left engine, powered the plane around in a complete 360-degree rotation, spinning on its nose like a top before angling over and landing on its back.

Fitch continued his description from his point of view in the now separated cockpit: "The windshield lightened for a split second, darkened a second time. Heat and humidity and violence beyond any words I could ever hope to put forth. My next recognition was being still. I was upside down, I had mud in my eyes and my ears, I couldn't hear, I couldn't see, I couldn't move. I could feel the blood flowing up my face to my ears and up to my hair. Tremendous pain. My ribs were broken and they punctured my right lung cavity and stuck in there. Just couldn't get a breath of air." Indeed, his punctured lung would almost kill him that first night, and the repair of his severed radial nerve would eventually require a nine-hour operation.

As the crew waited for someone to notice the cockpit, the controllers in the tower stared in silence at a scene they could scarcely comprehend. Bachman turned away from his position and fell to his knees on the floor of the tower, hanging his head, as Zielezinski and the other controllers gaped in horror. "And it was just, it was just surreal," Zielezinski said. "I mean, there was smoke floating past the tower, and you could see paper and pamphlets and whatever just floating in the smoke, you know, it was just, it was—*really eerie*."

Zielezinski put his hand on Bachman's shoulder, recalled Bachman, and he "told me that I had done everything I could."

Bachman stood up, quaking and ill, and went unsteadily down the tower stairs and burst into tears.

As Bates and Zielezinski and the others watched, the sunny scene of summer in Iowa turned to a gray and wintry landscape. "The thing that struck me the most," Bates said, "was the shower of paper. It was like snow." Then the sirens began their keening wail, as dozens of pieces of equipment began to move.

Bates said, "Here's this fire, this plane that had broken into all these pieces, and the snow coming down. Millions of pieces of paper and Lord knows what else—clothing—and it fell on the field like snow. It was just amazing." As the fire on Runway 17-35 burned out where fuel had spilled, Bates raised his binoculars and saw a set of two seats out on the concrete. "There was a man and a wife sitting in two seats. Their legs were pointed at ridiculous angles. His left shoulder was dislocated and [his arm] wrapped back around behind his head, and all I saw was red."

Charles Owings, the local controller, broke the silence and broadcast an announcement to all aircraft on the frequency that Sioux Gateway Airport was closed. Luckily, the traffic was light. Then the emergency dispatcher radioed the helicopter, saying, "MAC, I, we have the airplane down one half mile from the airport. Start that way please, the plane is on fire." Owings called the pilot, too, saying, "You'd better get in here, it's real ugly."

The pilot said solemnly, "We see."

As the controllers watched the chaotic scene below them from their glass-walled crypt ninety feet in the air, in a vortex of blowing ash and paper, the tower returned to silence.

"We were totally helpless," Bates said.

CHAPTER SEVEN

Brad Griffin had his hands on the first class seat in front of him, which was the first row in the airplane. Gerald Harlon Dobson, a retired state trooper from New Jersey, sat with his wife Joann, dressed in their festive Hawaiian clothes directly across from Rene Le Beau's jump seat. Griffin had been meditating. He felt no fear, even though he could feel how unusually fast the plane was going. "And when we hit the runway," Griffin recalled, "my seat belt pops." He was stunned for a second, free in his seat, and he turned to look at Michael Kielbassa on his right.

"If this is as bad as it gets," Griffin said, "we'll be okay."

It took but a second. When he turned to look forward toward Le Beau, as he later recalled, "the plane's disintegrating. Everything's starting to turn gray, because of the particles and whatever parts of the plane are falling apart. And it's getting hard to breathe." The cockpit was separating from the rest of the plane, and angels of fire were roaring around the open tube of the fuselage, even as the first class cabin began tearing away from the remainder of the craft. As fire bloomed in the air, it consumed all the oxygen. Griffin could feel himself suffocating and could feel the air heating up around him, as the fire from the fuel spraying out behind him moved forward and expanded into a deflagrating cloud. Looking ahead, he could distinguish less and less of the structure of the airplane, as the identifiable parts—the bulkhead, the galley, the jump seats for the flight attendants—were being transformed into dust. Griffin watched it all with detachment.

Then he was launched into flight. "I'm free in the air. When that plane breaks into pieces, I'm thrown out of the plane and I see the fire. And as I'm leaving the plane, I think, 'If I go in that fire, I'll be a dead man.'" He believes that he traveled 150 or 200 yards. "I land in a cornfield, and I'm unconscious for a minute or so—maybe two minutes, I don't know. I'd worn sandals, and I'm feeling this coolness on my feet, and I go, 'Oh, that feels good.'" He didn't yet know that he had broken the bones in his feet. His feet had also sustained second- and third-degree burns from passing through the cloud of fire. "And I go, 'No, that's fuel, stand up.' And I stand right up, and I look around. The plane's far from me. And I go, 'Well, what should I do now?' And my brain just said, 'Go in slow motion. Just lie down.' I lie down, and I hear people yelling for help around me. And I yell for help."

Greg Clapper had left his wife, Jody, and his daughters, Laura and Jenna, in the car on the side of the highway after urging them to go back to the mall to see *Peter Pan*. They watched Clapper run down the shoulder toward the airport half a mile distant, and then Jody pulled out into traffic and drove away. Clapper ran on for a time, reflecting on how little he knew about the mission he had set for himself. He had his PhD from Emory University and was teaching at Westmar College a few miles up the road in Le Mars. He was the chaplain for the Air National Guard. But he had no real-life experience to prepare him for an event of this magnitude. All at once, he was filled with misgivings about his role. He had been to Garrett-Evangelical Theological Seminary at Northwestern University, but he hadn't even been to the military chaplain school yet. He was merely an ordained minister. What resources could he fall back on? What help might he bring?

He stopped running. He looked toward the east at the angry

vortex of smoke and debris. He threw his hands up to heaven and said, "Lord, make me an instrument of your peace and help me to be your servant here." And then on he ran toward whatever tasks awaited him. He knew that the situation would be bad. At the least, he'd be dealing with people who were severely shaken from the task of retrieving the dead.

He reached the gate and introduced himself to Chuck Sundberg, the director of Siouxland Health Services, the ambulance company for the local area.

"I'm glad you're here," Sundberg said, and offered his hand. When they shook hands, a look of surprise crossed Sundberg's face. "Wow," he said. "I just got goose bumps shaking your hand."

"You know, this isn't the kind of thing you can prove," Clapper said many years later, "but part of me wants to think, somehow, that holy spirit that I asked to come into my life was palpably noticeable to Chuck when we shook hands."

Sundberg quickly prepared an ID for Clapper and recruited someone to drive him onto the field. Within minutes, he was walking through a scene that was beyond anything he could have imagined. Papers were blowing everywhere, and the sunny day had turned gloomy and overcast and gray with ash and smoke. Streamers of computer tape had come loose from the spools that had been packed in the luggage bay and now made shimmering serpents around his ankles as he walked. He squinted to make sense of the scene. Across the runway he went, stepping around a bank of seats in which the people lay beyond all hope. He passed the dead in all their ranks, in all their spectral attitudes. Some lay supine, mouths open in attitudes of near ecstasy, one upon the next, embracing. Some had bowed their heads as if in deep meditation or prayer. Others had been ground to pulp against the concrete and conveyed no expression at all. Clapper stepped off the far side of the runway and saw what was clearly a human form lying at the edge of the corn where the body had evidently smashed the stalks flat on impact.

Clapper crossed to the form and knelt. The man was not only alive, he was conscious. He was also badly injured.

Clapper asked, "What's your name?"

"Brad," Griffin said.

"I'm the chaplain, Brad. Just keep breathing in God's spirit, and people are going to be here to help you."

When the command to brace came, Susan White and the other flight attendants took up the chorus: "Brace! Brace! Brace!"

"And as I'm yelling it," White recalled, "I'm saying the Lord's Prayer in my head and focusing on the bright light, the tunnel—that swirling tunnel that takes you to heaven—the harps and everything peaceful that I had imagined heaven to be like." She looked out the window and saw that they were passing through a layer of clouds, so fluffy, so white, so beautiful, and she felt her love of flying once more. "Right before impact, I said, 'Okay, I'm in your hands, Lord.' And I had no fear at all. No fear. I took a deep breath. . . ." And then she felt the devastating concussion and saw through the porthole in her exit door that a ball of fire had engulfed the plane. "And I calmly said to myself, 'I'm burning to death. That's how I'm dying.' And the fire was there. And then we started tumbling, and three times I remember it hitting on my door."

The flight attendants always locked the bathrooms before landing so that someone trying to escape wouldn't walk in there by mistake and die. Now as she watched, the lavatory doors exploded open, and the blue water from the toilets spewed out into her face and across her chest and legs. As the separated tail screamed along the runway, metal grinding concrete, "I thought, 'Oh, gosh, how many people went to the bathroom in there?' And I could hear the tanks: Clunk! Clunk! Clunk! I have my hands on my head, my legs are up in the air, as we're tumbling around, and it was kind of . . . I don't know, I would describe it as being in a tornado with the amount of soot and dirt that we were scraping up, and then pieces of metal were just flying around the plane. Something came and hit my leg and my butt and it tore my pants and sliced my shoe. I left my eyes open, because I wanted to block everything that was coming my way to protect myself." The fire she had seen was gone now, and she fleetingly wondered where it went. She could see Martha Conant to her left, but she could not yet see what Conant would see when the tail came to rest. Since Susan was facing aft, she couldn't see that the plane—the entire plane—was gone. "I kept saying to myself, 'Hang on, Hang on,' as I'm battling, and all of a sudden it was silent, and it just hit me, Oh, my gosh, I'm alive!" She immediately reverted to her training and began shouting, "Release your seat belts and get out! Release your seat belts and get out!"

Runway 17-35 formed a complex intersection where it met the old Runway 04-22 and Taxiway Lima. When the tail snapped off, it went rocketing down Runway 22 and came to rest at that intersection, mostly on the concrete of Taxiway Lima but with its open end on the grass easement. It had come to a stop on its side, tilted at an angle so that Dave Randa and his mother were suspended twelve feet or so above the torn and jagged metal of the hull. Still strapped into their seats, they were leaning sharply to their right, "looking down into scrap metal," as Dave put it. "And the only way down is to jump." Looking forward he saw a seat, "maybe two, and then a bunch of mangled metal. And daylight." Despite the impact, the scraping and plowing and tumbling of this fragment of the aircraft, the row immediately ahead of him was intact, but beyond that, everyone was gone, the seats all gone.

Susan White continued to shout, "Release your seat belts and get out! Release your seat belts and get out!"

Susan Randa said, "I remember opening my eyes and thinking, 'Oh, my God, we're alive. How could we be alive?'" But she saw "absolutely nothing. It was just gray. There was no space, I don't remember the seat. I remember Dave there. I still had my arm around him. But I did not know that we were up in the air." A second, two seconds, may have passed when, hearing White's words, Dave's mother released her seat belt as directed. The boy watched his mother's body recede in slow motion, growing smaller as she went. She landed in the jagged metal below.

Dave later said, "I look around, asking, All right, what's going on? My mom dropped. She stood up and looked at me."

On the way down, she hit something, "and I hope to this day that I didn't hurt anyone," Susan Randa said. She rose unsteadily to her feet. "And then I looked up, and I just saw Dave up there so high, and he had this blue shirt on, and all I could see was gray, plus his blue shirt, and I'm like, 'Oh, my God, you left your kid up there. How are you gonna get him down?'" Susan Randa's eyes would sometimes turn flame red as we talked. But when she spoke of leaving her son, she broke down and wept in the restaurant where we sat talking.

She called up to Dave, warning him to hold on before releasing his seat belt. The boy was athletic, big for his age. He braced against the seats and positioned himself so that he could drop feet first. His mother stepped back so that he could fall where she had fallen. She watched as he maneuvered, hung for a moment, and then let go. "Thank God, he did it," she said. Some of the torn metal cut his ankle, but he was otherwise unhurt.

"So we're in the metal," Dave said. "We're walking through metal. We see daylight." Dave and his mother stepped out into a blaze of sunlight. They saw a fire truck grumbling at idle nearby. They walked fifty feet or so to the truck, and Susan asked the fire fighter, "Where should we go?"

"Go back in there and help those people," he said, clearly unaware that she was from inside the plane and not some wandering volunteer. Susan held Dave's hand and led him to a lighted sign on the taxiway. It was a metal box about thigh high with translucent illuminated panels. The markings on it meant nothing to her. She and Dave sat on the sign and watched the people come and go. As they waited in the midst of the unfolding catastrophe, Dave complained to his mother that he had lost his favorite Cubs hat and lamented the fact that they might miss the game.

Nearly a quarter of a century after the crash, Susan Randa told her son, "All I could think of when you said that, was 'OMG, you're lucky to have your head.' Fortunately my parenting skills were working to the max that day and I said nothing. Still makes me laugh when I think of it!"

Dave told her, "What can I say, Mom? I started young with good priorities. . . ." He wanted to get to a Cubs game.

In those first few seconds of silence after the tail came to a stop, as Susan White was shouting for people to release their belts, she could not release her own. She was trapped. "I kept grabbing and grabbing and grabbing, and it wasn't releasing." Her every action was reflex from her training. But the jump seats on this particular aircraft had latch mechanisms that were different from the one she had used in training. She deliberately stopped herself to take stock of her situation. She was soaked with septic blue toilet water. The visual cues before her, the lavatory doors, were straight, and yet she felt as if gravity wanted to pull her at an odd angle to her left, and not down toward her feet as it had always done before. Concentrating on the task, she looked down at the clasp on her harness and realized that it was a different attachment. Now that she was focused, she was able to rotate the clasp. The belts released. She hung in her harness, still at that odd angle. She hooked her left arm into the shoulder strap and swung her leg around the way gravity took it. Thus dangling from her harness like a circus aerialist high above the crowd, she planted her left foot on her jump seat and braced her right foot on the magazine rack. Now she saw for the first time that the plane was gone. She had fully expected to turn and see the familiar cabin and all her people, but there was nothing. She saw seats torn asunder, people dangling, people falling, but no airplane. She saw Dave and Susan Randa below, departing across the grass. White had no memory of seeing John Hatch. Then as she was preparing to release herself and drop, she saw that a man was trapped beneath a piece of metal below her. He couldn't get out. If she let go, she'd fall on him and crush him further. Someone, a woman, was with him. It was most likely the couple who had been sitting next to Martha Conant, Karl and Marilyn Walter of Denver.

"I'm stuck!" called the man, who was sixty years old and had injured his head.

White reached down for his hand but couldn't span the distance. She took hold of the metal and pulled, but it wouldn't move.

"I'm stuck!" he called again.

"Wiggle!" White shouted. "Wiggle, wiggle, wiggle!"

The man followed her orders: "He wiggled. And he got out from underneath that metal. And the minute he got out from underneath that, I jumped down on that metal." Facing yet another drop, White jumped once more and found herself face to face with Donna McGrady. When they were calling for people to release their belts, White had become convinced that McGrady had been crushed. Indeed, that part of the tail had been crushed, and now nine-year-old Yisroel Brownstein lay beneath Richard Howard Sudlow, who was twitching on top of the boy as he breathed his last breaths.

"And it was terrible," Yisroel recalled, "just terrible." Sudlow's successful effort to use his body to shield the nine-year-old had cost him his life.

Down below, when White saw McGrady, she later said, "it gave me so much energy, because I knew she was alive!" White still didn't realize how completely they had been detached from their craft until this moment, as she turned toward the opening. She immediately started running—yet another reflex—but then she heard voices, so she ran back to the cockeyed tail, towering above her. She could see Jerry Milford and his seven-year-old son, David, hanging from their seat belts. Blood was running down the father's face. Against White's advice, he had put his glasses in his shirt pocket. Then he put his head down, and under the extreme forces of the crash, something—perhaps his own knee—drove one of the temple pieces through his lip. Across the aisle, in seats wrenched nearly free of their mounting rail, sat Jerry Milford's sister Kari and his other son, Tom, who was nine.

White took McGrady's arm and said, "We have to go back in the plane, there's still people in there."

Inside the tail once more, she shouted up to Jerry Milford to release his seat belt, and he shouted back that he'd fall. "Release your son and we'll catch him," White called. The father held David's arms and released his belt and dangled him down to the two flight attendants, who broke his fall. Then Jerry Milford was able to hold onto his seat and release himself in a controlled fall. Kari and Thomas were able to let themselves down, and by then the tail was swarming with rescue workers. White backed out into the hot sunlight. Being nowhere near the fuselage, they were not beneath the snowy overcast of ash and cash and smoke and paper. (For mysteriously, money had begun to appear in the blowing debris, in addition to a large number of pineapples that had gone tumbling across the field.)

Inside the tail, Yisroel Brownstein looked out from his position trapped beneath the dying man. He could see flames burning on the runway in the distance where fuel had been spilled. As if from a cave, he watched as the fire diminished and flickered and went out. He said that the silence was like none he has ever heard since then. "I thought maybe this was death. Like if there was a waiting room for death. I felt like that's where I was." He smelled burned foam rubber. As his senses began to return, he was overwhelmed by that smell. "One of the most terrifying nightmares I have on a regular basis is us rolling and that smell."

Then he heard an urgent voice saying, "Don't move, don't move, don't move! We're going to get you out of there. Stop moving!" Yisroel didn't realize that he was struggling.

The rescue worker tried at first to save Richard Howard Sudlow but quickly realized that it was not possible. Within a minute or two, he had died. His daughter, who was Yisroel's age, had come home from school and was waiting for him in Carol Stream, Illinois.

The rescue worker turned his attention to Yisroel, who had begun screaming, "Thirty-five thirty-five West Winona Court!" The man who was trying to free him started laughing, but he kept reassuring the child, saying, "You're gonna make it, you're gonna make it."

In the meantime, Yisroel caught sight of his own hand and had to look away because it was so obvious that he was severely injured. "I was losing a lot of blood."

The rescuer was at last able to extract Yisroel from his seat and place him on a stretcher. "One of my clearest memories is lying on the concrete screaming my address and my parents' phone number. I knew something was ridiculously wrong with my arm." As his head lolled to one side, he saw the tall stalks of corn leaning away, as the afternoon wind kicked up to fifteen miles an hour. Then he looked up and saw the towering clouds marooned in the blue dome of the sky. The beautiful face of a weeping woman appeared over him, as if in a religious icon. But no, Yisroel realized, she was not an apparition. She wore an Air National Guard uniform and carried him on a stretcher with someone else holding the other end.

Susan White had backed out of the tail to make way for the rescue workers, and now she saw a woman lying on the ground, facedown. "She had a dress on. Her dress was up. Her nylons had big holes in [them]." White turned to one of the rescue workers and said, "We have to get that lady."

He said, "Come on. We've already checked her."

"What happened to the rest of the plane?" she asked.

He shook his head. "It just disintegrated. You're the only survivors."

Because White had taken the tickets in the boarding lounge in Denver, she had met everyone face-to-face, had spoken to each person individually. Now the full impact of it hit her. Thinking of Sister Mary Viannea, she could not imagine that a nun could die while she was spared.

"What about the cockpit?" Susan asked.

"It disintegrated," said the rescue worker.

Oh, Dudley!

When Jan Brown was about to give the final briefing, her mouth was so dry she could not speak. Standing beside her jump seat, microphone in hand, she found that her lips had literally stuck together as if they had been bonded with glue. She leaned around behind the bulkhead and reached into the galley. The microphone cord was barely long enough to allow her to push the spigot in the galley sink and drip water onto her fingers. Then she brought her fingers to her lips and wet them so that she could talk. She keyed the microphone.

In that brief moment of delay, Haynes began his final announcement. For reasons unknown, what he said was not recorded, but Haynes was certain that he began his announcement by saying, "I'm not going to kid you." He doesn't remember the rest. Many passengers recalled that he said it was going to be the roughest landing any of them had ever experienced. Maybe worse.

For once, Brown had what she had wanted for all those years: The full attention of her passengers. All those years of businessmen reading the *Wall Street Journal* right through every word she spoke, of people sleeping—snoring!—ignoring her. Those seasoned travelers, they thought she was there to serve them coffee, bring them pillows. And now here they were at last, like little children, looking at her with imploring eyes: *just tell me what to do, and I'll do it.* "They were right there in the palm of my hand," Brown said, "because the minute he stopped, I went right into it before they had a chance to bat an eye."

Here is what Jan Brown said:

Ladies and Gentlemen, this is your first flight attendant. While we prepare the cabin, pay attention as we use a checklist to review some very important safety information with you.

At this time, extinguish all cigarettes; bring seatbacks to the upright position; stow all tray tables; make sure seatbelts are low and tight about you.

Take the safety card from the seat pocket and look at the protective positions shown on the card.

With your seatbelt low and tight, lean forward and grab your ankles.

If you cannot grab your ankles, cross your arms, lean forward with the palms of your hands against the seatback in front of you and press your forehead against the back of your hands.

Flight attendants, check passenger protective positions.

Brown paused as the other flight attendants checked their passengers, going up and down the aisles to see if they were bracing properly. Then she resumed:

> Ladies and Gentlemen, the signal to get into your protective position will be given by the captain about one minute before landing. The signal will be, "Brace! Brace! Brace!" and the flight attendants will shout the word "Brace." Remain in your position until the airplane comes to a complete stop. The flight attendants will then shout, "Release your seatbelt and get out!" Leave your belongings and get out through your assigned exit.

As she finished the briefing and hung up the microphone, she heard from behind her, "Psst! Psst! Psst!" She looked into the galley and saw Jan Murray, knees bent, hunched over with an oxygen bottle in her arms like a baby. Brown had completely forgotten about Vincenta Eley and her heart attack. Murray had gone back to give her oxygen and now, in an urgent whisper, she asked Brown, "What should I do with this? Should I throw it in the lavatory?"

Brown imagined the heavy steel bottle bashing around in the bathroom and firing through the wall like a cannonball during the crash. "No," she said, "put it in a cart."

Brown strapped into her jump seat. She tried to think if she had covered everything in her briefing. "And then I come back on and I see parents, lap children," and she made the announcement, telling them to put their children on the floor. "As I'm saying this, I'm like, 'Oh, my God, this has got to be the most ludicrous, *ludicrous*, thing I've ever said in my life.' I'm telling people to put their prize, treasured possession on the floor? In other words, let's just hope for the best. Everybody else has a seat belt. I was so appalled at what I was saying."

Then her cabin fell silent, save for the restless uneven throbbing of the engines. For help with the door, Brown had recruited the three people closest to her, Upton Rehnberg, a big mountain of a man;

Helen Young Hayes, the investment analyst from Denver; and John Transue, the businessman across the aisle. Brown's work was done. She could only wait now. She looked across at Hayes, who held her fingers pressed to the side of her head as if she had a headache. Brown watched her, wondering what the woman was thinking. She looked beyond Rehnberg to the window by his head. She could see a sliver of the earth ripping past at a tremendous speed, like a green ribbon slithering through a fabulous machine being driven out of control by a maniac.

The time had come at last. Haynes made the call. And Brown and Murray began echoing him in alternating shouts as if in some twisted ritual gone amok: "Brace! Brace! Brace!" If she shouted it enough times, it ceased to have meaning. What does *brace* mean, anyway? *Brace*. Such an odd word. It comes from the Latin *brachium*, meaning arm. It means, at its heart, to embrace. It was a hug. A hug good-bye.

"When we yelled 'Brace!'" Brown said later, "I always described it as if you watched a wind come across a field of wheat and everything bends. That's how it was. Everybody went down. It was like a field of wheat being blown over." She said she never trusted the alternate position for bracing—hands on the seat in front of you and head on your hands. It's convenient, but "I always said you'll survive the crash and get killed by your luggage." Some people in that position broke their hands with the impact of their heads. Even fully bent over, some suffered black eyes from the impact of their faces with their knees.

Brown and Murray noticed two or three heads pop up at the back of B-Zone as people who were curious about their fate stole a glance out the windows. Together the two flight attendants yelled, "Get your heads down and stay down!" They well knew that this one simple precaution could mean the difference between life and death.

Brown watched the heads go back down, "and then we just smashed into the earth. I remember just involuntarily closing my eyes and then opening them again and thinking, I can't believe all the body parts are still connected. It was *so hard*. And I think I saw an overhead bin or two open up and I just passed out, because I thought, There's nothing I can do right now. I think I'll just check out for a minute." She entered a state of deep dissociation. Later she had the impression that she had been unconscious, but she could also remember everything about the crash, the noise and feel and smell of it. "All of a sudden, I realize that we're starting to tilt, and I'm like, 'Oh! I don't want to do this! I don't do roller coasters, I don't do Ferris wheels, I don't do any of this stuff!'"

Then as the door separated from its frame, a fireball came through her exit, and the flames washed over her. "I'm thinking the whole time, 'Oh, jeez, you know, as if this isn't bad enough, now I'm in fire. Oh, really! This is great!'" That's Jan Brown all over: cynical, humorous, and ironic unto death. She could feel the right two-thirds of her body being flamed, as the hair on that side of her head shriveled to nothing, and her stockings melted between the cuffs of her slacks and the tops of her shoes. "Two-thirds of my body is in fire," she said. "I was engulfed in the flames. And I just said, 'Well, this is how I'm going to go.'" Death, it seems, can come to us tenderly. "It was the most serene moment of my life," she said. "There was no fear, there was no pain, nothing but total peace." And then Jan Brown was in limbo, suspended in her harness, neither awake nor asleep.

CHAPTER EIGHT

Even before 1819 Uniform was within sight of the airport, Bob Hamilton, chief of the Sioux City Fire Department; Gary Brown, director of WCDES, representing the three-state area of Siouxland; Jim Hathaway, the fire chief for the Air National Guard and the Sioux Gateway Airport; and Chuck Sundberg, the director of the local ambulance company, were preparing their emergency responders to move into action. When John Bates made the call from the control tower, announcing that the airport was experiencing an Alert Three emergency, roughly thirty-one fire departments and thirty-five ambulances responded. In addition, several hundred Air National Guard men and women were on alert to help in any way they could. Twenty-six law enforcement agencies also showed up, and forty communities sent emergency equipment of various kinds. Long before the plane arrived, all of those resources were arrayed across the countryside surrounding the field. Because Haynes thought that the plane might not reach the runway, emergency equipment waited along Highway 20 and at varying distances from the airport. Even so, everyone hoped that the craft would somehow arrive safely. Many rescue workers imagined that they would escort people off the field once the passengers slid down the yellow evacuation slides. The radio chatter, however, betrayed how keyed up and nervous many of those emergency workers were. The voice of the woman who was on duty as fire department dispatcher that day had already taken on a tone of weary and tremulous resignation. "All rigs in route," she began and gasped—"to the airport, be advised this is now an Alert Three. I repeat, it's an Alert Three. They're advising that a DC-10 is five miles south. They won't be able to make the runway." She meant *north*, not *south*, but nearly everyone was in a state of confusion at one point or another during that afternoon.

As Dvorak was broadcasting the two-minute warning to passengers, the dispatcher transmitted in a trembling and broken voice, "All rigs, this aircraft is about six miles east of Hinton and still descending."

A fire fighter some five miles northwest of the field radioed, "Red Dog Four has the plane in sight at Lawton. He's descending." And through it all cut the scream and whoop of sirens and the sound of heavy static.

One of the reasons for the level of the response and its coordination—rather than pure chaos—was that for many years before this emergency, Gary Brown had lobbied for a disaster plan for Siouxland. Specifically, he wanted to have a drill that simulated the crash of a jumbo jet. People rolled their eyes and referred to Gary as Chicken Little. They thought it made no sense. Sioux City was a small town, and big things don't happen out in the Iowa cornfields. But Gary was a young and energetic bulldog of a man who believed in his mission, and with some crucial help from fire fighters, the Air National Guard, and the two hospitals in town, he managed to stage a full-scale exercise on the airfield in the fall of 1987, simulating a plane crash with scores of people injured. They performed the simulation on Runway 22, on the spot where United Flight 232 would come down.

Gary grew up in Siouxland at the confluence of the Missouri River, the Floyd River, and the Big Sioux River. He grew up in Sioux City, to be sure, but Siouxland includes South Sioux City, Nebraska; the towns of Dakota Dunes and North Sioux City in South Dakota;

Sergeant Bluff, Iowa; and numerous other communities. The three rivers flood frequently, and the people by necessity have learned the art of resilience.

Sitting in his cluttered office in 2013, at the back of his wife's gift shop, George Lindblade told me, "Sioux City's greatest moment is when there's a disaster. And this dates back to time eternal." Lindblade, a photographer and videographer, had made it his business over the years to document big events in the town's history. He became the unofficial custodian of memorabilia from the crash of United Flight 232. "Sioux City is a town that's been plagued by floods throughout its history, and the town has always pulled together. It's like an Irish family. They fight like hell among themselves. They want nothing to do with each other. But you throw a disaster at them, and they're all shoulder to shoulder and they'll do whatever it takes. They don't stop for one minute to think what their personal cost or toll is going to be in it, they just do it." During a flood in 2011, the Federal Emergency Management Agency came to town to teach kids how to fill sandbags. Lindblade laughed. "There isn't a kid born in this town who don't know how to fill a sandbag."

Gary Brown said, "I never paid any attention to the way the community pulled together until 232. That caught me off guard. I had been in this mode of, I'm the disaster preparedness guy, and I gotta prepare for every possible thing that we need to do—food, water, porta-pods, traffic control, medical, blood—oh, my God, I got all these parts to make sure they're gonna come into motion. But what you really find is: get the hell out of the way and let them things happen."

That, more or less, is the definition of Siouxland, and the crash of United Flight 232, said Lindblade, "defined Siouxland." It was the finest moment for these people to show what they were made of. And the people of Siouxland stepped up to the plate, drawing admiration from all over the world.

In the control tower, Kevin Bachman was telling Al Haynes that he might want to try landing on I-29, which the police had closed off for

him, the roadblock that Greg Clapper and his family had encountered after driving from the movie theater in the mall. As the plane
came within sight of the airport, one of the fire fighters transmitted,
"We have a DC-nine, er, ten coming across Morningside Avenue.
We've got him in sight here." Southern Hills Mall, where Clapper
had stood watching the plane, was two miles below Morningside
Avenue.

The assistant fire chief, Orville Thiele, watching from the
ground, radioed to his chief that he too had the plane in sight, and the
commander said, "Ten-four, he's descending now. We hope he can
make it in here, but what happens when he gets in is another thing."

Then Thiele transmitted, "He's comin' down real fast!"

And another shouted, "Okay, all rigs stand by!"

Then someone keyed a microphone and screamed, "He's on
fire!" and for a moment the frequency was silent as people watched in
disbelief while the plane exploded and pitch-poled up onto its nose,
breaking apart. Then everyone tried to talk at once, and the transmissions became unintelligible.

"Come out and give us a hand out here!" Chief Hathaway
screamed. "This aircraft is gone!"

The emergency vehicles began to roll.

As the ambulances and fire trucks and pickup trucks and cars rum-
bled across the ramp and out onto the runway in the moments after
the pieces of the plane had come to rest, the storm of papers began
rising on the heat waves above the main body of the fire. The smoke
and ash and debris turned in a slow rotating vortex like a mythical creature and began drifting down around the fire fighters. "We
encountered dense smoke and a snowstorm of paper that came out
of the aircraft," said Hathaway.

Fire was eating away at the center section of the fuselage in
the cornfield, where Jerry Schemmel and the ex-Navy fighter pilot
Charles Martz were escaping from opposite ends. Emergency vehicles trying to reach the burning wreckage were stopped by the
debris and by survivors who were wandering around in shock. A
fire fighter named Larry Niehus drove a crash truck while another

fire fighter named Jerry Logemann walked ahead of the truck to move debris and allow Niehus to reach the main section of the fuselage, where Rod Vetter and Margo Crain, John Transue and Bruce Benham and Garry Priest, Clif Marshall, and Ron Sheldon, among others, were popping their seat belts and dropping to the ceiling of the inverted coach cabin.

"It was very hot," said Bob Hamilton, "because we had a running fuel fire inside the aircraft from the ruptured fuel tanks." He estimated that the fire was burning at 1,800 degrees Fahrenheit. He said that although the fire fighters knew where the fuel tanks were, they could not pinpoint all the pressurized containers in the plane, such as fire extinguishers and oxygen bottles. "There were numerous explosions during the fire and this did pose a serious hazard to our fire fighters."

As Niehus and Logemann began spraying foam on the fire, trying to knock it down, they sprayed the passengers as they came out the rear of the plane, thus protecting them from the flames as well as they could. The two men soon realized that they were going to have to fight the fire the same way they fought house fires: they would need to put on their silver proximity gear with self-contained breathing equipment. As Niehus crossed the ground between his truck and the fuselage, Records was looking out from the crushed cockpit and likely saw him. Niehus passed the cockpit, heading into the burning fuselage dragging a hand line. The belly tank above and forward of him was pouring fuel on the fire he was trying to fight. As he worked, he grabbed people and pulled them out as fast as he could. Some were already free of their seats, but he had to reach up and cut seat belts to release others. Fire fighters outside the fuselage took the people as Niehus dragged them out. "We had pulled a couple of little kids out of there," Niehus remembered, "and one of them, a little girl, was about the age of my daughter at that time, and I had a really hard time with that." She was dead in his arms, and he was still thinking about her more than twenty years later. He said that while he was inside, fighting the fire with a hand line and dragging passengers, dead and alive, out of the plane, the fuselage was melting in on him. It gradually closed around him, forcing him to back out. "It was collapsing all the way around," he said. "It got to where we couldn't see the passengers anymore, and it was pretty much collapsed down to where you couldn't actually get into it." He could no longer help those who were left inside. Their one avenue of escape had closed.

Meanwhile, staff members at the hospitals were preparing to receive casualties. In the minutes before the crash, nurses at Marian Health Center lined the halls with gurneys, IV stands, drugs, dressings for wounds, IV kits, surgical packs, and sterile linens in anticipation of the arrival of wounded passengers. All patients who could be released were sent home to make more beds available. All elective surgery was canceled. The same scene was being repeated at St. Luke's, the other hospital in town. Between four o'clock in the afternoon and nine o'clock that night, the food service staff began carrying out the two-day emergency menu plan by making seven hundred sandwiches and distributing them, along with eight hundred cans of soda and forty dozen cookies. The first patients arrived within twenty minutes of the crash, as helicopters landed on the pad at Marian and ambulances screamed up to the emergency room doors at St. Luke's. The first two patients to reach St. Luke's were children. At one point Cathie Deck from the Community Relations Department at St. Luke's was holding a telephone to each ear, giving simultaneous interviews to reporters in Japan and Australia. Eighty-eight people arrived at Marian for treatment. Five were pronounced dead on arrival, and an additional two died during the night.

Sheryl Dieber, a nurse at St. Luke's, was ministering to a six-year-old boy in traction. The boy motioned to Dieber to come close. "I'll tell you a secret," he said. "Get closer." She moved closer. "Come closer," the boy insisted, and Dieber leaned in. "Come closer," the boy said again, and she put her ear right up to his lips. "My mommy died in the plane crash," the boy whispered. And together they wept. The little boy was Brandon Bailey, son of Frances, brother of Spencer.

The acting Woodbury County medical examiner, Dr. Gene Herbek, felt overwhelmed by the job before him: he'd been told to expect two hundred victims or more and wasn't sure how to handle that many. "When I got to the scene, the numbers quickly reduced to 120, which is still a large number," Herbek recalled. "The victims who were on the field, their injuries were of severe trauma. Just tremendous force injuries, broken bones, head injuries, neck injuries." Herbek realized fairly quickly that the bodies would have to be left on the field for the night. Others would independently reach the same conclusion. The sun was going down. No one had the ability to assemble the people and equipment needed to begin recovering bodies before nightfall. They could not work in the dark. They might make mistakes in identifying bodies. People might be injured on shredded metal. In any event, there was nowhere for the bodies to go. No morgue yet existed. As much as United Airlines and McDonnell Douglas and General Electric wanted the dead out of sight, it was not yet possible. As Herbek characterized it, "That's one of the things I had done that was very unpopular with a lot of people. Fortunately, it was a cool night." By morning, the temperature had dropped to 59 degrees. "The thing that I had learned in my training," he said, "was that you wanted to leave things where they were and that included all personal effects."

Some time that afternoon, a forensic pathologist named Brad Randall, thirty-eight, had been at his office in Sioux Falls, "doing pathology things," as he put it, when someone came in and asked if he had heard about the plane crash. He had not. He turned on his radio and listened for a while. Then he picked up the phone and called the Iowa Department of Public Safety (DPS), under whose authority the medical examiner operated at that time. Dr. Thomas Bennett, the state medical examiner, was testifying in another state, and someone at the Iowa Department of Criminal Investigation (DCI), a part of DPS, urged Randall to volunteer. He made the hour-long drive south to Sioux City and was directed to a conference room at Graham Aviation, the hangar where private planes were serviced. There he found "several people sitting, standing, somewhat confusedly. Gene Herbek was very happy to see me show up." In fact, Herbek asked Randall to be the director of the morgue, and Bennett later approved of that decision.

At about six o'clock that first evening, Herbek took Randall, along with a woman named Marliss DeJong, on a tour of the wreckage to try to anticipate what lay ahead. Herbek knew that they would have to create a reference system of some sort to map the location of each body and body part on the field. A fifty-two-year-old lieutenant colonel named Lawrence Harrington, joining the tour along with Gary Brown, would be instrumental in arranging for all the equipment the mortuary team would need. As Randall explained to me later, when he saw the condition of the charred fuselage, he said, "Oh, my. This is going to be an archeological operation. We're going to have to get down there and start sifting through all this ash for bones." Then someone told him that nearly everyone in the section he was looking at had survived. This was where Margo Crain, Rod Vetter, Ron Sheldon, Clif Marshall, Aki Muto, Gitte Skaanes, and Sister Mary Viannea had been sitting. Randall was astonished.

Once they returned to the conference room, Herbek gave Randall his blessing and told him to take anyone he needed and go to another conference room to work out how the morgue was going to be run from start to finish. During that organizational breakout session, Randall remembered one of the most prominent forensic dentists in America, E. Steven Smith from Northwestern University. The year before, Smith had come to Sioux City to give a talk at a seminar that Randall held. Smith's talk had been about responding to mass casualties. He had even warned the attendees that since Sioux City was in the middle of the nation, it was beneath the flight path of thousands of aircraft and could well find itself facing the crash of a large plane one day. Now Randall told the group in the breakout session, "I know who I can call. [Steven Smith] can put a whole team together and be here tomorrow."

Randall later said, "I just made one phone call to him, and he said, 'I've got it handled.'"

He recounted how the operation got organized. "One of those people [who] deserves more credit than anybody else in this whole thing is Marliss DeJong." United States Senator Chuck Grassley kept an office in Sioux City. DeJong worked there as a liaison between local communities and the Federal Emergency Management Agency. She was also on the board of the Red Cross and a member of the local Emergency Planning Committee. She was well known for her organizational skills, and it was said around Sioux City that if you wanted a stickler for paperwork, you sought out Marliss DeJong. Now she went off with Brad Randall to formulate a plan for setting up and operating the morgue. "She knew how to make information flow between places and to secure things and to make sure that stuff didn't get screwed up in a bureaucratic mess," said Randall. "And I knew that the worst mistake that we could make was to do something quickly."

At about nine that night, Randall and DeJong began diagramming how a deceased person would be wheeled in, then inventoried, along with any clothing and possessions. The person would have to be photographed and x-rayed and fingerprinted. Each process was added to the developing flow chart, even as Randall and DeJong discussed how information would be collected and filed and protected. DeJong conceived a scheme for making sure that each file of paperwork remained with the correct body so that under no circumstances could the identities of two people be switched. If someone requested paperwork, it would be photocopied. The original would remain in the file. With this system in place, with the flow chart they had created for the morgue, and now with Steven Smith's resources on the way, it had begun to appear as if the task of processing the dead might be possible.

In the meantime, the base commander for the Air National Guard, Colonel Dennis Swanstrom, forty-six, in consultation with his right-hand man, Lawrence Harrington, began making arrangements to convert the physical space of the fuel cell hangar into a temporary morgue. During all their planning and training, Gary Brown and his team at WCDES had designated Hangar 252 for mortuary operations. It was ordinarily used to repair fuel cells for the A-7s. Now that the real disaster was upon them, Herbek recalled, "that's one thing that we didn't have to worry about or think about, and believe me, having that worry out of the way was a very, very big help." Hangar 252 was in a fairly remote location on the military base and was easy to cordon off. It had a concrete floor with drains in it. The large hangar doors could be opened for ventilation, and movable partitions could be brought in to divide the giant room into protected areas for each step in the postmortem procedure. Herbek called it "ideal.... The disaster committee planned well." In addition, a double-wide house trailer, or modular home, was already parked north of the hangar. Swanstrom and Harrington turned it over to Herbek to use as office space.

Harrington, Gary Brown, DeJong, and others in the meantime began ordering banks of telephones and dividers to partition off the open space, as well as all the myriad people, tools, and equipment needed for the task before them. (Greg Finzen, the Executive Director of the American Red Cross chapter in Sioux City, was out on the field within minutes of the crash on Wednesday, and through the following days would be instrumental in sending his people not only to work in the morgue but to provide food services there and at other locations, as well as to bring supplies to any person or working group that might need them.)

At about ten o'clock that evening, Randall recalled, "the doors opened and a group of suits came in and announced themselves as United Airlines representatives and told us that we needed to start body recovery *right now*."

"It's the middle of the night," Randall told them.

The United spokesman said, "We don't care. We'll get lights out. We'll get whatever you want. We want those bodies out of there right now."

"We very politely told them," Randall said, "that they could go . . ." And here he implied telling them something impolite indeed, but in our conversation he said only the word "whatever." He went on: "And they did. They huffed and they puffed and then they left. It was clear they did not want those bodies left . . . for all the press to see the next day."

Across the field at his WCDES command post, Gary Brown was hearing the same thing from his bosses and from the county administrator. They were telling him that someone named Stephen Wolf from United Airlines was insisting that the bodies be removed immediately. After a number of frustrating calls, Gary stormed over to the terminal building and went to the basement where he found a conference room jammed with employees of United Airlines. "And I walk in," Gary later said, "and I didn't look good, I didn't smell good, and I was *not* in a good mood."

Gary shouted, "Who the fuck is Stephen Wolf?" The room fell silent, as everyone turned to look at the bull-like visage of Gary Brown.

A deceptively mild-looking man in round tortoise-shell spectacles, with reddish brown hair falling toward his bushy eyebrows and sporting a graying walrus mustache, Wolf said, "I'm Stephen Wolf. How can I help you?" He was the CEO of United Airlines.

"You're making my life miserable," Gary said, "and you need to stop." Wolf then assigned Gary Brown a United employee as liaison to the command post, "and it was very smooth after that," said Brown.

At about eleven o'clock that night, Randall felt that a workable plan was in place and that he could be of no further use until morning. Because of the scarcity of hotel rooms, a college called Morningside had opened its doors to house many of the technical experts and investigators who had come to town. Randall retired to a room in the dormitory for a few hours of sleep.

CHAPTER NINE

The great fan at the front of the CF6-6 engine pulls air into the compressors. Once the air is compressed, it has to enter the combustion chamber. That super-heated air, however, is moving at about four hundred miles an hour at that point, far too fast to sustain a flame. Moreover, that flame will burn at more than 3,000 degrees Fahrenheit, hot enough to melt the nickel alloy that the combustion chamber is made of.

In 1989, Nicholas Edward Cherolis was an engineer at General Electric, specializing in what's known as failure analysis. He worked on the team that investigated the crash of United Flight 232. He was one of the detectives who figured out what went wrong with 1819 Uniform and GE engine number 451-243. I asked Cherolis to explain jet engines to me, and he did a good job right up until we reached the subject of the combustor. Then he began talking about "the black art of making the fuel nozzles themselves mix the fuel and the air that's coming in around it into the perfectly combustible mixture that they need." When I asked him about the aerodynamicists who design the swirl and vortex patterns of air and fuel that the combustor had to produce to make flight possible, he said, "That's all voodoo to me. I have no idea what they're doing." It was as if I had asked him to describe the work of the devil. He was expressing not an ignorance of his profession but the sharp cultural divide that has existed since the early days of NASA between those who design the interiors of jet engines and those who perform autopsies on them after they break. "They're combustion designers," Cherolis said. "I don't talk to 'em." He said the air flowing through the engine doesn't really stop, but the flame stands still, or else the necessary fire would travel out the end of the engine and be gone: a flameout.

Here's what happens: The fans and compressor wheels blow air backward. When some of that air reaches the combustor, it hits a diffuser. The diffuser performs several functions. The pattern of tiny holes slows the speed of the air so that the flame isn't blown out, but it also allows the air into the combustion chamber in a complex aerodynamic dance that makes efficient combustion possible. Some people spend their whole careers studying those vortex patterns and the holes that make them. The well-respected primer on turbine engines by Bill Gunston says, "It is usual to design each fuel burner so that [the flame front] is situated in the center of a strong swirling vortex. The reduced pressure in the center then tends to suck air back into it, causing a region where the flow is in the upstream direction, providing conditions for stable burning with the flame effectively anchored in space."

In addition, those patterns of holes spray a layer of cooler air across the inner surface of the combustion chamber. This cooler air protects the metal from the 3,000-degree flame. Only by the most intricate and clever ducting of cool air through those holes can the engine be saved from self-annihilation. If flame should touch metal, the walls would turn to slag, and in a fraction of a second the whole chamber would flow guttering into space, reducing the engine to a heap of scrap. That presented another possibility for what might have gone wrong with Flight 232.

That stable flame front forms a hoop of fire held in place by competing aerodynamic forces and extruding its white hot fluid out the back of the combustor and on through the turbine blades, driving them to power all the wheels up front that create the wind. The big fan in front—the number one fan—provides 85 percent of the thrust. The turbine wheels extract almost all of the energy from the burning of fuel and transmit it forward. Any energy that still remains in the exhaust gas helps to push the plane forward.

It is a marvel that such a contraption can hold together for one flight, let alone tens of thousands in its lifetime, but it generally does so because the engineers are smart and the testing is rigorous. And yet several of the investigators of the crash of 1819 Uniform had already begun to suspect that the failure was caused not by the combustor but rather by the spinning wheels.

One of the designers of the CF6-6 engine, Martin Hemsworth, said, "We elected to design the rotor [fan disk] for 54,000 cycles . . . with the expectation that we would follow the FAA guidelines and assign an initial operating interval of 18,000 cycles;* in other words, one-third."

"A major engineering concept regarding strength of parts," explained Robert Benzon of the NTSB, "is that you design something, test it until it fails, then make it 50 percent stronger to ensure that it doesn't fail."

And the designers do not guess. They don't stop with calculating what the engine can withstand. They test it aggressively and even destructively. Hemsworth explained, "For example, when bird resistance is evaluated, that has to be done in a complete engine, and pneumatic guns are set up in front of the engine and the four-pound and pound-and-a-half and small birds are shot at the engine at a rate and location that is specified in the FAA regulations to evaluate damage tolerance."

The engineers also are simultaneously pushing toward the absolute limits of the materials involved—the hottest temperature, the thinnest blades, the fastest speeds, the highest altitudes, the longest service life—and yet are ever vigilant concerning the need to kill as few people as possible.

Ben Bendixen had been a pilot in the Navy, as well as a medical officer and an aircraft accident investigator. When he left the Navy, he

---

* A cycle equals roughly one takeoff and landing.

went into private practice as a physician in Denison, Iowa, about sixty miles from Sioux City. He joined the Air National Guard and worked as the medical officer for the 185th. His normal schedule with the Guard was to fly a training run early on Wednesday mornings so that he could be seeing patients at his satellite clinic in Ute, Iowa, by 1:30 in the afternoon. For reasons he was never able to learn, he was scheduled to fly at 1:30 in the afternoon on July 19, 1989. Although he was irritated by the change, he decided to go ahead and fly the hop and then stay late at his clinic that night.

When he and his lead pilot, Al Smith, returned from their practice run over Kansas, Bendixen recalled, "I had just taxied into my parking place and crawled out of the airplane and started walking up the ramp." In the meantime, the other four A-7s had landed but could not move from their position on Taxiway Lima between the two main runways because the DC-10 was too close to the airport. "If you've ever heard an airplane crash," said Bendixen, "it has a very distinctive sound, a very distinctive thoomp! Muffled thump." He was describing the bursting of the thin balloon of the aluminum skin as everything—pressurized air, fuel, paper, people, glittery computer tape, hundred-dollar bills, and pineapples—came bursting into the open. It was a wet and tremendously powerful sound. It had the same reflexively nauseating quality as hearing someone vomit. "I looked up and here's this great big black cloud up at the north end of the field with flame inside it, and I remember saying to myself, Oh shit, they won't need me now."

He continued up the ramp. At fifty-one years of age, he was the lone medical officer for the base, but he assumed that everyone on board had been killed. They'd be needing pathologists, mortuary services, and Greg Clapper, that new chaplain they'd hired. Bendixen said he was walking "sort of slowly. And then I thought to myself, you never know." Bendixen hurried across the ramp. Inside the maintenance control building, he struggled out of his torso harness and his G-suit. He ran outside. "And just by chance, my ambulance and my medics happened to come driving across the ramp. So I waved them down, threw the guy in the right front seat into the back, and away we went." As his crew sped away toward the smoke, he silently said a prayer in much the same way that Clapper had done. He later recalled saying to himself, "God, I've never been in this situation before. Give me some guidance."

As the ambulance rolled onto Runway 22, Bendixen spotted several banks of seats from the coach cabin. He ordered the driver to stop. The shredded red-and-black-checked upholstery of the coach seats was stained with blood and disgorging its foam rubber padding. By Bendixen's reckoning, the dozen or more people before him were either dead or not long for this world. He passed his expert eye over the people one by one, and assessed them in his mind. Using endotracheal tubes, he and his medics established airways for those who were still alive. Most had severe head injuries, but "there was one woman at the end of the row who was alive and obviously conscious, with a little boy sitting beside her on the ground."

"Is this your little boy?" Bendixen asked her.

"No," she said, "but would you check my husband next to me?"

Her husband was dead beside her. The woman may have been Lydia Atwell of Santa Fe, New Mexico. Bendixen said, "She really didn't appear to need treatment."

At about the same time that Bendixen began his impromptu triage, Bob Johnson, the triage officer with Siouxland Health Services, arrived on the scene and began acting in his official capacity in accordance with the WCDES disaster plan. Ward Palmer, Johnson's paramedic supervisor, was on the field as well. "We have basically four different groups," Palmer said later. "We have red, which is the critical. Yellow, which is moderate injury. Green, which is basically your walking wounded. And then there's black, which is the mortally injured or dead." Palmer had reached the field so fast that not all of the mortally wounded had died. "That's one of the problems we had," he said. "We were sitting there waiting for it, so they didn't have that time to die." For example, Palmer came upon a man who was lying on the runway. "He basically had both legs and both arms amputated. He asked me, 'Am I gonna live?'"

Palmer told him, "We're gonna do what we can for you," but he knew that he could not save the man. "He stayed there until he passed. He was one of those, you know: he didn't have the time to die."

Palmer stayed in one place, while Air National Guard men and women with backboards and stretchers brought the wounded to him. He would then assign each victim to one of the categories—red, yellow, green, or black. A transport officer would assign them to an ambulance or helicopter or some other means of transport for the trip to the hospital. Through this system, Palmer was able to move all of the seriously wounded people to the hospital within about forty-five minutes after the crash.

While Palmer and Bendixen worked with their teams, many other members of the Air National Guard responded as well, doing whatever they could to help. Among those volunteers, Jim Walker, twenty-five, was a full-time lieutenant flying the A-7 Corsair. Walker happened to be standing on the ramp with a few other pilots when they saw the DC-10 line up with the old Runway 04-22.

"Wow," Walker remembered saying to his fellow pilots, "this guy's really going to be embarrassed. He's landing on a closed runway." Then he did a double take and thought, "My God, he's awful fast and extremely shallow." The plane disappeared behind some buildings and then "just a moment thereafter [I] saw an enormous fireball and then saw the aircraft cartwheel and another fireball and just a huge amount of debris. Oddly enough, it looked like it was paper."

Walker assumed that no one could have survived, but a few minutes later another pilot, Norm Frank, pulled up in a pickup truck and said, "Get in, we're going to pick up survivors." And with that, Walker's life was changed forever, as he was swept up in the rescue. He boarded the truck, and Frank raced onto the field.

"There were bodies everywhere," Walker said.

Frank stopped the truck, "and we just sat there looking at all these dead people," Walker recalled. Most of them were lying in the grassy easement between the concrete and the crops. "And the most surreal thing I've ever seen in my life happened next. It actually looked like something from *Night of the Living Dead*, because many of these dead bodies all of a sudden started sitting up and standing up and I remember saying, 'Is everyone else seeing this?' "

Many others confirmed what Walker saw. "That's absolutely true," Gary Brown said. "Because I was there, and I saw it firsthand." Brown elaborated: "As the aircraft passed in front of me, I pulled out there, and I literally saw people getting up, injured, and looking around, walking toward me."

James Hathaway saw it too. He later said that as he arrived in the seconds after the crash, "there were a lot of people that stumbled up the runway and slid up the runway in seats; and those people—some of those people that were uninjured were simply unbuckling their seat belts and getting out of their seats and walking toward the sirens."

Walker watched in amazement as a businessman in a suit stood up and looked around as if searching for something. "He walked over and grabbed his luggage," and walked away.

Overcoming their shock, Walker and the other pilots left the truck and began trying to render first aid. Some of the people who had been ejected from the plane were, according to Walker, "relatively unscathed." But a woman in her fifties "sticks in my mind forever," he said with a voice full of sadness and regret. "I hate it. Her skin was just shredded. She obviously had broken bones, but she was walking in shock. I couldn't figure out where to grab her to help her without hurting her more. It was terrible. It was hard to tell what was skin and what was from her nylons."

While Walker and others were ushering as many wounded as possible to triage, one of Bendixen's fellow pilots approached him and said, "Doc, we've got three people trapped in the wreckage over here. Would you come over and supervise getting them out?" He could see a tangled pile of wire and metal on the side of Runway 17-35, but if he had noticed it before, Bendixen had dismissed it as inconsequential. It didn't look large enough to contain a person, not a live one, and certainly not three people. In fact, it contained four. As Bendixen approached, Chaplain Clapper knelt beside the wreckage with his hand thrust inside it, touching the top of Records's head and saying, "Keep breathing in God's spirit. Keep breathing in and out. That's your job. Everybody's working as hard as they can to get you out of there."

"Great, thanks," Records said, sounding as chipper as can be. "I'm glad you're here."

Bendixen found it hard to believe that anyone was alive inside the tangled mess. "Here was this pile of aluminum and wires, and I couldn't figure out what it was. And I sort of peered into there, and they were actually conscious, talking to us." Now the question was how to get Haynes, Records, Dvorak, and Fitch out of that mess of agonized metal without injuring them any further.

Upton Rehnberg worked for Sundstrand, which had designed the power system that was producing the electricity flowing through the hundred miles of wire all around him as he sat across from Jan Brown's jump seat. In addition, the plane carried the Sundstrand model AV557B cockpit voice recorder and the Sundstrand model 573 flight data recorder. The investment analyst in the aisle seat next to Rehnberg, Helen Young Hayes, wore a miniskirt and nylon panty-hose. Rehnberg wore a Dacron polyester short-sleeved shirt. Across the aisle from Hayes, John Transue felt lucky because the seat on his right was empty, giving him a bit more elbow room. He had grown up in Milwaukee where his parents lived. From his home in Denver, Transue had driven his wife Jacqueline to Wisconsin for a vacation, along with their two daughters, Michelle and Lindsey, who were three and eight at the time. He left the car there so that Jacqueline could drive the kids around, and he flew back to Denver for his work. Now he was returning to Milwaukee by way of Chicago to pick them up and drive them home.

When Jan Brown appeared in the galley doorway with her pink emergency manual and her microphone in hand, Rehnberg leaned over to Hayes and said, "This is a very bad sign." Then Brown asked the three to be her "door helpers" in case she couldn't open the door "for some reason." Transue tried to brace, clutching his ankles and putting his head in his lap. It was awkward at best. Rehnberg looked up and saw Brown a few feet away. She sat in her jump seat facing him, snug in her harness, having finished her briefing. Her mobile face went through contortions as if she might burst into tears at any moment, another bad sign, Rehnberg thought.

He later said, "We hit the ground really, really hard." As we talked at his kitchen table in Rockford, Illinois, Rehnberg sighed and said, "Oh, dear," and hung his head. Rehnberg has a powerful build, yet he was unable to keep hold of his ankles during the crash. The forces were so great that he had no control over his limbs, which were thrown straight up into the air. As that happened, he saw the fireball come through the door and closed his eyes in time for the mist of flaming fuel to wash over him. The fire passed him and flashed over Hayes, melting her pantyhose into the flesh of her legs before moving across the aisle to Transue.

Transue recalled that "the noise was just a calliope of screaming metal." He was trying to hold his ankles when "the belly hit the ground, and then it started to roll, and something came flying through the air and hit me in the top of the head. At that point, everything started to be surreal, like it was moving in slow motion. I let go of my ankles, and as the plane started to roll down the runway, the fire came in where the doors crushed. There were big gaps on both sides of the door, and a wall of flame came in right across the galley in front of me." The fire lit up the dark cabin, "and I could see that my hands and my feet were above my head in the air. I was pin-wheeling."

Transue couldn't remember where he had learned not to wear synthetic clothing on an airplane, not to expose any more skin than necessary. He wore woolen dress pants, a long-sleeved cotton shirt, wool over-the-calf socks, and leather Florsheim shoes. The fireball burned one of his socks down to the skin, but the natural fibers ultimately protected him from sustaining the second-degree burns that Rehnberg and Hayes suffered. In those long seconds of this catastrophic sequence, Transue had a simple thought, as he later reported: "I don't like this part."

Brad Griffin, who had been meditating in seat 2-E, was gone by then, flying into the cornfield. The crushing and burning of the first class cabin killed most of the people in A-Zone, but the crushing also dissipated a tremendous amount of energy and acted as a shock absorber, protecting Jan Brown, Upton Rehnberg, Helen Hayes, and John Transue.

The wall of flame had passed through the coach cabin, which fell into darkness once more. The metallic screeching had stopped, and now Transue began to hear a noise that he described as "dut-dut-dut-dut-dut-dut." Very fast. "Dut-dut-dut-dut-dut-dut." He wondered what it could be. Whatever hit Transue in the head had knocked him senseless, and he watched dumbly as the people in his row dropped to the ceiling below and fled. When all the motion had stopped, Rehnberg found himself hanging from his seat belt, hair and beard singed, arms and face and chest burned, his Dacron shirt melted. He had no recollection of how he escaped from his seat belt, but he moved toward the light that fell from one side. He entered a familiar passageway. He saw that first class was gone. He was looking into the corn through a jagged hole beneath the bluest sky he had ever seen. He paused and gazed around in amazement. The world looked like an overexposed photograph, though when he turned around, he saw the wintry scene of ash and smoke and the swirling snowstorm of paper and money.

Still inside, Transue had begun to regain some of his senses. It was dark, save for a faint glow of sunlight. He was alone, or so he thought. The galley was still in front of him. Smoke coiled in the air. "I just kind of hung there suspended for a while," he said. "I didn't yet have full use of my brain." Finally Transue released his seat belt and fell onto his head and hands and knees. "I wasn't awake enough to catch myself." But he was down. The smoke was up. And with each breath, he regained some of his reason.

He recalled making a promise to himself before the crash: he would clear his row of people before leaving. Now he checked once again. His row was empty. He was about to bolt for the rays of light when through the smoke he made out the dim figure of a woman hanging upside down near the 2-Right exit. "She wasn't really conscious or unconscious. She was in that in-between state where I was for a while." Transue watched her slap ineffectually at her chest, trying to release the clasp on her harness. He could see now that she was a flight attendant, and it was clear that she would not be able to escape without help. "She just hung there when it didn't release." It was dark enough that Transue had to bring his face close to her chest to see the mechanism. He turned the rotating clasp, and Jan Brown fell right on top of him. All the hair on one side of her head was singed away, but that hair had saved the skin of her face. The right side of her white cotton blouse had been singed to the color of toast.

At that point, she seemed to come to life. She stood up and her training took over. She shouted, "Get out! Get out!"

Transue said, "I just thought, Thank God I'm released." To his left he saw fire. He crawled through the wreckage where first class had been. As he went through the breach in the fuselage, he faced a tangle of cornstalks and realized with a start what that rapid "dut-dut-dut-dut-dut-dut" had been. As it skidded along in the mud, the torn fuselage had been cutting corn stalks.

Still in something of a daze, Jan Brown began yelling for people to get out, as a steady stream of passengers made their way across the ceiling, struggling over the spilled contents of the overhead bins. Thus with the evacuation in progress, Brown stood at the opening, where she and Upton Rehnberg held a bundle of wires out of the way, and she ushered people out. Many years later, sitting in her kitchen eating her chocolate chip cookies, I told Brown that a number of people had commented that her demeanor was crisp, courteous, and professional, as if the plane had been parked at the gate, and she was saying, "Thank you for flying United. Come see us again soon."

And with a puzzled expression, Brown exclaimed, "I had the same feeling!"

After a time, the procession of people slowed and stopped. Brown was actually standing just inside the wrecked cabin. She happened to look up. "I'm looking up at the floor, which is now the ceiling, and I mean—you know how you see pictures of tornadoes that are moving across [the land]? Well, this was like that." She watched a rolling vortex of greasy black and gray smoke undulate toward her. "I have never ever seen anything so deadly looking." From the time of the crash until the last survivor escaped, only minutes had elapsed. The fire fighters in the rear of the plane estimated that the fuselage burned through and melted down in about ninety seconds.

The fire was everywhere now. It was so intense that the oxygen bottles and the fire extinguishers had begun to explode, sharp concussions and blossoms of white smoke. Brown's training asserted itself once more. The instructors had always told her, "Where the water's too deep, the fire's too hot, or the smoke is too thick, get out, get out!" And Brown knew the first rule of rescue operations as well: don't create more victims. "So I had to leave." As she began moving away, she saw Sylvia Tsao coming toward her. "Before she said anything, I just blocked her."

"I have to go back," Sylvia said. "My son's in there."

"There are men that'll get him," Brown said without much conviction.

"You told me to put him on the floor and it would be all right," Sylvia cried bitterly. "And now he's gone!"

"It was the best thing to do," Brown told her. "It was all we had." But as Brown looked at the bereaved young mother, she thought, as she later said, "I'm going to live with that for the rest of my life."

Lieutenant Colonel Harrington was trained for disaster preparedness in nuclear, chemical, and biological warfare. He had been in his office when he heard the All Call put out by the base commander, Dennis Swanstrom. As Harrington rushed toward the scene, he began passing the destruction on Runway 17-35. "There'd be like three people in a seat, one would be dead and two alive." He saw Swanstrom driving out and intercepted him. Swanstrom told Harrington to round up as many survivors as he could and bring them to the mess hall so that they could get water and make phone calls. Harrington returned to his office and began the monumental task of coordinating everything that would have to be done, from requisitioning buses for the transport of survivors to securing a supply of paper cups for water. Within the first hour, the walking wounded and the uninjured survivors congregated in the mess hall. Workers from restaurants in town began arriving with truckloads of food and drink. No one had to ask for it. The local television news anchor asked for donations of blood, and the people of Siouxland formed a line out the door and around the block at the blood bank. At the next commercial break, the same anchor had to ask people to stop donating blood.

The most urgent job Harrington had before him was to begin coordinating with Gene Herbek. As Harrington watched the people swarming the mess hall, he picked up the phone and called the Iowa State medical examiner's office in Des Moines. He was told that a full-body X-ray machine would be needed. One of the reasons why Swanstrom valued Harrington so highly was that he knew how to get things done. Harrington now recalled that a C-130 heavy transport plane, rigged as an air ambulance, happened to be parked on his ramp that day. It had stopped in Sioux City for the night. Its crew had been staying in a downtown motel, watching TV, as 1819 Uniform approached. Seeing the emergency developing on the news, they had rushed to the airport to re-rig the plane for litters in case it was needed to transport patients. Harrington asked the crew if they would fly down to Offutt Air Force Base south of Omaha to pick up a full-body X-ray machine for the morgue. Harrington also called someone who knew a lawyer who knew someone in the Nebraska coroner's office, who knew a dentist who had a portable dental X-ray machine. Moments later the phone rang in the Omaha office of Robert Sorenson, a legendary dentist who was self-taught in the discipline of forensics and was also a chain-smoking deputy sheriff. A very short man, he made an impression wherever he went, which was often to the scene of a crime in the company of a whole lot of police.

Then Harrington began calling various organizations to acquire enough gurneys for a mass casualty. "You never want to set a body on the floor," he explained later. "Because the juices run into the floor, and the only way you can get that smell out is to tear the floor out. So we wanted to make sure all the bodies were set on gurneys and not on the concrete floor." He had to canvass mortuaries from the entire region to secure enough gurneys for the job. Despite his effort, the morgue came up short.

As the day wore on, Harrington called Marx Truck Trailer Sales in Sioux City and another company called Acme to ask about renting refrigerated tractor-trailer trucks. They would be parked right outside Hangar 252. Those trucks would be used to refrigerate the dead.

CHAPTER TEN

In 1989, the *Sioux City Journal* was an old-fashioned daily newspaper steeped in a tradition that began in the 1860s. By necessity, all thirty-one staffers wore many hats. Marcia Poole was food editor and responsible for the Sunday Living section as well. "We were vacation thin, of course, in July," she recalled. Four reporters were on duty, along with three photographers and two interns.

Cal Olson, the editor, was a character right out of central casting in Hollywood. With a generous head of wavy hair, and not much pepper left amid the salt, he had a vigorously frank and friendly face. He wore sharp conservative suits and big glasses that accented his black bushy eyebrows. His smirk could either wither you or fill you with warm confidence, depending on what you had done to deserve it. He made a habit of asking his reporters, "How does it smell out there?"

Poole had returned from interviewing a poor family that was trying to make the most of its budget for food. She had stopped in at Dean's Drug Cafe to order a grilled cheese sandwich and a Coke to go and hurried back to the paper to write her story. She could barely hear the murmuring police scanner, which sat on the desk of one of the newsmen. The city editor, Glenn Olson (no relation to Cal), had been listening when the distinctive musical tones signaling an Alert Two came over the air. It was becoming apparent that a jumbo jet was in genuine distress, as the scanner picked up increasingly alarming chatter from police and fire departments. The musical tones now announced Alert Three status. Poole left her frustrating story and her sandwich and crossed the room to the scanner. She knew that jumbo jets didn't land at Sioux City. As the skeleton staff gathered around, word came over the air that the plane might have to land on U.S. Highway 20.

Glenn Olson picked up the phone and called the new library, where John Quinlan, a reporter, and a photographer named Gary Anderson were covering a news conference about the opening of the nearly completed building. Someone at the library called Quinlan to the phone, and the city editor barked, "Get back to the newsroom." Even as Quinlan and Anderson drove the short distance from the library to the *Journal* offices, Ed Porter, a photographer at the paper, was sitting in his car in front of the old Carnegie library, listening to his police scanner. Mark Fageol, the chief photographer, also heard the announcement that the plane might land on a road. Porter put his car in gear and headed straight for the airport, while Fageol headed out of town on Highway 20.

As Poole and the staff listened to radio chatter, Cal Olson stepped out of his office and said to the newsroom in general, "Get your stuff and get out to the airport. I don't care what you're doing, just drop it."

Even though Mark Reinders was a copy editor, he left for the airport. "I had no idea what I was going to be doing." But he knew that Marcia had sent an intern, Shari Zenor, a girl of barely college age, to the fire department to write a feature story for the Living section on a typical day in the life of a fire fighter—what Cal Olson called a popcorn piece, pure filler. Chances were that nothing at all would happen, and she would struggle to fill the space describing yawning firemen watching daytime television. The high point of the story would be a firehouse lunch. Now Reinders couldn't imagine where the poor kid would wind up.

Poole, in a kind of daze, ran out of the newsroom and into the street, still not convinced that a DC-10 could be coming their way. Standing before the *Journal* building, she found herself looking at the sight that caught Greg Clapper's attention as he led his family to the movie theater to see *Peter Pan.* "I could see the plane riding low to the southeast," she said. She watched 1819 Uniform vanish behind the intervening buildings. The town seemed completely silent, as it does after a deep winter snow. She heaved a sigh of relief. They had made it in safely. *Thank God*, she thought.

Minutes before, Gary Anderson had rushed into the *Journal* building to get his telephoto lens. He was now going seventy miles an hour on Interstate 29 north of the airport, and at the same moment when Clapper and Poole saw the plane, Anderson too saw it out his window. Without taking his foot off the accelerator, he picked up the Nikon F2 and began firing off frames with the motor drive. The silhouetted shape, shark-like and huge, rose over the bluffs, ballooned above the Southern Hills Mall, and dragged in over the intervening trees. As he fired away, he kept thinking that everything would turn out all right, making a good tight local story with a happy ending.

He cranked the steering wheel over and stopped on the shoulder. He leapt out. He could see the DC-10 vanish behind a hill. As he brought the camera to his eye, "I got the fireball," he later recounted, "then I felt sick thinking there were a lot of people dead, right at that moment, right there. How could anybody be alive?"

Bill Zahren, a young reporter, stood with fire fighters at the south end of the airport and watched 1819 Uniform come in low and fast. He lost sight of it behind a building, "and I heard this rumble like a tympani drum, and I saw the wing shoot up in the air and saw fire running off the wing like water runs off a butter knife," he said. Zahren began running toward the terminal. When he reached the fence beside the building, he saw Dave Boxum, a cameraman from KTIV TV, Channel 4. Standing beside his tripod and camera, his hair and eyebrows were so blond that they seemed incandescent in the sun. He looked pale and shaken.

"Hey!" Zahren called, "did you get that shit?"

"Yeah, I think so," said Boxum, and Zahren ran on. He realized that he had to get on the field. As he ran, he recalled a story he'd recently researched about someone who had built his own airplane.

He had met him at Graham Aviation, where all the private planes parked. He remembered how easy it was to get on the ramp. "You just had to go through a shop door, turn left, and there you were."

Fageol had been on his way out of town on Highway 20 when a police car, lights and siren going, passed him and pulled over to the shoulder. Fageol slammed on the brakes and pulled in behind him. He stepped out with a 200-millimeter lens on his camera and aimed up at the mammoth shape passing overhead. Clearly the plane wasn't going to land on Highway 20. The police car turned around and headed back west toward town, and Fageol followed. He was going well over the speed limit, he recalled, when a sheriff's police car passed him as if he'd been parked.

Poole stood before the *Journal* building, watching the dome of black smoke billow into the sapphire sky and begin leaning away to the south. She went inside to tell the city editor that she'd go anywhere he needed her, as every phone in the newsroom continued ringing. She picked one up and said, "*Journal* newsroom, Marcia Poole." She heard a scratchy, long-distance voice say, "You're on the air!" The call was from a radio station in Toronto. Only two reporters remained unassigned, Poole and the court reporter, Kathy Hoeschen Massey, but when word came over the scanner that some people had survived the plane crash, it became immediately obvious where they should go. From previous stories she'd done, Poole already knew people at St. Luke's Hospital, so she went there, while Massey went to Marian Health Center.

Out on the freeway, Anderson returned to his car and barely made it past the first roadblock. When he saw a second roadblock, he drove through somebody's front yard to reach the road to the airport. Going through the main terminal would be hopeless, so he headed to the opposite side of the field where the private planes parked at Graham Aviation.

As Bill Zahren ran toward Graham, he saw Anderson. They walked through as if they knew what they were doing. As at most small airfields in the 1980s, no one stopped them.

At the same time, Ed Porter, an ex-Marine with more than

thirty years of experience, was pulling up to the Air National Guard entrance on the north side of the airfield. By chance Swanstrom had issued the All Call moments before. Porter, a month shy of his fifty-fifth birthday, was swept through the gate with everyone else who was responding. The sentries weren't even checking IDs. A bus was waiting, and Porter boarded with the rest of the Air National Guard men and women, many of whom were not in uniform. He was the only reporter on the scene with experience photographing air crashes. He had been a Marine Corps photographer from 1954 through 1957. As he put it, "I knew what the outcome was when you stick a jet into the ground."

When the bus stopped on the debris-strewn runway, Porter emerged with the other men and women and paused for a moment on the elevated step to look out over the scene. He saw ribbons glittering and rippling across a snowscape bedecked with human bodies "and then two or three people just kind of walking. That's the first image I remember."

He stepped down and took a few photographs before heading across the runway toward the tail of the aircraft, which lay on Taxiway Lima. Before he reached it, a United Airlines employee accosted him, "and he and I got into a fight, because he was trying to stop me from taking pictures. The last frame I got is his hand over the lens of my camera. He was trying to take the camera away from me." As the two struggled amid the revolving paper and ash and smoke and money, the Sioux City chief of police, Gerald Donovan, approached with several officers.

"Get them out of here," Donovan told his officers.

No sooner had Gary Anderson run out onto the airfield than he saw the most incongruous sight: a middle-aged man in a suit, looking as if he'd stepped out of his office. The man walked right up to Anderson and said, "Have you ever seen anything like this? I was on that plane. Is there a bar around here?" Anderson could barely speak. He pointed at the terminal building. The man walked on as if nothing had happened. He was later found drinking at the bar.

Anderson continued to take photos. More and more people came wandering out of the smoke. He turned and shot and turned and shot. "There was so much out there," he later said, "but I couldn't just shoot randomly. I couldn't panic. I had to have some sense of what I was getting and how it would all go together to tell the story." Then he caught sight of a guardsman carrying a small blond boy unconscious in his arms. Anderson let off a burst of exposures with his motor drive. The boy's name was Spencer Bailey, son of Frances, brother of Brandon.

Moments before, a woman named Lynn Hartter, forty-four, had run onto the field in the company of several other members of the Air National Guard. "We ran out there," she said, "a whole bunch of us. There was a civilian man kneeling by this group of seats." The bank of seats was tipped over so that the people who were strapped in were face-down on the concrete. "We went over there, and you could hear a noise. And then we realized that it was a child." Two of the guardsmen reacted instinctively and "pulled the seats back. I mean it was just sheer adrenaline, they couldn't have done that the next day." Hartter squirmed up under the seats as the two men held them back. The civilian man pulled out a knife, reached up under the seats, and cut the seat belt, and three-year-old Spencer Bailey fell face-down into her arms. "And then I wiggled out and stood up and got the kid turned over." Then she was running for an ambulance, dodging debris and bodies.

As the supervisor of flying for the Air National Guard that day, Colonel Dennis Nielsen had witnessed the crash from a distance of less than 200 yards. Now he was astonished to see any survivors at all, let alone this little boy who had been ejected from the plane, with his mother and brother, in a detached bank of seats. "Lynn Hartter was carrying him," said Nielsen, "and there was a lot of debris on the ground. It was difficult to walk. Spencer was not a small child, and Lynn Hartter was in her mid to late forties, tiny gal. I knew Lynn, and she was stumbling through the wreckage, and she wasn't going to make it with this child to wherever she was going, and she just yelled, 'Colonel Nielsen, Colonel Nielsen, help me!' And the child fell into my arms. I walked about a hundred feet or so and put Spencer into an ambulance." During those few moments, while Nielsen relayed Spencer from Lynn's arms to the ambulance, Gary Anderson spun and snapped off several frames with his telephoto lens.

Lieutenant Jim Walker was searching for bodies with a group of Guard men and women at the edge of the corn and happened to turn and see Nielsen carrying Spencer. "I was within twenty yards of him when he walked out of the cornfield, and I remember thinking, Man that would make a great picture. And then I was just stunned when I saw that on the front page of the newspaper." That photograph was published around the world and became the model for a life-size bronze statue that commemorates the crash on the river walk in downtown Sioux City.*

Anderson was barely getting started constructing his story. He had shot perhaps two dozen frames when the police came down the runway with Ed Porter. The two photographers saw each other at last.

"I think I've got something!" Anderson called.

"That was good enough for me," Porter said later. His main concern was getting off the field with their film and cameras intact, "because Gary [Anderson] was hot. He was mad. I was trying to keep everything calm and collected until we could get out of there."

Anderson said, "I was just hoping I had something in focus." He drove back to the newsroom, marveling at the fact that he had started his day with a stultifying news conference at the library and then had been launched into "the biggest story I've ever covered in a matter of minutes." And it was over almost before it began.

In the immediate aftermath of the crash, Mark Reinders, carrying no more equipment than a notebook, found himself stymied by the dozens of vehicles blocking the main gate to the airfield. He took back roads, which he knew well, and parked near the north end of the airport. "I assume the statute of limitations has run out," Reinders

---

* Colonel Nielsen visited Spencer Bailey in the hospital and was met by reporters as he left. One reporter shouted, "How did you save the child?" Nielsen responded, "God saved the child—I just carried him!" Those words are inscribed on a plaque near the statue.

admitted to me a bit sheepishly. "But I literally climbed the fence." Coming from the north, Reinders first reached an area that a number of the passengers later called the Grassy Knoll. The rise in the land where no corn grew made a home for a few gnarled and aging scrub trees, some weeds and grasses, a boulder, and the running killdeer and creaking red-winged blackbirds. A gravel road curved into the distance. A vast cornfield separated the knoll from the wreckage, but many of the passengers, running through the corn, were led there by the arrangement of the rows. As Reinders approached, he saw a few people sitting on and near the boulder and called out, "Hey, what are you guys up to? Are you with the airport?"

"No," one of them said. "We were in that plane that crashed."

Reinders was "speechless and dumbfounded." An FAA technician had already discovered the passengers and radioed for help. Soon Air National Guard men and women escorted the survivors to triage. The rescue workers wanted to take Reinders to triage too, but he told them that he was not a survivor, he was a reporter. They told him to go away, "and there was no way I was going away."

Fortunately, the Guard members had their hands full, and Reinders slipped into the cornfield. He bashed his way through the stalks as survivors hurried past in the other direction. The heat was steaming him inside his clothing as he slogged through the rows, while a helicopter thundered overhead. He ducked down to avoid being seen. After the helicopter passed, he pushed on toward the wreckage. "And your adrenaline is just pounding the whole time," he recalled.

Emerging from the rows of corn, he concealed himself in the spaces among the emergency vehicles, which were parked haphazardly in every direction. From that vantage, he said, "I just took it all in." By then the police had rounded up all the other reporters and photographers and ejected them from the scene. Reinders was the only official witness left. All except for Shari Zenor, the young intern, who was concealed within Orville Thiele's fire department SUV. Although she had a box seat for the biggest show ever to hit Siouxland, the fire fighters had told her to stay in the vehicle, and she obeyed them. Marcia Poole later wrote, "It's doubtful, however, that any of the experienced reporters or photographers would have obeyed orders to stay in the fire department vehicle. The extreme circumstances would have compelled them to get out of the truck and go to work."

Zenor, however, was in shock, and she remained in shock throughout the afternoon, trapped in the vehicle, taking desultory notes as the scanner emitted bursts of static and frenzied voices. People were trapped in the fuselage as Larry Niehus, Jerry Logemann, and the other fire fighters tried to put out the fire with foam. Zenor could taste the oily smoke and hear the sirens and helicopters and the roar of the angry fire. She took in the dead bodies in their seats, even as survivors streamed out of the murk toward her. One of those survivors, a man wearing a blue Oxford shirt and a tie, came to her window and asked for water. Zenor opened the door and stepped out of the car to point the man in the direction of the triage area. For many years, Zenor would see that man's face in her dreams.

Thiele had his driver move the vehicle several times in the first hour after the crash. By that time, the injured were gone. Thiele asked Zenor if she wanted to get out and look around. She stepped down into the wintry scene and tried on the unfamiliar cloak of the reporter. "I saw bodies and body parts," she later wrote. "We had to drive around and through them. Most hadn't been covered. Some of them were still in their seats. I can shut my eyes and see those people."

Mark Reinders was in shock as well. When I asked him to tell me what he saw out there, all the air went out of him in a loud rushing hiss. He was rendered speechless for a moment, as the memories rushed back in. He described it as "similar to a tornado, where you just see so many personal items, purses and books and clothing and blankets and everything else just strewn out over the runway—wallets, napkins, necklaces, credit cards, and things like that, just—forever. And the wind was blowing and a lot of that stuff was blowing across the runway in the grassy areas." He surveyed the scene, scrawling in his notebook, "Two sets of golf clubs, a wallet photo insert depicting a pretty brunette in her prom dress, a Reebok tennis shoe, a purple hairdryer, pages and pages ripped from magazines, a dozen pieces of luggage, a signed graduation card, one woman's black high heeled shoe and a collection of Marilyn Monroe photos."

While he crept among the emergency vehicles, catching glimpses of the scene from his concealment, Reinders was struck by the endless computer tape that draped the site, as if it were a festive bunting for this unclean event. In the dim and smoky atmosphere, "it was like tinsel at Christmas with people dead in their seats," he later said. Pat McCann, a young police officer who was on the field, said it made him think of some sort of diabolical parade.

Reinders wrote in his notebook that the heat of the fire had withered the cornstalks and seared off their tops in a vast swath to the south of the main wreckage. He mentioned the strong smell of kerosene. He noted that even when the bodies were covered, it was obvious that some had been torn apart. The advantage the reporter has over the photographer is that his equipment is in his head. He need only open his eyes and see. And by now Reinders had seen it all. Moreover, all the survivors had been taken away by then. So he took in the blackness where a wall of flame had passed over the runway and the grass. He let the overwhelming heat and toxic smells of burning jet fuel and plastic and of the people who had not made it out of the fuselage seep into him and find a permanent place there, and he filed those things away where he could retrieve them later on.

When the time came at last, as Reinders knew it would, the police escorted him off the field. He returned to the newsroom and found "a chaotic mess" because everyone was trying to make the deadline for the next day's paper. Reinders wasn't even sure that he had anything to contribute because he hadn't really interviewed anyone in an official capacity. But Reinders had something more valuable than mere facts or quotes. He had a human view of the scene, and Cal Olson recognized that and told him to write it. "And that is what I did." Reinders served the role of official witness to a great historic event.

Everyone at the *Journal* scrambled to develop film and print photos. They pounded out copy and even managed to answer the ringing phones and make room in their darkroom for photographers from other news organizations. The bulldog edition of the paper went to bed at ten that night. Then Mark Fageol transmitted photos electronically to various news organizations for a few hours. He packed up a couple of hundred prints and set out for the airport in Omaha at about two in the morning. Some news organizations, such as *Time* and *Newsweek*, required prints for the higher-quality images they offered. It fell to Fageol to get them to the Associated Press in New York as fast as possible so that organization could distribute them to the magazines and other outlets. He reached the airport in Omaha at about three o'clock. At first the only plane he could find bound for New York was a United flight. He hesitated. Fageol understood that if he shipped a box of photos from the *Sioux City Journal* to the Associated Press, it might never arrive. "It would be one of those lost luggage things," he said with a laugh. He found another flight later that morning, made sure the package was on board, and began the return trip home. "By the time I got halfway to Sioux City, it's sunrise."

Even before Fageol began his drive to Omaha, many of the reporters had gone to Miles Inn, the local hangout for journalists, and ordered drinks. The team from KTIV, the local television station that had been co-founded by the *Journal*, was in attendance as well. The pub was small and crowded. As the *Journal* staffers drank and watched the coverage on television, the footage of the crash came flaming across the screen above the bar in horrifying color. Dave Boxum from KTIV had stood right behind Gary Brown, with the airport fence between them, and had caught the fiery breakup.*

"And it was kind of unfortunate," Reinders said of that night, "because . . . [the KTIV team] kind of cheered. They were proud of what they had caught on camera. But there were some other people in the tavern who found that offensive. There wasn't a big row, but it was kind of like, You heartless bastards, people died in that plane crash." Yet it was understandable that they wanted to acknowledge their achievement. They had caught on video what was never caught on video at that time: the crash of an airliner full of people.

In fact, all of the reporters at Miles Inn that night had helped to

---

* Go to laurencegonzales.com to watch the video.

document a unique event in history. As Reinders said of the ensuing days and weeks of round-the-clock work, "It was fun. It was invigorating. Long, long hours, because it was taking so much space and time, and nobody cared. Because that's what we do in the newspaper world. I remember being very proud of the next day's coverage. We were heartbroken for all the people that lost their lives and proud of the people that were on the scene and helped out, but we did our role as well, and to me there's nothing wrong with that." In the aftermath, Reinders worried that he might really be a heartless bastard. But when Cal Olson sent him to cover the one-year anniversary of the crash, he said, "I cried like a baby."

Just before the crash, a volunteer with WCDES, a local businessman named Dave Kaplan, was flying one of his company's airplanes inbound to Sioux City. "I was actually airborne at the time and witnessed the smoke plume from far away," Kaplan recalled. Since the airport was closed right after the crash, he landed at another field and caught a ride back to Sioux City. "I reported to Gary [Brown] when I got there and he sent me to a pile of wreckage to check it out." As he approached the pile, he saw fire fighters standing around examining passengers and asked, concerning the unrecognizable pile of debris, "What's this?"

A voice came out of the pile: "It's the cockpit. There's four of us in here."

Years later, Kaplan recalled, "It scared the be-Jesus out of me when I heard voices calling for help out of that pile."

Jim Allen, a lieutenant with Engine 5 of the Sioux City Fire Department, and two of his fire fighters gathered around with Kaplan and started talking with the eerie voices emanating from within the tangled mess. Allen, wearing a neat mustache and cleanly trimmed brown hair flecked with gray, gave a sad smile as he ruminated on the difficulties his crew faced that day. The flight crew, he said, was "trapped in this wreckage that to the naked eye did not resemble a cockpit area whatsoever." They were used to people being trapped in cars or trucks, which presented known "points of access," as he put it. "There was nothing to go by. We winged it." It seemed to be nothing but a giant ball of wire. Indeed, the amount of wire in a DC-10 could stretch from Sioux City to Omaha and beyond, and it all came together in the cockpit, the location from which the plane was supposed to be controlled. As the plane rotated up onto its nose and as the cockpit was sheared away from the first class cabin, those wires were pulled from the walls and floor of the aircraft and were left trailing. Then as the cockpit tumbled down the runway at better than a hundred miles an hour, it wrapped itself in those wires.

Allen and his crew used hacksaws to cut the wire. Once the fire fighters had unwrapped the cockpit from its shroud, they were able to reach in through the broken windows and cut the pilots' seat belts. Chaplain Clapper knelt beside the wreckage, his hand thrust inside to touch Bill Records's head. A paramedic reached through a broken window to give Records oxygen. "I was on the bottom of the pile, and it kind of revived me," Records said. The rescue workers tried to lift the wreckage but it wouldn't budge. Allen radioed to one of the WCDES vehicles that carried AMKUS tools, powerful hydraulic clippers used for cutting the tops off of wrecked cars. But when they tried to use those cutters on Records's side of the pile, it began squeezing Haynes, and he screamed in pain. When they tried it on Haynes's side, Records called out.

"We stopped that immediately," said Allen, "and I called for a forklift." He thought that if they could lift the structure straight up with no side loads on it, they might succeed.

At about that time, one of the Air National Guard pilots saw Bendixen across the 150-foot-wide runway and asked for his help. Bendixen marched across the runway and began to look for ways to give assistance. He peered inside and saw living, breathing men.

"I was face-to-face with this flight surgeon," Dvorak recalled. "He was peeking into the crack and talking to me."

The Air National Guard sent Allen both a crane and a large forklift. As Bendixen inspected the wreckage to see where each person was located and to assess his condition, Allen chose the forklift. He had the operator put the forks above the cockpit. "We strung a chain around the forks and down throughout various trusses of the wreckage," said Allen. One man was assigned to each pilot to watch him and to alert the operator to stop lifting if the movement was crushing anyone. Then Allen ordered the forklift operator to lift the wreckage six inches. A guardsman stood on the forks looking down to ensure that the pile of debris came straight up. The pile rose a few inches off the ground. Bendixen and Allen checked with each monitor. It appeared that no one inside was being injured, so Allen gave the order to resume lifting, and Fitch came out, as Allen put it, "almost immediately, almost under his own power."

"We didn't hear any noise from him anymore," Dvorak said.

"I felt a hand just tap me on the chest," Fitch recalled.

The hand belonged to a guardsman named Brian Bauerly, who said, "Don't worry, buddy, I've got ya. You're gonna be fine, we got ya."

While the forklift was adjusting and readjusting, the wreckage separated somewhat, and "I decided that I could crawl out of there," Dvorak said. He was the second person to be freed. As he squirmed out, Susan White was making her way across the field in a glow of adrenaline. He said, "I crawled out, they put me on a stretcher and hauled me over to triage." He blew a mass of blood and snot out of his nose as White appeared. Dvorak believed that she was "grossed out by that," as he later said, but after being told that the cockpit had disintegrated and that no one had survived, she was overjoyed to see him alive. She wiped his face and gave him water.

Al Haynes was the most difficult to rescue. Somehow in the tumbling of the cockpit, his head had been trapped by the yoke. His leg had been thrown up and over the control column as well. "We had to cut the yoke," Allen said. After Bendixen crawled inside and pushed Haynes through the small opening onto a backboard, he turned to Records, who was trapped in his collapsed seat.

An ambulance from the Cushing, Iowa, fire department was moving along Interstate 29 by then, not making much progress. The paramedics had encountered a wall of parked cars with people standing on their hoods and roofs, trying to see the wrecked plane. The crew had to drive on the grass to get around the roadblock.

Nevertheless, the ambulance arrived in time to transport Records. As the paramedics prepared to leave, one of the rescue workers leaned inside the open door and asked how many people had been in the cockpit. Records held up four fingers, and then Allen, Kaplan, and Bendixen knew that everyone was out. Records suffered some of the worst injuries of any member of the flight crew. As he later said, "I was pretty much out of commission for almost a month there. I was in critical condition for about the first week. Then they moved me down a floor to Intensive Care for another week. It was several weeks before I was even able to talk to the investigating team. I was unable to talk because my ribs were broken and I was full of fluid, and [I was] trying to keep from coughing."

Haynes and Dvorak shared an ambulance. As it pulled away, John Transue stood by in his undershirt with an ice pack on his head and his crushed briefcase under his arm. Inside the ambulance, as it jolted across the debris and the uneven ground, Al Haynes winced in pain at every bump. He groaned and said to Dvorak, "Tell the driver to go back. I think he missed a pothole."

At the same time, Jim Walker and his fellow A-7 pilots, who had been moving wounded people to triage, formed lines and began walking through the corn to make sure they hadn't missed anyone in the confusing scene. Walker had begun to notice, "a large amount of cash blowing around, piles of it. Even days later you could find small drifts of various denominations against a fence or wherever the wind left it." As soon as the plane crashed, people all over the field had begun to notice that thousands of hundred-dollar bills were swirling around within the snowstorm of paper and were drifting in piles, as the wind picked up through the long afternoon. The plane had been carrying an exceptionally large amount of U.S. currency. No one knew why. (The large number of pineapples was easier to understand, as many passengers coming from Hawaii were carrying them as gifts.)

Gary Brown said, "There was enough cash turned over to me that I could have paid off my house. I had one of our big Ford rescue trucks out there, and people were bringing me handfuls of hundred-dollar bills." He was seated in the truck, using it as a temporary command post. He reached over and rolled up the window on the passenger side and locked the door. As people brought him the money, he threw it on the floor. He filled the passenger side of the truck with the bills.

Dave Kaplan, one of Gary Brown's volunteers, said, "I filled a body bag with crisp hundred-dollar bills. People were just walking up to me and handing them to me. I can't begin to image how much money I handled in those two to three days on the field. Later someone from NTSB mentioned to us they were amazed that we turned that money in. The thought of keeping it didn't cross our minds." When I asked Gary if he knew where the money came from, he laughed. "We think we do. Nobody will admit to it. There was a lot of money on that aircraft. There's a reason that nobody wants to talk about it from an official agency, because they don't want people to know that large amounts of cash are being transferred on commercial airlines." I asked him where it went. "The FBI took it," he said. United Airlines issued a denial that the money had ever existed.

After Haynes and his crew were taken away, Bendixen crossed the runway once more. He returned to check the victims who had been left where they were because he or a medic had determined that they were too seriously injured to save. He found three or four people who had been thrown clear of the wreckage and now lay in the corn, still breathing. "We put 'em on a backboard, carried 'em out of the corn to the nearest ambulance, and let the ambulance go from there."

Bendixen's best friend Bill Shattuck lived in town, and he went to stay with him and his wife Marie that night. Bendixen was at the Sioux City airport for six days straight "with just my underwear and my flight suit. And every night, Marie would take my flight suit and my underwear and put it in the laundry and give it back to me the next morning, and away I'd go." He said that to this day, he marvels at the fact that he was on the scene. "There was just no logical reason why I should have been there that day. I had been flying for two years before that, and they never scheduled me in the afternoon."

CHAPTER ELEVEN

Margo Crain, thirty-one, was on her way to Chicago for training in her job at an insurance company. That morning she went down the hall from her office to visit Ellen, her travel agent. Crain wore a light-blue mid-length skirt with a long-sleeved white blouse, sheer hose, and light-pink high heels. She and Ellen chatted for a while. Ellen told her that she was seated in the back of the plane. She asked if Crain wanted to move forward.

"Sure, why not?" When Crain smiled, a dimple formed on the left side of her mouth.

Ellen told Crain that she would seat her over the wing. "It's safer over the wing." Ellen wished her a safe trip.

Then Crain visited another office to say good-bye to Sandy, an old friend from high school. At the time, they were both struggling with failing marriages and felt fortunate to be so close, both emotionally and geographically. Each of the women had two children. They talked about what it was going to be like as single mothers. Crain hugged Sandy good-bye and then left for the airport for what she expected to be a smooth flight on a beautiful summer day.

In the terminal, Crain walked down the wide corridor, following a flight attendant she had noticed because of her brilliant red hair with the big blue bow in it. The boarding lounge was overrun with people, especially families. "A lot of children. A lot of activity," recalled Ron Sheldon, who would sit next to Rod Vetter and Margo Crain. "Typical summertime activity. The plane was way overbooked." Sheldon saw Ruth E. Gomez, thirty-five, with her children running around, John A., ten; Paul, seven; and Leah, four. Ruth wore a ring inscribed with the words *Con todo mi amor* and signed "Anthony" with the date "1974." John was wearing an orthodontic retainer. That afternoon, Chaplain Clapper would find Paul and Leah in the Air National Guard mess hall, looking lost and in shock without their mother and brother. He remembered Leah's teddy bear earrings. Paul needed to go to the bathroom, so Clapper took him. "We were washing our hands, and the blood and mud was going down the drain together," Clapper said later, "and that image always stayed with me."

As Crain waited in the crowded boarding lounge, she watched Jerry Schemmel and Jay Ramsdell looking agitated at the ticket counter. She didn't know that they had been trying without success to get on a flight all morning. She could see that Schemmel was steaming, frustrated by the delays. She saw Garry Priest and admired him. He was twenty-three, a big good-looking executive dressed casually in jeans, traveling with his diminutive boss, Bruce Benham, thirty-seven. In fact, Priest looked quite a bit like a young Marlon Brando.

Crain boarded through exit 2-Left behind first class. She stepped over Upton Rehnberg's feet, passed Helen Young Hayes, the Chinese American investment analyst in her miniskirt, and headed down the port aisle. She found her seat on the aisle next to Rod Vetter, thirty-nine. Vetter rose from his seat and stowed her suitcase for her. They sat three rows ahead of the bulkhead that separated B-Zone from C-Zone.

When the engine blew, Sheldon, seated to Vetter's right, said, "Oops! Sounds like we lost an engine." Then he added, "Well, we've got two other engines. We'll just keep on going, it's just gonna slow us down a little bit." He seemed preternaturally composed under the circumstances.

Crain was not nearly as sanguine. "They served chicken fingers," she said. "And to this day I can never eat chicken fingers without reliving that moment and feeling the fear." Crain began to pray. "I pictured my children growing up without me. I thanked God that they were not on the plane with me." Memories of her children began playing "like a movie" before her eyes as she watched them grow from infants to their present ages, Bryson, ten, and Molly, seven.

About that time, Sheldon began to watch the spokes of sunlight revolving in the cabin—first appearing on one wall, then migrating slowly across and painting the backs of seats, then angling around the cabin and up the other wall—following them like a cat.

Although Rod Vetter was a former naval aviator, he had no idea what was going on in the cockpit. Even later, when the captain told the passengers that the flight was diverting to Sioux City, he didn't think it was so odd. The captain also said it was going to be a "very difficult landing," and Vetter wondered why. Then something happened that made his blood run cold. Dudley Dvorak emerged from the cockpit and rushed down the aisle. "He was white," Vetter said later. "Absolutely white." Then he noticed that the flight attendants had gone rigid in their movements, their faces strained and pale, and "you could tell that this was a severe situation." He turned to Ron Sheldon and Margo Crain and said that when this thing was over, they were going to have a drink together. They all agreed.

"It took us several years to do it," Crain said, "but we did have that drink."

As the airfield drew near Vetter tried bracing, he realized that because he was big and tall, he couldn't fold his body over correctly and so had to bend to one side. He was thinking to himself, "God, I'm going to break my neck." And in another few minutes, that is what he did.

To make a useful engineering material out of naturally occurring titanium requires almost super-human effort. The ore has to be dug out of the ground. One type of ore, called rutile (titanium dioxide), though inexpensive, is 95 percent titanium. Titanium is valuable only because it is lighter and stronger than any other metal, but to be strong, it must be pure, and to make it pure is difficult and costly.

Mixed with chlorine gas and petroleum coke, rutile produces Tickle. At that point, the Tickle is in the form of a gas. That gas—titanium tetrachloride—is put through a series of condensers and purification towers to produce liquid Tickle that is more than 99.8 percent pure. The liquid Tickle, which looks like water but is in reality metal, is stored in tanks filled with inert helium.

Although Titanium Metals of America, TIMET, had its headquarters in New Jersey in the 1970s, the facility that fabricated the metal was located in Henderson, Nevada, near the Hoover Dam, because the process of extracting titanium from ore requires large amounts of both electricity and water. To convert Tickle to a pure metal at that time, four parts by weight was combined with one part of molten magnesium at about 1,800 degrees Fahrenheit in a giant vessel flooded with argon gas to keep air out. That so-called reduction, known as the Kroll process, produced one part titanium metal and four parts magnesium chloride. On February 23, 1971, more than eighteen years before the crash of United Flight 232, TIMET used the Kroll process to produce a mass of some seven thousand pounds of what's known as titanium "sponge." It's called that because it looks like a sponge: it has holes in it. Once the reactor had cooled, the sponge was removed and crushed into small pieces. Then the magnesium chloride was leached out with acid, and the pure titanium metal was dried.

James Wildey, the senior metallurgist at the NTSB at the time of the crash, explained that "pure titanium, by itself, is not a useful engineering material because it has such low strength and is very expensive to process. However, adding aluminum and vanadium significantly changes the properties to give a much more useful alloy, one that is very resistant to corrosion, has by far the greater strength-to-weight ratio of any other metal alloy, from room temperature up to several hundred degrees Fahrenheit, and excellent resistance to fatigue and cracking. This combination of properties makes titanium alloys the material of choice for the large disks and fan blades at the front of high-bypass jet engines." To achieve that transformation requires what the makers of titanium themselves call an art. It requires a person, known as a melter, who has a sixth sense of how to make that metal. The textbook *Titanium* says, "There is a significant 'art' content involved in the melting operation."

In early 1971, TIMET had to blend the fragmented titanium sponge with other materials, such as recycled Ti-6Al-4V—an alloy of titanium containing 6 percent aluminum and 4 percent vanadium—as well as aluminum shot (small spheres of the metal) to make up the raw material that would ultimately be melted. About a third of that mixture came from scrap titanium—plate, bar, and the leftovers from previous melting operations. Technicians in great domed helmets with green glass visors wielded gas torches to cut this material into four-inch pieces. They then chemically cleaned the chunks and crushed all of them once again into small bits and then mixed and remixed the bits and mechanically pressed them into solid masses, each weighing about 310 pounds and shaped like cylinders cut in half lengthwise. The technicians then welded those half-cylinders together to form a long mass called an electrode. The melting process was called "vacuum consumable arc remelting" because it consumed the electrode. In fact, each melting operation consumed two of them. The first electrode was put into a water-cooled copper furnace, a columnar chamber twelve or fifteen feet long. Some titanium turnings were placed in the bottom. The furnace was sealed and all the air evacuated from it. Then, as General Electric's own report on the crash put it, "an arc of specified amperage and voltage, was struck across the bottom of the primary fabricated electrode and the bottom of the crucible, and the first fabricated electrode melted." After the furnace had cooled, the second electrode was loaded into the furnace and melted on top of the first. After the furnace had cooled once again, a giant overhead crane picked up the mass of metal and removed it for cleaning with acid to eliminate impurities. The crane then inverted the ingot and inserted it into a furnace crucible for a second melting. The temperature was raised several hundred degrees Fahrenheit above the melting point of the metal in the hope that this would melt away any remaining impurities, which have a higher melting point than titanium itself. Some impurities would disappear during that so-called double-melt process. However, like a meteor passing through the atmosphere, if an impurity were big enough, some of it could survive intact. Each melting operation, when complete, was known as a heat, and each heat was given an identifying number. On that February day in 1971, the heat TIMET melted was given the number K8283.

From Henderson, Nevada, heat K8283, was shipped to the TIMET facility in Toronto, Ohio, to be turned into what's known as a billet. Technicians there heated up the column of metal and worked it until it was sixteen inches in diameter. They then ground the surface of the ingot and put it through a contact ultrasonic test. That test is similar to the ultrasounds used in medicine. The technicians put a transducer on the surface of the metal and moved it around, looking for defects in the interior structure of the billet. They were searching for places where the material hadn't melted completely or had been contaminated by gases, such as nitrogen or oxygen. General Electric, the ultimate customer for this metal, had not ordered the best quality of titanium that was available at the time. In 1966, TIMET had introduced the triple-melt process, which produced purer titanium, less likely to have defects. Donald Cooper, the vice president for technology and quality assurance at TIMET, said, "There's basically two levels of quality: Premium and non-premium." The metal for the engines at General Electric "was ordered to a non-premium quality." Cooper went on, "We have always found that . . . the [triple-melt] material had a lower rate of anomalies or irregularities." (That said, the accident may have happened even with triple-melt titanium.)

The technicians at TIMET removed six and a half inches of metal from the outer surface of the billet and discarded that material. Then they cut a slice from either end of the billet and cut each slice in half across its diameter. They "upset" it in a forge to see if it was workable. The word *upset* means they mashed it. Working metal could be compared to working bread dough. Forging operations involve kneading and mashing the metal.

The technicians then impressed the identifying label "K8283" into the top of the billet, which weighed 6,208 pounds by that time. Heat K8283, now about fifteen feet long, left the TIMET facility at Toronto, Ohio, on March 26, 1971, along with certificates of testing that guaranteed the purity of the material and its suitability for the spinning disks that would be made from it. It left on a Glen Cartage truck along with four other heats, each weighing about six thousand pounds. Heat K8283 came with papers describing its exact chemical composition. The metal, said this pedigree, was mostly titanium. But it contained 6.2 percent aluminum and 4.1 percent vanadium, close enough to the formula for rotating aerospace parts to satisfy the customer. It also contained trace elements that couldn't be avoided, such as .026 percent carbon, .18 percent iron, and .008 percent nitrogen— all within allowable limits.

Throughout the long journey of this bland hunk of metal, with all its hidden mystery and its curious properties, everyone involved in the process knew that it would ultimately be subjected to tremendous forces once it went on duty carrying people and families and sisters and lovers and children and pregnant mothers aloft in the heavens.

TIMET trucked that billet of metal to ALCOA, the Aluminum Company of America, for the next steps in manufacturing the number one fan disk, serial number MPO-00385, that would wind up on the General Electric CF6-6 engine with the serial number 451-243 on the last flight of 1819 Uniform.

Terri Hardman boarded United Flight 232 with her sixteen-year-old daughter Sheli and her fourteen-year-old son Ryan. Her husband Fred had stayed home to work until Friday, when he would join them in Illinois for a wedding. Their other daughter, Christine, wasn't planning to attend because she was involved in softball playoffs. She would stay with friends. Since the Hardmans were originally from Illinois, Terri was excited for the chance to visit family.

Terri and her children had been assigned seats in row 28. When Fred Hardman led them to the gate, he asked if they could move forward. Luckily, seats opened up ahead, to the right of Rod Vetter, Margo Crain, and Ron Sheldon. Like Vetter, Terri wasn't really concerned about the explosion until Dvorak came rushing past, between her and the two teens, who were seated across the starboard aisle from her. A number of passengers called out and reached up to Dvorak to learn what was going on, but he was fixed on his task and kept going. Terri thought his behavior was strange. She later described the cabin as "very quiet. I think everybody was listening." Deep down, she knew now that they were in trouble. She reached across to Sheli and squeezed her knee. "I love you," she said. Sheli gave her a strained smile. She reached farther across to squeeze Ryan's knee and Ryan pushed her hand away, saying, "Mom, don't do that." Terri withdrew, thinking of thirteen-year-old Christine at home. She felt relieved that she had not brought all three of her children. At least Fred could raise one child.

After Haynes had told the passengers how rough the landing was going to be, after Jan Brown's dire, if formal, briefing, Terri insisted on touching Ryan again and saying, "I love you."

This time, Ryan gripped her hand and whispered, "I love you too."

Once Terri and her children were bent over, bracing, she recalled, "I peeked up a couple of times, I have to admit."

Jan Brown and Jan Murray saw her head come up and shouted, "Get your heads down and stay down!"

"It's amazing what things run through your mind," Terri said. As she bent to brace herself, she said, "Your mind races. I thought I should have got my purse and got my pictures out. I should have written something down and put it in my purse to Fred and to Chris. Then when we hit, it was a severe bump and something popped up in front of us on the floor." It was one of the aluminum floor panels, firing up and away with the force of the crash. The moment it was gone, Terri said, the air around her was suffused with the smell of spring and freshly mowed grass. Then the grass and earth began spewing out of the newly opened hole in the floor, and Terri closed her eyes and held onto her legs as tight as she could, hoping to God that her children were doing the same.

Rod Vetter found himself hanging upside down from his seat belt with the aft bulkhead collapsed onto his intact row of seats. Because the cabin was inverted, he was actually above the bulkhead. When he opened his eyes, he could see fire and smoke and a hole in what had been the floor, which was now above him.

"Margo, are you all right?" Vetter asked.

"Yeah, I'm fine," she said. "Let's get out of here, this place is on fire."

Ron Sheldon had already released his belt. Sheldon had an advantage over many of those around him. He had been an infantry soldier in Vietnam and had seen friends lose their lives. He had nearly lost his own life in rocket and mortar attacks. Now he deeply believed that he was going to live. He could see sunlight through the windows, "very dusty, hazy." He began reaching up to people who were still strapped in. He pushed them upward to relieve the tension on their seat belts so that he could unsnap them, saying, "Come on. We've got to get out of here."

Vetter searched for the nearest exit, but all he saw was fire. He unbuckled his seat belt and didn't fall because of the collapsed bulkhead pressing against his back. He checked for the hole in the floor that he had seen above him. He saw feet going out of it, so he knew that a person could fit through. He squirmed out of the space between the bulkhead and his seat and made it into the aisle. He saw another hole with people streaming out of it. This second hole was more attractive because he could simply walk over the debris to reach it.

"That way," he told Crain. "Go. Get out and keep going." But Vetter himself stayed behind.

On the far end of their center section of seats, Clif Marshall had

been on his way home to Ohio from a meeting of his industry association in Denver. Marshall sat on the starboard aisle. Two colleagues
from his company had also attended. Ron Rohde sat directly behind
him. Robert Boese was far in the back in C-Zone.

About the crash, Marshall said, "It went ker-bang, and it felt like
my teeth were falling out of my head." He ignored the instructions to
brace himself. He instead looked out the window and saw something
amazing: a shower of sparks streaming back from the right wing. The
oxygen masks dropped, and as the plane rotated upward and rolled
right, the overhead bins opened up, and as Marshall put it, "Shit was
flying all over the place." He said that when the plane rolled over and
went up onto its nose, that it was "sort of a very soft going over and
landing on the back." He described the sound the fuselage made as it
entered the cornfield as "swishing"—a loud whispering noise, as if a
bucket of pebbles had been thrown into the sea.

"Comes to a stop," Marshall said. "Then it gets quiet as hell,
and everything's very dark." Marshall dropped from his seat and
stood up. He saw the exit over the right wing, but the crash had
deformed it. Flames rose beyond the window. Marshall began to
think that he had survived the crash only to die in the smoke. His
story, as well as his life, might have ended there, as many others did
in that area of the fuselage, but "it so happens that I looked up, and
a panel of the floor had fallen out in the aisle, which was now right
above my head." Marshall was looking up through a luggage bay and
out a hole about sixteen inches on a side. "And I see blue sky!" He
thought, "I know where I'm going." He was looking through the hole
where the aluminum floor panel had blown out between Sheli Hardman and her mother Terri, filling the cabin with the shocking aroma
of freshly mowed grass.

While Marshall was trying to figure out a way to get up there, Ron
Sheldon stepped forward and knelt before him like a knight before a
king. He interlaced his fingers, making a stirrup of his hands. Marshall was about to step into Sheldon's hands when he saw eight-year-
old Alisa Hjermstad standing nearby, looking lost. He picked her up
and boosted her into the hole. Then he stepped into Sheldon's wait-

ing hands and climbed up after her. Sheldon began urging people to step into his hands and climb into the luggage bay.

Inside that luggage bay, Marshall picked up Alisa and lifted her out through the hole in the fuselage. He had to jump to reach the edge of the hole. He caught the jagged lip of metal, performed an adrenaline-charged pull-up, and climbed out after her. The metal of the airplane's skin was hot to the touch.

Marshall found himself standing on the bottom of the inverted fuselage, out in the hot July sun in the middle of an Iowa cornfield, twenty feet or more off the ground in the company of a little girl. It was like standing on the roof of a two-story house. Only it was a house in hell. The world was on fire. He turned and looked all around him, at the wreckage, the overcast of smoke and windblown papers and money, seats wrenched apart and scattered in the distance. Marshall looked at Alisa, who seemed to have gone mute. He saw how concerned she looked. His first thought was to get away because the plane might blow up, but he looked down and saw more people in the luggage bay who were trying to jump up to the hole in the fuselage. They had climbed into the trap and doomed themselves. Marshall peered into the smoky murk and saw their imploring faces.

"So I started reaching down and grabbing hold of their hands and pullin' 'em out." In the next minute or two, Sheldon boosted up—and Marshall pulled out—at least eight people, perhaps more, among them Alisa's brother Eric, eleven, and their father, Lawrence Hjermstad. Marshall had no idea that he was working with Sheldon. He peered between his feet and pulled out anyone who appeared in the hole. Sheldon knew that he had a partner up above, but he had no idea who it was. Yet working together, they also helped to rescue Terri Hardman and her two teens. (Terri stayed back to help Sheldon with her children, then let Sheldon boost her up.) Once on top of the inverted fuselage, "we went across the belly of the plane," Terri said. She and her children slid down onto the wing and jumped. While the Hardmans were escaping into the corn, Marshall pulled out the teenage girl from Norway who had annoyed Joseph Trombello with her pop music turned up so loud that he could hear it, even though she wore earphones. Trombello, forty-two, a corporate auditor, had been seated ahead of Crain and Vetter, across the aisle on the port side. Before takeoff in Denver, Trombello had been settling in, planning to read his newspaper, when Gitte Skaanes, seventeen, of Trondheim, Norway, sat down next to him. A striking blonde, she wore a short sleeveless black dress. Trombello found it hard to concentrate with her music blaring. He communicated with her using hand signals, and she turned down the volume. They fell into conversation. Skaanes had spent the summer in Wyoming as an exchange student and was on her way home. Now Marshall reached down between his feet through the broken fuselage and pulled Skaanes out.

"She was next to last," Marshall said. "And the last one I pulled out was Aki Muto, a nineteen-year-old Japanese girl." Marshall said that he used to have vivid memories of the faces of those people he and Sheldon rescued from United Flight 232. They came before him frequently, floating up like spirits in the night or while he daydreamed. He could picture them with great clarity up until the 1990s. Even after that, he saw a few of them from time to time, but then those ghostly yet living companions began to grow dim, and by the time I talked to Marshall in 2012, they had faded into mist. As he put it, "That brain cell is dead." And he laughed about it.

Once Skaanes and Muto were beside him, Marshall reached down for the next person, but only Ron Sheldon remained, too far below to reach. Sheldon had no one to boost him up and no one else to boost. "You go ahead," Sheldon called. "I'll find a way out." Those rescues had taken place in the first speedy seconds after the crash. Vetter had seen one of the pairs of feet going up through the hole. Now as Sheldon watched Marshall's face disappear from view, he looked around the smoky cabin and noticed a human face between his feet. He paused to make sense of the odd apparition. It was the face of a Catholic nun.

"Oh, my gosh, Sister!" Sheldon said. "Are you okay?"

"I think so," said Sister Mary. "But you're standing on me."

"I jumped out of the way and started to pick her up," Sheldon said. "But she was pretty heavy." He had seen her board the plane in a wheelchair, so he knew that moving her would not be easy. He asked if she could walk, and she said she could not. Bruce Benham, Garry Priest, and Rod Vetter saw Sheldon struggling and joined him in helping Sister Mary out.

On top of the fuselage, Marshall said, "My thought was that everyone had died of smoke inhalation, and being the coward that I am, I wasn't going back in there and gettin' 'em." Marshall now turned to Muto and Skaanes, and he had the John Wayne moment of his life. "All right, sweethearts," he said. "Let's get the hell out of here." They slid off the fuselage, ran across the wing, and jumped into the corn.

Marshall led the girls toward the terminal buildings that he had seen from their elevated position on the fuselage. But in doing so, he had to cross the debris field. As he put it, "There was shit all over the place. Parts and pieces and bodies." Yet Marshall was somehow able to put it from his mind and prevent it from affecting him. "I did not focus on it, because I knew it would be kind of grim, and I just didn't want to keep that in my head." He kept his eyes on the distant terminal, even as he marched past his dismembered fellow passengers. He saw a place where people had gathered—the triage area—and he steered the girls toward it. Muto and Skaanes sat on the ground, and Marshall knelt between them with a hand placed protectively on Muto's shoulder and Skaanes's back, as she held her blonde hair out of her eyes against the wind. They were eventually taken to the mess hall. He called his wife, who thought he was dead. She had seen the crash on television. Like so many others, she could not believe that anyone had survived.

Marshall spent two nights in the hospital for smoke inhalation and a bruised heart. It took until Friday morning before his pulse would drop below 100. He returned home by way of flights from Sioux City to St. Louis and Ostrander, Ohio, northwest of Columbus. While we talked, he sometimes choked up, as the powerful emotions that he had held in check for nearly a quarter of a century surged through him again. "This is pulling out emotions from me," he said at one point. And "you're pulling stuff out of my brain that's been sitting back in the back for a while." Yet once he reached home, he found that he was able to put the disaster in its place in his life. "I don't dwell on it much," he said. "[I have] too many other more important things to deal with."

Marshall's colleague Ron Rohde, in the seat behind him, survived as well, but his other colleague, Robert Boese, had been seated on the other side of the plane from Jay Ramsdell. The fuselage fractured across those rows. Boese's neck was broken and his brainstem cut in half. His aorta was lacerated by a piece of debris that went through his chest. He could not have survived his injuries.

On balance, Marshall felt that he had been through the worst that life could possibly offer him. Everything else was gravy. Why not enjoy it?

At the time of the crash, Aki Muto had been an exchange student living with an American family in Fort Collins and studying English at Colorado State University. At first, she wouldn't write to me in English, saying that her English was too poor. The first letter I received from her was in Japanese. However, it quickly became apparent that her English was just fine, and we enjoyed a long correspondence.

"There was a queue [of people] who wanted to get out from the airplane. I know [Clif Marshall] pulled out all of them, because I was the last one. He made sure that there was no one else there, and then he evacuated himself with me. I was 19 years old at that time and was very skinny. But there was a quite big lady in front of me, and it was amazing how he could pull her out. I really respect Clif for what he did on that day. He saved many people's lives. Without him, I am not here today."

Although all the hotel rooms near Sioux City had been booked, the dormitories at Briar Cliff College, high up in the hills in a bucolic setting, were empty for the summer. Margaret Wick, the president of the school, opened the rooms to the survivors, as well as to the families that would soon arrive in search of the living or the dead.

"I was taken to the dormitory," said Muto, "after some medical checking at the hospital. They provided me the room and the Norwe-gian girl was there too." Both being about the same age, Muto and Skaanes were given a room together, but "somehow she was away from the room and I was there alone. I felt very lonely and scared. So I went out from the room and found the space where many of survi-vors were gathering. I spent rest of time there. There was a boy who was eight or nine years old. I spent most of time talking and playing with him. He was with his younger sister. . . . I was very happy to be with them." I wrote back and reminded Muto that Lawrence Hjermstad was traveling with his two children, Alisa and Eric. They had been seated next to Terri Hardman.

Muto wrote back, saying, "I now remember it was Eric!! He was much, much younger than I, but he was very gentle. I received sev-eral calls from Japanese media. One Japanese TV company visited for the interview. I did not want to appear on TV but they strived to do it and I finally accepted. [Eric] saw that I had a trouble to refuse the TV interview. When I finally accepted the interview, which was taking place on the first floor of the dormitory, he came downstairs with me, saying 'I will protect you. If they do what you don't want, I will punch them!' When I accepted the interview, they promise that they were not going to film me. I was not comfortable to been filmed, because I looked very miserable, you know. They were filming after all without me and Eric knowing. They filmed me and Eric from our back and it was on TV news all over Japan."

In describing her night in the dorm, she wrote, "Both of my phys-ical and mental condition were not normal. I could not have the sense of time or hunger or sleep. I did not eat much. I did not sleep almost at all. What I thought there [in the dorm] was [that] I wanted to go back to Colorado as soon as possible." On the other hand, she was well cared for by the staff and by the volunteers at Briar Cliff. "There were many volunteer people there and they provided me the food and clothes. I could take the shower there too."

Meanwhile, back in Japan, reporters were mobbing her parents' home. "My parents did not know I was on that flight. They learned it from the media people. They were very quick, and they were waiting for my parents in front of their house. My parents had a very hard time to handle the media people. There are so many arrived in my parents' house and it was totally a mess. My photo was stolen. Next morning, they learned it had been stolen because it was on the front page of the newspaper! I was lucky that I was not in Japan, but I feel so sorry for my mom and dad." She could have called her family, but in her state of confusion she thought it would be too expensive. "I did not have any money with me."

Alisa Hjermstad had a ball of yarn, and the three of them made string figures, such as a cat's cradle and a Jacob's ladder, to keep their racing minds occupied. Muto became a child again and allowed herself to be comforted by Alisa and Eric.

During the flight, Muto had been seated next to a kindly woman, Velma Wright, and during that first night, Velma's brother drove from Denver straight through to Sioux City. In the morning, Muto accepted a ride with them so that she could reunite with her "American parents" in Colorado. Her mother and brother flew in from Japan. Muto continued studying English in Fort Collins and returned to Japan in March of 1990. She took up the study of English linguistics and graduated from Sophia Junior College in 1991.

As the clock struck midnight in the dormitory at Briar Cliff College, Gitte Skaanes turned eighteen. Once she reached home, she did not get on an airplane again for another seventeen years.

CHAPTER TWELVE

Robert MacIntosh left his office at NTSB headquarters and drove to his home in suburban Virginia. Some time during that ride, November 1819 Uniform crashed. MacIntosh arrived home to find that his wife and their two daughters, eight and three, had already seen it on TV. His wife entertained the girls while MacIntosh quickly packed in the bedroom. Anticipating being in hot July cornfields, he tucked in hat, gloves, and sunblock among his blue shirts with the NTSB logo on them and his other items of clothing. He kissed his wife and daughters and in minutes was making the five-mile run down Old Keene Mill Road to the interstate. By the time he reached the big Department of Transportation hangar, known as Hangar Six at Washington National Airport,* about two hours had elapsed since he left his office.

Inside the hangar, he walked between the two parallel lines painted on the gleaming gray floor. "You can eat off the floor in Hangar Six," Robert Benzon said.

A couple of other Go Team members had beat MacIntosh there. They sat on a couch watching television. "And sure enough," said MacIntosh, "we were able to see the aircraft come down and do that famous pirouette. . . . And that was sobering, because it appeared to

_____

* The airport was renamed Ronald Reagan National Airport in 1998.

us that, indeed, there would be no survivors." As they watched CNN, the magnitude of the crash began to sink in. MacIntosh said, "Wow. This is gonna be tough."

The waiting was tough too, as the administrative staff back at headquarters on Independence Avenue discovered that the FAA had no airplanes available to take the Go Team to Sioux City. They had to scrounge up a Coast Guard Grumman Gulfstream Turboprop, which would be slower than an FAA jet. They also had to locate a fresh crew. The crew then had to generate a flight plan and obtain weather briefings, and stragglers on the Go Team had to get to the airport. Some would make a quick stop at McDonald's or the 7-Eleven for a meal to eat on the flight. "To its credit," Benzon said, "the FAA runs Hangar Six like an executive VIP passenger operation for obvious reasons. They fly cabinet secretaries, congressmen, the FAA administrator, and the like around as their main job. Passengers deposit their bags at the entry door for handling by the FAA staff. The pilots always wear white shirts and ties. Airplane interiors are immaculate, and the service is really first class. With one exception: no food. Not even a stale pretzel. Ok . . . coffee, but that was about it." And while members of the Go Team traveled first class to the crash, they returned home by whatever means they could find. Theirs was the Go Team, not the Go Home Team.

Theirs was not the only Go Team in action that day either. General Electric had no trouble finding a Lear jet to accommodate the flight safety engineer, William H. Thompson, and a flight safety investigator, along with the CF6 systems manager, and a representative of GE Products Support Engineering Department. The Lear jet left Cincinnati Lunken Airport and landed in Sioux City at about 9:30 that night, almost before the NTSB Go Team had left Washington.

United Airlines sent a Go Team as well, and an investigator from the NTSB was on board. As soon as his plane arrived that night, he approached Gary Brown at the Woodbury County command post, which by then operated out of the hangar at Graham Aviation. "He was a big boy," Gary Brown recalled. "And he wanted to go out and collect the flight data recorder." Gary was reluctant to let him do it because he didn't know the man. "And he unfolded a badge. It was the biggest badge I'd ever seen. It was impressive." The big boy went out onto the field with a flashlight and found the flight data recorder and the cockpit voice recorder, and Gary put them in the back of his big Woodbury County rescue truck and assigned guards to stay with it overnight.

United Airlines also activated its crisis room, which was set up like Mission Control at NASA. The manager of external communications at United Airlines, Rob Doughty, described the facility at the headquarters. "It was high-tech. There were two or three tiers of tables, all facing the front of the room. There would be a center section, and the two sections on the side were angled a little bit. And then there were two, maybe three, huge screens where we could display all kinds of things. One of them had data about the aircraft, another we could throw up video, we could have a live television feed from CNN. And then we all had our own individual computers. Everybody had a station and there were phones at each station with multiple lines." No one would have ever suspected that, in the bland and anonymous industrial complex in Elk Grove Village, Illinois, this United mission control was in full operation day and night in the days after the crash.

By the time the NTSB Go Team departed, the mood was fairly grim, as the craft rolled down the runway and angled into the encroaching darkness. The Gulfstream was luxurious, with leather captain's chairs that could swivel into the aisle for more leg room. A table for each pair of facing seats could be folded out of the wall. Two people could sit comfortably on a couch in back near the small galley and toilet. A phone hung beside one of the seats.

A Board member was always included on the Go Team, and that day it happened to be the chairman of the NTSB, Jim Burnett. Burnett was appointed by Ronald Reagan in 1981. As Benzon put it, "He grew up pretty quickly into the accident investigation business soon after he was appointed. The Potomac River crash occurred about a half mile from our headquarters within a short time of his appointment." Air Florida Flight 90 attempted to take off during a snowstorm with ice on its wings and in its engines and crashed into the river in January of 1982. "He stepped up to the plate, and over the years became a very good advocate for aviation safety . . . much better than later chairmen." Although he was a young man, around forty at the time of the crash of United Flight 232, Burnett walked with a cane sporting a dog's head for a handle. "He said that was so he could point his cane head at bureaucrats to bird-dog the Federal Aviation Administration and other government transportation agencies," said Benzon. "In short, he didn't care much who he pissed off." Burnett would serve such functions as appearing on television to give interviews and presenting to the public the face of the Board, while providing the working investigators with a shield against the press. As such, he would work closely with Ted Lopatkiewicz, the public affairs officer, who sat beside him on the plane. Lopatkiewicz opened what he called his Go Bag and took out a list he always carried, which showed the worst airline crashes in history. Burnett studied the list for a moment. With a start, he understood that with 292 fatalities this would indeed be the largest death toll for an air crash in U.S. history. That was the number that Haynes had transmitted in response to Kevin Bachman's request for "souls on board." (The actual number was 296.) The next worst crash had occurred ten years earlier. American Airlines Flight 191—another DC-10—had crashed on takeoff from Chicago on May 25, 1979. The nation was shocked at the death toll: 273. In the vernacular of the NTSB, such accidents are called Crowd Killers.

Most airplanes at that time had a navigational radio called an ADF, for automatic direction finder, that operated on the AM radio band. MacIntosh asked the flight crew to tune it to a local AM radio station so that the team could listen to the news on the cabin speaker. "It was unbelievable to us," said MacIntosh, "as we passed places like Pittsburgh and Columbus and Indianapolis and so forth, to hear that there were survivors—many, many survivors—being taken to local hospitals." Cruising along in the dead of night, accompanied by the rumble and whine of the Gulfstream's turbines, the glow of flame gently tailing out of each engine, they sat in their captain's chairs, listening incredulously to that news. Lopatkiewicz said that Chairman Burnett was "flabbergasted."

Ten minutes before 1819 Uniform crashed, Jerry Schemmel craned his neck around to meet the eyes of his best friend and boss, Jay Ramsdell. Ramsdell grinned and gave him a thumbs-up. Schemmel smiled and returned the signal, as fourteen-year-old Tony Feeney watched. Then silence fell and the long wait began. Every emotion was represented in those aisles. Three rows ahead of Ramsdell, Charles Martz, the ex-Navy fighter pilot, was growing more and more angry. He usually flew himself around the country in the business aircraft he leased. Linda Pierce, seated across from Garry Priest, the young businessman traveling with Bruce Benham, was petrified. Priest tried to comfort her. Priest described himself this way: "I was twenty-three years old, bulletproof, big 'S' on my chest, a red cape behind. Pretty invincible at the time. I'm ten feet tall. And I guarantee you one thing: At that time? *Planes. Don't. Crash.*" He didn't believe the plane was going to crash until it crashed.

Pete Wernick, a bluegrass player known as Dr. Banjo, was holding his six-year-old son's hand and trying to comfort Ellen Badis on his right, whose two-year-old, Aaron, had fallen peacefully asleep with gum in his mouth. Sharon Bayless, seated across the starboard aisle from Aaron, leaned over and suggested to Ellen that she take the gum out of the boy's mouth.

A few rows forward sat the Mobley family, on their way to North Carolina to attend a reunion. Amy, nineteen, sat in the starboard window seat next to her eleven-year-old brother Rusty. Amy had married Doug Reynolds nineteen days before the flight, and this trip was doing double duty as their honeymoon. Rusty's cousin Marci sat across the aisle from him, with his brother Dustin on her left. Amy was thrilled for her new husband, as she explained later, "because that was his first time flying. He got to watch the Kentucky Derby," which was playing on the video screens throughout the plane. Doug was having the time of his life too. Pretty women were serving him food and drinks, and he was living in the lap of luxury. Amy said that although Doug had been afraid of the whole idea of flight before-hand, he could hardly believe that he was having such an exotic experience, traveling miles in the sky near the speed of sound with his whole new family of in-laws. He was a small-town guy. He worked drilling oil wells. Amy went on with a sigh. "It was just a dream come true for him. He just never ever got to do anything like that before." She paused. "It just wasn't quite what he was expecting." She laughed softly and then said, "Now we don't do it at all."

Sister Mary Viannea Karpinski, across the aisle, was still praying with her red rosary beads.

When the order from the cockpit came at last—"Brace! Brace! Brace!"—time went into slow motion for Schemmel. He reflected that he felt strangely at peace. "I felt good," he said. "I felt ready for whatever was going to happen." But he could not remember if he had told his wife about the new life insurance policy that he'd recently bought. He opened his briefcase, found pen and paper, and wrote this note:

> July 19, 1989
> Aboard United Flight 232.
> Whoever finds this note,
> I have a new life insurance
> policy. The papers are in
> my guest bedroom closet.
> Jerry Schemmel

He put the note in his briefcase and placed it beneath the seat ahead of him. Like so many people who wrote notes, he never saw it again.

Then began the breaking of the great aluminum ship, ripping and screaming across the ground, bursting into flames as it went. People were crying out. Schemmel was thrown against his seat belt. He watched in amazement as "a woman, still strapped in her seat, flew past me on the other side." He saw a body fly through the air. A ball of fire roared down the aisle above him as Schemmel tried to cover his head, to make himself small. Then the vessel arched into the air, breaking up further as it angled over, pirouetted, and slammed down onto its back. Schemmel felt pain searing through his spine, up into his neck, and down into his legs. Hanging from his seat belt now, jerking like a rag doll as the open cylinder of metal tore through the corn, he wondered if he'd broken his back, as the plane slid on and on. A concussion sent an intense pain through his head, and Schemmel was lying on the playing field after being hit by one of his teammates in a high school football game. He opened his eyes and looked up at his coach and at the teammate. All the world was silent.

Then he was back in the plane again, hanging inverted, watching the lazy smoke illuminated by flickering flames in the darkness. He released his seat belt and dropped to the ceiling. His eyes began to adjust. The man sitting behind him, Walter Williams, the twenty-eight-year-old with perfect teeth, had received fatal wounds to his chest. Some of the people were dripping blood. One person's severed arm hung down, held only by a strip of skin. Schemmel's eyes darted all around. So many bodies lay in disarray on the ceiling, bereft of their seats in this smoky cave. He looked for Sylvia Tsao, who had been seated ahead of him with her grinning toddler Evan. They were nowhere to be seen in the smoke. He saw no way out. The darkness was punctuated only by the dancing firelight. Many of the windows were still intact, but the force of landing on its back had partially crushed the fuselage so that many windows were flat on the ground, pressed into the mud or the corn, admitting no light at all. In some places the ceiling had been crushed enough to trap people in their seats, alive but unable to get out. To Schemmel's left and just behind him, going back from row 22 through 31, in the two-seat section on the port side, nearly everyone died of the smoke.

Now the filigree of flame had grown angry. The smoke, so wispy at first, began to turn and curdle as if the air itself were clotting. Schemmel began to choke. He helped seventy-nine-year-old Wilbur Eley down from his seat. He didn't notice Wilbur's wife, Vincenta, who had thought she was having a heart attack. The elderly man and woman began picking their way over the spilled luggage, moving

slowly through B-Zone toward Jan Brown, who was politely ushering people out. Schemmel saw a spoke of sunlight lance through the
smoke. "I knew at that moment that I was not going to die," he later
wrote.

As he began to move toward the light, he saw a woman heading
back into the depths of the burning plane, into the syrupy coils of
smoke. Schemmel struggled over the debris to reach her. He took her
arm to guide her out. Then he saw that it was Sylvia Tsao, and he
understood the horror in her eyes. Evan's face rose up in Schemmel's
vision.

"I can't find my son!" Sylvia shrieked at him. "I can't leave without my son!"

Sylvia had done as Jan Brown had directed. She had put Evan on
the floor and now he was gone. As she said later, "I remember being
in the brace position, with my son's head tucked between my knees,
my left hand holding his ankle, my face pushing down on his head,
my legs outside his legs." But then "suddenly, the world seemed to
end. I saw for an instant my son's body floating and flying at a high
speed down the right aisle towards the back of the aircraft, his head
first, his face away from me."

Now as flames lapped around the plane, Schemmel tried to think
of what the correct action was at this, the moment of truth. He saw
that Sylvia would go toward the rear in search of Evan and die in
there. Desperate to get her out of the plane, Schemmel said the first
thing that came into his head, the words that he knew would move
her: "I'll find your son. But you have to get out yourself. Now." He led
her to the forward galley, past the lavatories, and out of the open fuselage where first class had been torn away. Two men ushered her out.

Schemmel had said what he felt he had to say to save her life. Now
he stepped down from the burning plane and felt the softness of the
earth. He smelled a familiar scent from his childhood, and those
memories snapped the scene into focus for him: he was in a field of
corn in Iowa. As that realization descended on him, he also understood that he was standing next to a burning jumbo jet that might

explode.* He prepared to run. But no sooner had he taken a step or two, than a sound stopped him. It was the voice of a baby crying from within the plane. Without thinking, he headed back toward the plane where he had told Sylvia not to go. A man tried to stop him, shouting, "No! We've got to go!"

"There's a baby!" Schemmel said. Perhaps it was Evan. Perhaps he could find Sylvia's son. He jerked free of the man's grip and found himself back inside the darkened plane, choking, blinded by the smoke. As he went deeper into the burning wreck, the smoke grew so dense and toxic that he clenched his eyes shut, closed his mouth, held his breath. "I know I couldn't see anything and I do remember homing in on the cries. 'Keep crying,' I remember saying to myself. 'Please, keep crying.'" Schemmel groped toward the breathless wailing, hands out, feeling along the ceiling beneath his feet. He lifted away something that felt like a duffel bag. He pulled out a long piece of cloth, realizing as it passed through his hands that it was an airline blanket. He picked up something heavy made of metal and tossed it away. He reached down into an opening and felt flesh, soft and warm. It was an arm. He lifted the baby out, pushed the small body to his chest. Then he was outside once more, gasping for air in the sunlight. At last, he was running, clutching the baby, bracing himself for the explosion that he felt sure was coming.

When the order came to brace, Margo Crain held her ankles tight. She was slim and limber and was able to tuck deep down between the seats. Her first thought as she was blown along, so out of control, was, as she put it, "My kids! My kids!" She believed that she was about to die, and like Cindy Muncey ten rows behind her, Crain worried about who would take care of them. She hoped her husband would raise them right. Yet a feeling of inexplicable calm descended

---

* Many people believed that the plane would explode. Many even reported that it did explode. In fact, it did not, although oxygen bottles and fire extinguishers burst in the fire.

on her. She silently told herself, "Okay, ride it out." She held on "for dear life" and managed to keep her body in a tight tuck. And with that, "things came to an abrupt stop."

Crain remembers that she reflexively unbuckled her seat belt and fell on her head. "It was dark and smoky and dusty." She called Vetter's name, and he was calling hers and then "I saw his hand reach under some debris and grab mine." He had to move debris to clear a path. Vetter told Crain to follow him, and together they crawled on hands and knees away from the collapsed bulkhead toward the light. As she passed a window, Crain could see flames outside, "glowing, menacing." She called them "flickering, coppery, fiery." She couldn't seem to stop coughing. During the breakup of the ship, it was as if a great hand had come down and shaken out a rug, releasing all the dust that had accumulated for years in the upholstery and carpeting.

After pausing to watch Vetter, Sheldon, and the other men drag Sister Mary forward, Crain followed them past ten rows to the break in the fuselage that was their exit. She stepped out past Upton Rehnberg and the wires he held. "I came out and I looked around and it was this beautiful bright summer day, and I felt like Dorothy in *The Wizard of Oz* when she came out of her house after it had been through the tornado." As she stepped into the cornfield, she told herself, "I am going to change a lot of things in my life."

She followed the rows. The tassels on the stalks were high above her head. It was like a green, green dream. "The heat of the July summer day, combined with the heat from the fire of the plane, plus the unsettled dust made the air around me very suffocating. I felt like I was in some kind of dense, overgrown jungle." She emerged at last onto an open field. In one direction she saw radio towers, a parking apron beside them, and a gravel road leading away into the distance. In the other direction, she saw the Grassy Knoll, where others were gathering and where several aged scrub trees provided a bit of shade. Someone sat on a small boulder as if in a pastoral painting from another era. She went toward the people and the shade and climbed the rise in the land. She turned around and saw the pall of smoke, the wreckage, the tornado of money and ash that was turning the sunny day overcast. For the first time, she understood that the plane had actually crashed. Many years later she said, "The one scent I could really, really smell so strongly that it probably will never leave me is the scent of burning flesh."

Jerry Schemmel felt at last that he had put enough distance between himself and the plane to feel safe from an explosion. He paused to examine the baby in his arms. It was not Evan Jeffrey Tsao. It was "a little girl in a light blue dress." He checked her all over but found no sign of injury other than a small scrape on her cheek. And then she gave Schemmel "a big, beautiful smile." He would later learn that her name was Sabrina Lee Michaelson. Schemmel hurried through the corn and eventually found himself at the Grassy Knoll. He saw a young woman who seemed uninjured, standing on the rise in the land in a light-blue skirt and a white blouse.

As Crain stood contemplating all that had happened, she saw a man in a suit and tie walking quickly toward her with a look of determination on his face and a baby in his arms. "Here," he said, holding the baby out to her. "Can you hold her? I rescued her from the plane, but I don't know where her family is."

"Sure," Crain said, taking Sabrina Lee from Schemmel. "Being a mother," she told me, "I just held her. Her diaper was gone, but she just had a little bruise on one cheek." As Crain watched the man recede into the corn, she held Sabrina on her hip and consoled her. The child seemed so content. "She wasn't even crying." Then Crain heard a voice call out, "Oh, my God, my God! You've found my little girl! My baby! My baby! There she is!" Mark Michaelson came running out of the corn toward Crain with his hands outstretched, saying, "Thank you, thank you!"

"You're welcome," Crain said, as the other members of the Michaelson family emerged from the corn, Mark's wife Lori and their other children, Andrew, four, and Douglas, six, and all of them uninjured. By Friday, baby Sabrina and family would be on *The Oprah Winfrey Show* with Margo Crain.

But even as the Michaelson family was being reunited, Crain heard Sylvia Tsao screaming, "My baby! Where is my baby?" Crain turned toward the voice and saw Sylvia crawling on her hands and knees as if to find the lost child beneath the very earth.

For Schemmel everything happened too fast that day. After giving baby Sabrina to Crain, he took off in the direction of the burning plane "for what possible reason I do not know," as he later recalled. Schemmel ran to the plane and found that the fire had completely enveloped the fuselage. Yet he was still faced with the nagging sense that he had left some important business unfinished. It was too late. No one was going in now. No one was coming out. The rest of the day was one surreal experience after another for him. People were dazed and wandering, covered with blood amid the intense and beautiful green of the corn. One man knelt beside Sister Mary Viannea, praying.

When the engine blew up, Sister Mary later said, "I grabbed my rosary and said, 'Dear Lord, this rosary is for everyone on this plane. Please keep us in your hands.'" Miles below, a woman named Terry Moran was driving her car up the long sweeping hill of Floyd Boulevard, headed for the high bluffs above Sioux City, where an old boys' school, Trinity College, stood abandoned. In the early 1980s, a group of Catholics had joined together to devote themselves to the Virgin Mary. They wanted to tear down the old college and build a center in her honor on the highest bluff in town. A priest named Father Harold Cooper led the effort. Their first bid for the property had been rejected some time earlier. Then Father Cooper buried a statue of Saint Joseph on the property and brought the group together to say the rosary every day in the hope that the Virgin Mary would hear their prayers and intercede on their behalf. When the group later made a lower offer—about half of the original bid—it was accepted. Into this atmosphere of hope, Terry Moran, one of the co-founders of the Marian Center at Trinity Heights, drove her car as fast as she could. She screeched to a halt and leapt out, shouting, "Start the rosary right away! A plane is coming in to make a crash landing right now!" Father Cooper began to lead the prayers for the fifteen or so people gathered there. They harmonized with Sister Mary Viannea, praying so high above them, as the DC-10 staggered in and exploded in flames on the runway.

Now Sister Mary sat on the ground in a cornfield surrounded by survivors. Several people reported seeing her methodically working her rosary beads through her fingers and saying Hail Marys one after another in both Polish and English. On the other hand, her red rosary was gone. "Mine was lost in the crash," she said. Someone gave her another one to use in the aftermath. But she credited her special red rosary with saving all the people who survived. A childhood friend had bought it in Assisi and had it blessed in Fatima before giving it to Sister Mary. "I give credit to the rosary," she said. "It was the rosary that saved us. I know it." Terry Moran and the others who had prayed the rosary on the high bluff before the crash also credited the rosary with saving many lives. "It really was a miracle," said Sister Mary.

As Schemmel wandered through the chaos, Air National Guard men and women in green fatigues materialized out of the corn like apparitions in a dream. A helicopter hovered, sharp and thunderous, reanimating the clothing on the corpses as if to raise the dead. Volunteers approached Gary Brown's white truck with offerings of hundred-dollar bills. Schemmel meandered here and there, then came upon several seats in a pile and a woman sitting in one of them with a girl of eight or nine beside her. He ran to help them out of their seat belts, thinking that they had been overlooked in the confusion. When he reached them, he saw the tags on their wrists and realized that they were dead.

CHAPTER THIRTEEN

When the billet of titanium known as heat K8283 arrived at ALCOA in Cleveland, Ohio, technicians cut it into eight blanks weighing about seven hundred pounds each. Those blanks were destined to become fan disks for General Electric CF6-6 engines. The blanks, squat cylindrical columns sixteen inches in diameter and twenty-two inches deep, were put through a series of processes to prepare them for shipping to General Electric. The first was a forging operation that would make the blank the right shape to fit into a die. It would also knead the metal like bread dough to improve its microscopic crystalline structure. Then the blank was put through blocker forging to yield a crude approximation of the finished shape. Finisher forging gave the metal nearly its true shape but with enough excess material to allow for the fine machining it would undergo at GE. Heat treatment refined the crystalline structure of the metal further and gave it the right balance of strength and ductility for its life of spinning. Heating and working metal also helps dissolve impurities and further homogenizes the crystals. Gregory Williams, the manager of quality assurance in metallurgy for ALCOA, said, "All of the preforming work was done on a 3,000 ton hydraulic press between closed dies, typically heated to 500 degrees F. The forging stock was typically heated to 1,700 to

1,750 degrees F for these operations." As the blanks went through these processes, technicians wrote serial numbers on them in crayon.

A ring of metal was cut from around the bore of each blank—the hole in the center—and another from around the outer edge. The inner ring was tested for purity and strength. The outer ring was not. Thus did the eight blanks made from heat K8283 obtain another set of papers certifying their suitability for the flight. The blanks were shipped to General Electric in May of 1971 to be machined and finished into CF6-6 fan disks and put on airliners. Those blanks now had a pedigree from TIMET and another from ALCOA. They had papers saying that they had been tested and were of a material suitable for service on a jet engine that would propel a plane carrying hundreds of people.

Those papers were wrong.

At GE, the blanks were forged to what's known as "sonic shape" or rectilinear form. As James W. Tucker, the general manager of product operations at GE, put it, "The sides are parallel. . . . There are no dovetails machined in it." The disks were then given another ultrasonic inspection. During this first stage of the process at GE, the technicians who were performing the ultrasonic tests could see something below the surface of the metal on one of the eight disks that had been cut from heat K8283. No one knew if it was a real defect or an artifact of the ultrasonic test itself. In the past, false-positive findings had caused GE to waste money and cut up perfectly good disks to look for defects. But the disk was pulled out of production just to be on the safe side. These slugs of metal, now weighing about 370 pounds each, were nearly ready to commit to the audacious act of spinning into flight and soaring high above the earth.

Of the eight blanks that ALCOA had made, GE machined seven into working fan disks. The disks were given serial numbers MPO-00382 through MPO-00388. Fan disk MPO-00385 was entered into the GE manufacturing cycle on September 13, 1971. It was inspected by immersion ultrasonic testing on September 29 and passed the test. (Immersion ultrasonic testing, using water to conduct sound waves, is a more reliable way of detecting flaws.) Still in the sonic shape, it was subjected to a process called macroetch in which it is submerged in nitric hydrofluoric acid. This burns away some of the metal to reveal the grain structure. A technician inspected the grain of the metal and gave the disk a clean bill of health. During the week beginning December 1, 1971, the workers machined 00385 to its final shape—a large disk with a hole in the middle and dove-tail slots cut into the outer edge. The day after the disk was finished, technicians subjected it to fluorescent penetrant inspection (FPI). In this process, the disk is submerged in an oily liquid that will seep into any cracks that might be present. A powder is applied to draw the penetrant out of the cracks. The dye fluoresces under ultraviolet light, making cracks easier to see. Disk 00385 passed that test.

Two weeks before Christmas, the GE technicians put the disk through a finishing process called shot peening, in which tiny beads of metal are flung at the surface at high speed. They then used grit blasting and metal spray on the dovetail slots that would hold the fan blades. The finished disk was given a final inspection on December 11. Mechanics fitted the new disk with thirty-eight finely crafted fan blades, surgically precise in their ability to move air without undue turbulence. You can hear their almost ceramic ring and howl, an echoing bell-like sound that tolls when the captain pulls back the power as a big jet flies overhead on its way to landing. Mechanics then installed fan disk 00385 on a new CF6-6 engine. That engine, in turn, was sent out to Douglas Aircraft in Long Beach, California, on January 22, 1972. Douglas installed the engine on a brand new DC-10 to carry people to and fro across the heavens.

At that point, anyone inspecting the disk could be confident that it had no defects because of all the previous testing it had undergone and all the certificates guaranteeing its integrity. In fact the fan was a beautiful and otherworldly object made of a gleaming and silver-gray and perfectly smooth metal that existed nowhere without the hand of man. With all that it had been through, with all of its papers in place, who would be tempted to look at it with too jaundiced an eye?

Yet inside the bore of disk 00385, less than an inch from the front edge, a tiny pit, a cavity, existed on the finished surface. Shortly after TIMET melted heat K8283, General Electric changed its specification to call for a different type of furnace to be used in making titanium. It also required that the metal be melted three times instead of two. In addition, the use of scrap was no longer permitted. By then, however, heat K8283 had already been made, and a piece of it—fan disk 00385—had embarked on the long and winding road that would take it to 1819 Uniform and onward toward its long fall in two big pieces into the green corn of Buena Vista County, Iowa. By another bitter twist, 00385 and its seven sister disks were the last CF6 fan disks ever made with the old-fashioned double-melt titanium process. In 1989 passengers had no way to tell if they were boarding a plane bearing new technology or old. The same is true for passengers today.

Tony Feeney, the skinny fourteen-year-old boy with the big glasses, was traveling alone on United Flight 232. He was on his way to visit his grandmother and to attend Michael Jordan's basketball camp in Chicago. When the engine exploded, Feeney recalled, he was eating his lunch, listening to music on headphones, and reading a heavy-metal magazine. When Dudley Dvorak rushed back to look out the window at the tail, Feeney made the sign of the cross and prayed, "Holy angels, protect us." Priscilla Theroux, twenty-seven, seated across the aisle, gave him a religious medal. The businessman on Feeney's left tried to comfort him. Reynaldo Orito, forty-nine, told Feeney that he took this flight twice a week. "He gave me his Oreo cookies from his lunch and said that everything was going to be okay," Feeney said.

 With Orito's reassurance and Priscilla's sacred medal, Feeney felt more confident that the plane would land safely. As he held his ankles, though, and waited, "there was a loud impact," he told me, "and it kind of threw everybody back in their seats, and I remember seeing the back of people's heads as we were all kind of thrown out of the brace position and into the backs of our seats." He was jerked upward. His arms and legs went into the air, and his body was wrenched into odd contortions that he could not control. "And the next thing I remember is just rolling along on the runway. I was thrown from the plane at impact, out of my seat." He had no recollection of how he came out of his seat belt.

A week after the crash, Marcia Poole of the *Sioux City Journal* visited Feeney in his hospital room at St. Luke's. "The teenager clearly remembers," wrote Poole, "noticing two men several rows in front of his 32-G seat seconds before the crash." As Feeney watched them, they gave each other the thumbs-up sign.

"I thought they had a plan," Feeney told Poole, "or maybe they knew they were going to die."

As he watched, the right wing struck the runway and the plane began coming apart around him. Then, according to the story he told Poole, he saw Schemmel and Ramsdell leap out of their seats and wrench open the emergency exit. "I saw them bail out," he told Poole. Then he leaped up and followed.

"Tony described the struggle up the aisle," wrote Poole, "against a force that was pushing him back. When he reached the exit, he hoped there'd be a cushioned ramp to jump onto."

"But there wasn't," Feeney said. "And I just jumped."

Not long after that, *Life* magazine interviewed Feeney, and he told a different story. "After impact, I made my way through an exit," he said, "but I missed the emergency chute and fell to the ground." By whatever means, Feeney came free of his seat, the fuselage broke apart immediately in front of him, and he wound up on the easement between the runway and the corn. A startling number of people who were thrown out of the plane lived, including the man seated next to Brad Griffin, Michael Kielbassa, and thirty-nine-year-old Paul Olivier, who sat in the row behind Feeney on the port side next to sixteen-year-old Nina Skuljski. When Olivier's seat came to a stop on the runway, he was alive and Nina, still strapped in beside him, was dead.

Feeney told me that as he hit the surface of the runway and began tumbling, "I fractured my skull. Hit my head pretty good. I have bits and pieces of memory from coming in and out of consciousness as I was tumbling and rolling." He remembered "rolling along the side of the runway. And I remember a specific thought being, When am I going to stop rolling?" I asked how he thought he might have survived. "I was a super scrappy, skinny little kid," he said. "I kind of came to a stop on the side of the cornfield. A rescue worker had come around that area of the crash and found me. He picked me up like you would pick up a baby. My back was broken, so I remember screaming in pain. He put me in the back of his truck and drove me to triage, and from triage I was taken to St. Luke's Hospital" because that hospital had a burn unit. "I had third-degree [friction] burns all along the right-hand side of my body."

His father drove about twelve hours straight through from Casper, Wyoming. He found his son in traction. Tony was in St. Luke's Hospital for more than a month. He said that when he returned to high school that fall, he "received a lot of attention." He tried as much as possible to have a normal experience at school. But at the same time, the crash marked his life, and it "began to be how people knew me: Oh, he's the kid from the plane crash." In fact, he soon acquired the nickname Skip, owing to his traverse along the runway and perhaps to the tale he told Marcia Poole.

Feeney said that when he was eighteen or nineteen years old, he saw the movie *Fearless* and, "that had a large impact on me." The film was based on the novel of the same name by Rafael Yglesias, which was loosely inspired by the crash of United Flight 232. The main character, Brad Klein, played by Jeff Bridges, borrowed some elements of Jerry Schemmel's story. In the movie, Klein emerges unscathed from the crash carrying a baby. He comes to believe that he can't be killed. Klein takes a number of risks that endanger his life, such as driving his car into a brick wall and eating strawberries, to which he's allergic. Feeney said he started to do "stupid things like that," such as sitting on the edge of the roof of a tall building at night, tempting fate to take him.

"I went through periods of extreme recklessness, almost invincibility-type behavior." Looking back at his actions during those years, "I thought: 'Really? I was doing that?'"

When I asked him to be more specific, he said, "Well, you know . . . I jumped off a train."

I said, "That's an interesting choice. How fast was it going?"

Feeney laughed. "I don't know. Pretty fast." He had the idea that he could run in the air and then run out the speed of the train once he touched the ground, as you might imagine a cartoon character doing. It was a real-life reenactment of his dreamscape fantasy: following Schemmel and Ramsdell and jumping out of the crashing plane. And instead of successfully running, he experienced the same traumatic tumbling that he'd gone through when he was ejected from the plane. "I was all beat up and bloodied and couldn't breathe. I had bloodied my face and bloodied my hips." As the train roared off into the distance, he started crawling. After he caught his breath, he was able to stand and begin walking. Once he came to his senses, he realized that he had leapt off of a train in the middle of a desert in Wyoming. He walked back to the last town the train had passed through "and bought some pancakes and coffee and called some friends, who drove out and picked me up."

During that period of his life, he might wake up in the middle of the night and just take off and drive across the country for no reason. "I guess that's even how I got to Latin America. I just sold off all my possessions and ran away one day." When I spoke to him, he lived in Costa Rica.

Both Reynaldo Orito, who gave Feeney his Oreo cookies and reassured him, and Priscilla Theroux, who gave him the religious medal, were killed after being thrown from the plane. They lay dead on the runway when Charles Martz, the ex-Navy fighter pilot, walked past.

In the moments immediately after the crash, the control tower was quiet. After the intensity of Kevin Bachman's dialogue with Captain Haynes, the drama had been snatched away, and the tower cab became an odd and uncomfortable sanctuary high above the sea of suffering and smoke and the tiny human figures running to embrace the calamity. Occasionally the silence would be broken by a radio transmission from a pilot overflying the area high above. The controllers who had been working the crash were relieved from their duties by other controllers. Matt Rostermundt had taken Dale Mleynek's position on ground control.

Then Rostermundt answered a call from the field, startling everyone. Sam Gochenour, a technician from the FAA, helped maintain the electronic equipment on the field and in the tower. The communications antennas that many survivors had noticed near the Grassy Knoll were his responsibility. A small building sat inside the array of four antennas (a fifth was added later), with a parking apron next to it and a gravel road leading away along the perimeter of the airfield. Those antennas, known as the remote transmitter / receiver, or RTR site, carried all of the frequencies used by the Sioux City airport. Gochenour, in his mid-fifties, had been in a lower floor of the control tower all day realigning the thirty-six channels of continuous tape recording that captured everything that was said over the air. "Here I had all the voice tapes," Sam said, "but I wasn't listening to 'em. I was just doin' my job."

Just before 4:00, he signed off the work he'd done and crossed the ramp beneath a pile-driver sun to FAA vehicle number 636, a late-model Jeep. He made the short drive down the ramp to the FAA shop, which served as the headquarters for the technicians. As he parked his car, he noticed several people standing outside the shop, watching the sky. Gochenour stepped down from his Jeep, and one of the other workers told him about the emergency. He stood beside his car and watched the horizon. "I seen it come in," Gochenour said, "and I seen it tryin' to land. I seen it blow up. I seen it flip in the air."

He knew that his first order of business was to make sure that the crash had not harmed any equipment that was vital to flight operations. He returned to his car and drove to the gate. Then he saw the mobs of people and emergency vehicles. As he was considering how to reach his equipment, a recently hired technician named Tim Norton pulled up behind him in FAA vehicle number 637, a yellow late-model Dodge Caravan. Gochenour stepped out and went to Tim's window. "Tim," he said, "let's go around back. Let's don't go through that mess up front." They turned their vehicles around, and Tim followed Gochenour to a gate that led onto the perimeter road and about two miles around the south and west sides of the field, away from the wreck. They parked on the gravel apron beside the radio antenna towers. The RTR site was on the north side of the vast cornfield, on the far side of which the plane lay burning. Most of the emergency vehicles were approaching the crash from the south and east sides. Gochenour and Norton could see the boiling black smoke on the horizon, but nothing more beyond the horse-high corn, which blocked their view. As they stood watching, Norton, twenty-five, saw Helen Young Hayes walk out of the corn toward them. A moment later, an older man emerged behind her.

"God," Norton said, "talk about rubber neckers." He thought the people had come from I-29 and jumped the fence to gawk at the crash. As Hayes drew closer, though, Norton was struck by something odd about her. He realized that her synthetic clothing and her sheer nylon stockings were melted onto her body. She was burned. She had been seated between Upton Rehnberg and John Transue when the fireball came through the 2-Left exit. Norton watched her advance toward him and further realized that she was in shock. She could only mumble and stammer her response when they asked her to sit down. Then the elderly man caught up with her and said that he was having pains in his chest. When they looked up, there were dozens of people streaming out of the corn, some running, some staggering, and others moving in the rigid, awkward gait of shock.

Gochenour crossed to his Jeep, picked up the microphone, and called the tower. Matt Rostermundt answered, listened for a moment, and then turned to Mleynek. "Sam says he's got survivors out there." Mleynek gave him an incredulous look.

"They thought I was nuts," Gochenour later recounted. "He thought I was crazy."

While Gochenour called for help, Norton opened up the air-conditioned electronics building and began guiding people into the small room. He let some of the passengers drink the water that was used to refill the batteries. And then the first class flight attendant, Jan Murray, came walking out of the corn.

Before the plane crashed, Murray recalled later, "I went up to the front bathroom, because I wanted to pray. I got down on my knees in that dirty bathroom, and I just remember praying. I don't know what I was praying for. I was just praying, I guess, to get us there safely." She came out of the starboard first class lavatory and walked back through A-Zone to exit 2-Right, where she strapped into her jump seat. Across the airplane at 2-Left, Jan Brown strapped into her seat as well. Murray waited, listening to the strange sounds around her. "My whole life was going through my mind. I mean I thought . . . I thought probably that this was the end of my life." And she was filled with "yearning," she said, "to be with my mom and dad, just *yearning* to be home and be safe. I wanted my mom and dad so bad, it was awful, it was just an awful yearning." Telling me this, Murray heaved a trembling sigh and began weeping. She fell silent for a long time. When she resumed, she said in a whisper, "I can remember looking at the two guys, the gentlemen that were facing me." Bill Mackin, fifty-one, sat in the window seat with Craig Koglin beside him. As she watched Koglin, forty, he began limbering up for what was to come. "I could see him stretching and kind of getting ready for the game. You could just see him trying to relax his body and that sort of thing."

"How close are we?" Murray asked Mackin, who had a view out the window.

"Pretty close," he said, as he gazed at the ground rushing up.

Murray braced herself. Then both she and Jan Brown began screaming, "Brace! Brace! Brace! Stay down! Stay down! Stay down!" at the top of their lungs, and Murray found herself looking out over what appeared to be an empty cabin. "Boy," she said with a sigh. "That was eerie, to look back and not see a head. That seemed like an eternity while we were hollering 'Brace!' And then . . ." She paused, as if to try to think if she had any more to say. When nothing came to mind, she said, with simple finality, "We hit."

She heard no sound at all, but in the vivid light that poured in through the hole where the tail had broken off, she watched the doors to the overhead bins blow open, and "bags started flying everywhere." When the tail and nose tore away, a storm of dirt and runway grit began blowing through the cabin with hurricane force, and all of it still going in slow motion. Then she was dangling upside down in her harness. The force of the crash was so great that it drove the round steel clasp of her harness into her flesh and up under her ribcage, breaking several ribs. In the confusing smoke and haze, she could feel people moving around her. "It was smoky and it was black and it was nasty." She dug the clasp out of her ribcage and somehow managed to open it. The straps had wrapped around and around her arms, "like an ACE bandage. And I couldn't get down. I heard people scampering by and I had heard voices. Then I remember flailing my arms, and finally I dropped to the floor. And . . . I couldn't see anything and I was on my hands and knees and I didn't know which way to go and I looked up and there was this tiny pole of light, so I just started crawling for that light."

Then Craig Koglin was beside her, calmly saying, "I think we can get out here."

As her eyes adjusted, Murray saw corn jammed up into the area where the light leached through. Koglin pulled at something, and a space opened up, and they stepped out into the high corn. "It smelled like fresh-cut grass," she said with an astonished tone of voice as she recalled those first moments of release. "There was nowhere to go but to follow the rows of corn."

Murray again began to weep. She said in a high keening voice, "And the sky was blue—beautiful, beautiful blue—and the clouds were puffy white clouds. I thought we were in heaven." She fell into silent weeping for a time and then said through her tears, "I said, 'Are we alive?' and he said, 'Yeah, but we've got to run.' We just ran and ran and ran. We just followed the rows. The corn was higher than I was." When she staggered out of the corn, she was at the Grassy Knoll. She took her place among the other passengers, climbing the little hill with Margo Crain and looking back at the destruction.

"The plane looked like it had exploded, and I thought that we were the only survivors." She could barely speak through her tears as she said, "There were about . . . maybe twenty passengers on that bank." She had no idea that the plane had made it to an airport. As far as she could tell, they had crashed in a cornfield in the middle of nowhere. "It was just surreal." She called it "a peaceful little bank after what we'd been through." She was also unaware that the two FAA technicians, Gochenour and Norton, were trying to bring order to this chaotic scene, which spread from the Grassy Knoll to the RTR site.

She took stock of the people around her and realized that a number of them were seriously injured. Working alongside Georgeann del Castillo, her fellow flight attendant, Murray decided to triage the survivors for quick transport. She observed "a lot of blood," she said. "It was hard to tell what the injuries were, because it was really messy," but "We literally had a line ready. It's incredible that we did this."

An Air National Guard nurse named Pam Christianson had arrived on the field to help with triage. Her exact location was unclear, but she gave a sense of what sort of injuries people had sustained. She said, "The first lady I saw was literally scalped from her eyeballs back. When I first looked at her she was talking to me. I told her: 'Don't open your eyes. DO NOT open your eyes . . .' I put my hand on the back of her neck and felt her scalp and hair all in a clump. I pulled her scalp back over the top of her head as gingerly as possible."

As Murray and del Castillo moved among the badly wounded people, they encountered Norton and Gochenour, who were also trying to organize the passengers. People had begun asking after lost relatives, and Murray looked for something on which to write their names.

"We didn't have any paper," Norton said, "so we were using our legs and arms and the backs of shirts. So we started writing as much information as we could down." Murray, who was still wearing her apron from serving lunch on the plane, began to write names and telephone numbers on that.

Gochenour said, "People would come up to her and write their name and their number on her blouse."

Norton loaded some of the most seriously injured people into his van and left for the hospital. While Murray and del Castillo helped the victims, Gochenour was faced with onlookers trying to climb the fence. "I had to go down there and run them off," he recalled. He returned to the RTR to find a man climbing one of the towers. A woman with her two-year-old son was tearing her blue dress to give the man a piece of cloth to wave. The man on the tower was trying to draw attention to the survivors. Gochenour ran up and yelled at him to get down, help was coming.

A fire engine appeared out of nowhere and seemed to be heading right into the cornfield. Gochenour stood in front of the engine and put his hands out. He said, "You can't go in that damned cornfield. Park it." The fire fighter who was driving stepped down and looked around at the survivors. He saw two people he thought ought to go to the hospital immediately. He asked Gochenour if he could use his Jeep to take them. Gochenour gave him the keys, and the fire fighter loaded the victims. As he drove off, he called out to Gochenour, "When you leave, bring my fire engine!"

About forty minutes after the crash, a blue Air National Guard bus hove into view and parked near the RTR site. Murray and del Castillo said good-bye to Gochenour and joined the passengers as they filed on board to be transported to the triage area amid the wreckage. When the bus rolled away in a cloud of smoke, Gochenour sat in the heat alongside the fire engine and not a soul around. The only sounds came from the killdeers and red-winged blackbirds that flickered in and out of the torn-up corn. Gochenour went inside the air-conditioned RTR building and picked up the phone to call his boss. He explained the situation, then said, "You'd better come and get me, cause I'm not going to drive the damned fire truck."

Gochenour waited, watching the smoke rise into the blue sky that was columned in all quadrants with the cumulus that grew out of the afternoon heat. Soon his supervisor came driving out along the perimeter road towing a rooster tail of dust from the sun-dried gravel. They drove back the way he had come, avoiding all the wreck-age and carnage that Gochenour preferred not to see. "My logic was, there was enough people working on that. They did not need me. And I never seen a dead body, because I didn't want to see one, because you have to forget it. My supervisor come and got me and we went back to the restaurant [in the terminal] and had a cup of coffee."

CHAPTER FOURTEEN

Wandering around inside the McDonnell Douglas plant, where 1819 Uniform was built, I had an overwhelming impression of sheer size: everything seemed forty times larger than normal. What philosophy, what intent or craft, I wondered, could inspire building on such a monumental scale? By golf cart, an executive from McDonnell Douglas and I glided among the clean brown-and-tan-colored buildings, buildings so large that I couldn't quite gauge their scale until we drove inside of one and I saw, as we passed from yellow sunlight to a blue fluorescent haze, the sign warning, IT TAKES SIX MINUTES TO OPEN OR CLOSE THIS DOOR.

I stood in a room—a single room—that contained ten DC-10s. That was but one room in a complex in which the workers traveled by bicycle from one desk to another, while others could be seen hitchhiking during the lunch hour. Some of those workers were third-generation employees of Douglas, where planes had been built without interruption since the early 1920s. That could not be said of either Boeing or Lockheed, the two competitors that were making jumbo jets at the time of my visit.

Long before United Flight 232 crashed, at about the time that Dave Randa and Yisroel Brownstein were infants, I was writing about airline crashes and airline safety, and I had the opportunity to visit the Douglas plant where DC-10s were being built. To get there,

I flew in the cockpit of a DC-10, sitting in the jump seat behind the captain, as Dudley Dvorak would do during the final minutes of United Flight 232.

The DC-10 was built in stages, and each plane took eighteen months from start to finish. Some parts were made elsewhere by other companies. For example, engineers at Convair, a division of General Dynamics, designed the fuselage of the DC-10. The Convair factory built it. Other parts were fabricated right there in the McDonnell Douglas plant. Eventually the whole plane would emerge on the flight line at Long Beach Airport, and one day John C. Brizendine, who was president of Douglas at the time, would step forward for the traditional presentation of the new plane. One sunny day, I watched him deliver a snow-white DC-10 to the airline that had ordered it. Because of the time of year, the craft had a red Christmas bow tied around its entire sixty-two-foot girth. It had taken twenty million hours of engineering effort and fifteen hundred hours of flight testing to create this ship and its sisters.

We hummed along in a golf cart, my minder and I, to another building to watch a section of fuselage arrive on a special vehicle that one might have called a truck if it had not been so big. This was the same component as the section of fuselage that would wind up inverted and on fire in a cornfield, a piece of midsection made by Convair that would be fitted with a cockpit and a nose assembly, with wings and a tail: a marvelous cylinder of aluminum skin and skeleton, still displaying its coating of yellow-green strontium-chromate corrosion inhibitor. Apparently, even the employees were not used to the remarkable size of their own operations. Workers all over the area stopped to watch when the safety horn sounded, signaling that the great crane was lifting the object and moving it a few meters to its cradle at the end of a long line of partly finished fuselages. Since each airplane took a year and a half to build, the workers didn't assemble them one at a time. They built them in gangs.

After two days in the Douglas plant, I had no doubt that the men and women I saw there were as dedicated and sincere, as talented and well trained, as any group of technicians in aviation. And out there beneath the Long Beach sun, in the spick-and-span, designer-toned atmosphere of the Douglas plant, watching the workers assemble the unimaginably complex DC-10 airplane, I found it difficult to imagine those sleek ships doing anything but flying off to greater glory. One of the passengers who escaped the burning wreckage of 1819 Uniform, Amy Mobley Reynolds, said that in the minutes before the crash, she was admiring the craft that was carrying so many of those people around her to their deaths. "It was such a *beautiful* plane," she said with a sad sigh. (It was so reminiscent of the *Titanic*, a ship that, like 1819 Uniform, was unique and beautiful and had also carried a fatal flaw hidden deep within its structure. Charles Burgess was the last member of *Titanic*'s crew to retire, after forty-three years at sea. He was the baker on the *Titanic* and later sailed all the great ships, including the *Queen Elizabeth* and *Titanic*'s sister ship, the *Olympic*. He said that no vessel that ever sailed could hold a candle to *Titanic*. "She was a beautiful, wonderful ship.")

I went to look at the electrical assembly line for the DC-10 and the DC-9. The room was so large, the DC-10s themselves so large, that the new Douglas Super 80s and a number of DC-9s in various stages of construction seemed like toys tossed into corners by forgetful children. Except that I could see the tiny workers swarming over them and hear the echo of rivets popping like machine-gun fire throughout the vaulted space. I could smell the flux of solder and see the arc lights glittering and the giant spider shadow of a welder cast high up onto the ceiling.

The man in charge of wiring was explaining how they create and then move the wire harnesses, and I couldn't shake the feeling that what I saw before me was awfully spooky. Computers checked the accuracy of the connections, all of which were made by hand, mostly by women from the look of the assembly line. I was staring at a virtual wall of white wire that was but one-quarter of one section of an embryonic DC-10's nose. "One hundred miles of wire in a DC-10," said the man in charge. All that white wire, coiling endlessly, was mesmerizing. When the cockpit ripped away from 1819 Uniform, when the first class cabin was torn off, what remained for the passengers in coach to face—Upton Rehnberg and Garry Priest, Helen Young Hayes and Ellen Badis—was this wall of wire. And beyond that, strewn across the fields, as they emerged through the white curtain, they found the entire inventory of 270,000 parts that had once been collected into a whole and stuck together by two million fasteners, nuts, bolts, rivets, solder, thread, glue, and hope.

While Susan White and Donna McGrady stood in the sun by the broken tail, watching the people flowing across the field, the paper and insulation blowing down the runways, and the ambulances and helicopters coming and going, White had a surreal and adrenaline-fueled sense of purpose, as if she had been put there by God himself to help. Then she began walking through the debris, past the broken pieces of the plane and the people who had tumbled across the scene in their seats, and saw her own tote bag on the ground. She hesitated. She felt that it would be somehow blasphemous to walk through all this destruction carrying one's belongings. Triage had been set up amid the wreckage, and more people were being delivered there by Air National Guard buses all the time.

More helicopters were landing now, and the great swirling mass of smoke and soot and papers revolved around her as she went forward, she knew not where. Air National Guard men and women were running, and ambulances tore through the scene, their lights revolving, as she came upon a girl whose leg was split open, the muscle pulsating out of the gash in her skin. White leaned down and touched her and said, "Hang on. Someone's going to be with you."

As White and McGrady went among the dead and wounded, McGrady came across a woman who was badly burned, her synthetic clothes completely melted to her body, her hair singed away, leaving her skull blackened. One of her legs was so badly broken that the foot was up at the level of her waist. Her face was deeply burned, McGrady recalled. She was conscious, but "she was dying. She was saying something, but she couldn't hardly say anything." The woman may have worn dentures. McGrady said that her teeth had melted. She had most likely inhaled fire. "And at that time the only thing that I could think of was just to try to soothe the pain." McGrady knelt beside her, trying to think how she might help. Emergency workers flowed around her, treating patients they thought they could save. McGrady looked around the scene of blowing debris, swirling money. Then she lifted her face to the sun beyond the sooty gloom and began singing an old spiritual song to the woman before her. She sang and sang out there in the smoke and the sunny overcast until a team of medics came at last to bear the woman away.

Nearby, Susan White had set up an improvised clearing station for people emerging from the smoke. Her uniform attracted those wanderers in search of a mother, a husband, a son. Schemmel approached, remembering her from the boarding lounge and from the walk down the Jetway in Denver.

"Do you remember my friend?" he asked.

"Of course, I do."

"I can't find my friend," Schemmel said.

White promised to keep an eye out for Jay Ramsdell.

Susan Randa approached and hugged White, saying, "Thank you for saying 'Release your seat belt,' because I would have just waited for someone to come rescue me."

"That's just what we're trained to say," White explained.

Jan Brown came out of the corn, pale and shaken from her encounter with Sylvia Tsao. In the middle of that green maze of cornstalks and blowing pollen, she had run into Lori Michaelson carrying Sabrina Lee. She had called out to her, "Were you able to hold her?"

"No," Lori called back. Reflecting on the crash a year later, Lori said, "I had to put her on the floor and once the plane hit, I was able to hold onto her, but once it flipped, then I lost her. And she was lost for a half hour or so."

Jan Brown had not yet heard about the rescue, and she wondered how Lori came to have possession of her baby. As Jan moved through the rows of corn, unable to see anything but green, her mind drifted back to the movie she'd seen the previous week, *Field of Dreams.* And when she emerged at last, she found Susan White and Donna

McGrady and Jan Murray, who had arrived by bus from the grassy knoll, and the four flight attendants hugged and leapt around, glad to see one another so impossibly alive.

When White saw Brown, she cried out, "There's a priest here! I'm going to get him to give us a blessing." White went away and returned with a priest, who dutifully proceeded to give each flight attendant a blessing, one at a time. But when he had gone, White cried out, "He didn't give me one!"

Her mind kept returning to her tote bag and her car keys. She asked a rescue worker to escort her back to the tail. As she walked through the carnage, she saw Tim Owens being carried on a stretcher. White was "jumping up and down, I was so happy to see him." In fact, she had assumed that he was dead, and Owens, having seen the tail break off and depart with White in it, had assumed the same of her. He was so excited to see her alive that he vaulted off the stretcher and ran to her.

"Yeah," Owens said, reminiscing, "that was one of the biggest hugs that I've ever gotten or given anybody. I'll never forget that. It was almost like one of those running-through-the-fields romance type of things."

As Owens and White embraced each other, she saw Georgeann del Castillo too. But no one saw Rene Le Beau.

Owens returned to the stretcher and allowed the guardsmen to take him to an ambulance. Then White continued on to the tail and retrieved her bag. Feeling better about having her car keys, she came running back to the triage area, crying, "Donna! I found my bag! I found my bag!"

"Can you find mine?" McGrady asked.

"Sure!" White said, and off she went. Approaching the shattered tail, she saw McGrady's purse on the ground, its contents spilled. A dead man lay nearby, legs and elbows cocked in an attitude of fleeing. She scooped everything into the bag and ran back to McGrady.

By then, White was in a frenzy of helping, charged with adrenaline. "I just couldn't do enough," she said. She was accosting paramedics saying, "Lemme do something, lemme do something," and they'd send her to fetch supplies or anything to get her out of their hair. As she ran back and forth through the triage area, she had been unaware that the pile of debris nearby was the cockpit. But once Jim Allen's team, along with Dave Kaplan and Ben Bendixen, had freed the crew, the pilots were laid out nearby. In one of her transits across the area, White saw Dvorak lying on a backboard. "I was so happy to see Dudley. He was all bloody." She hurried over and trickled water on him and wiped his face. Kneeling beside him, she dripped water into his mouth. She watched the paramedics take him away and load him into an ambulance. Then she crossed the field to the Air National Guard headquarters building.

As she entered, she put her hands in her pockets and realized that she still had the paperwork for an unaccompanied minor in her apron. She drew it out and saw that it was for thirteen-year-old Cinnamon Martinez. When a parent puts a child on a commercial airliner alone, it is with the clear understanding that one specified member of the crew will be responsible for that child: If you get out, my child gets out. Yet when White had turned around from her jump seat, the plane was gone. She'd had no chance to look out for Cinnamon. White stumbled into the building in a welter of confused emotions and was greeted by flight attendants who had not been in the crash. They had been at the airport on a layover. When they saw the crash on the news, they crossed the airfield to help. They took Cinnamon's paperwork from White. She went to a bank of phones to try to call her mother. All the lines were busy. Greg Clapper, who was passing by, stopped and introduced himself.

"I'm just trying to call my mom, and I can't get a line."

"You can come back in my office with me," said Clapper. "I'll help you call."

"Oh, thank you so much." White breathed a sigh of relief that she was the one being taken care of for once. "It was just so touching to me. I was so grateful."

Clapper took her hand and led her back to his office, where they sat in chairs knee-to-knee. He continued to hold her hands. "Let's pray," he said. In telling me this, White broke down and cried, saying,

"It always makes me cry." She tried to call her mother again, but the line was busy. Her parents were divorced, so she was able to try her father at a different number. Although White did not yet know it, her father had had a premonition that she was on United Flight 232. He had called her mother, who tried to calm him, but he kept saying, "No, she was on there. I feel it, I feel it." He had called United, but they refused to tell him anything, which convinced him that she was, indeed, on the flight.

"So by now the phone rings," White said, "and my dad answers, and he has this deep 'Hello.' He had been crying, I could tell. And I said, 'Daaad?'" White's voice crept up into a high and trembling register.

"Susan!"

Four of White's five sisters happened to be at her father's house, and she could hear them scream in unison in the background. Her father was weeping over the phone, saying, "I knew you were on that plane."

And White said in a quaking whisper, *"I'm alive!"*

Clapper was fixed on her, watching what appeared to him to be a genuine miracle. White started sobbing so hard then that she could no longer talk. She handed Clapper the phone. Ever since the engine exploded, she had tried not to break down. She had wanted to cry while attending the last moments of Cynthia Muncey's life, even as she believed that she, too, would perish. She had held back her tears as she hugged Cindy and comforted her. But now at last, in the privacy of this office, in the company of the chaplain, and in contact with her family, she let go.

Jan Brown was still on the airfield when John Transue came by wearing nothing but his undershirt and slacks. Transue had been guarding a woman with a compound fracture of the leg. As passengers rushed away from the burning plane, some had accidentally stepped on her. When the woman complained that the sun was hurting her broken leg, Transue took off his shirt and covered her with it. Now as he was about to exchange a word of greeting with Jan Brown, he spotted his briefcase lying on the runway. He tried to make his way through the debris toward it, but a fire truck came roaring out of nowhere, smashed it flat, and went chugging off into the smoke. Transue picked it up anyway. He was wandering around on the airfield in his undershirt, carrying his crushed briefcase, when someone noticed that he was bleeding from the head and led him to an ambulance. He accepted an ice pack from a paramedic. Then stretcher bearers arrived with Captain Haynes and placed him in the ambulance. "He was face down," Transue recalled. "He had towels on his head, because he was bleeding. He was *covered* in dirt. And he was weeping. He said, 'I killed all those people, I killed all those people.' And I said, 'You didn't kill anyone. You saved us.'" Then Dvorak arrived on another stretcher, and the paramedics slid him into the ambulance and rushed the two pilots to the hospital.

Transue was put on a crowded bus and driven toward the Air National Guard headquarters, where Clapper was helping Susan White call her father. As the bus moved slowly along the runway, Transue looked out the window and saw "torsos, arms, legs, all scattered along the runway. There were corpses and parts of corpses everywhere. I saw torsos with no arms, no legs." A pretty woman in a blue dress went from corpse to corpse out there, peering into the faces of those who had faces. She clutched a small child in her arms.

"I started looking away then," Transue said. "I didn't want to look anymore." But the images had been burned into his brain. Yet even among all the wreckage, both human and mechanical, a banjo lay on the runway, its leather shoulder strap still attached. It belonged to Pete Wernick, Dr. Banjo, who played bluegrass music in a band called Hot Rize. He was traveling with his wife Joan and their son Will and eleven large pieces of luggage, including that banjo and a steel guitar. He said he had some "pretty pricey possessions." He had packed a laptop computer and a video camera, which were exotic and expensive gadgets at the time. Out of all that luggage, United Airlines returned only their still camera and the steel guitar. After a thorough restoration, "I still play that instrument on stage, scorch marks and all," said Pete. The camera was "completely fried." Pete soon replaced everything he had lost in the crash, including the computer and video camera. As a traveling musician, he flew regularly, and two weeks after the crash, he packed all his suitcases and instrument cases and checked his new luggage for a flight to a concert in Oregon. United Airlines lost his luggage for the second time. Of his newly acquired possessions, nothing was ever seen again.

In addition to playing with Hot Rize, Pete also sold instructional videos to teach people how to play the banjo. As it happened, the executive director of the Sioux City airport, Randy Curtis, was learning to play banjo using one of Pete's videos when Dr. Banjo himself came crashing down out of the sky in an unscheduled fiery entrance. The day after the crash, Curtis walked out onto the runway and picked up the banjo. He found the case and put the banjo in it and shipped it back to Pete. He eventually wound up attending one of Pete's banjo camps.

Ellen Ayers, thirty-two, worked in the cardiopulmonary unit at St. Luke's as a neurodiagnostic technician. She was also qualified as a certified respiratory therapist. If you could not breathe, Ayers could breathe for you. She could make you live. She could put a tube down your throat and force air through it with a bag or a machine called a ventilator. Ayers was ready to go home at 3:30 on Wednesday afternoon when word came that a plane was in trouble and was headed her way. She called her husband Mark to say that she'd be late.

"I went to the ER, because I do the CPR." She was prepared for major injuries, but what happened next was anticlimactic. "I recall a lot of just . . . hanging around, not knowing what to expect. There was a lot of excitement, because this is something that had never, ever happened before." Ayers, however, had dealt with trauma in her previous job in Arizona. "I kind of felt calm." She believed that she knew what to expect. So she checked and double-checked to make sure that the emergency room had all the necessary equipment for CPR, including endotracheal tubes and bags, "crash cart, suction, oxygen, and that those kind of things were in the room, and then it was just quiet and waiting." The hospital staff, meanwhile, was dismissing all patients who weren't in need of immediate attention and canceling all nonemergency surgery. The whole hospital fell silent except for the clicking and beeping of equipment and occasional announcements over the loudspeakers.

"And of course," Ayers said, "the worst ones came in first."

She thought she had seen enough trauma to be inured to it, but the first person to come into her care shocked and humbled her. Gerald Harlon "Gerry" Dobson, forty-six, from Pittsgrove Township, New Jersey, had suffered second- and third-degree burns over 93 percent of his body and had fractured his right tibia and fibula. Dobson, on his way home from a dream vacation in Hawaii, "was severely burned. We had intubated him, and I was bagging." His wife Joann and their companions, Bill and Rose Marie Prato, were dead on the field, the muumuus and Hawaiian shirts singed and melted away. They suffered severe injuries to the head, neck, and chest.

In describing Dobson's condition when he came through the emergency room, Ayers said, "There's a lot of swelling. Just like if you burn your finger. It puffs up immediately, a lot of fluid underneath. His face, his arms, his legs, I mean, we're talking, almost his total body was burned. If that was somebody that I knew, I would not recognize them." Dobson's heart was going like mad. The doctors stabilized him as well as they could. Ayers continued bagging. She ran alongside the gurney as the team pushed it down the hall and into the elevator, which took them to the burn unit. Ayers helped to put Dobson on the ventilator that would continue to breathe for him through the hours and then the days and the weeks to come.

"His lungs had gotten burned too," Ayers said. The burned lung tissue swells, closing off airways and making recovery unlikely. He was eventually moved to Crozer-Chester Medical Center in Upland, Pennsylvania, across the Delaware River from New Jersey. His sons Arret, eighteen, and Emory, fourteen, rushed to his side. Dobson couldn't talk but was able to communicate by squeezing their hands.

After Ayers had put Dobson on the ventilator, she returned to the emergency room. And then "it started to really get crazy. I mean, people were coming in left and right." Doctors and nurses and technicians were rushing around pushing severely injured people on gurneys with ventilator bags going and IV bottles swinging, even as off-duty doctors, nurses, and technicians of every specialty arrived and tried to find some way to help. As Ayers made her way through this madness, dodging doctors and patients, she saw Kathy Shen, twenty-six, a flight attendant who had been deadheading in first class. She lay on a gurney with her stockings melted to her legs and a head wound. Ayers stood aside as she glided past. Shen was destined to remain in a coma for the next six weeks and to wake with no memory of United Flight 232 and none ever to return to her. She pieced together her own story by talking to many people over the years. Shen would likely have been killed if Jan Brown hadn't moved her from her first class seat. When she asked Jan where to sit, Brown was busy and pointed to a seat and said, "There." It happened to be the portside inboard jump seat, in which Shen was thrown clear of the plane. It was a random choice, but it saved her life.

"That was my fate," Shen said. "My assigned seat was vanished."

Ellen Ayers returned to the emergency room and began bagging patients who couldn't breathe on their own. Then the off-duty respiratory technicians began to arrive. They had not seen much trauma, and this was new for them. They were so excited that they shoved in and took over from her. "It wasn't rude. It was just excitement, wanting to be there and do something and help." She could see that these wild-eyed, adrenaline-powered young technicians needed to feel that they were part of the action, so she busied herself bringing clean sheets and blankets and towels. "I kind of backed off on what my job truly was and started to do more of the menial little things." By then the halls were jammed with people, and she felt as if she were in the way. In fact, nurses showed up from as far away as Minneapolis and Omaha. Nurses and specialists who happened to be visiting from San Francisco, Florida, and Colorado volunteered at either St. Luke's or Marian Health Center. After a while, Ayers decided that it was time for her to go home to her husband.

With Mark as a sounding board, Ayers tried to decompress from the experience. "Going home was the best part," she said. "Being able to tell Mark about what I had seen was a release for me. He would listen to my stories, he was kind of my therapist." That evening she saw the video of the crash on television. "It was incredible," she said. "Unbelievable those were the people I had just seen. I had no idea exactly what had happened until seeing the footage. I only knew there was a plane crash, people were hurt and coming into the hospital. It did not really sink in for weeks." As she prepared to retire for the night, however, the hospital called.

She returned to St. Luke's to find a young man who lay unconscious. "He had a lot of head trauma," Ayers said. The man, in his twenties, was engaged to be married. His fiancée was on her way. When Ayers entered the room, she was immediately stymied. She needed to perform an electroencephalogram on him. But to measure his brain waves, she would have to attach the electrical contacts to his head. Doing that involved measuring the distance between his ears to identify the points of contact. "And the man had no ears," she said. "It looked like he had slid down the runway. Both ears were scraped off. His hair was burned off. Or scraped off, either one. Parts of his skull were showing."

Ayers picked up the phone and dialed Dr. James L. Case, the neurologist on staff. She said, "I can't measure this patient's head, Doctor. Has no ears."

"What do you mean he has no ears?"

"He has no ears. They're gone."

Ayers said, "I remember saying it several times, because he couldn't understand. I told him, 'I think you need to come up and see this gentleman.'"

When Case arrived and saw the man's condition, he decided that it was imperative to determine if he had any brain activity. He told Ayers to try her best. In the end, she said, "I just guesstimated where I should put the wires." Once the electrodes were glued to his head, she found "very minimal brain waves." She watched the pen scratch feebly back and forth as the paper scrolled out of the machine. She could see that he was virtually flat-lined. A good brain wave is like a heartbeat. She would expect to see medium-strong voltage pulsing up and down eight to twelve times a second. A page took thirty seconds to scroll beneath the pen, and she saw scarcely two-dozen blips on each one. "With brain death," Ayers said, "it may be one or two cycles per second."

The patient was nevertheless admitted to the hospital and kept on a ventilator until July 23. On that day, Ayers was called to repeat the test to see if he had improved. By then his fiancée was by his side, trying to hold up against the waves of grief washing over her. Ayers arrived and attached the electrodes once more. She asked his fiancée to talk to him, thinking that she would have the greatest chance of eliciting a response.

The young woman told him that she loved him and was looking forward to the wedding and to seeing him return home. She implored him to get better.

"And I tried so hard not to cry," Ayers said, "because I could see. I don't think he ever truly was there. They left him on the runway. And I just had her keep talking to him." He was taken off the ventilator.

But then Ayers was called to the pediatric intensive care unit and asked to perform the same test on a little boy in a coma. His name was Spencer Bailey—son of Frances, brother of Brandon—and he "had some scrapes but otherwise seemed so precious. I loved working with children," Ayers said. She measured the distance between his ears and placed the electrodes. She tuned her instrument and talked to him and gently shook his shoulder. And there on the roll of paper, the pen began scratching out the pattern that she loved to see, big looping arcs filling the page with spikes of voltage a dozen times a second. When Lynn Hartter had run out onto the field with her fellow National Guard volunteers, she had seen the men lift the bank of seats, weighing hundreds of pounds, and had crawled under it to catch the little boy after he was cut free from his seat belt. She had run across the field with the two-year-old in her arms. As she tired of running, Colonel Dennis Nielsen took the boy from her and continued on to a waiting ambulance. Gary Anderson chose that moment to swing his telephoto lens around, creating the image seen around the world. And Ellen Ayers now determined that the little boy in that photograph would live.

Jan Brown wound up in the company of Jan Murray. Brown had walked to triage amid the wreckage, while Murray had been bussed there. Now they began to understand that their job was over—their shining ship in ruins—and that they were through with this filthy field with its blood and its blowing money and its scorched pineapples scattered here and there like severed heads. They saw a hangar in the distance and hitched a ride. As they were jolting across the uneven ground, Brown realized something that had been in the back of her mind since before she shouted the order to brace. "I always waited too long to go to the restroom before landing," she said. At Graham Aviation, the two flight attendants were shown to the restroom. Courteous to a fault, Brown let Murray go first. When it was her turn, she avoided looking in the mirror. She knew that half of her hair had been singed off. She didn't need another fright. She found Murray outside smoking a cigarette. "I had quit smoking four days before this," Brown told me.

"You know," she said to Murray, "if you've got another one of those, I think I'd like one, because there are other things that are going to kill me."

She and Murray were taken to the hospital, Brown said, "and the first thing I asked them was where the smoking section was. That nurse gave me the most stricken look." The nurse told Brown and Murray that the hospital had instituted a ban on smoking the week before.

Brown looked at her and said, "There's *always* a place to smoke."

By that time, Donna McGrady had arrived, and the three flight attendants were put in separate examining areas. After a few minutes, a nurse pulled the curtain and said to Brown, "Your husband's on the phone."

"I don't have a husband."

The nurse gave her a puzzled look and "she walked away so fast that it went click." Brown realized that the husband of "the other Jan

The landing. This is a still frame taken from a video of the crash. The black spot at center above the smoke appears to be a bank of seats with people still strapped in. To view the video, see laurencegonzales.com. *From the collection of Gary Brown*

Just moments after the crash, emergency vehicles and volunteers swarmed the scene. The truck with the sign that says, "Follow Me," is ordinarily used to direct small aircraft to the parking ramp.

Fighting the fire in the minutes immediately after the crash. In the interior of the plane, the temperature rose to an estimated 1,800 degrees Fahrenheit (982 degrees Celsius), melting the structure and burning the people inside beyond recognition.

Firefighters use a forklift to raise the wreckage of the cockpit with four pilots trapped inside. For half an hour, people walked past this debris not realizing what it was.

Dr. Romaine "Ben" Bendixen (in the flight suit, center) looks down at one of the pilots freshly extracted from the cockpit.

Lieutenant Jim Allen of the Sioux City Fire Department (in the red helmet) calls for a backboard for the injured pilot. Dave Kaplan (in sunglasses), a volunteer with WCDES, was among the first to realize that the pile of wreckage had people in it.

Minutes after the crash, survivors, some without a scratch, others fatally wounded, were taken to triage. Colonel Dennis Swanstrom, the base commander, is on the far left. Lieutenant Colonel Lawrence Harrington (wearing a hat) is in the center. The sign for Graham Aviation can be seen between the two, and the control tower is in the background, at the far right.

Air National Guard men and women prepare to search for bodies in the cornfield. The tail of the aircraft is in the background with two rows of seats still attached inside. The tail broke away and tumbled down the runway at more than 200 miles an hour, yet most people in those seats survived.

Above left: July 20, 1989, the day after the crash: The path of destruction from first impact on Runway 22. The view is approximately to the south. The burning fuselage came to rest inverted in the cornfield, in the upper left. Note the patches of unscarred ground in the middle where the jumbo jet bounced on its nose as it pirouetted.

Above right: The reverse view of the path, with the fuselage in the foreground and the point of impact in the background. *Photos by John Bates*

The tail where it came to rest on Taxiway Lima, with passengers and flight attendants still alive inside. It broke away when the aircraft hit the ground traveling at almost 250 miles an hour. *Photo by John Bates*

The burned-out fuselage on the day after the crash. Dozens of the dead were still inside. A perimeter had been cut in the cornfield to make it easier to guard the wreckage during the night. All of the dead remained on the field through the night. *Photo by John Bates*

Passenger seat. Note the skid marks showing paths taken by seats. The two stains are from bodies that lay on the runway overnight. The pink numbers are case numbers. Each body was given a unique number before identification. Tags bearing these numbers were wired to each body. *Photo by Pat McCann*

A typical arrangement of seats that had been ejected from the plane. Some passengers survived in these banks of seats, but the pink number and the stain on the concrete show the location of a fatality. *Photo by Pat McCann*

The seats where Dave and Susan Randa sat, along with John Hatch, Martha Conant, Yisroel Brownstein, Richard Howard Sudlow, and the Milford family. Susan White's jump seat (not visible) faces aft behind the seats at the top of the image.

Left: The electronics building and the radio transmitter-receiver (RTR) towers where some survivors gathered after running through the cornfield (background). *Photo from the author's collection*

Below left: Hangar 252, the temporary morgue, with refrigerated trucks awaiting the dead. Note the double-wide modular home on the left, where the white boards were set up and paperwork was done.

Below right: Inside Hangar 252 before it was transformed into a morgue. Guardsmen gather to prepare the tags that would be wired to the wrists or ankles of the dead.

Several trackers stand before three body bags that had been set on the floor because the morgue ran out of gurneys. Left, two dentists (red shirts) work in the dental section. In the upper left, FBI technicians take fingerprints. To the far right, funeral directors embalm a body. Behind the blue partition in the foreground, pathologists perform an autopsy. Note the body bag labeled *E* awaiting autopsy. Only one body at a time was handled at each station.

Thomas Randolph was a DCI special agent who worked both in the crime lab and on homicide investigations. He suffered severe post-traumatic stress after having to photograph all the victims as they were admitted to the morgue. He died at the age of sixty-four in 2005 and was considered by friends to be a casualty of this crash.

One of the most prominent forensic dentists in America, E. Steven Smith, came to Sioux City from Northwestern University. He brought with him Apple SE/30 computers, a new addition to the practice of forensic dentistry at the time. The new technology made the process of identifying bodies easier and faster.

The last two rows in the plane, 37 and 38, remained inside the tail as it broke away from the fuselage on impact. Most of the people in those seats survived. But 41-year-old Jasumati Patel was in 35-A, and the plane broke apart across her row, inflicting multiple fatal injuries. Her jewelry was used to help identify her.

Left, top: An attempt to record the remains of a passenger.

Left, bottom: In the office space beside the morgue, forensic dentists and volunteers work to identify a victim. Just above the woman on the left is Robert Sorenson, a legendary dentist who was self-taught in the discipline of forensics. On the right, center, with the bald head, is Raymond Rawson, a forensic dentist who helped to identify the eighty-five people killed in the fire at the MGM Grand Hotel in Las Vegas. In the upper right, with his hands on his hips, is Forrest Lorz, the programmer who wrote ToothPics, the computer software that helped to identify victims.

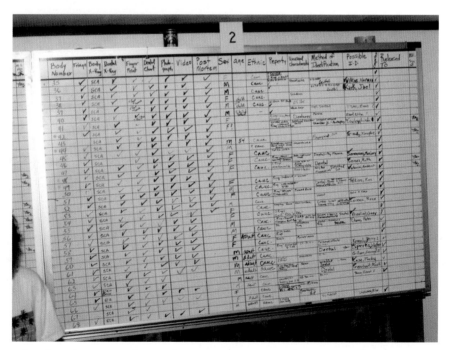

White boards were used to track any information that might help to identify a victim. The check marks show that a body had been processed through the various stations in the morgue.

When National Guard employees returned to work Monday morning, the halls were lined with caskets in shipping containers ready to be shipped home to the families awaiting the remains of their loved ones.

Left thrust reverser and cowl

Fan frame

Forward end of driveshaft

Engine pylon

Right thrust reverser and cowl

The seven-foot titanium fan on the front of this engine was mounted on the driveshaft, seen here sheared away at the center of the circular structure. As soon as investigators saw this, they knew that they would have to find the pieces of the broken fan, which had fallen into the summer-high corn somewhere to the northeast.

The tail, already separated from the rest of the aircraft, is lifted into position to be brought into a hangar for reconstruction. Robert MacIntosh, the Investigator in Charge, ordered the pieces of the tail reassembled and then had ropes strung from the origin of the explosion to the holes in the horizontal stabilizer, so that each piece of shrapnel could be accounted for.

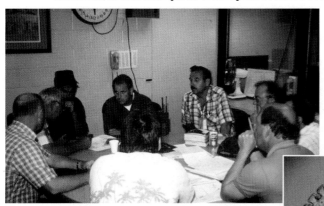

Above: Once investigators determined that the titanium fan was missing, Colonel Dennis Swanstrom, the base commander (center, in uniform), convened a meeting to try to formulate a plan for finding it.

Right: The search for the missing fan failed. The fractured parts were found by accident during the harvest. The pieces were moved to the black security room, known as Cell 10, at General Electric in Evendale, Ohio. Analysis of the metal began immediately and went on all night and into the following days. *Photo Courtesy of GE Aviation, US*

The defect that caused the fan to fracture was found on the inside of the hole, known as the bore, in the center of the disk. To the left of the numbers 51406, the shape of the cross section can be seen where the disk was cut for examination. That shape is shown below. *Photo Courtesy of GE Aviation, US*

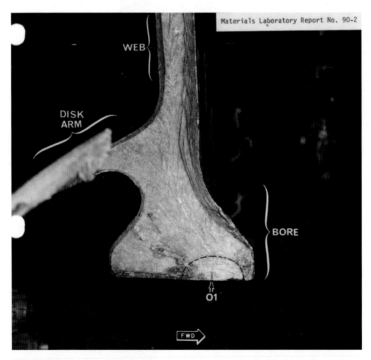

The fan disk was cut from bore to rim to expose the defect, shown at the arrow labeled 01. (See cut fan disk above.) *From NTSB Docket 437*

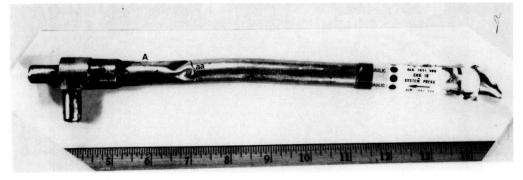

Technicians used an electron microscope to identify smears of titanium metal at the locations where the stainless-steel hydraulic lines had been punctured. The evidence proved that parts of the fan had cut the lines. *From NTSB Docket 437*

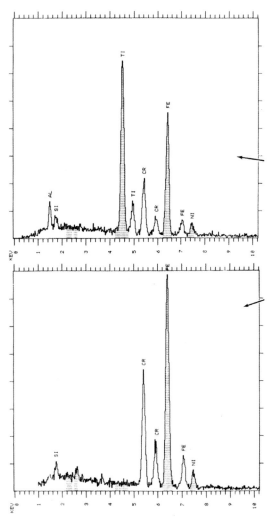

Two spectral plots produced with an electron microscope. The lower spectrum shows the stainless steel that the hydraulic lines are made of, which is mostly iron (FE). The upper spectrum shows the smear from the impact of a fragment of titanium (TI). *From NTSB Docket 437*

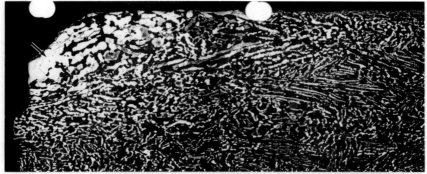

Figure 16. Microstructure on the eighth step polish. Arrow indicates an area of stabilized alpha below the cavity. X100, Kroll's etchant.

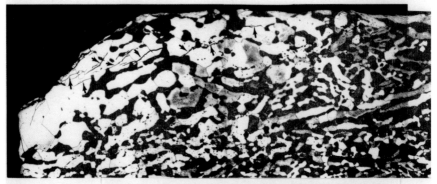

Figure 17. Same view as figure 16, but at twice the magnification. Arrowheads indicate microcracks. X200, Kroll's etchant.

The team of analysts zeroed in on the defect that started the cascade of failures that ended in the crash. The right side of figure 16 shows a normal matrix of titanium, aluminum, and vanadium in a proper alloy. The arrow, in the upper left, shows how the mixture, contaminated with nitrogen, fused together into "hard alpha" during manufacture and then cracked. Figure 17 shows a higher magnification of the same area. It was conclusive: the sequence that led to the crash began with defective titanium. *From NTSB Docket 437*

Back row: Donna McGrady, Bill Records, Tim Owens. Middle row: Kathy Shen, Georgeann del Castillo, Barbara Gillaspie, Dennis Fitch, Jan Brown. Front row: Susan White, Al Haynes, Dudley Dvorak, Jan Murray. *Photo from the collection of Jan Brown*

During a visit to the Sioux City Airport in 2012, Dennis Swanstrom (pointing), former base commander, recalls the events of 1989 with Jim Walker (center) and Lawrence Harrington (right). Walker, an Air National Guard pilot who volunteered on the scene, was one of the first people to respond. *Photo from the author's collection*

Cynthia Muncey (*left*) wrote this postcard to her sister, Pam, shortly before boarding a plane in Hawaii that would take her to her connection with United Flight 232 in Denver. *From the collection of Pamela McDowell*

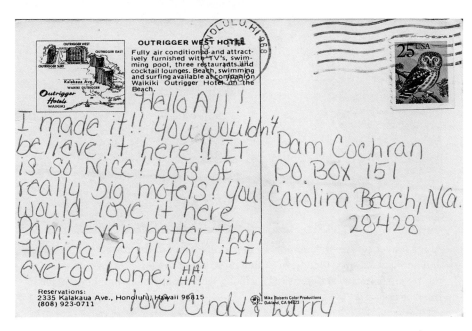

Susan White, twenty-five, comforted Cynthia Muncey during the last minutes of her life. White then survived in her jump seat in the tail and went on to rescue and assist others. *Photo from the Collection of Susan Callender*

At the prayer service in honor of the first anniversary of the crash, Susan White and her fiancé, Dan Callender, a United pilot, asked Gregory Clapper, chaplain of the 185th, to preside at their wedding along with the pastor at their church. *Photo from the Collection of Susan Callender*

Brown" was calling for Janice-Long Brown and their eleven-year-old daughter Kimberly. "They're mixing us up," Brown said, "right to the very, very end."

She was treated for the burns on her ankles where the fireball had melted her stockings in the gap between her slacks and her shoes. Then a nurse was kind enough to take her outside in a wheelchair and give her another cigarette. After that she was wheeled to the cafeteria, which was teeming with passengers, and for the fourth time that day she saw Sylvia Tsao, who wasn't even speaking anymore. She was in shock. Joan Wernick, Dr. Banjo's wife, crossed the room and put her hand on Sylvia's back, but the bereft mother of Evan could only stare into space.

Brown heard that United Airlines was going to fly survivors of Flight 232 to Chicago that night. She asked to be put on that flight. Someone drove her to the airport. Brown and Murray sat in the nearly empty boarding lounge, chain-smoking the pack of cigarettes that someone had given them. Brown watched the crusty old captain of the special flight come down the hall. She wondered why they hadn't left yet. By then the NTSB Go Team was en route, and Robert MacIntosh, the investigator in charge, had sent word ahead that all crew members from United Flight 232 were not to leave town before being interviewed.

"If I had known then what I know now," Brown said, "I would have just walked on the airplane and said, 'You'll have to get me off here kicking and screaming, because you know where I live. Just come and interview me.'"

Someone found a hotel room for Brown, but she didn't feel much like being in it. She and Murray were asked if they wanted something to eat, but Brown said, "I'd really like a beer." She tasted no beer that night. The two flight attendants smoked their last three cigarettes. Neither could sleep. Late that night, Brown managed to doze off for a couple of hours. In the morning, she wandered the halls looking for cigarettes, until she stumbled onto the United Airlines crisis team in a conference room. Charts on the wall listed the names of surviving passengers. She went in to see if she could find Janice Brown and Kimberly. Sure enough, she found a Jan Brown on the chart: her friend was at St. Luke's Hospital. Brown breathed a sigh of relief. She felt sure that if the mother escaped, then the daughter survived as well.

Satisfied that her friend was safe, she left. She had to be questioned by the NTSB and make arrangements to go home. "And I don't know where I was when it clicked that that was me that they had on that board from St. Luke's." She hurried back to the conference room. She scanned the board, but the name Jan Brown had been erased from the list. At last she knew that Janice and Kimberly were dead.

CHAPTER FIFTEEN

At one or two o'clock on the morning of July 20, when the Grumman Gulfstream touched down at the Sioux City airport and taxied to the ramp, more than a dozen people descended the stairs, including the chairman of the NTSB, Jim Burnett, and a young engineering intern from Auburn University named Laura Levy, with her laser transit packed in its case. Immediately after their arrival, while everyone else retired to hotels and motels, MacIntosh and Benzon took a group on a tour of the crash site. The group included Ted Lopatkiewicz, Jim Burnett, Randy Curtis, Gary Brown, Frank Hilldrup, and Dennis Swanstrom, among others.

"Indeed, it was nasty," MacIntosh remembered years later. As they walked through the night swinging flashlight beams, their feet shuffling through blowing paper and yellow insulation and sparkling computer tape, they passed the throttle quadrant that the crew had used to fly the plane. About the cockpit, Benzon said, "Well, it wasn't there. It was twisted-up seats, pilot seats, and part of the throttle quadrant. We were aware that the crew had survived, and we were very, very surprised after looking at what was left of the cockpit."

Frank Hilldrup, twenty-nine, chairman of the Structures Group, had joined the NTSB the previous fall. Wielding a flashlight, he made his way across the naked swath where the broken fuselage had skidded, cutting corn. He came to the severed end of the coach cabin from which the tail had departed. He stepped inside amid fire-fighting foam and melted metal, and shined his flashlight around to see the condition of the plane. He was shocked to see people hanging upside down or sprawled on the ceiling—many, many people, who some nine or ten hours earlier had been eating chicken fingers and watching the Kentucky Derby. His flashlight set the shadows of the people dancing, arms thrown up as if in some gruesome mockery of jubilation. He felt "a jolt," he said, and backed out of there.

MacIntosh followed Runway 04-22 all the way to the threshold where the right wing hit. There he saw a long hole a foot and a half deep gouged through the concrete by the right landing gear, and he understood the tremendous force with which the plane had hit. Again he shook his head, marveling that there was anything left of the plane and its passengers. This was definitely a Crowd Killer, and yet most of the crowd had survived.

Under a bright moon that had been full the day before, augmented by floodlights, the group proceeded down Runway 22, across the uneven slabs of concrete, mismatched and shifted through the decades. They stopped at the intersection of 17-35 near what remained of the tail. MacIntosh cast his flashlight beam up into the seats where John Hatch and Martha Conant had been sitting. He saw the torn and twisted metal, the tangle of wires hanging down, the fiberglass batting inside ripped aluminum foil, the bent magazine rack on its side where Susan White had braced her foot, and the lavatory thrown open where the blue toilet water had vomited out at her. In the jaundiced illumination, they saw the stains on the upholstery where Susan and Dave Randa had been splashed with someone's blood.

One of Gary Brown's volunteers, Dave Kaplan, watched as an investigator from the NTSB recovered the cockpit voice recorder and the flight data recorder and brought them to the command post. "I remember holding the CVR thinking to myself the answer to what just happened here is in my hands," said Kaplan. The devices were put in Gary Brown's truck and another WCDES volunteer, Don Dandurand, was assigned to keep them secure. "I should add,"

Kaplan said, "that Don spent the night on the field in the truck, surrounded by the dead, the wreckage, the smell and keeping an eye on the CVR. Don later told me it was the worst night of his life."

They all knew that there had been an explosion, but no one suspected that it was "nefarious," to use MacIntosh's word. It was the failure of a machine, which by design had a large amount of energy roaring around inside it. That energy, which normally bled out the back of the engine in a controlled fashion, had somehow come bursting into the open all at once. Beyond that, they knew little, and they were not inclined toward speculation. They couldn't work until dawn, and the hour was late.

Benzon and MacIntosh drove across the river to the Flamingo Motel in Nebraska. "We had to pass near a cow rendering plant," Benzon said. "It actually hurt your nose to take a whiff as we drove by. By the time we arrived in Sioux City, all the motels were so crowded with reporters and their entourages that Bob MacIntosh and I had to room together." The Flamingo was, as Benzon called it, "a dump of a place. Flamingos in Iowa? We called it the Flamin' O, as one letter of the neon sign was not working or was always blinking, and so it had, well . . . a scatological connotation." Benzon described their evenings during the investigation as "two middle-aged guys sitting around in their underwear, discussing what to do and where to go next and watching the late evening press coverage on an old black-and-white television."

Margo Crain was not sure what happened after she returned baby Sabrina Lee to the Michaelson family. By that time, fifty to seventy people, by her estimate, were milling around the area of the Grassy Knoll a short distance from the RTR antenna site. Sam Gochenour had called for transportation, and now Crain found herself riding through the wreckage in a National Guard bus, "with not a run in my hose," as she put it. She said the ride "seemed to take an eternity. The gruesome, violent aftermath that . . . the bus had to pick its way through, was enough to turn anyone's head. However, instead of turning away, I couldn't help but stare."

Once at the mess hall, Crain sought out a quiet corner and sat on the floor by herself. She had been driven through a field of dead bodies and was in shock. She had lost track of Rod Vetter, the only person with whom she had any acquaintance. Now she sat with her knees ricked up and her arms clasped around them, watching the people circle aimlessly. Garry Priest, the young executive she had admired in the boarding lounge in Denver, approached. She had followed him down the Jetway, remarking to herself how handsome he was. She was not quite ten years older than Priest, but he looked young to her. He had a black eye and a burst blood vessel that caused the white of his eye to turn a shocking crimson. He looked like a wounded warrior, stoic and brave. Now he squatted down beside her in his tight jeans and asked if she was all right.

"I guess," she told him. "As well as can be expected." Priest sat beside her on the floor. To Priest, Crain seemed a much older, if exotic, woman. She looked at him and said, "Actually, no. I'm not. I don't think any of us are really all right, are we?" The two sat staring at each other, and in that moment Margo Crain and Garry Priest were fused as if they'd been welded in the fires of the crash.

"It's amazing," Crain later observed, "how in one instant you are complete strangers and the next instant you are bonded for life due to a life-changing split second. Your body chemistry and outlook on life are forever altered."

A guardsman announced that phones had been set up. Crain and Priest took their places in line to make calls. When her turn came, Crain couldn't remember any phone numbers, but in time she found her sister Babette's number.

"Babette," she said. "It's me and I'm all right!"

"What do you mean? What happened? Where are you?"

"Have you been watching television?"

"No."

"Our plane crashed. I'm in Iowa."

"What!"

"Yeah, I'm sure it's all over the news by now. Don't worry though, I'm fine. I walked off without a scratch. So if you're watching TV, there's coverage, and I just wanted you to know I'm all right. I'm in one piece."

Babette tuned in the news and gasped as she watched the plane break up and explode and burst into flames. Crain reassured her that she was not injured and asked her to call the family. Her mother-in-law was taking care of her children.

"Are you sure you're all right?" Babette asked again.

"Yes, I'm fine. There are a lot of people here helping us. I love you. I'll see you soon. I'll call you again when I have a chance."

Crain wanted to be with Priest. But they were separated at St. Luke's Hospital. Priest was taken to one doctor and Crain to another. Then Crain found herself in an ambulance with several other uninjured people. She did not know where Priest had gone. The ambulance wound its way up into the hills around Sioux City to a stately edifice on a bluff surrounded by pine trees and with a view of the city below, as if she flew in an airliner once again. While she watched out the window, she felt a deep sense of disorientation. The other passengers were chatting in that nervous, manic way, saying, "How do you feel?" and "Where were you?" or "What did you see?" One passenger, a woman Crain called Chatty Cathy, could not seem to stop herself from rambling on and on about the crash and the inconvenience and how she was supposed to be at home by now. "And I just wanted her to shut up."

Once in the dormitory at Briar Cliff, where Aki Muto was making string figures with Eric and Alisa Hjermstad, Crain was calm but also in such a state of shock that everything seemed surreal. She said she had sudden powerful surges of emotion in which she felt invincible and capable of anything. The room was like a nun's cell in a convent with drab white curtains, a boxy rectangular shelf on the wall for school books, a narrow desk at which to do homework. Two single beds and a napkin's worth of floor space. A volunteer from the Red Cross had given Margo Crain and her roommate Ruth Pearlstein soap and shampoo. Crain also received a pink sweat suit two sizes too big and tennis shoes that were far too large for her feet. Her own clothes were covered in mud and blood and smelled like burning flesh and kerosene. She didn't know what time it was. "My eyes burned like I was still inside the burning plane. Everything was blurry and it hurt to keep them open." Yet she was afraid to take out her contact lenses, because then she would be unable to see at all. "I needed some form of vision to make sure that things were real and not just a dream." The night was hot and humid, and the dorm was not air-conditioned.

At last she went to the communal shower and took off her reeking clothes. While she stood under the cascading water, the adrenaline high faded, and the feeling of invincibility drained from her, leaving behind the reality of what had happened. She gave in to uncontrollable sobbing, as the carnage came rushing back, along with the realization of how close she had come to dying on that ordinary Wednesday afternoon.

Richard Swetnam, thirty-seven, was on vacation on his farm across the line in Nebraska. He had recently visited his family in Kansas City and attended his twentieth high school reunion there. Now he was spending a pleasant, if sweltering, day spreading gravel on his driveway. Late in the afternoon, Swetnam dumped one last load and returned to the house. His kids were watching cartoons on the TV. He stood behind them and saw Charles Kuralt interrupt the program with a news bulletin: a DC-10 had crashed at the Sioux City airport. Swetnam's heart kicked into a canter. He thought the reporters were mixing up Sioux City and Sioux Falls. Then the phone rang. It was a friend calling to ask if he knew anything about the crash. Swetnam looked out the window and saw his neighbor's truck coming up the drive. Like Swetnam, Brad Risinger was an air traffic controller. Swetnam put the phone down and hurried outside. When he approached the truck, Risinger said, "They're going to need your help."

"Lemme just get out of these filthy clothes," Swetnam said, and ran back into the house. He kissed his kids good-bye and within a few minutes was seated in Risinger's truck bouncing along the new gravel and out onto the narrow country road. Risinger had been an

air traffic controller in the Army before he went to work for the FAA.
He'd had experience with fatal accidents. Now he tried to give Swetnam an idea of what to expect. One thing was certain: the controllers
who witnessed the crash would have to be relieved as soon as possible. As they headed north on Main Street and then northeast along
170th Street to U.S. Highway 20, Risinger snapped on the radio,
and they heard the first rumors that someone may have survived the
crash. The two air traffic controllers exchanged a skeptical look.

They reached the control tower at about 5:00. "You climb the
stairs, you know," Swetnam said to me, "and then as you round the
corner on the stairs, you know, y-you look to the north and—" Air
traffic controllers do not—must not—stutter. They speak clearly
and precisely, and they talk fast. But when Swetnam told his tale, he
was reduced to a barely coherent stammer, as he was thrust back into
that deeply shaken state. "And, uh—and the, you know, there was
still smoke—and there was just—just . . ." Words failed him, and he
fell silent. "You know. Debris everywhere. And I-I, the one thing I-I
remember—uh—was, ah, just. . . . You know, there was a little bit of
a breeze, and there was just—ye—it's amazing from one airplane
how, how—much, ah, ah—it seemed to be tape or something. It just,
it just, they were, it, they kinda shined in the sun, it was blowing.
And-and-and it just it, it was, it was weird, you know, a-a-and it just,
it was everywhere. You know and there was paper blowing and stuff
like that, but I-I-I remember the—the tape."

Swetnam took over the approach control position that Kevin
Bachman had been working. Risinger took over local control for aircraft that were landing. Everything had been deathly quiet for a long
time, "and then it got busy," Swetnam said. "Helicopters were coming in from everywhere." Even though the airport was closed, the
emergency flights were allowed to operate. In addition, Swetnam's
position, covering the thirty or forty miles out from the airport,
was flooded with requests from the news people who had rented all
manner of aircraft. "Everybody in the world was flying in," Swetnam
said. "And everybody wanted to take pictures of the crash site before
they landed." The airspace was closed up to five thousand feet, but

Swetnam couldn't stop planes from flying over the field above that altitude. To avoid the possibility of another crash, he put the aircraft in holding patterns from five thousand feet up, with one thousand feet between the aircraft.

As the news organizations finished their work of documenting the scene from above, they began requesting that Swetnam direct them to airfields where they could land, "which was another problem, because some of the bigger planes required runways that we didn't have. The other two airports around Sioux City are just for small airplanes." Sioux City had runways that were long enough, but the airfield was closed. Handling a dozen aircraft at any one time, Swetnam began sending the smallest airplanes to nearby Martin Field, an airport for light planes. He had to send the larger planes thirty miles northeast to Le Mars or thirty miles northwest to Vermillion, South Dakota, where the runways were longer. Once he sat down to work, Swetnam recalled, "you forgot that an airplane just crashed here." He handled one aircraft after another for an hour and a half, and then he rolled his chair back and took a breath. He looked around, "and all of a sudden, reality hit again, and you realize, Aw, yeah, we just had a crash here."

The press planes were gone long before dark. That evening and into the night, only three planes arrived. One was the 727 that brought in the Go Team from United. It would later carry Charles Martz, Martha Conant, Rod Vetter, John Hatch, and other survivors who wanted to fly to Chicago. The Lear jet carrying the Go Team from General Electric landed around 9:30. The Go Team from the NTSB would arrive in the early morning hours.

By 10:00 that night, Swetnam said, "Everybody else was gone. I was the only one there." After the departure of the United 727 the scene fell silent. Swetnam sat staring out the window at the grim vigil under the nearly full moon, the arc lights, as the sheriff's police and Air National Guard stood watch over the scene. Swetnam had been too busy to feel or think until then, but now there was no escaping it. "They set up all these big floodlights to keep the place illuminated. And you know, you just have time to—to really think about things and-and-and that—yeah," he said with a sigh. "And then, and then, you know that they didn't move any of the bodies. So you know that there's a-ah lot of dead people out there. And ah, and so, yeah, that-that was probably the first time for me that it affected me. You could see, you know, sheets out there, and you knew, you knew that the sheets were covering people." It was probably two in the morning by his estimate before the Gulfstream carrying NTSB Go Team landed on Runway 31. And that was the end of Swetnam's turn as the lone controller for Sioux City that night. A controller named Rod Hensel arrived to relieve him.

John Bates said of Hensel, "He was a good friend to every single one of us there at Sioux City." The fact that everyone loved him made it doubly painful when, five days before the crash, Hensel's four-year-old daughter had died suddenly of a fast-moving infection. He had been on funeral leave. Sioux City, however, is a small town, and the tower ran out of controllers. Hensel was called to duty. Bates said, "What happened to him was a crime. You can imagine what sitting there with [all those] bodies on the field was like."

Bates had gone off duty from the control tower some time after nine o'clock. The temperature had fallen to 73 degrees, but the air was still humid as he crossed the parking lot toward his car. When he arrived home, all of his neighbors were out in the street with six packs of beer, waiting to greet him. As Bates spoke of this twenty-three years after the crash, he choked up and his voice cracked as he said, "It was one of the kindest things I ever saw." Bates, though, gently urged his neighbors to go home, then he went inside, "and told my wife everything. *Everything*." They stayed up late together, talking, and then Kevin Bachman called, weeping and saying it was all his fault. Bates spent the better part of two hours on the phone, trying to convince him that he had performed bravely and professionally. Neither Bates nor Bachman slept much that night. "All I could see in my head was the friggin' plane crashing over and over again," Bates said.

While Bates was replaying the crash for his wife, Mark Zielezinski, still in the control tower, "had to continue moving the traffic." He was not relieved because he was technically management and not a controller on duty during the crash. Late that night, with Swetnam on duty, Zielezinski was able to go home at last. "The adrenaline was flowing so high," Zielezinski recalled, "that when I got home, it was probably eleven o'clock that evening and at that point I finally came to the realization of what had happened." And then he let go, and as Bachman and Bates and so many others had done, he wept.

Leo Miller, the Sheriff of Woodbury County, faced the daunting task of securing the scene for the night. The plane crashed in an inherently secure area, the surface of an airport. By late afternoon, the DCI— the Department of Criminal Investigation—had strung a bunting of yellow ribbon, emblazoned with the words *Crime Scene*, around everything, as if to cordon off heaven and hell alike. In addition, Miller decided to place a ring of protection around the crash site. He was concerned not only about people who might try to get into the crash site—reporters, looters, morbid curiosity seekers—but also about animals who might come to prey on the dead. "We also put a security net around the inside, around the wreckage itself," he said. "It was quite difficult for two reasons. One, the amount of distance which it covered." The debris was spread over more than thirty-five hundred feet of ground. Another difficulty was that bodies and parts of bodies, as well as pieces of the airplane, lay obscured in the corn. The sheriff ordered a combine brought in to cut a wide swath around the wrecked fuselage so that no person or animal could creep up on it without being seen.

In the hours after the crash, Chaplain Clapper had stayed at headquarters, talking to rescuers and fire fighters and lending a sympathetic ear to anyone who needed it. He listened to a fire fighter tell of a woman he had found strapped into her seat, screaming. When he cut the seat belt, she fell apart. She was being held together by the seat belt. She died at his feet.

As evening came on, he decided that he needed to go home, clean up, and "put on my uniform so they could see the cross." Clapper hiked out to the road and stuck out his thumb. He said, "It wasn't hard getting a ride. I think people were in a helping mood that day."

At home, he indulged in a big hug from Jody. The girls were already in bed, but he went in and kissed Laura and Jenna anyway. They had enjoyed *Peter Pan* in the theater at the Southern Hills Mall. Then Clapper showered, put on his chaplain's uniform, said good-bye to his wife, and drove back to the base.

"I spent that night walking around the perimeter." He saw police, FBI agents, and fire fighters sitting out on their equipment watching for flare-ups from the wreck. The pools of yellow illumination from the lights somehow made the shadows seem that much deeper. As Clapper moved around in moonlight and arc light, he said, "I found that when you're keeping vigil with the dead, sometimes it can be a very emotionally noisy space." He would stop and chat with anyone who wanted to talk, "and they'd start telling me what they saw." In many cases, the crash brought back old traumas. The cops talked about bad road accidents. The fire fighters talked about their worst fires. Clapper spent nearly two hours with one member of his Guard unit. The man needed to talk about a child he had lost. "We carry all of our brokenness and our tragedy with us," Clapper said. "And when you open the door on tragedy, perhaps because a new tragedy has come into your life, all those old tragedies start spilling out."

On through the night he wandered among the dead and their attendants. And as a gray light bled into the eastern sky, Clapper strolled with one of the security guards in quiet contemplation. After a time, they came upon a section of the plane where bodies still occupied some of the seats inside. And in the long cables of newborn sun from the east, "I could see something that made me cry."

"Hey, Chaplain," said the security guard. "Are you okay?"

Clapper later said, "I guess that was the most okay thing I could do was cry. I had seen this large man. And he was embracing a young boy. Both dead. And to me, to catch that vision of love even at the moment of death was very powerful."

Once the sun had risen, Clapper went back to his office and slept on the floor for two hours. Then he splashed water on his face, found a cup of coffee, and went out to the ramp, where Air National Guard men and women and fire fighters were preparing with teams of pathologists, photographers, scribes, and volunteers to document and remove the dead. They were boarding pickup trucks for the ride out to site. Clapper climbed into the bed of one of the trucks and said, "Unless there's some objection, I just want to have a word of prayer before we start this." No one in the subdued and exhausted crowd objected. After a short prayer, Clapper began, "The Lord is my shepherd, I shall not want. He maketh me to lie down in green pastures. He leadeth me beside the still waters. He restoreth my soul. He leadeth me in the paths of righteousness for his name's sake." As he recited the twenty-third Psalm, he looked out over the crowd of workers and the destruction and chaos beyond, the torn metal, the scorched runways, and the rich land with all the people scattered there. And the chaplain saw, indeed, that "we were there, in the valley of the shadow of death." His voice cracked during the recitation. At the time he was embarrassed, but later he said, "Maybe sometimes God's word has to come through a cracking voice in this world."

CHAPTER SIXTEEN

The moon was still up, pale in the western sky, as Robert Mac-
Intosh, the investigator in charge, made his way to the first
organizational meeting of the NTSB on Thursday morning, July 20, 1989. He estimated that in addition to the press, 130
people showed up at the conference room in the convention center
downtown. Daniel Murphy, the postmaster, was among them. He
wanted to be permitted onto the site so that his workers could collect
the sacks of U.S. mail—nine hundred pounds of it—that were scattered across the airfield. Within thirty-six hours of the crash, all that
mail would be delivered with notes signed by Murphy explaining
the circumstances of the delay. In Montgomery County, Maryland,
a high school teacher received an orchid that he had ordered from
Hawaii. Like so many of the passengers, the flower was in perfect
condition, although Murphy's letter assured the teacher that it had
been through the crash.

Much of the NTSB meeting that morning was taken up with
assigning duties to members of the NTSB Go Team and then select-
ing representatives to work with whatever agencies or organizations
were concerned. So, for example, the Engine Investigation Group
for the NTSB was headed by Edward Wizniak, a senior aerospace
engineer. General Electric was asked to provide representatives to
work with him, and the obvious choice was William Thompson, the

flight safety engineer who had arrived with the GE Go Team on the Lear jet the night before. Since the engine was the obvious suspect in the chain of events, GE provided nine engineers for the group. McDonnell Douglas and the FAA each contributed two more, while United Airlines sent one.

Wizniak, who was seventy-eight years old when I interviewed him, could not remember the exact number of engineers who accompanied him when he left the convention center Thursday morning and drove out to the field for his first look at the number two engine, serial number 451-243. Thompson was there. He and Wizniak knew that the engine had fallen out of its mount upon impact and was lying to the east of Runway 4-22, on Taxiway Juliette just off the main ramp. The group drove through the gate and stopped at the Air National Guard headquarters, where they were shown the video of the crash. It was an unprecedented piece of evidence.

Then they drove to the northwest end of the ramp. They could see the engine even before they entered Taxiway Juliette. As they

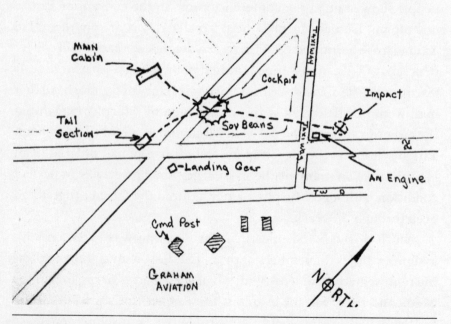

A sketch made during the investigation showing where various parts of 1819 Uniform came to rest. Engine number two lay on Taxiway Juliette. *From NTSB Docket 437*

closed the distance, the engine looked worse and worse. Being the orderly and linear engineers they were, they decided to start at the beginning and work their way back. Thompson described it this way: "We also were interested in getting a general overall feeling for what had happened . . . and this included taking a walk to the impact initial touchdown site and, more or less, walking down the runway to the end near the empennage [tail] area." Down the runway under the cool morning sun came the Engine Investigation Group, their heads full of engineering truths, as they attempted to wrest some orderly and analytical thoughts from the chaos before them. Even though what they really wanted to see was the number two engine, they encountered parts of the number three engine first and examined them. That engine appeared to have been running normally when the plane crashed. It had been wrecked by contact with the runway, on which its housing had left a series of symmetrical lens-shaped scuff marks. As they walked southwest, they encountered all manner of aircraft parts—flaps and wheels and rudders—among which lay the dead. At last they returned to Taxiway Juliette and the number two engine. "One of the first things that we noted," said Thompson, "was the absence of the fan rotor . . ." He meant the seven-foot fan on the front of the engine, known as the number one fan. It was gone. "The forward fan shaft itself had been fractured, and there was a small stub area remaining, sticking out at the center of the engine in a forward direction." The thrust reversers were banged open like a clam shell.

As Wizniak told me, "Walked up there, found the engine there, and looked—woah! Where's the—? First thing you notice, boy, the whole front end of the engine is completely gone. And nearby was the fan containment ring." Only half of it was present, the other half being in a cornfield about sixty miles away near Storm Lake, Iowa. That big hoop of stainless steel, which had encircled the front fan, was designed to stop a fan blade if one happened to be released. But said Wizniak, "You could see how it had split in half." The entire mammoth number one fan disk had burst into two pieces, tearing the heavy steel containment right in half as fragments escaped. Many of the thirty-eight blades attached to that disk had presumably escaped too. Neither Wizniak nor Thompson had ever seen such a thing.

MacIntosh also viewed the containment ring that first day of the investigation. "Right away you know you've got a rotating parts failure," he said. "Now, knowing *why* you had a fan disk rupture is the trick. And then trying to figure out how that damaged the aircraft to the degree that it did . . ." In fact, the damage to the engine was so severe, so unprecedented, that Thompson was moved to wonder if part of the cowling from the number one or number three engine had come off the plane for whatever reason and had then been sucked into the number two engine, destroying it.

As the giant fan disk split and broke through its metal containment, it left clear evidence of what had happened. Wizniak and Thompson could see "witness marks" across the surface of the containment ring, where the fan blades had made contact as "it just departed," as Wizniak put it. They could also see that once the disk failed, it went through three-fourths of a revolution as it burst through that containment ring. Studying it in the July sunshine, Wizniak was shocked to see that one of those fragments comprised about two-thirds of the whole disk. He later described his reaction: "Oh, my God. Lord above. That is really an impressive sight. And kind of sad." The engine towered above Wizniak, but even a tall man had to look up to examine it in the glaring light. He remembered saying out loud, "Oh, Lord, what happened there?" More than two decades later, he said, "The engine just tore it up and it was one big mess."

But most importantly, as soon as he looked at the damage to the containment ring and realized that the main fan disk had come apart, "I already knew it was probably subsurface fatigue origin," said Wizniak. He meant that he suspected that somewhere within the titanium disk that held those thirty-eight blades, a fatigue crack had originated in a flaw of some sort. "Yes," he said, "that's what happened. You knew it instantly."

Thompson and a representative of United Airlines stood beside Wizniak, who later said, "They all had bad looks on their faces. It was a shock."

Standing amid the wreckage, with the bodies still lying out in the sun, Wizniak's mind was drawn to an Eastern Airlines L-1011, the direct competitor to the DC-10. Like the DC-10, the Lockheed Tri-Star jetliner had an engine on each wing and one through the tail. As with United Flight 232, Eastern Flight 935, out of Newark, New Jersey, experienced an explosion of the number two engine in the tail.

A bearing around the driveshaft was deprived of oil, and as Wizniak put it, "The fan shaft became ductile and it just let go." The fan disk "just sort of walked out like a top. It's somewhere out there in the Atlantic Ocean still." The failure of the number two engine eliminated one hydraulic system. Fragments from the explosion penetrated the tail and cut the lines for two of the other hydraulic systems. "The fan disk came out and came within a hair's breadth of cutting all the hydraulic lines." The reason that November 309 Echo Alpha, the Eastern plane, was able to make an emergency landing at JFK International Airport on that September day in 1981 was that it had four hydraulic systems. McDonnell Douglas had designed the DC-10 with three.

Contemplating this possible scenario, Wizniak returned to Graham Aviation, where he called Washington. "And they couldn't believe it," he said. He told them that the number one fan disk had shattered and vanished from the number two engine. He ventured his opinion that the cause was a tiny defect that began the process of cracking the metal over a long period of time. He said that the disk had come out in two big pieces, "and they brought up all kinds of things, 'You're sure it wasn't birds?'" Even as late as the Saturday after the crash, the New York Times was speculating that the crash may have been the result of birds being sucked into the engine. The disk, however, had exploded at thirty-seven thousand feet, an altitude to which even the most ambitious birds would not aspire. The people at NTSB in Washington asked Wizniak if it might have been blue ice, which refers to the blue fluid in the toilets. In the past that fluid (which had splashed all over Susan White at impact) had leaked out and frozen in the cold upper atmosphere. Chunks of it had broken off and been ingested by jet engines.

The speculations back at GE headquarters in Ohio were extensive as well. John Moehring took charge of the in-house investigation. He and his engineers set out all the scenarios they could conceive of to explain what had happened. Their first thought was what he called "a major ingestion event, or that something has happened to cause a very severe obstruction." They considered whether the driveshaft itself could have failed or the bolts that held the disk to it. The driveshaft was a long tube that flared at the forward end into a cone. That funnel-shaped end was attached to the fan disk with twenty bolts. The engineers at GE evolved seven hypotheses to explain how the failure might have happened, and Moehring assigned a leader to each one. That leader pulled together a team of engineers that set to work trying to prove its chosen theme for explaining how the disk failed. Christopher Glynn, the manager of fan and compressor design at the GE jet engine plant in Evendale, Ohio, was assigned to lead the team devoted to proving that the "prime event in the sequence" was the fan disk itself, serial number 00385. He immediately began recruiting metallurgists, engineers, and "analytical people," as he put it, to help demonstrate that the disk could have fragmented, starting the sequence of events that led to the loss of control and the crash. There could have been any number of causes for the disk to burst. On September 22, 1981, a turbine disk exploded on a DC-10 at Miami, Florida, because a mechanic had left something inside the engine while working on it.

On the field on that first day after the crash, Wizniak felt that he knew in his gut what he was looking at. He left his betters in Evendale and Washington, D.C., to scratch their heads while he put together his group and went out to look for the part of the airplane they would need to prove their case. His intuition and logic told him that the way this fan disk came apart, they were not going to find it anywhere near Sioux City. It was out by Storm Lake where the engine let go, about sixty miles away, near Alta, Iowa, where the farmers had heard the bang and had looked up to see pieces falling off of the airplane. They were going to need another kind of investigator to find the disk. John

Clark, the senior performance engineer for the NTSB, would arrive later that afternoon.

In the meantime, Wizniak's crew walked the field, "from the initial contact point to where it came to rest," but they found nothing of interest where fan disk 00385 was concerned. Soon combines rolled onto the field and proceeded to cut down the soybeans that were growing along Runway 17-35 and 04-22. Then people began walking up and down swinging magnetometers in search of anything made of metal. They began turning up components from all over the aircraft. After all, more than a quarter of a million parts had spilled onto the field. (In fact, when I visited Sioux City in 2012, Colonel Dennis Swanstrom, by then retired, was still actively searching the cornfields for parts of 1819 Uniform.) The question in Wizniak's mind, as in the minds of the other investigators, was, Which of those parts could help determine the cause of the crash?

The searchers found three of the twenty nuts that had held the fan disk to its driveshaft. The threads were stripped. Two additional nuts had been fired like bullets into the acoustic panels that surrounded the engine. Yet another nut was found—again, fired like a bullet from a gun—embedded in the right horizontal stabilizer, the area of the tail that Dvorak had seen from his position near Yisroel Brownstein and Richard Howard Sudlow. Behind the big front fan was the number two fan. Spherical imprints on the front of it showed where the number one bearing raceway was ripped open as the number one fan disk fractured. That bearing fired its balls like grapeshot, as the big disk tore the number two disk apart.

Searchers found the bent bolts that had been threaded through some of the nuts that had held the fan disk to the shaft, as well as fifteen pieces of fan blades, both on the ground and embedded in the tail. Farmers out near Storm Lake had begun to find various pieces even before the plane crashed. Wizniak and his team started the laborious process of documenting all the pieces of the number two engine. Although the engine had torn itself apart, many of its parts remained within the housing or lay on the ground nearby. Within a short time, a great variety of pieces had been brought in from the farmland around Alta, including pieces of the engine bellmouth, which would have killed someone if they had fallen in a slightly different location. Chuck Eddy, the sheriff of Buena Vista County, stood inside one piece. Significantly, two pieces of tubing from the number two hydraulic system were found in a farm field. With those in hand, Wizniak knew how at least one of the three hydraulic systems had failed. Each engine had two hydraulic pumps attached. Each pump ran off of the power from its respective engine. MacIntosh said that they knew that the hydraulic flex lines of the number two engine had been ripped loose in the explosion. Pieces of the pump accumulators were found near Alta. So they knew how the number two hydraulic system failed. "But we didn't understand how we had lost number one and number three [hydraulic systems]," said MacIntosh. And although Wizniak thought he could guess how the other two hydraulic systems had failed, the NTSB wasn't in the business of guessing. He would need help from experts in a wide range of disciplines— flight controls, metallurgy, ballistics, and other specialties—for the team to make his hunch convincing.

At about six o'clock on the evening of the crash, well before sundown on that midsummer day, Dr. Gene Herbek, the acting Woodbury County medical examiner, had ridden out to the site in the back of an Air National Guard pickup truck with Marliss DeJong and other volunteers. On the ride, he turned to DeJong and said, "Don't I know you?"

Herbek later said, "Initially we met before the crash at a bridge club, so that's how I knew her." He also knew her reputation for organization and paperwork, and now asked if she would help Brad Randall run the morgue.

Other than at a funeral, DeJong had never seen a dead body before, but she told Herbek, "I'll do whatever you want." What she saw while touring the site with Herbek convinced her that she could do the job. DeJong said, "One thing that I remember on the field was seeing an arm." The woman's arm was lying on the concrete, but it had "beautiful polished long red fingernails." DeJong felt strong. She felt that she could handle what lay ahead.

Herbek said, "That's one of the smart things I did that night, was appointing her to help us organize."

That evening, back at Hangar 252, Herbek coordinated with Lawrence Harrington to prepare for the next day. They would have to document the dead on the field, then bag the bodies and move them to the refrigerated trucks. They would need to enlist volunteers to lift body bags and track bodies through the various stages in the morgue. At about eight o'clock that evening, Herbek picked up the phone and began to dial. He didn't finish all of his calls until three o'clock in the morning.

Brad Randall, too, picked up a phone to try to reach the most prominent forensic dental team in America, headed by E. Steven Smith. Smith in turn contacted his colleagues Larry Pierce and Raymond D. Rawson in Las Vegas. Pierce and Rawson had worked identifying the eighty-five people who were killed in the fire at the MGM Grand Hotel in 1980.

DeJong worked on setting up a system for the paperwork involved in identifying the dead, while fielding calls that were routed to the office space in the modular home outside the hangar. Dentists and pathologists from all over the country volunteered their services. Late that night Randall reached the team at Northwestern University at last and then retired to Morningside College for a few hours of sleep.

At about two in the morning, Dr. Thomas Bennett, the state medical examiner, arrived. Herbek briefed him, and Bennett studied the flow chart that Randall and his team had prepared for the operation of the morgue. It took the dead step by step from where they lay on the airfield to the refrigerated trucks that had begun to arrive and on into the vestibule in the fuel cell hangar that would be created the next day using moveable partitions. There each body would proceed through the stations to be subjected to procedures for identification and autopsy to determine the cause of death. The body would then be embalmed and put into a casket. The caskets to be used would soon be trucked to Sioux City from Batesville, Indiana. Herbek went home to rest at three in the morning, while the Sioux City fire chief, Bob Hamilton, drove DeJong home.

Herbek, Randall, and DeJong were back in the hangar at 6:30 Thursday morning for a meeting with Bennett, the Red Cross, the Air National Guard, and the DCI to plan the day's work. The first item to consider was how to map the position of the bodies that lay in this long and awkward swath of destruction. In early 1990, Randall presented a paper at the Forty-second Annual Meeting of the American Academy of Forensic Sciences in Cincinnati. During that presentation, he said,

> Conventional wisdom suggested constructing a traditional grid system to locate the bodies. Although workable in a relatively small, compact crash site, the traditional grid was not applicable to a crash site which was over 1½ km long and several hundred metres wide. A former highway patrol officer suggested that we use instead a linear reference line and pinpoint each body by its distance from a reference and its perpendicular distance from the reference line.

An arbitrary reference point was established by someone from the DCI. Randall described it this way: "First there was a reference point, and then from that point a reference line was drawn. A body's location was then plotted as the distance from the reference point along the reference line and then the distance above or below the line."

Herbek recruited guardsmen to number body tags from one to one hundred, and he personally took control of those tags. "One of the things we also did was made sure there was only one set of body tags. [We] did not want to get duplicates of numbers," Herbek said. "We had numbers one through one hundred made up that morning." Then an investigator from the DCI used a rolling measuring wheel to determine the distance from the reference line to each body. Thus would the dead be fixed in space and a scatterplot diagram be made of them, with each body represented by a red dot and a tag number.

Hangar 252 was not yet a morgue, and much remained to be done, as the guardsmen, squatting on the painted concrete floor with the orange demarcation lines on its perimeter, carried out their tasks. They were quiet as they passed lengths of wire through the holes in the tags. Any noise echoed sharply in the vast space with its white-painted cinderblock walls, pipes and girders running across them in every direction. In a room of such deliberate blandness, where the fuel tanks for fighter planes were serviced, the yellow emergency shower, placed there for someone who might accidentally splash himself with fuel or chemicals, suggested the urgent purpose of the building.

While the guardsmen prepared tags, DeJong had white boards brought in and set up on the steel racks that were used to store spare aircraft tires. Someone used a wooden yardstick and felt-tipped marker to rule horizontal and vertical lines on the white boards, forming cells for information concerning the dead. Each row would bear a number from one of the tags to represent a dead person in search of an identity. Then, reading across from left to right, the display would show each step in the process of identification, starting with the tag number, then body X-ray, dental X-ray, fingerprints, and so on, through personal effects and unusual characteristics such as scars or tattoos.* Near the far right of each line was a space labeled "Possible ID" for the person's name. Once the white boards had been prepared to receive this information, they were installed on the walls of the office in the modular home north of Hangar 252, to provide a quick reference that anyone could read at a glance.

United Airlines helped to establish communication lines and a phone number that the relatives of victims could call. Volunteers

---

* Many questioned why the families were not brought in to identify the dead in cases where the victims were not disfigured, but for reasons that were never made completely clear, only Jasumati J. Patel was identified visually.

called all of the families of those who were thought to have died in the crash. The families were told to bring dental X-rays to any airport, turn them over to any airline, and United would see that they reached Hangar 252 as fast as possible. FedEx set up a special account to handle those deliveries at no charge.

Herbek and his teams, including the DCI, returned to the field at about 8:30 in the morning and set about establishing the linear reference system, a process that took about two hours of working around the dead out in the sun. The morning had risen cool and clear. A light wind from the northwest still blew papers and the few remaining hundred-dollar bills around. As the teams worked, many other groups were toiling as well. Laura Levy set up her laser transit and began mapping the field of debris. Edward Wizniak and his group expressed astonishment at the condition of engine number 451-243. MacIntosh and Benzon surveyed the field to ascertain where "the four corners" of the aircraft had come to rest: the wingtips, the nose, and the tail.

Randall created three teams for the initial phase of recovering bodies. Each team was headed by a pathologist. Randall assigned one team to each of three areas where the majority of the bodies lay. "While there were three areas in this part of the body recovery," Randall told me, "the fourth area contained the bodies still in the burned-out portion of the plane." Lieutenant Jim Walker, the Air National Guard pilot who had been among the first to respond to the crash—who had watched in disbelief as the dead rose up out of their seats and walked—was assigned to that fourth team.

Working from the flow chart, DeJong directed workers to set up a maze of blue canvas partitions in the hangar to isolate areas for full body X-rays, for dental X-rays, for conducting autopsies, and so on. She ordered office supplies, surgical gloves, and disposable aprons, among other necessities. She arranged the flow of paperwork in the office and coordinated with Harrington, who provided secretaries from the Air National Guard to type and file. DeJong sought out help from the Red Cross and Salvation Army in setting up food trucks and tents outside, where the workers could eat and take breaks. The menu would include chili, sloppy joes, chips, and pop.

In the meantime, Gary Brown began to realize that despite their constant planning and training, they had overlooked some of the details. "Some of the things we really, really weren't prepared for were some of the things that were needed in the morgue—sawhorses, working tables. We had anticipated embalming tables, autopsy tables, but we really didn't anticipate workbenches and worktables and that they were going to need room dividers, that they would want to section off this morgue, so it wouldn't be quite as gruesome to everyone working in there. The more traumatic parts of it could be screened off."

Randall explained that if an accident such as this, or any mass casualty, happened today, the authorities would contact the National Disaster Medical System of the U.S. Department of Health and Human Services. Once that organization is notified, it assembles a Go Team, known as a Disaster Mortuary Operational Response Team (DMORT), composed of volunteers who are specialists in the fields of temporary morgue facilities, victim identification, forensic dental pathology, forensic anthropology methods, as well as the processing, preparation, and disposition of human remains. The DMORT would also include medical records technicians and transcribers, fingerprint experts, X-ray technicians, funeral directors, mental health specialists, computer experts, administrative support staff, and security and investigative personnel. The DMORT would come with its own "morgue in a box," known as Disaster Portable Morgue Units. These so-called DPMUs are always ready to be dispatched from warehouses on the East Coast and the West Coast. The DPMU contains all the equipment and supplies needed for the DMORT to create a complete morgue, with all its workstations for each step in processing a body, including all of the equipment and supplies that DeJong and Harrington had to assemble piecemeal from wherever they could find them. Under the DMORT system, no one would have to go looking for anything. Brad Randall credits

Marliss DeJong with creating the tracking system that is still in use by DMORT to ensure that no body is misidentified. Others say that Randall is too modest and deserves some of the credit. Either way, it is clear that the crash of United Flight 232 and the people of Siouxland had a lasting influence on the way we respond to disasters.

Out on the field at about 10:30 on Thursday morning, the DCI crime scene technicians finished the linear reference system, and Herbek directed his three teams to begin removing the dead. Each team was given a handful of tags to use. When they ran out, they had to come to Herbek for more. "We took pictures of the individuals as they lay," Herbek explained, "and also had scribes writing all the descriptive things that we thought were important besides taking the measurements from our coordinates." Staff from the Air National Guard, the DCI, and the medical examiner's office, along with many others, took hundreds of photographs of the scene and of the dead. Once a body was ready to be moved, someone would drive a numbered stake into the ground or spray-paint the tag number on the concrete to note its place. The operation ultimately required three cases of spray paint.

After the body had been recorded in that fashion, the Air National Guard took over to remove it. Each body was placed in a body bag. The number from the tag was spray-painted onto the bag. The first person, given the number 1, was twelve-year-old James Matthew Bohn, born May 7, 1977. He would have been a bit older than Dave Randa and Yisroel Brownstein. He had been seated in 35-J beside Lena Ann Blaha, who alerted Jan Brown to the damage on the tail.

The worst part, Jim Walker said, was removing bodies from the fuselage. In a report on the operation, Robert Monserrate and Dennis Chapman of the DCI wrote, "Two cranes were connected to the remaining landing gear to lift the plane while railroad ties were stacked to support the wings. The 47 bodies located in the fuselage were tagged, photographed in position and then removed. Some of the victims were still strapped into their seats. Because of tight quarters and a partially collapsed cabin, it was necessary to cut out and remove those seats from the plane before the victims could be removed from their seats. This process took five hours."

Drew Baier, a young Sergeant who worked for Gary Brown at the WCDES, was called to the field along with Dave Kaplan. Baier conceived the plan for removing the bodies that lay trapped in the aircraft. "Early morning, the day after the crash," recalled Kaplan, "we had a truckload of plywood sheets delivered that we could lay down on the sharp exposed aluminum of what was the inside top of the aircraft but was now what we were crawling on. Most of the bodies were still strapped in their seats with the heads touching the now crushed ceiling. Drew and I started early, as it was July and we knew it was going to get very warm. In full bunker gear and self-contained breathing apparatus, to protect ourselves both from sharp objects and smells, we crawled into the wreckage and using the Amkus rescue cutters (jaws of life) we would cut a row of seats out with the bodies still strapped in. Then we would wrestle the entire thing out where the remains, still in their seats, were photographed, and anything to further identify the remains was also photographed." Gene Herbek's mortuary teams then tagged the bodies, put them in body bags, and removed them to the refrigerated trucks.

Walker gave me his impression of the burned-out fuselage. "It had just been charred. There were some horrific scenes in there, people that were sticking maybe waist high above the burned debris and looked like something out of the Pacific World War II theater. Just burned, charred." He told of a young woman who was working on the team. Walker said she "was very, very businesslike in processing the people. I remember being in awe that she could do this, because I just couldn't handle it." That Thursday, Walker found himself working side by side with her. "And somehow in the midst of all that debris, they found an infant who was untouched. Of course, dead. And that same female coroner who was so stone cold picked up that baby and cradled it, and she just lost it. I mean, she was crying, sobbing, right out at the wreck."

As with pallbearers in a funeral, it took six Air National Guard men and women to move one intact adult human body, and the young men and women who volunteered to deal with that carnage carried people and body parts one after another to the middle of the main north-south runway and laid them out in neat rows to be picked up and transported in trucks.

The trucks took the dead across the field to the refrigerated semi-trailers that had been parked with their cargo doors facing the open door of Hangar 252. The bodies were placed in the first truck, to await processing. By noon on Thursday, the teams had removed fifty-three bodies from the crash site. The forensic dental team headed by Edwin Steven Smith had arrived. Randall said, "He had all the equipment, the computers, he was all ready to go. So it was almost a turn-key operation." In 1989, computers were a fairly new addition to the practice of forensic dentistry. As one forensic dentist said of Steven Smith's operation, "It was revolutionary."

CHAPTER SEVENTEEN

On February 24, 1989, United Airlines had enjoyed more than ten years without an accident. That day, Flight 811, a Boeing 747 jumbo jet bound from Honolulu, Hawaii, to Auckland, New Zealand, with 355 people on board, ended the streak of good luck. As the ship climbed out of twenty-two thousand feet, a forward cargo door on the starboard side of the plane blew off, ripping upward as it departed and tearing a hole the size of a garage door in the passenger compartment. The explosive decompression sucked nine passengers out. Within half an hour the Coast Guard cutter *Cape Corwin* was under way to the area to look for the passengers and debris, and more than a thousand people participated in the search during the next two days. The Coast Guard found two intact seats and assorted debris floating in the water, but those nine people were never found.

The last time United Airlines had lost a plane before that accident was on December 28, 1978. United Flight 173, a McDonnell Douglas DC-8 scheduled to fly from John F. Kennedy International Airport in New York to Portland, Oregon, crashed into a wooded suburb six miles from the airport. The plane had a malfunction of the landing gear on approach. The captain began circling the area to make sure that the gear were down. Preoccupied with that, Captain Malburn "Buddy" A. McBroom, fifty-two, ignored his crew's warnings that fuel was running low. When the engines began quitting, McBroom understood his mistake. The plane came down at the intersection of Northeast 157th Avenue and East Burnside Street, killing 10 people and seriously injuring 23 of the 189 passengers.

Those at United Airlines and the NTSB believed that the military backgrounds of most airline pilots at the time contributed to the crash. The captain of the ship was supreme, and the other members of the crew were expected to defer to him and keep their mouths shut. It was a maritime and military tradition going back hundreds if not thousands of years. This crash had a direct bearing on the fate of United Flight 232, because after the crash of United Flight 173, the NTSB recommended retraining flight crews in what came to be known as cockpit (or crew) resource management (CRM). United Airlines pioneered the training, in which captains were taught to listen to their crews, and the members of their crews were taught to be assertive if they thought that a hazardous condition was developing. United earned a reputation as one of the safest airlines and the company even trained the crews of other airlines. The CRM training was credited with helping the crew of Flight 811 out of Honolulu to return safely and with allowing the crew of Flight 232 to reach Sioux City, saving many lives. United Airlines helped to change the culture of the cockpit.

United also had another lasting influence on the industry. Before 1989, airlines were extremely averse to sharing information. When a plane crashed, airline employees were sent out to obscure the logos on the wrecked aircraft. (Some airlines still do this.) The airlines never talked to the NTSB, which was viewed as the enemy. And they certainly didn't like to talk to the press.

When Flight 232 crashed, Rob Doughty, thirty-six, who was manager of external communications at United, was in London, helping to open up that territory to the company's scheduled flights. British Airways gave him a courtesy flight home on the Concorde, the supersonic jetliner, and he was in Sioux City the next day. Doughty joined the United Go Team, and as he put it, he and James M. Guyette, a vice president at United, were "joined at the hip" for the next ten days. Guyette was the most senior person on the United Go Team. Some time before Flight 232, he "became concerned," Doughty told me, "because we hadn't had an accident in ten years, and the world had changed. Most notably, CNN would carry live footage of an accident almost as soon as it happened." The days of painting out the logos and clamming up were over. "It was very different from the last time we'd had an accident," said Doughty. Guyette realized that the Crisis Communications Plan for United Airlines was seriously out of date. He charged Doughty with revamping the company's plan for how to respond when a plane crashed.

When Doughty was devising the plan, he sought help from the Air Force, which had a wealth of experience in dealing with crashes, and he consulted the chemical industry, which routinely dealt with fatal accidents. "But none of the other airlines would talk to me about it," he said. In addition, at that time, executives from the airlines had no understanding of the NTSB and its work. At Guyette's urging, Doughty broke ranks with the airline industry and called the public information officer at the NTSB. As a result of that conversation, Doughty wrote a white paper on how an airline ought to behave after a crash.

"It was very important," Doughty said, "because it allowed us to anticipate things in a much more strategic fashion." For example, it was widely known in the news business that the NTSB held a press conference every evening at six o'clock during an active investigation. In February of 1989 in Hawaii, when the new United Airlines Crisis Communications Plan was implemented for the first time, Doughty became the first public relations executive from an airline to attend one of those briefings.

"Previous to the Hawaii accident," said Doughty, "the relationship between the NTSB and the airlines and the unions was very adversarial. Everybody was blaming everybody else and pointing the finger and so forth." When responding to a crash, the NTSB, the pilots' union, and the airline traditionally set up their headquarters as far away from one another as possible. But 1989 ushered in a new era. "Our communication strategy was to prove that, despite having an accident, we were still a safe airline." The airline needed to be open about what was being learned that could prevent future accidents. In Hawaii, United set up its operations in the same hotel as the NTSB. "And we talked to them," Doughty said, "which had never happened before,"

Until the 1980s, United had no concrete idea of what it wished to get across in its public communications. During its period of developing a new plan leading up to 1989, "I decided," said Doughty, "why not do it the way you'd write a marketing plan or a communications plan, which starts with an objective. What is it you want to accomplish at the end of the day? And so I decided that our objective was to show that we are a safe airline and to reassure our passengers that we are safe to fly on."

It worked. After the two accidents in 1989, United conducted market research and found that the public perception of the accidents was overwhelmingly the same: "It's surprising it was United, they're such a safe airline," as Doughty put it. In fact, after the crash of United Flight 232, for the first time in history, bookings did not decline. While the ultimate taboo in the airline business had been any discussion of safety, United not only talked about it but also began promoting it. When Barbara Walters wanted to film a segment for the show *20/20* about the training of airline pilots, no one would talk to her. United agreed to cooperate, and the show became, in Doughty's words, "a twenty-minute commercial for United Airlines." In the end, United Airlines, especially in its response to the crash of 1819 Uniform, changed not only the way airlines dealt with accidents, but also the way in which they marketed their services. The most important change of all, though, was the training that Haynes and his crew had received in cockpit resource management. Without their concerted cooperation during the crisis, there might have been no survivors.

When Yisroel Brownstein was in the third grade, he was not doing so well in school. He now believes that he had a form of dyslexia. Whatever the cause of his poor grades, his father told him that if he improved his scores, he could fly to Philadelphia to visit his best friend, who had moved there. Yisroel worked hard, and his father redeemed some frequent-flyer miles and gave his nine-year-old son a ticket as promised. Yisroel's parents saw him off with hugs and kisses in the boarding lounge in Denver, where they lived at the time. His father, an ultra-orthodox rabbi, gave him a prayer to say on the plane. It was a special prayer for travelers, meant to protect the boy. Yisroel entered the plane at exit 2-Left, stepping past Upton Rehnberg's feet. He crossed over to the starboard aisle and paralleled Martha Conant's path all the way back to the last row, where he took the aisle seat. Richard Howard Sudlow sat at the window. Sudlow was a marketing executive for a company in Altoona, Pennsylvania, and was on his way home from a business trip.

Yisroel had originally been assigned a seat in the front row of the coach cabin, but at the last minute, the Brownstein family was told that the boy had to sit in the last row. His father threw a fit at the gate, then his parents "got into a huge fight over whether or not they should change the seat," Yisroel said. Their fighting made the already nervous child even more anxious. When he reached his seat at last, he was eager to say his traveling prayer so that he could be protected. He had rehearsed it with his father. He knew that he was supposed to wait until the plane had climbed above the clouds before saying it. Yisroel had been on an airplane once before, but he had been an infant at the time and had no recollection of it. He turned to Sudlow, whom he described as "a really sweet businessman," and explained his predicament: he had a prayer to say and had no idea how to tell if the plane was above the clouds. Sudlow expressed a great interest in the prayer and even put his work down and took the time to learn the words of response from the nine-year-old boy in the yarmulke. After the plane took off and flew through a layer of clouds, the businessman and the child bowed their heads and recited the prayer together. Then they ate their lunch.

When the engine exploded behind his head, Yisroel went into a state of paralytic terror. The crash of United Flight 232 left him permanently scarred, not only physically but also emotionally. When

I met him, he was a thirty-two-year-old psychologist who smoked Newport cigarettes—not quite chain-smoking—and talked rapidly and urgently about his experience. Heavyset and baby-faced under a black yarmulke, he wore torn black jeans. "And no one in my community would ever wear jeans," he said. He wore his black hair spiked and had a generally edgy look about him that he said did not go over well in his ultra-orthodox Jewish milieu. He said that he was a born rebel. The crash had made him more so. When he was eighteen, he enlisted in the Israeli Army to annoy his father. The Israelis took one look at his medical records and threw him out.

Shortly after the engine exploded, Donna McGrady came down the aisle with a worried look on her face. She leaned across Yisroel to Sudlow and asked if he would be her door helper. The last exit on the starboard side, 4-Right, was directly behind Sudlow's seat. Yisroel stood and they switched seats so that Sudlow was on the aisle. Yisroel was quaking with fear, and the view out the window made it worse. The prayer was not working. As soon as McGrady left, Sudlow tried showing Yisroel how to brace, but Yisroel found it impossible to concentrate. He was rigid with fear. He later said that his mind kept screaming, "Please stop! Please stop! Please stop! I had this sensation of begging on a psychological level."

Although Sudlow had shown him how to brace, Yisroel could not help himself. When the order came from the cockpit and McGrady began screaming from her jump seat right behind them, "Brace! Brace! Brace!" Yisroel was unable to move. Sudlow said, "You have to brace, you have to brace. Remember what I showed you?" Yisroel could only squeeze his eyes shut and wait for death to take him. At the last moment, Sudlow took hold of Yisroel and shoved his upper body down to the floor, "and he put his body on top of mine," Yisroel recalled. Sudlow lay on top of the child, crushing him, forcing him out of harm's way. Then the crash began, and to Yisroel it seemed to go on forever. "It was probably a matter of seconds, but in my brain it was like an hour. I saw a lot of flame throughout." The smell of burning foam rubber was forever imprinted in his emotional system. He said, "It's the smell of like destroyed foam or something like maybe if somebody took it and scratched it for a long time and then you smelled it."

During the crash, he remembered, "The first five seconds were insanely loud. The second five seconds, also. The last five seconds, I still remember hating the fact that we were rolling." And then Yisroel leaned in toward me and whispered, "But it was silent. Almost like a comfort. But, oh, my God, we were still flying. We were still rolling."

The quiet was replaced by a ripping sound, "almost like if you took, let's say, like a snow plowing truck and take it onto this lawn and dig it into the grass and drive forward." As he told me his story, we sat in my backyard in the month of May, surrounded by lush greenery, a profusion of red roses. "You know that like ripping sound of weeds. I'll hear it, and I start shaking."

Then everything stopped.

As Yisroel looked out from his position trapped beneath debris with Sudlow on top of him, he could see flames burning on the runway where fuel had been spilled. But the fire soon died down and flickered out.

Three seats away, Martha Conant unlatched her seat belt, dropped, and stepped out onto the moist earth. Susan and Dave Randa also rapidly freed themselves and emerged. Susan White was shouting, "Wiggle! Wiggle! Wiggle!" and dropping to the ground. The Air National Guard arrived and entered the tail to look for survivors.

Yisroel's hearing began to return. A man was trying to save Sudlow, but the kind businessman's back was broken, his internal organs crushed, his lungs filled with fluid. He had acted as a shock absorber for the boy. Yisroel was hollering his address and phone number over and over again. Soon he was lying in an ambulance alongside a woman who was dying.

"I was torn to pieces," Yisroel said. "My right arm wasn't connected besides one of the bones. My whole arm was off." His skull was fractured in three places. His brain was hemorrhaging. On my patio, he took off his yarmulke and leaned over the wrought-iron table, "I still have a huge dent," he said. He showed me a white gouge in his skull where hair no longer grew. In the hospital, the doctors were reluctant to put him under anesthesia for fear that he might lapse into a coma and never wake. But he survived, and two weeks later he and another boy were doing wheelies with their wheelchairs in the halls of the hospital.

"I do a lot of MMA," he said, smoking his Newports as we sat drinking coffee. He meant mixed martial arts, the most violent and unrestrained form of boxing. Anything goes. "So I'm always, like, bruised and bleeding." When I met him, his right cheekbone was scratched and bruised from taking a blow to the face. It was as if Yisroel had managed to find a pursuit that would re-create, in a small way, one of his most formative childhood experiences, from which he could eternally rise like a phoenix. He was mastering pain, agony, blood, injury. "Anytime I get clocked," he said, "anytime I get hit in the face, I know exactly what it feels like. That's probably similar to what I felt [in the crash]." His response reminded me of Tony Feeney jumping from a moving train.

Jason Henry, a lifeguard at a municipal swimming pool in Sioux City, spent the morning of July 20, 1989, lifting the dead off of Air National Guard trucks and carrying them into the refrigerated semi-trailers. He had turned twenty in June. His boss had asked for volunteers to help with the crash. Henry had no idea what he was volunteering for, but he and his friend Brian Massey raised their hands. More than two decades after his experience, when Henry tried to describe the process, he choked up and could not speak for a time.

At one point, a pickup truck arrived and he and Massey lifted the body bag out of the bed. The driver told Henry, "Make sure those bags don't get separated." Henry looked down and saw a foot in a ziplock bag on top of the body bag.

While Henry, Massey, and other volunteers moved bodies throughout the morning, Brad Randall, Marliss DeJong, Lawrence Harrington, Gary Brown, and others were setting up the temporary morgue in the hangar. By noon the portable X-ray unit had arrived from Offutt Air Force Base, and soon the morgue was ready to begin operating. Out on the field by that time, most of the bodies had been removed, except those inside the fuselage, so Henry and Massey were recruited as "trackers."

Herbek said, "Once the body entered our identification area," meaning Hangar 252, "they were given a person, a volunteer with a file that was not to leave that body as it traveled through this whole process. We wanted to make sure we did not lose the file or get bodies mixed up in the process. . . . We called them trackers."

Henry was given a yellow apron to identify him as a tracker and was ushered into the morgue. "That was a tough one," he told me. Once again, he could not continue to talk for a time. He remembered finding himself standing at the head of a body bag, facing a maze of blue moveable dividers about six feet high. All morning he had been grateful that he had not seen what was inside those bags he'd been carrying. Now an investigator from the DCI, wearing a pale blue plastic Sanapron disposable apron, unzipped the body bag on the gurney before him to reveal a beautiful young woman with long straight blonde hair wearing jeans and a blouse. Thomas Randolph, seated on a four-step wooden ladder to one side, flashed a strobe to take a photograph of her, while the investigator, with rapid snips of surgical scissors, quickly cut off her clothes and tossed them aside. Stunned and shaken, Henry watched as a DCI agent took notes on a clipboard. Now before him Henry saw a beautiful figure, as in Botticelli's *The Birth of Venus*, who appeared for all the world as if she might stand up and walk away, her perfect breasts gleaming in the harsh light, the concavity of her pelvis, the rounded slope of her shoulder suggesting incipient movement. The DCI investigators turned her over, looking for scars, tattoos, any identifiable feature, but she was perfect in every way. He saw not a scratch on her.

Some people later criticized the operators of the morgue for allowing someone as young and sensitive as Jason Henry to do that job. But people younger than that go to war. And Thomas Randolph, the photographer, was a DCI special agent who worked both in the crime lab and in homicide investigations as a member of the Crime Scene Investigation team. Yet a year and a half after the crash, he was suffering so severely from post-traumatic stress so severely that he had to retire. His colleague, Robert Monserrate, told of Randolph having to help extract a mother and child from the burned fuselage. "We found them together still strapped to their seats hanging upside down," said Monserrate. It was most likely Claudia Ellis, thirty-eight, and her eleven-year-old daughter Jaime Brines. After finishing with the recovery of bodies, Randolph worked as a photographer in the morgue, and when that job was done, he became a tracker. He followed the mother and daughter through the process of identification. "The death of that girl really upset Tom greatly," said Monserrate, "as it did me. The difference was he never recovered after seeing her. Tom was on many psychological drugs delivered by several different psychiatrists. He tried working for Best Buy and Wal-Mart in their photo sections. I would see him sometimes when I would visit the stores but eventually stopped going to see him, because my presence would cause him great distress, since I would remind him of the crash." Randolph continued to deteriorate and died in a nursing home at the age of sixty-four on October 21, 2005. "Sixteen years of torment came to an end," said Monserrate.

As Henry tried to tell me about his own experience in the morgue that day, he broke down and wept and said, "I didn't know it was still in there," meaning the power of his memory of the youthful woman lying nude before him. Again, Randolph photographed the woman from his perch on the top step of the ladder, red trash cans with plastic liners on either side of him. Meanwhile, a DCI agent documented the dead woman's clothing and personal effects, and then women in civilian clothes, wearing white aprons, put the property into a paper grocery sack, stapled it shut, and laid it on her gurney.

Henry remembered her body number as being 8 or else "in the single digits," but the memory is probably wrong. Among the first ten body numbers, only two women were similar in age to the woman Henry saw: Priscilla Theroux, twenty-seven (who gave Tony Feeney her religious medal), and Connie Marie Kingsbury, thirty, bodies numbered 7 and 8. Kingsbury died of "severe skull and facial bone fractures," according to the autopsy report. Other injuries included "multiple abrasions and contusions of body surfaces." She also had a broken right arm and two broken hips. Her injuries would have been obvious. Theroux, too, died of so many injuries that Henry could not possibly have missed them. The next-nearest possible candidate, Elaine J. Asay, twenty-two, was body number 11, and she too had "severe abrasions over face and extremities," as well as other injuries that Henry would have seen. Herbek and Randall said that the woman lying before Henry most likely suffered a broken neck or a wound to the head that was not visible beneath her hair. Heather Rose O'Mara, twenty-four, was a captain in the U.S. Army, a lawyer working as a prosecutor at Fort Carson in Colorado Springs. She had dark wavy hair and thick dark eyebrows, so she was not the blonde Henry saw. In fact, no woman of the right age who died on that plane seems to fit Henry's description. In the end, we can't know who Henry accompanied through that mortuary maze. Call her Jane Doe then.

Technicians wheeled Jane deeper into the labyrinth of royal-blue partitions under the eerie high-intensity lights of Hangar 252. Surgical lights had been set up on tripods. Folding tables were scattered with papers, Diet Coke cans, fly swatters, coffee cups, and Apple computers and printers. Where folding tables could not be found, sheets of plywood had been laid across sawhorses to make more work space. Tall oscillating fans were blowing the air around, which had begun to smell strange, like a combination of fire and alcohol and something dark and forbidding, the bad breath of catastrophe. At the second station in the process of identification, Jane was subjected to a full-body X-ray. The films were whisked away to be processed. The machine would transform her beauty into ghostly skeletal images, which might reveal a broken bone that had healed years before, an implant, or some other identifiable feature of the anatomical figure that lay before the mystified boy. Henry was already confused by the process. Jane Doe was perfect, unscathed, so far as he could tell. Why not have her family identify her? But Henry was a volunteer. He was doing what he was told.

From the X-ray table, Jane was wheeled across the hangar to the enclosure where FBI technicians were taking fingerprints. They laid out small white paper plates such as might be used to serve cake at a birthday party. The plates were ranked in pairs, five sets on a table made of bare sheets of plywood on sawhorses flanked by buckets of cleanser, bottles of alcohol, and surgical scissors and tools, a puzzling array of devices, as Henry saw it, for what would seem a simple procedure.

As he watched, one of the agents wielded a pair of shears. They appeared to be for trimming trees but were in reality orthopedic clippers. The FBI technician lifted Jane's delicate hand and proceeded to cut off the first joint of each finger. He placed each severed fingertip on a paper plate, ten fingertips on ten plates. Henry was speechless, quaking, his mind a blank as he watched. "You had a body that was recognizable and you're making it less recognizable," he said. "They cut all the fingertips off and then fingerprinted them and then put them into a ziplock bag, which goes back into the body bag."

Randall later told me, "I know there was one of the guys in the fingerprint area that kind of developed a carpal-tunnel syndrome from snipping the fingers off all day long."

Henry followed the gurney with his clipboard in hand and watched in growing horror, as an attendant wheeled Jane into the forensic dental area. With quick strokes of a scalpel, a dentist cut back Jane's lips and sliced through her gums to reveal the bones of her face. He had to cut down to the bone, because the Stryker saw he was about to use could not cut flesh. "It looks like it's rotating," said Randall, "but it's not. It's just vibrating back and forth. It's the same one that people use to take casts off of you. You can actually put it onto skin, and it won't cut the skin."

While a cameraman from the DCI videotaped the procedure, the dentist used the screaming Stryker saw to cut out Jane's upper and lower jaws and remove them as if they were a set of dentures. The procedure is called a Le Fort osteotomy. An assistant then brushed Jane's bloody teeth with a toothbrush, and the dentist put her jaws into a ziplock bag with a numbered tag and put the bag on a table made of plywood and sawhorses. He placed the bag in a row with many other similar bags containing the jaws of other people, each bag clipped to a printed sheet headed "Record of Dental Examination at Autopsy."

E. Steven Smith, the forensic dentist from Northwestern University, had suggested that identifying everyone by dental X-rays would be the fastest and most foolproof approach. Herbek, Bennett, and Randall agreed. Once the dentists had cut out someone's jaws, technicians would make an X-ray. As the families sent the ante-mortem dental X-rays to Sioux City, they would be logged into the computer, and records would be made. The real test, however, came when a dentist laid one piece of film over the other and looked at them against a light. Fillings, crowns, and other restorations would match perfectly. Anyone who had gone to the dentist regularly was immediately identifiable. And most people who can afford to fly can afford to see a dentist.

By the middle of that first afternoon, in the chaos of the morgue, someone had realized how young and inexperienced Jason Henry was—a mere boy thrust into this gruesome duty. He'd served as a tracker for just one body, but he was released. He didn't remember much about the bus ride back to the municipal swimming pool. He was in shock and recalled sitting in the bath house with his friend, Brian Massey, "crying a bit and just staring ahead." He began having nightmares about being in plane crashes after that. He had trouble sleeping. He travels for his work with Dow Corning now, "and there isn't a time that goes by when I get on a plane that I don't think about that." He has seen with his own eyes the consequences of carelessness in the serious matter of powered flight. Yet he said, "If the same situation came up and I had to do it over again, I would. I don't regret doing it at all."*

---

* Numerous other lifeguards worked in the morgue as well.

CHAPTER EIGHTEEN

MacIntosh and Benzon and Wizniak, along with William Thompson of GE, quickly developed an idea of what might have happened to 1819 Uniform. They were not sure yet and would not publicize the idea, but they would talk about it among themselves. More than anything, this idea seemed the only possible explanation for the events that they knew had occurred: a big bang as fan disk 00385 departed, followed by a complete loss of hydraulics less than two minutes later. By the Friday after the crash, if not sooner, the investigators were contemplating this scenario: United Flight 232 had been cruising blandly along on autopilot at thirty-seven thousand feet when something made that disk burst. The seven-foot number one fan broke into two big pieces, as Wizniak had seen from the witness marks on the containment ring. In addition to the two big pieces, that explosion also unleashed a sleeting storm of other metal parts. Given that the disk had burst above and behind the heads of Martha Conant, Yisroel Brownstein, Dave Randa, and John Hatch, they and the other passengers seated in the tail were lucky they weren't hit by flying debris—or worse. In November of 1973, the number three engine on the right wing of another DC-10 had exploded at cruise altitude. A fragment hit a window and broke it. The passenger seated next to that window was sucked out as the aircraft depressurized. He was never seen again.

When the DC-10 was being designed, McDonnell Douglas assured the FAA that the possibility of an engine exploding and disabling the flight controls was, in the words of FAA Advisory Circular 25.1309-1, "extremely improbable." As Gilbert Thompson of the FAA explained it, that means "a failure condition that is not expected to occur over the entire life of an airplane type, total number of airplanes." The FAA and the industry even put a number on it: one in a billion. And indeed, modern jet airliners are reliable, yet it was already known at that time that some jet engines would inevitably explode.

In the hours and days after the crash, as Wizniak studied the number two engine lying sadly on the ground with its front fan missing, he was aware that smaller disks made of titanium, compressor disks, had failed catastrophically in the past. General Electric must therefore have known that it was likely that the big disk on the front of the engine might fail one day. In any event, the federal regulation known as 14 CFR 25.901 states, "No single failure [of a power plant] or malfunction or probable combination of failures will jeopardize the safe operation of the airplane." The CF6 engine known by serial number 451-243 missed adhering to that rule by a fairly wide margin. On the other hand, it was not the engine that ultimately led to the crash. The DC-10 itself, not its power plants, had to have a deeper flaw to bring down the whole craft. In spelling out "special conditions" for granting McDonnell Douglas certification for the DC-10, the FAA wrote, "Probable malfunctions must have only minor effects on control system operation and must be capable of being readily counteracted by the pilot."

Captain D. B. Robinson of the Air Line Pilots Association would later write to the NTSB, "This accident was never supposed to have happened." The accident, he said, "contradicts the design philosophy under which the DC-10, B-747, and L-1011 were predicated and certificated by the FAA." In addition, the FAA had recommended shielding hydraulic lines specifically because rotating parts were known to burst. MacIntosh, Benzon, Wizniak, and others now suspected that some of the parts that were liberated when the disk burst had gone through the tail and had cut the hydraulic lines. It would take a team effort and more than a year to prove that idea.

Now some two hundred people from various agencies were supporting that team effort, scattering all over Siouxland to accomplish the tasks that would ultimately contribute to the final report about the accident. Some were at the hospital interviewing passengers and members of the crew. Others had gone to the dormitory at Briar Cliff College to interview survivors there. Yet others had gone to Jan Brown's hotel room to interview her. Some of the investigators had begun to review the tape recordings of transmissions to and from the control tower, while others searched through the maintenance records kept by United Airlines. In addition to the NTSB, the FAA had numerous people working the crash, along with many other organizations already mentioned.

Some of them were walking up and down the airfield along the path of destruction and were beginning to find pieces of hydraulic tubing that might provide evidence concerning the hunch that Wizniak and others had. The stainless-steel lines appeared to have been sliced, but the investigators needed harder evidence. Since they were investigating a Crowd Killer, it wasn't good enough to stand out in a cornfield eye-balling the part and venture a guess.

Benzon told me that the NTSB wasn't in the business of proving what had happened. "Probable cause is our goal," he said. And yet the Board's meticulous work would look like proof to most people. MacIntosh, in his role as investigator in charge, felt personally responsible for amassing mountains of evidence. John C. Clark, an investigator who would play a vital role on the team, said, "I was impressed with MacIntosh. He knew how to run a good investigation and knew a lot about all of the disciplines. He would keep the various groups integrated and keep the parties in line."

Looking over the wreckage on Thursday and Friday, then, Mac-Intosh hit upon one step he could take in the process of clearly demonstrating the cause of this crash. He decided that he and his team would find all the parts they needed and then reassemble the tail. "There was a great reluctance," he said. "Not too many people were really interested in putting the tail section up." They thought they could determine all the trajectories using mathematics. But, said MacIntosh, "I was Mr. Nasty and said, Hey, we've got enough stuff here that we ought to be able to reconstruct that." United supported him, since that company viewed itself as the victim. "GE and Douglas were a little more reluctant to do that," he said, since it was their engine and airplane that had failed. United enlisted its Heavy Maintenance Group from San Francisco. MacIntosh arranged with Lawrence Harrington to acquire cranes to lift the tail. The team removed all the pieces of the tail from the airfield to a hangar and began putting the puzzle together to see what it showed.

MacIntosh, Benzon, Wizniak, Gregory Phillips, the chairman of the Systems Group, and others were hoping that this would answer the question of how the plane had lost all of its hydraulic fluid. However, the biggest concern gnawing at John Moehring of GE, as well as the NTSB investigators, was how and why that fan disk came apart in the first place. A piece of the plane could have broken off to be sucked into the engine. A mechanic could have left a tool inside the engine. Or a quirk of the titanium metal itself may have betrayed them all. To know the answer, they had to find the disk, which lay in pieces somewhere in the sea of corn and soybeans that is the state of Iowa. There had to be some way to reduce that area to a reasonable size for a concerted search to be conducted.

While Jan Murray, the first class flight attendant, hung upside down in the burning wreckage, trying to pry the harness latch from underneath her ribs, her father Don was fishing with a friend on a lake in South Carolina. As his friend watched in alarm, Don Murray turned white and said, "We've got to go home. Something's wrong with Jan." He put away his fishing gear and hurried to shore. When he arrived home, he saw a crowd of people at his house. His heart sank. He rushed inside.

"I just heard from Jan," said his wife Jane. "Everything's okay. There's been a plane crash, and she was on it." They knew their daughter was alive, but they did not yet know her condition.

Jan Murray, too, had had a premonition. The night before the crash, she had been flying to Philadelphia and was seized by an overwhelming sense of loss and separation from her family. She couldn't explain it. She loved her job and her traveling way of life, but that night she felt so desperately homesick that she called her aunt and uncle when she reached her hotel room. During the next day's flight, she was behind the bulkhead working with the equipment to start the in-flight movie, when she broke down weeping for no apparent reason. "It was just this lonely separation, and it was from my mother, and it was a feeling that I'm not going to see her again. I just broke down in tears. I gathered myself together before I came from behind the partition, but that was so unlike me."

Now in the hospital, she understood her premonition. She also learned that she had broken her arm and several ribs. Wearing a cast, she stayed in a hotel that night with Donna McGrady as her roommate. She wandered aimlessly through the hotel, unable to sleep. She stumbled into the conference room where Jan Brown had seen the chart with "the other Jan Brown's" name on it. "Even though I was in shock and nothing was really going in or out," said Murray, "I remember that being very upsetting."

In fact, she was in a state of shock for a long time after returning home. "I talked about it constantly, relived it constantly. You think about it constantly and you talk-talk-talk, and you probably wear your friends and family out about it. It's all you—it-it-it—it took over my thoughts. I just remember reliving, I guess, the acute part of the crash a lot, reliving the impact." She tried to return to her life, but "everything was exaggerated. It's like, things that we go through life, day in and day out, and sort of take for granted were just all huge." Her voice broke as she said, "It was like, just, you know, a tree was *beautiful*." And then she laughed and cried at the same time, overwhelmed by the vision she had, as if a gauze curtain had always hung between her and the world, and the crash had ripped it away. "It was like everything was so, so *saturated*, and . . ." And she trailed off to nothing. She found herself going through the motions, almost robotically, "for a good year," she said. "I wanted my life back as it was—I thought. I wanted to be innocent Jan Murray again, and I wanted to go back, because I loved my job—I loved it! And I loved the lifestyle. And I wanted it back. Like it was."

She went to therapy, and after about eighteen months, she returned to work. One of her best friends joined her on her first flight. "I was apprehensive, but I was determined." Yet she quickly discovered that any mechanical trouble with an airplane, any trivial hitch in her routine, would throw her into a panic. The last straw came in Newark, New Jersey, when she was about to fly on a Boeing 727. Although it was a terrific plane with flight controls that could revert to manual operation if the hydraulic systems failed, it had an engine through the tail, and for Murray that was reminiscent of the DC-10. As the catering crew brought the meals on board, one of them mentioned that there appeared to be fan blades missing from the number two engine, the one that was mounted through the tail. The flight was delayed while mechanics examined the power plant. United switched planes, "but that was the end of my career," Murray said. "That was the day that it was clear to me that I was not going to fly anymore. I wasn't the same person." She went back to school to renew her certification as a registered nurse. "I knew that I was going to have to make a different path in life."

She continued, "The biggest impact the crash had on me is I am so claustrophobic that I won't ride elevators, I won't fly, and that stays with me." To this day, if the right stimulus is present, Murray can go back there in an instant, into the middle of that wild slamming catastrophe. "It's not like I dwell on it on a day-to-day basis," she said. "From the get-go, I tried to just grab the good out of it. I mean, you gotta grab the good." While acknowledging how devastating this was for others, she said, "I tried to see that maybe this was playing into me having a different path in life." When she was flying, she had no time for anything else. During that time of frenetic travel, her best friend knew the man she thought would be a good match for Murray. Her friend kept saying, "When you're ready for the right person, I know who he is." Murray paid no attention. Once she realized that she could no longer fly, however, she took the time to meet him in

1993. They married in 1994. They have two boys, John and Hayden. She believes that if she had continued to fly, she never would have had that family. "I think I was left here to be a mom for these boys."

The plane crashed on Wednesday. On Friday an attorney named Philip H. Corboy filed the first lawsuit on behalf of Joseph Trombello in Cook County Circuit Court, naming United Airlines, General Electric, and McDonnell Douglas. The lawsuit alleged that United was negligent in its maintenance, that GE built a flawed engine, and that McDonnell Douglas manufactured a poorly designed airplane. Many more lawsuits would be filed in the coming weeks and months, and many would make similar allegations. But because of the curious nature of aviation litigation, no proof of those allegations would ever be made available to the public.

David Rapoport, who represented the three members of the cockpit crew and a number of flight attendants, told me that "The issues of fault were fully worked up and by that I mean there were exchanges of documents by all parties that were sued. There were expert witnesses disclosed and deposed. And much of the material that was generated in that several-year-old, multi-headed series of cases is under protective order that remains in place." In other words, General Electric, United Airlines, and McDonnell Douglas succeeded in convincing a court to keep all the evidence secret, even while they paid out millions of dollars to the victims to head off potential trials that would expose all the evidence in a public court of law.

Although the NTSB would amass thousands of pages of evidence and testimony in the months and years after the crash, none of it would be aimed at assigning blame. "At NTSB hearings," Rapoport wrote in a scholarly paper, "questions directed to issues of fault and liability are not even permitted." In fact, at the time of the lawsuits arising from the crash of United Flight 232, it was common practice for defendants to insist on an order of protection before they would produce any documents at all in discovery proceedings.

Today, said Rapoport, "the many depositions, the thousands of pages of documents that included many things in addition to what were in the public docket from the NTSB, are all still under protective order. My opinion is that there are important things that haven't made it to the public domain." Treading a fine line between telling the whole story and breaking the law, he added, "I think I could make the general comment that there was much information developed in the private litigation implicating relative degrees of culpability" of all major defendants. I suggested to Rapoport that McDonnell Douglas was at fault for designing an airplane with serious deficiencies, that General Electric was at fault for building a defective fan disk, and that United Airlines was at fault for missing the defect in its final inspection of the disk. "Does that ring true?" I asked.

"Yes," he said. "I think you have the right cast of characters." Although the investigators did not know it when that first lawsuit was filed, a mechanic had not left a tool in the engine to cause the explosion. Nor had a piece of the plane broken off to be sucked into the number two engine. The fan disk itself was defective and exploded, initiating the sequence of events that caused the crash.

Rapoport, who as a plaintiff's attorney had every reason to want to assign blame, said, "My way of thinking about it would place no or minimal culpability on" the man who last inspected 00385. "Because I believe the entire system of inspection was flawed. I am not convinced that he was asleep on the job. I do recall that plenty of energy went into blaming the airline." And indeed, in its findings of probable cause, the NTSB in effect blamed United Airlines.

> The National Transportation Safety Board determines that the probable cause of this accident was the inadequate consideration given to human factors limitations in the inspection and quality control procedures used by United Airlines' engine overhaul facility which resulted in the failure to detect a fatigue crack originating from a previously undetected metallurgical defect located in a critical area of the stage 1 fan disk that was manufactured by General Electric Aircraft Engines. The subsequent catastrophic disintegration of the disk resulted in the liberation of debris in a pattern of distri-

bution and with energy levels that exceeded the level of protection provided by design features of the hydraulic systems that operate the DC-10's flight controls.

It's difficult to know what that statement means. It seems almost deliberately murky. And indeed, the NTSB not only investigates, but also negotiates with the parties involved, those companies for which a great deal of money is at stake.

Rapoport concluded, "I would say that the engine was sold with inadequate instructions for use in order to ferret out dangers that the manufacturer either knew of or should have known about."

An aeronautical engineer who had worked in flight testing with Boeing in his early years, Richard F. Schaden went into law and for thirty years tried cases involving airplane crashes, both military and civilian. After 1819 Uniform crashed, he represented Brad Griffin, among others. "It was unique in that we knew the crash was going to happen close to a half hour before it did happen," he said. "So from a lawyer's standpoint, you have all that anticipation of disaster. . . . The intervening mental anguish was the big legal issue."

But, he said, of primary concern to him was the faulty design of the DC-10. A faulty GE engine could have blown up on other jumbo jets and might not have caused a crash, as was the case with the L-1011 departing Newark. Schaden flies the Falcon 900 EX business jet, which is a three-engine system like the one on the DC-10. "The basic configuration, I think, is a good design," he said. "The issue of having all the hydraulic systems go through one location where there's a single point of failure—that was the biggest design issue. . . . It was a lack-of-redundancy problem. It was a lack of failure analysis at the time of the design. The DC-10 is the only [plane] that I know that would have [the hydraulic lines] in that location where they were so vulnerable."

About the failure to find a defect that might have caused the fan to fracture—whatever that defect might have been—Schaden said, "The method used for inspecting [the metal] was pretty weak at that time, the nondestructive testing they used. Titanium as a metal doesn't really exist. It was a manufactured metal, and the manufacturing process was not controlled very well. The titanium billets that were made back in those days are pretty much all in golf clubs now. Just so they could get rid of most of that defective titanium. There was just so much of it around, and it was expensive to make."

Schaden's strategy for litigating his cases for United Flight 232 was to avoid the federal court system and what he referred to as "kind of a bad food fight." There was ample opportunity to make money, and "everybody started jumping in the business back in those days." Lawyers retired on the money they made on 1819 Uniform. He completely sidestepped that process, filing his lawsuits in the city court in downtown St. Louis because that's where the corporate offices of McDonnell Douglas were. "That allowed me to get a more effective jury for my clients as a plaintiff's lawyer and also to stay out of the food fight of the multi-district litigation." The defendants tried without success to kick him out of courts in St. Louis and force him into the federal courts. "We had pretty much an all-minority jury in an inner-city venue in downtown St. Louis," he explained. "And that was the last thing that the industry wanted. Federal court juries tend to be much more conservative. They tend to be suburban, because they can draw from a large geographical area."

Schaden said, "When I stood up to make an opening statement, they settled all the cases."

Jason Henry, the young lifeguard who worked in the morgue, was not the only person who was made uneasy by the methods used in identifying the bodies. "As we first got started," Brad Randall said, "a funeral director representative came up to us just in a panic, because we had sat down with Steven Smith and his colleagues, and we'd decided we were going to take the jaws out of everybody. And she [the funeral director] was just aghast." In her profession, she was ordinarily in the business of making people look better, not worse. Even one of the young forensic dentists questioned the need to remove all jaws and fingers. He went on in his career to help develop methods of identifying people by their teeth that did not disfigure the dead and would allow for an open coffin at the funeral. The fact that dentists removed the jaws of perfectly intact and viewable victims gave forensic dentistry a bad name for a number of years after that crash. And that scandal encouraged the development of new techniques. At the time of the crash, performing forensic dentistry on one person was not an easy task. Trying to identify more than a hundred dead people was daunting indeed. "Unclenching a dead person's jaw is *extremely* difficult," Randall said. "And it's a good way to break teeth and that sort of thing." However, techniques are available today that allow the mouth to be propped open and a digital X-ray taken without any disfigurement. Also, FBI technicians no longer routinely cut people's fingers off to obtain fingerprints.

Marliss DeJong and numerous others defended the practice of removing jaws and fingers, saying that it was the fastest and most foolproof way to identify someone. "When you have all these families saying I want my family member, you want to process them as fast as you can," she said. "And you cannot make a mistake." If they mixed up one identity, they would automatically have two that were wrong, and the entire process would fall into question. Indeed, the Omaha daily newspaper ran a headline three days after the crash saying, "Iowa Examiner Slow but Sure in Identification of Jet Victims."

Randall said, "Yes, we could have gotten by without doing that. It would have slowed things down and made it a lot more difficult for charting and X-ray. And we just decided that the cosmetics that were lost doing that were worth the increased accuracy we were going to get. And the families were more concerned about a rapid identification than having a body slightly disfigured."

After a body had been put through the stages of the process for identification, either it was returned to a refrigerated truck to await autopsy, or if a pathologist was available, it was sent directly to the table. At one point on Friday, nearly three dozen people were simultaneously operating the X-ray, fingerprint, dental, autopsy, and embalming areas of the big partitioned-off postmortem room, amid garbage pails and buckets used for fluids. Pathologists worked with their scrubs soaked in sweat, while others took photographs or made videotapes of the proceedings. Some wore flowered aprons that were clearly meant for a cheerful kitchen, presumably because the morgue had run out of surgical aprons. Many others wore jeans and golf shirts.

When a plane crashed, the medical examiner was required by law to autopsy only the flight crew. The pilots of Flight 232, of course, were alive. Nevertheless, Herbek, Randall, and Bennett decided to autopsy all of the dead. Randall said, "They were real quick and dirty autopsies. We were just opening them up, looking for trauma, looking for horribly obvious natural disease, and that was it." When an autopsy was completed, the body was moved across the hangar to the area where morticians and funeral directors waited with stainless-steel tables, "and they [the bodies] were immediately embalmed," Herbek explained. "And again, the trackers were with these people the whole time."

Patricia Collins, a forty-eight-year-old mother of four and a homemaker, worked part time as a switchboard operator in a local office building in Sioux City. She volunteered, as Jason Henry did, not knowing what might be asked of her. But her experience could not have been more of a contrast to Henry's. She said that the faces of most of the bodies she processed during her two days as a tracker in the morgue were covered with a black substance that Herbek believed to be the oily soot produced by imperfectly burned jet fuel. A member of her team would dip a cloth into solvent and scrub the faces clean before Thomas Randolph, sitting on a folded white towel on the wooden ladder, photographed them. If the clothes weren't already burned off, they were snipped off with scissors. Collins stood at the head of the body, as Jason had done with Jane Doe, while a DCI agent recorded any pertinent information, such as possessions, tattoos, and identifying marks or scars, as the team turned the body over for examination. The team catalogued anything the person was wearing, such as earrings, rings, watches, necklaces, even the change in their pockets. "No matter what was in the pockets—it could have been a toothpick, it could have been a screw—everything was taken and put into the sack for the family." Then the brown-paper grocery sack was labeled with the body number. Kenneth Berger, for example. His wallet held a Sears credit card, a Maas Brothers card, and a card for The Athletic Club. Fragments of his skull were placed, like broken crockery, in a ziplock bag.

Collins still carries the memory of a nine-year-old girl who came under the cameras. The only nine-year-old girl who died in the crash was Cynthia Myers. Collins may have been wrong about the age, but the girl she attended could not have been Cynthia Myers, who died of smoke inhalation and would have therefore been badly burned, according to Randall. She had been in seat 24-C. It was a bad place to be. The portside ceiling collapsed starting at about row 22 and going back through row 28, and some of the people in those seats were trapped, though alive. Cynthia Myers had blood carbon monoxide saturation of 70 percent and would not have been able to escape the fire.

Like the Venus attended by Jason Henry, the little girl Collins saw was perfect. "She was our son's age," Collins said, "and she had on the same Nike tight biking shorts that he wore. They were black with a blue and white stripe up the side of the leg. And they were kind of Spandex, kind of tight fitting. And every other fingernail was painted blue like a little kid would do." The girl was striking, because like Jane Doe, she seemed completely uninjured. She was barefoot. Her dark-brown hair was shoulder length. She wore two braided string friendship bracelets. "Beautiful, beautiful girl. Just a beautiful little girl that you or I would love to take home," said Collins. That face was still rising up before Collins more than two decades after the crash.

"And then the gums and the entire teeth [were] sawed out," Collins said. "That was put into a plastic bag. After they did the jaw and the teeth were extracted, then they went into another area, which I did not watch, but they took all the fingertips." Fingerprints were actually taken first: "And then from there, the body went into a holding area. My [identifying] sheet was attached to the bag, and the body parts were put into the bag, the bag was zipped and [wheeled] into an embalming area, and they were laid just right in a file—one, two, three, four, five—right down the rows."

She said that what impressed her most was the respect with which she felt the bodies were treated. "There was very, very little talking. We treated these bodies like it was our mother or our father. One of the bodies came in, and there was a cricket on it. And so I didn't say anything but I pointed to one of the helpers and I just kind of shook my head, and they went and took that cricket off. We had utmost respect for the bodies."

Robert Monserrate of the DCI also worked in the morgue and said nearly the same words. At the prayer service for the first anniversary of the crash, a man and his son approached Monserrate and asked how the investigators knew that the badly burned body the family had received in a casket was the boy's mother, the man's wife. "We sat down at one of the tables and I told him how we recovered the bodies from the runway, the plane. How we transported the remains to the morgue, how we photographed the bodies, looked for any identifiable marks or jewelry, how we did the dental [identification], X-rays, fingerprints and such. How we had the utmost respect for all their loved ones, how we assigned a person to follow their loved one through the identification process and how there was no question in my mind as to our accuracy in identifying everyone."

After accompanying five bodies on the day after the crash, Collins threw away her gloves, washed her hands, and sat idle in a separate room. "We did five bodies. Then we would take a forty-five-minute break. Five bodies, forty-five-minute break. And I did this for two days." She said everyone in the break room was contemplative and sad. "We felt that we were fulfilling a mission, felt that we were doing good, but it was a very sad time. And we smelled. The bodies that came in, they reeked with jet fuel. The bodies had not started to decay, but the odor from the jet fuel was horrible."

Collins said that working in the morgue, seeing the gruesome things she saw, caused no psychological trauma in the long run. Her husband Dick was in the Air National Guard, and he worked on a search team looking for bodies in the cornfields. At home in the evenings, they showered to try to rid themselves of the smell and then sat talking quietly together, sharing their experiences from the day. They became each other's psychological counselors. They sought no outside help and had no ongoing emotional troubles. She attributes this in part to her Christian faith and in part to the sense of a sacred mission that she felt in her work. "When they got done," she said of the morticians, "they would fold the people's hands over their stomachs. Everything was done very, very tactfully and very—really, devoutly. I'm a pretty strong Christian, and there's a lot of things about this that are so beautiful of the respect for the human body, and we did that to the fullest."

J. Kenneth Berkemier, a funeral director from Sioux City, helped in that process. He rolled his eyes when he contemplated the volumes of paperwork that needed to be completed. He was sixty-one at the time of the crash and owned a cemetery as well as a mortuary business. He dealt with many bodies in his career, but never so many all at once. "We had a staff of funeral directors," he said, "funeral directors' wives, funeral directors' mothers," and here he laughed. He had thinning brown hair in a dramatic comb-over and wore oversized glasses and a suit and tie that made him look very much the picture of a funeral director. He said they recruited "anyone who would be familiar with the technicalities of death certificates, burial permits, transit permits, cremation permits, all the necessary things that had to be done before that body could go out. And those things all had to be produced and double-checked last minute." Those documents then had to be put with the shipping papers and sent out to the location on the airfield where the body was placed in a casket. Although all the workers in the morgue were dressed in the most casual way, the funeral directors wore suits in the July heat out of respect for the dead. They drove the bodies one by one in hearses. The first bodies were recovered from the field on Thursday, July 20. By Sunday, all but three of the dead had been identified. Those three were identified on Monday.

As Patricia Collins and her team brought bodies to him, Berkemier dispatched them for embalming. Burned bodies were placed in a container called a Ziegler case, which is a casket of 20 gauge steel with a channel gasket in the lid that allows it to be hermetically sealed against the smell that Margo Crain and others would never forget. The Ziegler case was put inside a conventional casket, "and in this instance, we used sealed caskets also," Berkemier said, "so those bodies were double sealed." The casket was placed in a shipping case, all of the paperwork attached, and then the body was either flown directly out of Sioux City or transported by hearse to Omaha, Nebraska, or Sioux Falls, South Dakota, for shipping home to the family.

Collins said that she wanted to make sure that the families of those who lost their lives in the wreck of 1819 Uniform would "realize that we took the best care of their people. I did it joyfully and sadfully. I was very happy to do it, but it was a very sad thing. It was a sad day, a very sad day. And it was very humbling, and it's a day I'll never forget."

Monserrate said that having the opportunity to explain to the father and son what had become of the wife and mother was therapeutic for him as well. "I know that he was very happy to learn the facts of what we did and how we took care of their loved ones. What he did not know was how much he really helped me and met my need to know that we made a difference and helped bring closure to families that lost loved ones out there."

Ellen and Adrienne Badis were on their way home from Honolulu to the East Coast by way of Denver and Chicago. Ellen was about to turn thirty-six, and Adrienne had recently turned forty. They traveled with their two children, Eric, six, and Aaron, two and a half. Ellen wore a pale-blue sleeveless sundress, and Adrienne wore a striped dress shirt and black slacks. Ellen was thin and pretty with light brown hair. Dark and round-faced, Adrienne looked the Filipino he was. The couple doted on their two boys. Before they left for the Honolulu airport, they posed for a portrait wearing leis of pink flowers with the sunlit sea behind them. Ellen wore a small lei as a headband.

When they arrived at the terminal, they discovered that their plane had mechanical trouble and was not going to take off. By the time they arrived in Denver the next morning, most of the eastbound flights were fully booked. The only seats available were on United Flight 232. Moreover, the seats weren't together. Ellen and Aaron wound up in B-Zone, while Adrienne and Eric were in C-Zone. Eric had been given 23-G, and Adrienne was supposed to be seated in row 28. Hoping for the best, Adrienne led Eric back to row 28 and sat in the vacant seat beside him, 28-F. When Jerry Schemmel arrived, annoyed to see someone in his seat, Adrienne asked, "Do you have 28-F?"

Trying not to let all the frustration show from his long morning of delays, Schemmel said yes, it was his seat.

"This is my son," Adrienne said. "He's supposed to be in 23-G. We'd like to sit together. Would you mind taking 23-G? It's an aisle seat."

"Sure," said Schemmel. "No problem." He trudged forward to take Eric's seat, and probably saved the boy's life by doing so.

Eleven rows ahead of her husband, Ellen was concerned that her fidgety two-year-old was bothering Pete Wernick and his wife Joan. She switched seats with Aaron. When the engine blew, Ellen told me, "It was the loudest noise I've ever heard, still to this day." Although the plane climbed right after the explosion, her perception was that it "just nose-dived," as she put it.* "We immediately went down a mile, five thousand feet. And I thought that was it, we were all going, we were going to crash. And I started praying." Ellen broke down weeping, almost unable to get the next few words out. "And then he gained control of the plane." She gasped for breath, reliving the terrible moment, as she said, "and we leveled off . . ." Joan Wernick tried to reassure Ellen, telling her that planes can fly with two engines or even with only one. As Ellen watched the flight attendants telling mothers to put their children on the floor, she silently gave

---

* Although the plane climbed three hundred feet immediately after the explosion, many people had the sensation that it dove.

thanks that she and her husband had bought tickets for their children. She put a pillow beneath Aaron's seatbelt, and Aaron almost immediately fell asleep with gum in his mouth. As the plane neared Sioux City, Sharon Bayless, sitting across the aisle, leaned over and suggested that Ellen remove Aaron's gum.

"I felt terrible that I'd left gum in his mouth," Ellen said. "He was asleep and he's a child and a toddler at that." As she described to me what happened next, her voice became a low growl, as if she were struggling to push the words out, and those words became almost like a sad lamenting song. "I went down as far as I could and, and, and braced, and when we hit, I just, ah, said, oh, the sound is just more that you'll never forget, the sound of metal shrieking and of earth and dirt and the smell of the, of the rubber, and the, the, the fumes and the, um, it's just, uh, something we'll never forget, but, ah . . . And it was just so long. Just, it was just terrible. So I said, 'Oh, gosh. We—have—crashed,' you know. And then, and then—there was this . . . *smooth* . . . No more noise!" Here Ellen's voice became almost jubilant. "It was . . . I, and I thought to myself, 'Oh, my gosh, if this is—I'm going to heaven! This is—if this is it, then this is wonderful!' And then it came back again—the noise, the same noise. And it went on, and it seemed to go on and on and aw, I just could not, aw! I—and then after that—" Ellen's voice collapsed in on itself, as she ran out of words. She said she thought she might have lost consciousness in her seat.

Her next memory was the sound of Aaron screaming. She thought, "Oh, my gosh—I'm alive!" She looked to her left and saw Pete and Joan and their six-year-old son Will, a few weeks from his seventh birthday, and saw that they seemed uninjured. "We were all squished, leaning forward. We could not lean back." Her senses were not her own. She found that she was looking at Aaron's toes. His legs seemed to dangle up toward the ceiling. "It was dark," she said, "but I had some light that I could see that his profile was there. And I heard him crying, so I knew that he was okay." But her mind was awash in confusion as she thought, "Oh, gosh, what—what do we do? What do I do? How do we get out of this—How do we get out of these seat belts? What? Somebody help me! Because there we were, dangling from these seat belts, which were, of course, our lifesavers." She had yet to realize that she was upside down. She "fumbled and fumbled and got up in there where the belt buckle was up in our stomachs and I finally got it opened and fell—oh, my gosh! Fell down, and then I just didn't—I just didn't know what to do. I was just starting to say, 'Somebody help me, please, help me with my son!'"

People were now dropping from their seats in twos and threes. The crowd of bodies quickly became impenetrable amid the debris. What had been the left side was now the right, and the people a few rows back were trapped in the crushed ceiling as the plane filled with smoke. The people around Ellen began struggling and crawling toward the light, so Pete and Will Wernick and Ellen found themselves caught up in this mass of protoplasm, squirming in the disturbed hive. "And there were wires," Ellen said, "and there were bodies and lots of wires, and then I got to the opening and then there was corn. And then I jumped, and then I looked, and I just can't believe I didn't have my child." She had somehow escaped the burning ship without her two-year-old. Aaron hung somewhere inside that dark interior, dangling from his seat belt like a ham.

CHAPTER NINETEEN

John C. Clark, the senior performance engineer from the Bureau of Technology at the NTSB, arrived in Sioux City on July 20 to search for fan disk 00385. Clark, along with Edward Wizniak, William Thompson, Robert MacIntosh, and others, paid a visit to Dennis Swanstrom, the base commander, and informed him that critical parts were missing out in the cornfields around Alta, Iowa. "And within ten minutes," recalled Thompson, "his forces were at work acting." From that point on, Swanstrom, Harrington, and the Air National Guard would play a key role in aiding Clark's search for the missing disk. Based on what the NTSB and GE had seen of the number two engine, one thing was clear: if they wanted to pinpoint the cause of the accident, they had to find the missing disk. They strongly suspected that it lay in two big pieces in a field about sixty miles northeast of Sioux City, on ground obscured by midsummer crops.

Clark, forty-one, was an experienced investigator and well aware of the history of titanium rotating parts blowing up. If people wanted modern air travel, they had to spin big heavy wheels. And if they spun big heavy wheels, they would have to accept that some of them would fly apart now and then, as such wheels had done from the beginning. But Clark had never seen a situation in which the number one fan vanished, along with a good portion of its shaft and attachments.

He already had parts from the airplane that farmers had found and some reports from those who had seen components falling from the plane about eight miles north of the town of Alta. Other pieces were sighted about two miles east of Highway M31, which runs north and south along the western edge of Alta. The lighter materials would have drifted with the winds of the upper atmosphere. Clark immediately ordered all the meteorological information that was available. The wind had been roughly from the north, blowing forty knots at thirty-seven thousand feet. Some of the lighter debris was found to have drifted to the southeast from the point of the explosion, while a piece of the airplane's aluminum skin was found a mile north of Alta on the west side of M31. Clark was eventually able to confirm the speed of the winds aloft by looking at the radar data. As 1819 Uniform turned from east to north, Clark would learn, there was a drop in its ground speed consistent with a headwind of roughly the correct velocity.

Now he needed to use mathematics and the laws of physics to account for all the forces on the parts of the fan disk and to predict where those parts went. "I remember getting various parts and pieces," he said. As the pieces came in, Clark kept records and plotted those fragments on maps of the farmland. Working at a long table in a conference room at the convention center in downtown Sioux City, he began by calculating the trajectory from the approximate spot where the engine blew to the locations where the pieces that they had in hand had landed. Such recovered parts yielded a lot of information. They showed the real-world behavior of parts of given shapes, sizes, and masses. Each time Clark calculated the trajectory for another part, it added to his store of knowledge about how those big pieces of the fan disk might have returned to earth. He adjusted other calculations accordingly, even while he consulted with the GE engineers, who were as eager as he was to find the fan disk.

Clark went out to the fields where the parts had been found and used the services of Laura Levy with her laser transit to assign an exact location to each part. Then he returned to the conference room and again sat at his table spread with papers to solve trajectory analysis equations. It was pretty straightforward for someone versed in mathematics and ballistics. Gravity was trying to pull the piece down. The speed of the airplane imparted momentum to the piece, pushing it forward as it was released in the explosion. The pressure of the air against the piece, known as drag, acted to slow its forward motion as it accelerated downward. "And you just keep making repetitive calculations at various time increments," Clark said. As gravity accelerated the piece toward the ground, the drag increased, thereby reducing its acceleration. Within a few seconds of free fall, the weight of the piece would come into equilibrium with the drag, and the speed at which it was falling would stabilize and remain constant for the rest of the trip to the ground. Once drag had stopped the forward momentum, the piece would drop more or less straight down, except for the motion of drifting with the wind.

"What we've found over the years," Clark said, "is that it's best to put everything together that you think you know, do your calculations, and find that spot. You can walk right out and put your foot down right on that spot, and then start expanding your search from that point."

At the time of the explosion, the plane had been moving eastward at a groundspeed of 560 miles an hour. If the plane had dropped a bomb, it would have been easy to calculate where it fell using the speed of the plane and the speed of the wind. But this was more complicated. As the fan disk broke apart and came out of the engine, the pieces could have gone in almost any direction at speeds of almost four hundred miles an hour. In addition, the plane's forward velocity would have thrown the pieces toward the east.

Clark called his boss in Washington. Monty Montgomery also happened to be the chief of the Engineering Services Division of the NTSB and was an expert in computers and flight data recorders. "Monty," Clark said, "wrote code for me when I arrived at the Board. He wrote the basic program for trajectory calculations and plotting in Fortran. I modified the basic programs for each accident, customized if you will. I would call him with my new estimates, and he would run the programs to get the trajectory calculations. He would call me with the numbers and I would plot them on a large area map—county crop maps." Clark's mapping of the debris that had already been collected matched the ballistic calculations. Those calculations showed where they would expect the missing parts, both light and heavy, to fall.

Another factor Clark had to consider was what might be called the Frisbee effect. Even if the disk still had blades or broken blades attached to it, and even if the disk was fractured and missing a large segment, it might fly, given the tremendous speed at which it was traveling. It might not fly elegantly, but if it produced even a small amount of lift in its spinning descent, it could, Clark calculated, travel more than three and a half miles off of a ballistic, bomblike trajectory during the seven-mile fall to the ground.

Clark had other unknowns to ponder. How would such a titanium Frisbee, possibly weighing in the neighborhood of three hundred pounds, orient itself while falling? Would it approach the earth edge-on like a coin going into a slot? Would it dish out onto its flat side the way a space capsule enters the atmosphere? What happens if you drop a paper plate from a balcony? What if you sail it instead? "Is it flying pointed end first or flat side into the wind or whatever, and that changes your drag characteristics," Clark said.

By the Friday after the crash, he said, "radar data started coming in, so that pinpointed us down pretty close to where the event occurred. Then I started getting [information] in from the flight data recorder, and with that I knew exactly at the moment when the engine blew, and then I could marry that up with the recorded radar data and get a very precise position over the ground where the engine let go." The fan disk and other parts had separated in pieces large enough to reflect a radar signal, and Clark could see the parts coming off at thirty-seven thousand feet. If he had his scope set up for it, James Michael Rohde, the air traffic controller at Minneapolis Center in Farmington, Minnesota, might have seen the dark images fluttering down his screen beginning at thirteen seconds after 3:16 on that Wednesday afternoon.

Clark performed some calculations and called Monty Montgomery again to feed him the data. The computer run showed that parts of the fan disk had most likely fallen to earth in either section seven or section eight of Scott Township in Buena Vista County, roughly between Rembrandt and Truesdale, two towns with a combined population of 419 people at the time. The two sections of farmland were each a mile square, but taking other factors into account, such as the Frisbee effect, Clark set the boundaries of the area to be searched, including those two sections, at eighteen square miles. Although Clark would give it an honest try on more than one occasion in the coming weeks, not all the people in Scott Township could have searched an area that large. But Clark hoped to get lucky. On Saturday he recruited the Iowa Public Service Bell JetRanger helicopter. Guided by Clark's calculations of the areas they needed to search, the pilot flew slowly back and forth about thirty feet above the ground. Clark stared down at the corn blowing this way and that in great sweeps of downwash from the rotors.* He could occasionally see the ground between the rows, but he was also aware of the blind spot beneath the helicopter and the ease with which he could miss something that was probably at least partly buried in the Cannisteo and Nicollet and Clarion loams of those fertile fields. Throughout that Saturday, he scanned sections four through nine in Scott Township without results. In addition, Clark understood that the disk could have landed in a pond and might never be found.

That Saturday, the Air National Guard at Lincoln, Nebraska, sent out its RF-4 Phantom fighter planes to take infrared and black-and-white photographs along the flight path that United Flight 232 followed. They used both vertical and oblique cameras, but only the ones looking straight down could see anything on the ground. Most people have never seen an F-4 up close. The planes are huge, and they are extremely loud. By all accounts, those RF-4C missions scared the daylights out of every living thing for miles around, especially peo-

---

* After the harvest, some farmers claimed that the helicopters damaged their crops while others said that the wind helped to pollinate the corn. The area enjoyed a bumper crop that year.

ple who were already nervous about the crash. The Southern Hills Mall, where Greg Clapper's wife and daughters saw *Peter Pan,* was deserted the day after the crash because people had heard that 1819 Uniform had flown right over it.

That night, teams of analysts and photo interpreters at the 155th Tactical Reconnaissance Group in Lincoln pored over those recon photos until dawn, trying to identify anything on the ground that might have been made of metal. In the morning, they gave Clark the maps they had drawn and directions to the targets they had identified as promising.

Sunday morning bright and early, John Clark, Edward Wizniak, Laura Levy, and Jim Walker, along with pilots, crew chiefs, and nine other volunteers from the 185th, stood out on the ramp ready to board the Hueys that were parked there on loan from Army National Guard bases in Boone and Waterloo. (Huey is the nickname for the Bell UH-1 Iroquois utility helicopter that was used during the war in Vietnam.) The volunteers and investigators boarded for the short flight out to the area around Rembrandt and Truesdale, and as Walker put it, "It seemed like we landed wherever we needed to, and I'm not sure how the farmers felt about that." As soon as the helicopters dropped them off, Walker and the other volunteers formed lines and began walking up and down section twelve on the eastern edge of Elk Township, which was the area adjacent to and west of section seven, where Clark thought the fan disk might have fallen. Walker was not prepared for the conditions that day. The corn was pollinating itself, and the air was thick with the yellow dust. "I have hay fever," he said, and after several hours of searching, "I couldn't even breathe, and somebody took pity on me, and when it was time to go home, I got to ride in the air-conditioned Bell helicopter with the leather seats."

John Clark said, "On one of the searches, Laura Levy and I had been out most of the morning, and it was hot with no wind. The corn pollen was really bad, and the corn was over my head. We stopped at a gas station on a section corner, out in the middle of nowhere, it seemed. Laura needed some water to rinse out her eyes. Her contacts were giving her fits. We went in and there were a number of gents sitting around. They went outside to the pitcher pump, and with a few pumps we had all the well water we needed."

Clark and Levy and the others were attempting to follow the directions from the photo interpreters, who had provided maps of suspected metal objects. The work was frustrating and fruitless. Clark would usually find something, but never what he was looking for. Often the team members were chasing shadows. They found pieces of metal. They found a feed sack. One time they found an object that was round and dark and had no corn on it. On the photograph, it looked as if it might be a big disk. When Clark and Levy slogged through the corn, covered in the choking yellow pollen, to reach the spot at last, it turned out to be an anthill. The search turned up nothing of value, but it demonstrated to Clark that the effort required for searching on foot was prohibitively large. Clark and Wizniak rode in the Hueys as they continued to fly up and down, back and forth. The investigators sat in the open doors, wind blowing around them, feet resting on the skids, and watched the corn blow.

Clark did go out to the spot where he had calculated fan disk 00385 to be, and he did put his foot down on the ground there. He didn't know it that day, but he was only a few hundred yards from the disk 00385. In the vastness of the sea of corn, that amounted to near pinpoint accuracy. But being close to the disk didn't make the search any easier. He returned to the Hueys and continued staring at the corn flowing past the door. "And I think we probably flew over that part down in that corn twenty, thirty, forty times," he said.

Through the frustrating days and then weeks after the crash, Clark was groping around for any kind of help he could get. It was essential to locate those parts if the people involved in this event were ever to be certain of what had been done to those passengers and why and by whom. In fact, most of the investigators from the NTSB, the FAA, United, GE, and McDonnell Douglas believed they knew what had happened. But United Airlines, General Electric, McDonnell Douglas—they had killed 112 of the 296 people on that plane. (Gerald Dobson was not yet dead but soon would be.) They had destroyed countless lives. The investigators could not simply hazard a guess as to what they thought might have happened. They had to compile the best evidence they could find. The people at General Electric wanted to know as badly as anyone. They wanted Clark to find the parts so that this type of accident might never happen again.

While Clark and Wizniak and the GE engineers were searching for the missing fan disk, John Young, an investigator from the NTSB, flew to Cincinnati, Ohio, near Evendale, where General Electric made its jet engines. There he worked with GE engineers, who were poring over records. Young was joined by David Cookson from United Airlines, who was in charge of searching and sequestering records for the airline anytime there was an incident or accident. Young and Cookson had had occasion to work together earlier in the year, when United nearly lost another jumbo jet, Flight 811 out of Honolulu, the accident in which nine people died. "We had a bad year that year," Cookson said. "John Young and I established a pretty good relationship. He was very professional." While John Clark wanted to know where that fan disk had gone, they wanted to know where it had come from. James W. Tucker, the general manager of Product Operations at GE, an engineering expert in turbines, even traveled to the offices of some vendors to dig through what he called "their dead letter file."

The records from that period of time at both ALCOA and GE were in a fair state of disarray, with some documents missing while others contained outright errors. Young and Cookson, Tucker, Moehring, and others were trying to determine the origin of the metal that was used to make fan disk 00385. In its final report, the NTSB called the records "contradictory" and "deficient." It said, "The records on a large number of [General Electric] disks are suspect." The report further stated that "several anomalies appear in the records [of General Electric], which call into question the reliability or accuracy of all the disk records from the same period. For instance, there were no records found indicating receipt of the fan disk forgings by the [General Electric] plant."

Despite the consistently sloppy practices at General Electric,

NTSB investigators came to realize that in 1971, a company called Titanium Metals of America out in Henderson, Nevada, had cast a cylinder of titanium weighing about seven thousand pounds. The missing fan disk had been cut from that column of titanium and then forged by ALCOA and machined by GE into the finished part. Disk 00385 from 1819 Uniform was one of eight that had been made from the same batch of metal. All of those pieces had been tested, and during those tests, one of the disks, not yet finished, had fallen under suspicion of having a defect. It never went into service. The seven others passed the tests, and six of them were still flying on DC-10s at the time of the crash.

"Within the very first few days after this event," said John Moehring of GE, "we researched the records . . . of all of the disks that had been manufactured from this . . . batch of titanium . . . we sent out an order to . . . withdraw those disks from service and bring them back to the factory."

In the evenings, after MacIntosh had led the daily meeting at the Sioux City Convention Center to review the findings of all the groups, Thompson of GE would call Moehring in Evendale and have what Moehring called "a long conference" about their progress toward an understanding of the appalling blunder that had been made in the General Electric aircraft engine factory.

Bruce Benham, thirty-seven, and his young colleague Garry Priest, had very different reactions to their impending arrival at Sioux City. Priest told me that he was not afraid. He later said that he was thinking, "Hell, this might even be kind of cool. Because, hey, we might get to go down the slide. I've never done that before. That might be kind of neat."

Benham, Priest's boss, on the other hand, was gripped with fear when he looked out the window and saw "how fast we were still going." He bent over and braced himself, and "to be honest, [I was] wondering when I would be killed. I was consciously thinking about when the end is going to come, because I thought it was done. The end."

When the wreckage came to a stop, Benham and Priest popped their seat belts. "I look around me and it just seems to be pitch black," Priest said. "Any direction I look is just darkness."

Benham echoed his assessment, describing "confusion, disorientation, darkness."

Gradually Priest saw silhouettes of faces. "No bodies, just faces. Really kind of eerie. And at some point, off to my right, I see the orange ember of what turns out to be a fire." He heard someone yell, "Fire!" and people began pushing past him in the opposite direction. He looked the other way and saw "a ray of sunlight. And it just made sense to go to it." He raised his voice and said, "Calm down and go to the light."

Benham had begun to follow Priest's lead, when he noticed a boy still strapped in across the aisle from his seat, alone in the thickening smoke. Benham had seen the boy's mother moments before, but now she was gone. Pete and Joan Wernick, with their son Will, were gone too. Ron Sheldon was boosting Aki Muto up into a hole in the floor a few rows back.

"I pulled him out of the seat and grabbed him," Benham said of the boy. "I didn't know the little guy's name. I just said, 'Son, please, please put your arms around my neck and hold me real tight. We're gonna get out of here.' His eyes were the size of a half-dollar. Beautiful little guy. He wasn't crying. I could tell he was scared. But he did exactly what I asked him to do. He put his arms around my neck, and I took him outside." With the boy in his arms, Benham struggled toward the hole, stumbling over luggage.

As the fuselage filled with smoke, Ellen Badis, the thirty-five-year-old mother of two, stood in the sunshine in her light-blue summer dress and came to the realization that her two-year-old, Aaron, was still inside. She turned to go back in, but the group of survivors who were ushering people out of the plane blocked her way. Now Ellen stared helplessly into the growing smoke.

Upton Rehnberg was holding back the bundle of wires that had been assembled by the hands of women at the Douglas factory in Long Beach. Rod Vetter and Jerry Schemmel were now joined by

Garry Priest in helping people out. John Transue stood with Jan Brown, while survivors, many of them injured, hurried away from the burning plane in different directions. Benham stepped out into the sunlit cornfield bearing the two-year-old in his arms. He moved away from the fire and smoke and almost immediately stumbled into a woman in a torn blue sleeveless sundress, standing in the sun and staring as if in a trance.

When Ellen Badis told this story, her voice dropped until it was nearly inaudible, the terrible confession, the unspeakable omission: "I just can't believe I didn't have my child." Then her voice rose almost to a scream as she said, "And then there he was! *There was Aaron.* And he was being held by this gentleman. The men were up on the broken fuselage, and they were helping folks off." She was seeing Clif Marshall on top of the inverted plane, pulling people out of the hole, Aki Muto and Gitte Skaanes and the Hjermstads, Alisa and Eric.

Benham handed Aaron to Ellen Badis, reuniting mother and son in the corn.

The crash happened on Wednesday, July 19. By Friday, July 28, everyone concerned—GE, the airlines, the NTSB, and many other manufacturers of parts that go into making an airliner—knew that jumbo jets were flying around that might have potentially deadly flaws in their engines. John Young from the NTSB, along with James Tucker, John Moehring, and others had already been poring over dispatch orders, inspection records, check sheets, ultrasonic inspection logs, discrepancy reports, and correspondence. They had come to realize what a mess the records were in. From this mass of material, they nevertheless managed to trace fan disk 00385, along with its seven so-called sister disks, to heat K8283.

As the sister disks came in to the Materials and Process Technology Lab at GE, they were subjected to ultrasonic inspection, and it soon became apparent that the disk labeled 00388 was indeed defective. Ultrasound showed the equivalent of a tumor in the flesh of the metal. It was a sick area within the crystalline structure. They called it an "indication," a spot in the metal where sound waves reflected in an unexpected way, indicating that the metal was somehow different at that location. Titanium kept jealous hold of its impurities, and here in 00388, the sister of 00385, was clear evidence of its true nature.

Pure titanium is silver-gray to the naked eye, white as snow under the microscope. The metallurgists call it alpha, the beginning of all the alchemy that will produce flight at unprecedented speed and height. With this special metal—the only metal strong enough and light enough for those spinning wheels—everyone from the towns of Rembrandt and Truesdale could be flown aloft at once, nearly to the edge of space, in a single ark.

James Wildey said, "Ti six-four (titanium with 6 percent aluminum and 4 percent vanadium) is an alloy composed of two phases. Phases are regions in the material with different crystallographic structure." He was talking about the way the atoms are arranged to create the microscopic crystals that make up the metal. At room temperature, for example, titanium crystals have the shape of a hexagon. Pure titanium is made of grains, and the grains are made of those hexagonal crystals. When more than half a percent of another substance is added to the pure metal, the structure of the titanium changes to accommodate the new material. When titanium is melted with aluminum and vanadium and then cooled to room temperature, the alpha (pure titanium) and beta (aluminum with some vanadium) freeze back into their own crystal structures and form interleaved sheets or lamina. Under a microscope, it looks almost like living tissue, a strange weave of fibrous grains, elongated and intertwined. In titanium, "the whole thing just transforms pretty much instantly as the temperature drops," said Wildey, "and this is what the resulting structure is. It freezes in place. And actually that's what gives you some of the strength, because it doesn't want to change. It's locked into place there. Whereas the alpha is a nice, gentle, softer material, and it gives you the toughness, because it can deform a little bit and take the impact, the (transformed) beta gives you the strength, resisting it."

Yet titanium can change its nature entirely. Magnified five hundred times, titanium can look like a bacterial infection in a petri dish. Add a little nitrogen when the titanium is being melted, and it suddenly looks like ice on a winter window. The area is much harder and more brittle than the material should be.

Wildey traveled to Evendale to examine the disk known as 00388. He would much rather have been working on 00385—the disk from Flight 232—but John Clark had yet to find it. (And indeed, Clark, along with the other people who were searching for the disk, never would find it.) So Wildey worked with metallurgists and technicians at GE to cut the sister disk 00388 into pieces to expose the tumor. The team then subjected that metal to nitric and hydrofluoric acid, industrial CAT scan, X-ray and neutron radiation, as well as ammonium bifluoride etching. They put pieces of it in a scanning electron microscope and bombarded it with a beam of electrons in a process known as energy dispersive spectrography, or EDS. In EDS, the electron beam bypasses the outer shells of electrons in the material and hits the inner shells. In that interaction, the atoms give off X-rays, which are high-energy photons. Wildey said, "Each atom will produce X-rays at a very specific energy based on the differences between the energy levels of the various electron shells in the atoms. So it's a pure atomic interaction. It looks at the differences in the electron shells in each atom." By reading the energy level, he could identify the element.

An electron microscope is a formidable instrument, unlike any other manmade object. It is a stainless-steel tower, perhaps a foot in diameter, with many knobs and devices bristling off of it. A thick cable enters the tower at the top. The tower is set in a platform the size of a businessman's desk but made of stainless steel and weighing a great deal to prevent any vibration that could blur an image that's been magnified many thousands of times. (Electron microscopes are often installed in basements, because the concrete floors tend to dampen vibrations.) At the bottom of the tower is a vacuum chamber with thick glass windows, and surrounding the tower are various other instruments aimed at that chamber. The big cable at the top carries twenty thousand volts of electricity into a tungsten filament to produce electrons, which are then accelerated downward in a vacuum through a series of electromagnets. The magnets act as lenses to focus the beam as it travels to the chamber where the specimen waits. The instruments around the chamber collect the X-rays that come off of the specimen under electron bombardment. The room is kept dark except for the displays, which give off a cold blue glow, while tangles of electrical cables snake in every direction from the various devices.

When Wildey's technician activated this suite of instruments and beamed electrons into the heart of the tumor in that metal, right down to the inner electron shells of its atoms, he found something curious indeed. When he read the X-ray signature of the atoms, he found titanium, aluminum, and vanadium, as expected. However, in addition to the strong energy levels from those elements, he saw the energy of the X-rays peter out, dwindle away, to weak uncertain signals. Something else had contaminated the metal, but its signal was not strong enough to read. Wildey had his thoughts about what the material might be, but he was going to have to change his technique if he wanted to be certain of what had caused that tumor.

Ellen Badis, with Aaron freshly delivered into her arms by Bruce Benham, was convinced that the burning plane behind her would explode. She began running down the muddy rows of corn, in her sandals. "The corn was so tall and beautiful," she said. She recalled the soft feel of the damp ground. She broke down weeping again as we talked. "I ran on and ran on, I didn't think I'd ever—oh, my gosh, we ran and ran and—and finally we came to the opening." Then Ellen said with great wonder in her voice, "And there was a tower down there. And a lot of other passengers were congregated. And one man was starting to climb the tower. We didn't know where we were. And I said, 'Here, you want part of my dress to use as a flag?' I had a light-blue dress on and it had been ripped a little. We wanted to let folks know we were out here." The man took a strip of blue cloth from Ellen's dress and began waving it in the hope that someone would take notice. Sam Gochenour, the technician from the FAA, ran over and yelled at him to get down, help was on the way.

As the adrenaline began to wear off, Ellen said, "I had to go pee so bad. It was just the worst." Someone offered to watch Aaron while she went down to a grassy bottom where trees grew, "and I just went down there behind a tree and relieved myself." She returned to the tower and joined the group, and a blue bus eventually came from the Air National Guard. "I just assumed my husband and Eric, my oldest son, were burning, were dead," she said. By the time she and the others were dropped off at the triage area, "I was desperate, looking for my son and Adrienne." She found herself rushing around, clutching her remaining son, "looking at every wounded person, every body. I was just desperate to find them. I didn't care in what condition, I just wanted to find them." While she was peering into the faces of the dead, John Transue rode past in a bus, staring out in horror at the tableau of corpses and body parts and the dissonant image of the mother and child hurrying among them.

As Transue passed by, Ellen peered into the face of a man who was taking his last breath. A United Methodist minister named Duane Churchman, who was volunteering on the scene, saw her. He took her arm and gently pulled her away, saying, "You don't want to do this. Come with me. I will take you somewhere."

Beside herself, she screamed, "But I've got to find them!"

People gathered around to reassure her that her husband and son had probably been taken to the hospital. It meant nothing to her. Her husband and son were dead, and she just wanted to see them one last time. The clergyman took her to the mess hall. "And I was just slowly going into psychological shock," she said. She burst into tears once more as she relived those moments. She recalled people sitting on the floor with blankets, despite the heat of July. "And there was a TV over in the corner," she said. She asked if someone would turn on the television, thinking that she might see Adrienne and Eric. Someone turned it on and Ellen stood watching the jumbo jet explode.

"And then I lost all hope after that," she wept. "I just couldn't believe anyone else could have survived." As she went into shock, paramedics loaded her and Aaron into an ambulance.

Before the Badis family left Hawaii, Adrienne's mother had bought the boys matching T-shirts in shades of blue and turquoise. The shirts bore the smiley face symbol and the words "Don't Worry, Be Happy." Both boys wore those shirts on board the plane. At the hospital, "when the ambulance doors opened, Aaron was handed off first," Ellen said.

Before Aaron's feet even touched the ground, an X-ray technician saw his shirt and made the connection. She approached the ambulance and asked, "Is this Aaron?" Ellen could barely speak through her tears as she recalled what the technician said to her: "They're here, and they're okay."

"The knot that I had in my stomach was so—was just so relieved," Ellen said. "I could just not believe it." Now the technician led Ellen and Aaron into the X-ray department. "And we were reunited, and it was the best feeling we've ever had."

By the time the Badis family reached the dormitory at Briar Cliff College, all the beds were taken. They had to sleep on the floor. Nearly everyone in the area where Adrienne and Eric were seated was killed, the Feeney family from Denver (no relation to Tony) and Cindy Muncey, Ruth Gomez and her ten-year-old son John— it was a bad place to be—yet father and son walked away from the crash virtually unhurt. (When I interviewed her, Ellen still had not learned how Adrienne escaped, because he had never been able to talk about it.)

While Bruce Benham's superficial wounds were being treated at the hospital, a producer from ABC News arrived and asked him if he would appear on a television program called *Nightline*. Benham, Schemmel, and Priest appeared on the show and then spent the night at the house of a local weatherman. No one could sleep. Schemmel stayed up all night making phone calls to try to find Jay Ramsdell. At one point, about 3:00 in the morning, the United crisis line reported that Ramsdell was in the burn unit at St. Luke's. "I called the hospital for a half hour," said Schemmel, "and couldn't get through." When he reached someone at last, he learned that Ramsdell was not at St. Luke's. In fact, Jay Ramsdell lay dead on the field. Television producers recruited the three survivors to appear on another show, *Good Morning, America.* When the show was over, a producer drove them back to the airport so that they could fly home to Denver.

Once the Badis family had returned to their home in the Raleigh-Durham area, "It felt like we had been born again," said Ellen. "We saw things in such a wonderful light now. Everything just felt new, being back in our home again." From then on, the Badis family never let a day go by without expressing their love for one another. "Because," as Ellen put it, "you never knew how quick your life could be cut short."

But the initial euphoria wore off. Ellen began to feel the symptoms. She had difficulty concentrating and developed digestive trouble. She lost her ability to function at work. By 1991 Ellen Badis had quit her job as a nurse, never to return. Ellen developed a whole range of emotional triggers that could set off a panic reaction again, such as low-flying planes or any type of concussion or explosion. "I've got a terrible, terrible startle reflex," she said, "and I have to apologize in the store, if somebody drops something." And of course, she said, "we don't fly."

CHAPTER TWENTY

By the first week in August of 1989, executives at General Electric came under increasing pressure to find the missing fan disk. John Clark was eager to have it too. He knew where it was and felt confident that he would find it. He also had the means at his disposal, he thought, to search as effectively as anyone could. The executives at GE, however, were impatient. They sent out one of their investigators to comb through plat books for the names and addresses of the people who owned the land underneath the path that 1819 Uniform took to Sioux City. GE worked with a local law firm, Mack, Hansen, Gadd, Armstrong, and Schiller, in Storm Lake, to send out about fifteen hundred letters to landowners in Buena Vista County and elsewhere, offering cash rewards to anyone who found parts of the airplane. The farmers in that area thought the whole idea was ridiculous. By mid-August GE had upped the offer of rewards to more than $250,000. The larger segment of fan disk 00385 would fetch $50,000. Individual blades might be worth $1,000 each. But Chuck Eddy, the sheriff of Buena Vista County, admitted that except for people from GE and the NTSB, no one was looking for the missing parts. Steve Lullman, who worked at Mellowdent Hybrids where a big piece of the tail had fallen, expressed the opinion of the local farmers when he said, "I think it's a waste of time."

In the meantime, John Clark had checked and rechecked his bal-

listics calculations and had sent all the revised data to Monty Montgomery in Washington in an effort to refine the trajectories. He
realized, though, that in order to understand how a fan disk would
fall, he would have to take one out and drop it. When I asked how
he did that, Clark laughed and said, "It was pretty crude." United
Airlines offered up two fan disks that had been retired from service.
Clark took one, and as he put it, "We basically just put a strap around
it and slung it up under a Huey, climbed up to altitude, and then just
pickled the load—cut it loose." They timed the fall of the disk from
twenty-five hundred feet and photographed it and observed how it
flew. They didn't need to lift it any higher than that, because, as is
true of any falling body, the forces of gravity and of the air acting on
the disk stabilized fairly quickly.

They carefully marked the spot where it fell to avoid the embar-
rassment of having to search for two titanium fan disks that were
lost in the corn. Then they landed and trudged over to it through
the crops and looked at how it had hit the ground. It had buried
itself about fifteen inches into the soft earth, but it was partly above
ground and plainly visible. In fact, the disk had oriented itself flat
side to the flow of air, dishing out like a paper plate dropped from a
height. Disk 00385 would have tended to drift with the wind. Clark
had to think about how the disk fractured and make some estimates
of what would happen depending on the various ways it might have
come apart. The disk he used in the test had no blades, but in all likelihood, fan disk 00385 tore away from the engine with quite a few
blades still attached. That could produce drag that might turn the
disk edge-on toward the earth and cause it to drop more directly
down instead of drifting. His team also studied how the disk had
buried itself in the soft loam, to develop an idea of what they ought
to be looking for. Clark's team concluded that the broken fan disk
ought to be visible from a low-flying helicopter—if the observers
were lucky and happened to see the ground instead of corn.

John Moehring from GE coordinated with the NTSB, Lawrence
Harrington, and others to get the number two engine documented
and then lifted onto a lowboy tractor trailer for transport. The driver

of the semi left on Wednesday, August 2, for an all-night run to Evendale, arriving there at about 3:00 a.m. on Thursday. The engine went into a high-security room at General Electric known as Cell 10. "There are guards at the door," Moehring said later. It was a cell where engines were tested for "a black program," such as the B-2 bomber. The engineers hoped that even without fan disk 00385, a close examination of what remained of the number two engine would yield a more precise picture of how the disk had burst. Moehring had appointed Christopher Glynn to head the team that would try to prove that the fan disk itself had initiated the sequence of events that led to the crash. Glynn in turn assigned each of the experts he had recruited to examine a portion of the engine. "We asked those people," Glynn said, "to go off, look at the hardware, map the damage, try to put the pieces back together, and basically arrive at a time line where we could say, 'This happened first, this happened second, this happened third,' and try to deduce the correct sequence."

Meanwhile, back at the Sioux City airport, John Clark had been offered the use of the latest high-tech spy planes from the military to see if those planes could find the missing disk. Each of the two Spanish CASA C-212 Aviocar aircraft had a top-secret suite of sensors that included such devices as forward-looking infrared radar and infrared line scanner, which were meant to be used in guerrilla warfare in the jungle. Each plane had three gimbal-mounted cameras with lenses of different focal lengths. Known as the Grisly Hunter program, the crew and its equipment arrived in Iowa with a telemetry van that raced up to the high bluffs for line-of-sight mission control and for the monitoring and acquiring of data in real time. Clark took one of the fan disks that United had given him and had it placed in a cornfield so that the Grisly Hunters could fly over it and see what it looked like and calibrate their equipment. In fact, when they knew where to look, they could easily see the fan disk. Now they would try to find one whose location they did not know beforehand.

The Grisly Hunter pilots flew at night. Strobe lights were set up in the corn, flashing eerily across the tassels and illuminating the blowing stalks. The silhouetted forms of the teams on the ground made throbbing shadows as the strobes fired off. While the Grisly Hunters flew one path, the ground crew moved the strobes 250 feet over, and the planes flew the next line. The two aircraft flew back and forth going north and south, then flew more passes going east and west. For five nights, the aircraft searched in a grid pattern over sections seven and eight of Scott Township and over all the sections surrounding those two. The Grisly Hunters also made video records and created grid maps of the area. Since Clark's team was going to search on foot on the ground for anything the spy planes detected, the experts in the spy van could work up those locations at night and have them ready in the morning. Then Clark's group would spend the day walking up and down through the fields. At the end of the day, they would bring their data to the conference room at the convention center to discuss what they had accomplished. As Clark studied that mass of data at one of their meetings, he remarked to the group, "The signature we're looking for off of that fan disk is remarkably like a pig feeder." Years later he commented, "And boy, there were a lot of pig feeders in Iowa."

Although they flew right over the fan disk, the high-tech equipment missed it. Clark was understandably frustrated. He knew where the disk was with a fair degree of accuracy. Lighter debris drifted with the wind more than heavy debris did, so he could see the pattern in the pieces that had already been retrieved from the fields. And the line made by the lighter debris would invariably point to the spot where the heavy debris was to be found. This was the same method that had been used to find the *Titanic* on the bottom of the Atlantic Ocean in 1985.

Clark's team would go back to their motel, exhausted at the end of a long hot day, and see the Grisly Hunter pilots sitting out by the pool drinking iced tea, getting ready for their night flights. Walking the fields, Clark's team found about fifteen objects sighted by the planes, none being parts of 1819 Uniform. They searched and searched and failed to find many of the other targets that the Grisly Hunters turned up; the grid maps weren't precise enough. In time,

Clark gave up and surrendered the videotapes to a private company for review. But all the effort and the untold sums of money yielded nothing.

By that time, Glynn had worked with his group at General Electric to tear down the number two engine. They had puzzled over the witness marks—the scratches and smears and tears—and saw what appeared to be conflicting evidence. "We had a significant penetration of that containment ring," he said. "But then approximately 180 degrees away from that, we had a different sort of a separation, not due to penetration. It was just an overload kind of a separation. We had great difficulty in the early going in understanding what that could have been produced by." Moreover, Glynn and his team had studied the driveshaft that had been torn asunder. "That joint is a very strong joint. It has about a half million pounds of clamp, and yet we had failed these bolts." A tremendous amount of energy would have been needed to create the kind of damage they saw.

They were ultimately able to make a successful analysis through techniques ranging from the simplest to the most sophisticated. On the simple end of the scale, a moving part would leave an impression on a stationary part. They put the parts together where they saw damage, and if the parts fit like the pieces of a jigsaw puzzle, they could be pretty certain that one part had hit the other and left that imprint. To back that up, electron microscopy revealed traces of the metal that the moving part had left on the stationary part. (All this time, another team of experts at the NTSB labs in Washington was conducting a similar analysis of other parts that were not from the engine itself, such as the stainless-steel tubing from the hydraulic systems.)

Glynn's team, working on the number two engine, conducted its work at GE but with members of the NTSB present and participating. His group would meet each morning to discuss and debate the various theories, comparing them with the physical evidence from the previous days' work. During the afternoons—and often long into the night—Glynn's engineers "would go back and try to perform fundamental calculations to see if the velocities, masses, loads that separate pieces were in reasonable agreement with the kind of damage that we saw." They performed their calculations based on the idea that momentum is conserved. Glynn's team was able to estimate the approximate size and speed of the two main fragments of the missing disk. They were able to read witness marks that showed that one segment still had fan blades attached. In addition, by knowing the momentum of the spinning fan and calculating the forces needed to inflict the kind of damage they saw, they realized, as Glynn put it, "that the mass times the velocity of the small piece should equate in the early going to the mass times velocity of the large piece, and that the angular momentum of the system should be conserved as well." Their numbers compared favorably with the original momentum of the intact disk spinning in cruise flight. Glynn's team, working with GE engineers, was able to tell, step by step, where each piece of bearing, blade, or structure had gone and at what speed. The entire event took five to six milliseconds, far less than the blink of an eye.

As Glynn's team fed this new information to John Clark, he made new ballistic calculations and passed them to Monty Montgomery in Washington for another run through the computer. Clark drew a new map of where those two pieces of fan disk 00385 ought to be. And although everyone was still unable to find them, they were pretty much where he said they should be. By then it was September, and he had retuned to Washington to write his first report on the search. The harvest began September 11.

When Martha Conant first came out of the broken tail of the aircraft, she believed that she was the only passenger left alive. She was in such a high state of alarm that she didn't even notice when John Hatch and Susan and Dave Randa dropped from above. She saw nothing but her longed-for earth, and then she ran away. When a stranger stopped her, she turned and looked around at last. She saw people streaming toward her. She saw the couple who had been seated to her right, Marilyn and Karl Walter. "He had some burns on his hands," she recalled. Susan White had shouted at him when he was somehow stuck: "Wiggle, wiggle, wiggle!"

Conant's thoughts and perceptions were in disarray. She saw Dave and Susan Randa sitting on a lighted sign and was amazed that they were alive. The boy no longer had his Cubs baseball cap. She saw John Hatch. Except for a few scratches on her leg, Conant was uninjured. People were wandering with uncertain looks on their faces. A number of them were thinking, *Am I in heaven?* Conant did not see Yisroel Brownstein or the businessman who sat next to him. People continued to stumble out of the corn, while rescuers came out to meet them. Someone helped her into a car. She was taken to a hospital, where a doctor cleaned up her minor cuts. "And then I was just kind of left to my own devices." The images flowed past her, and the scenes in which she found herself changed as if in a dream, with no logical transitions. She found herself in a room where food had been laid out on tables. A television on the wall kept playing footage of the crash.

Conant happened to strike up a conversation with Sylvia Tsao, a scientist from Albuquerque whose two-year-old son Evan had been wrenched out of her grasp during the crash. Sylvia had seen him flying through the air. She still had not found him. Hearing this, Conant began to understand what had happened. "I just felt so helpless," she said. "I mean, there I was with just a scratch, and there were people with just horrendous injuries and losses."

A social worker approached her and said, "God still has work for you to do."

"I didn't want to hear that," Conant said. She found it insulting, as many people did in the aftermath.

She waited, still in shock, still not completely sure whether or not she'd been through that surreal series of events. Late that night, United Airlines put her on a plane to Chicago. Rod Vetter was on board, his neck in a brace. John Hatch, who had tried to comfort Dave Randa, was sitting next to Vetter, "in a daze," as he put it. "It was a terrible flight because it was stormy," Hatch said. "I'd say we held hands," he said with a laugh, "but we didn't. We consoled each other. He was really a good guy."

Conant stayed overnight in a hotel, hallucinating in dreamtime, and flew back to Denver from Chicago in the morning. Time, it seemed, had come unmoored from real events. Her husband picked her up and took her home, and she stood in her house, looking around at the strangeness of her own environment and feeling as if it hadn't really happened, that monumental thing that had taken so many dozens of lives only the day before. Yet that same event, that great invisible force, had returned her unharmed to the earth as she had requested: *God, if you let me out of this alive, I'll clean up my act.* In her mind, that very God had blown away the entire airplane from right in front of her in a storm of biblical proportions and had placed her feet carefully, gently, onto the wet green earth.

She tried to adjust over the weekend. She was back at work Monday, telling her story to those who asked, "again and again and again and again. And every time I tell it, there's that sense that it wasn't really me."

She experienced no nightmares. When she went for counseling, the psychologist asked her what her worst fear had been before the crash. Conant said it was a fear of being in a car, heading into a brick wall, and knowing that she was going to die.

"Well," said the counselor, "then you've faced your worst fear. You have nothing more to fear."

"She was right," Conant said. "That was very helpful. I looked death in the eye and walked away." At that point Conant laughed and corrected herself: "Ran away."

She had put her purse and briefcase under Kari Milford's seat, which had been partly ripped out of its mounts. When Kari's seat bent to the right, Conant's purse and briefcase flew out onto the runway. Running across the field, she had lost one shoe. United Airlines eventually sent her suitcase and her purse back to her. "The suitcase was in fine condition, my purse was pretty beat up." But, she said, "I just got rid of them. They smelled of jet fuel, and jet fuel is a trigger for me." Even today, if she smells kerosene, she relives the crash, the people ahead of her being torn asunder, the entire scene. She also developed a fear of slippery roads when she experiences that wallowing feeling that she identified with the forty-four minutes before the crash.

A month after the crash, she made the trip to Philadelphia that she had been trying to make on July 19. Her youngest son Patrick rode along to keep her company. United seated them in first class and gave them "the royal treatment," but she was "scared to death," she said. "Scared to death." After that trip, she asked to be moved into a job that required less travel. And she remembered the bargain she had made with God. She began to change her ways. She described the change as "like an ocean liner turning. It doesn't turn on a dime. But I started making changes in my life. And I wanted deeper connections with people. My husband, my children, my friends. And I had not been that kind of person. I had been more private and more self-contained." As she described the transformation she experienced, her voice grew melancholy and dropped to a hoarse whisper. A long groan came out of her as, "Ohhhh, gosh." She heaved a weary sigh. The pauses between her words stretched out as she gathered the strength to speak. "I, um, started doing a little exploration of spirituality."

I asked her if she felt that the crash had changed her life for the worse, and she said, "No, no. It wasn't a *good* thing. It's not anything I would wish on anybody. For me, however, I've made it a good thing. I struggled for the longest time with, Why did I survive? And another person from Fort Collins didn't survive, and his widow, I've heard, committed suicide. A couple from Greely were very badly injured." Her survivor guilt "hit as soon as I was running and realized I was the only person on the field at that time, and it persisted for a *long* time. Until I realized that I was asking myself the wrong question. I was asking myself, Why me?" She gradually realized that she could ask a different question: What do I do as a result of having had that experience? "That was the big shift: What now?" She became almost breathless as she tried to explain the changes she experienced once she had shifted from "Why me?" to "What now?"

Her eldest son Rich has a PhD in botany and does research into global warming. His wife Beth gave birth to a healthy girl and boy. They live nearby. Her middle son Rob earned a PhD in electrical engineering, married Sarah in 2006, and they also have a girl and boy. "And I introduced them," Conant said with pride. "I'm very pleased about that." Her youngest, Patrick, and his wife Brittany also have a girl and boy and live nearby. "I'm incredibly fortunate," she said. Her marriage came back together and grew to be "very intimate and connected. I have wonderful relationships with my sons, my daughters-in-law, my grandchildren. I'm just incredibly fortunate."

Conant retired from Hewlett-Packard in 1998 and now works at her church—another big change. The crash in effect engaged her in a struggle and sent her on a journey that led to family and to God.

Within two weeks after the crash, most of the NTSB investigators had completed their work and returned home to write their reports. During that time, Colonel Swanstrom, along with Lawrence Harrington, engaged the Air National Guard members under their command to clean up the snowstorm of paper that had inundated the field. (Many other organizations joined the 185th in the operation, including the Iowa Public Service Company and the 134th Infantry of the Iowa Army National Guard.) The work was done by hand by these ordinary men and women wearing civilian clothes, walking back and forth over the ground, carrying white plastic garbage bags and bending down to pick up paper, over and over again, all day long, until their backs ached and their minds cleared. They worked around pieces of the airplane that still lay on the field. They worked around the pink spray-painted numbers that showed where bodies had been, the stains of blood, and the looping scars where banks of seats had skidded along like sleds from an amusement park ride gone amok. "It took us ten days to get the last piece of paper picked up off of the field," Swanstrom said. One of the people who helped with the cleanup told of finding little bottles of liquor all over the field. He said several people drank them on the spot. In fact, Jan Brown showed me two that she had picked up and kept. One had no cap. The seal on the other one had been broken, the contents removed, and the cap replaced.

Swanstrom's superiors wanted to return the Air Guard men and women to their regular jobs and let civilians clean up the airfield, but Swanstrom prevailed upon them to let everyone be part of the effort. He felt that by allowing his people to participate, they could get a feeling of completing the job they had begun under such trying circumstances. He was influenced by studies of post-traumatic stress that were being published at the time. In asking people such as Jim Walker to go out onto the field and deal with the dead, the mutilated, the severely injured, Swanstrom had asked them to make a sacrifice, to take a risk with their own emotional health. In allowing them to walk that ground again, purifying it, he felt that he could in some small measure help them to begin the process of healing. Each afternoon when the cleanup operation was over for the day, all the volunteers would gather on the field where a sound system had been set up, and someone would make a presentation. A psychological counselor might talk. Clapper or another chaplain might say a prayer. Swanstrom said that one of the lasting effects of the crash was to help people understand that it was natural to have strong emotional reactions to such events.

"One morning I'm sitting on the throne at home and I'm reading the morning paper," he said. "For some reason, it just hit me. I mean, I was real tired. I hadn't had much sleep. And I just broke down and cried like a baby." Swanstrom, a tall, athletic officer, commander of one thousand, told that story to his people, and they were grateful to know that their own emotional reactions were normal. "They didn't have to be macho about this thing."

At the time of the cleanup, Harrington was trying to decide how to handle the refrigerated trucks they had used to store the dead. "Those were road reefers that hauled beef and everything else in 'em like the day before." And now, he said, "there could be body juices there and stuff." He called the Department of Agriculture to ask for advice, but in fact, Harrington had been a federal inspector before he went into the service, and the department told him that he was as qualified as anyone to make a decision. "So I made sure they got on the wash rack there and they cleaned them out with disinfectant and everything and then took 'em over to a truck place and made 'em clean 'em all again. And I told everybody exactly what we did. Because you couldn't throw those trailers away. I let everybody see that they're cleanin' 'em out on the wash rack where we washed airplanes."

While Swanstrom and his people were cleaning up the field and the morgue operation, Gregory Phillips, the chairman of the Systems Group at the NTSB, worked in a hangar alongside Frank Hilldrup, head of the Structures Group, to reconstruct the tail of 1819 Uniform. Hilldrup and Laura Levy had meticulously recorded all the damage to the airplane and mapped the location of all the parts in painstaking detail. With that documentation in hand, all the fragments of the tail were brought to a hangar. The tail itself, where Susan White had sat in her jump seat, was too tall for the hangar. Mechanics cut off the top of the vertical stabilizer so the tail would fit. Then Robert MacIntosh's team used cables to connect the major section of the tail to the floor and ceiling and built a wooden scaffolding to hold pieces of the horizontal stabilizer at the correct angle for cruise flight. They built a wooden disk two feet in diameter, as John Moehring put it, "to simulate not the disk, but the center of mass of any fragments coming off the disk in the bore-to-rim split." Once the tail had been reconstructed, the team strung yellow ropes from the wooden disk to the horizontal stabilizer to show the trajectory of each piece of shrapnel. The starboard side suffered forty punctures, while the port side sustained thirty-eight. But that tail provided another set of data points, positive evidence in the conclusion that they would draw about how 1819 Uniform met its end.

In the meantime, the parts gathered by Gregory Phillips's on-site team had arrived at the NTSB labs in Washington. While Christopher Glynn's team was analyzing the number two engine at GE, Jim Wildey's crew of metallurgists began taking a closer look at pieces of the stainless-steel hydraulic tubing that had been found inside the tail, along the path of the wrecked airplane, and in the corn and bean fields between Rembrandt and Truesdale. The tubes had been bent, torn, punctured, and cut by something. And they bore obvious smear marks, evidence of what had happened. Long before then and long before the tail was reconstructed, everyone knew, at least at a gut level, what had happened up there at thirteen seconds after 3:16 p.m. on July 19, 1989, at thirty-seven thousand feet. You didn't need to be an NTSB investigator to figure it out. In fact, by the morning after the crash, Bob Hager on *The Today Show* had the scenario reasonably correct.

After the dead had been removed from the field, Ed Porter, a photographer for the *Sioux City Journal*, was allowed to photograph the wreckage. When MacIntosh and Lopatkiewicz led him to the tail before it had been moved to a hangar, Porter could see what had happened. He described it in an article that appeared in the paper on Saturday, July 22.

> The duct work for that engine shows scars where the engine rotar [*sic*] blades apparently sliced through it. And the horizontal stabilizer, located near where the engine should be, is riddled with holes from blade fragments.
>
> Inside the horizontal stabilizer, you can see hydraulic lines that looked like they had been severed while the plane was still in the air. Other lines were bent like straw, preventing anything from being able to flow through.

Porter wasn't alone in drawing those conclusions. The day after the crash, the *Omaha World-Herald* newspaper said, "FAA officials said the hydraulic failure in the spectacular crash Wednesday may have been triggered by an uncontained failure in the tail-section engine of the three-engine plane." Although the NTSB wouldn't release its own conclusions for more than fifteen months, Porter had accurately summed up what happened: Engine blew up. Shrapnel flew out and cut the hydraulic lines. The plane was left with no steering. End of story, it would seem.

But it wasn't the end of the story. Important questions remained. For example, did the investigators know with absolute certainty that fragments of the missing fan disk or its blades had cut the hydraulics? Wildey knew of a way to prove that. A metallurgist in his group, Joe Epperson, prepared specimens from the bent and twisted stainless-steel tubes. To begin with, Epperson could see with unaided eyes the areas he was most interested in viewing in the scanning electron microscope. Those areas showed the smears of a different color from the base metal—the 300-type stainless steel that the tubes were made of. It was Epperson's job to identify what caused the smears, which were the result of what's known as adiabatic heating. One part is moving so fast, with so much energy, that when it hits something, the parts heat up enough to become soft. One part leaves a smear on the other.

Epperson cut the areas of interest from the tubes with a saw and mounted the pieces for viewing in the electron microscope. One of the tubes was bent, and when he unbent it to examine it, it broke. He bombarded the smears with a high-powered beam of electrons, probing down to the inner electron shells of whatever atoms were there. In the darkened room, in the bluish white glow of the screen, various signature energy levels of X-rays came back showing the iron and chromium and nickel of the stainless steel. But above them all, shooting almost off the chart, came another tall spike of energy that was unmistakable: titanium.

Now they could fully understand one of the deep flaws in the design of the DC-10. To begin with, when the titanium fan disk exploded, it blew off its own hydraulic pumps, eliminating the number two hydraulic system. Then parts made of titanium scattered outward, cutting through the stainless-steel lines for hydraulic systems one and three. The screaming pumps on engines one and three, which Jan Murray described hearing, then poured all of the hydraulic fluid overboard, leaving the plane with no steering. That's what Captain D. B. Robinson of the Air Line Pilots Association meant when he wrote, "This accident was never supposed to have happened." He said the fact that a DC-10 could not fly without hydraulic fluid or that the hydraulic systems were not adequately protected constituted "a design flaw." And "the accident history demonstrates that hydraulic system integrity cannot be assured." In the 1970s a number of airline captains stepped down from flying the DC-10 and took pay cuts for this very reason.

By the time John Transue reached the Air National Guard mess hall, he found himself with a young German man in his twenties, babbling and laughing maniacally. "We were so happy to be alive and so high on adrenaline that we were laughing and chatting and just giddy." He had never felt so good in his life, Transue said.

A psychologist who had been called in to counsel survivors approached the pair and said, "You know, you're not going to feel like this later."

"And the German and I just looked at each other like we were Superman and this guy was crazy," Transue later said.

After a time, Transue was taken to the hospital. A doctor stapled his scalp closed where a flying object had knocked him senseless. The nurses cleaned up the cuts on his hands. They treated the minor burn on his leg where the fireball had burned through his woolen sock. During the hours since the crash, he had noticed that his back was hurting more and more, but an X-ray revealed nothing broken. He boarded the late-night flight to Chicago with Martha Conant, Rod Vetter, John Hatch, and others. When he reached his hotel in the early hours of the morning, he called his brother, who was a therapist at a hospital in Alaska. "I was so happy to be alive that I was laughing on the phone and joking around with him."

His brother listened for a while and then said, "You're having an adrenaline rush now. But within twenty-four hours, it's probably going to wear off."

Transue said, "Maybe, but I feel great right now."

He was at last reunited with his family at his parents' home outside of Milwaukee, but the press wouldn't leave him alone. Neither could he sleep. He told his wife Jacqueline, "Let's get the hell out of here and drive back to Colorado." Once they were on the road, peace descended at last. They drove west into the setting sun and watched it burn low on the horizon. Jacqueline was at the wheel. John sat in the front seat beside her. Their two little girls, Michelle and Lindsey, were snug in the back. As the family passed the Sioux City exit on the highway, Transue felt chills at the thought of the people, both living and dead, who remained there from the crash. Jacqueline drove late into the night, and Transue dozed at last, as the miles reeled out beneath the singing tires. Then something changed. "It was probably eleven or twelve at night," he said. "And that's when the adrenaline wore off. I woke up screaming." Transue had walked through Armageddon to become a berserker for fifty-six hours. And now he'd come back to earth at last. "I was having a nightmare that I was flying through the darkness and that my chest had been ripped open and I was going to hit a wall, and I woke up screaming. That's when the nightmares, the flashbacks, and all the bad stuff started happening."

He tried to get on with his life. He had to travel for work, yet when he boarded an airplane, he would look at the other passengers and see corpses, "sometimes decomposing corpses. I'd look out the window and see corpses down on the ground." He began taking tranquilizers when he had to fly, and that afforded him some relief. "But then I'd be driving around town, and I'd stop at a red light, and my car would fill up with fire. I'd have to sit there and say, 'You're not on fire. You're not back in the crash.' "

In those early days at home in Colorado, he would drive his car as fast as he could up the switchback mountain roads, getting closer and closer to the edge. Like Tony Feeney and Yisroel Brownstein, he was trying to re-create that euphoric adrenaline high that he experienced immediately after the crash. He took his motorcycle up in the hills and rode it in the same death-defying way, but he could never recapture that feeling. Gradually the pain in his back drove him inside himself. Between the nightmares, the flashbacks, and the constant pain, "I thought about the crash constantly. And I thought about suicide all the time too."

Although his flashbacks and nightmares stopped after about two years (a fairly normal outcome for post-traumatic stress) the pain from his injured back only grew worse. The chronic pain almost ruined his marriage and set back the development of his relationship with his children, he said. "I just came home from work, and I lay on a heating pad all night." He had been an avid skier. He missed riding his motorcycle. "I gave up my backpacking friends and my cross-country skiing friends." He liked bow hunting, and he lost contact with the hunters he had known. The pain isolated him from society and made it difficult for him to concentrate at work. He suffered through the untreated pain for eight years before admitting to his doctor that he was seriously considering killing himself.

"I said I really didn't want to kill myself with my mother being alive and my kids little, but I wasn't going to live like this. I'm at the end." His doctor relented and prescribed him a powerful opiate called OxyContin. At last Transue was able to experience relief for about ten hours a day. "And that's when I finally stopped thinking about it constantly," he said. "That was a pretty awful eight years." More than two decades after the crash, I asked him what his life was like now. "I'd say it's terrible."

One day at the airport he ran into Jan Brown coming off of a flight. She asked how he was doing, and he told her that he couldn't fly on DC-10s. If he even looked at one, it precipitated an attack of anxiety. Brown led Transue to a gate and told the agent at the podium that she and Transue had been on Flight 232. The agent nodded. Jan punched her security code into the locked door. She took Transue down a deserted Jetway. As they entered the cabin, he smelled the familiar smells and saw the familiar sights and realized that he was in a DC-10.

"See?" she said. "Easy."

Years later Brown said, "I just thought that this would have some meaning, even if he never flew on a DC-10 again. It might bring some healing."

They went to the seat where Transue had sat on United Flight 232, next to Rod Vetter and Margo Crain, not far from Jan Brown's jump seat at the 2-Left exit. They stood talking softly for a time. When the crew came on board for the next flight, Brown and Transue quietly left the plane.

On one other occasion, Transue saw Brown coming out of a Jetway with five or six flight attendants. Brown had been telling her crew about how Transue rescued her. And as if she had conjured him, he appeared. She took his arm and introduced him, beaming and saying, "This is my savior. This is the guy who saved my life." Brown believes that if Transue hadn't unbuckled her harness, she most likely would have died.

For Brown, the most difficult part of coming home after the crash was the knowledge that "the other Jan Brown" and her daughter Kimberly were dead and might have lived if only she had moved them to row 9. Of course, she had no way of knowing where the safest place in the cabin would be during the crash, but she felt guilty nonetheless. She had a few dreams about the crash. In one, she found herself once again in "the darkness that I woke up to" when the plane came to rest. "Every morning when I woke up, I cried." She dreamed of Janice standing beside her in a white sun dress with appliqués on it. And for a moment she could be happy again. Then she would wake and remember that Janice and Kimberly were dead. Jackhammers on the street sent her into flashbacks. "Initially, you think, well, this'll be over in six months and we'll get back to normal. And then at six months it was like: Well, maybe a year. And then you get to a year. And it was never over at work."

Brown gave her work an honest try. "Three months after the crash, I went back to work," she said. She continued to fly, but the crash had taken its toll. Her privacy was gone because everyone wanted to hear the story of United Flight 232. And because of what she now knew about small children on airliners, she began to have trouble with parents who brought babies on board without proper protection. On more than one occasion, she tried to get a parent to put a child in a seatbelt rather than hold him. And on more than one occasion, parents took offense, as if Brown had questioned their competence. Some lodged complaints against her. "It was unpleasant when I'm wanting to help make a child safe, which is my job, and they're taking it as criticism of their mothering." Brown gradually realized that she had been given an impossible job: to keep all passengers safe. Yet she could never protect one class of passengers: babies.

In 1998 she retired earlier than she might otherwise have done and began to devote her energies to establishing a requirement that children be given equal protection under the law. As she departed United Airlines, she had nothing but praise for her colleagues. "I could never say enough to acknowledge the goodness and support of my peers. My flying partners really tried to help me. My superiors were wonderful." Yet at the time of this writing, despite her efforts, the law has not been changed. In response to repeated pleas from the NTSB to protect babies, J. Randolph Babbitt, the administrator of the FAA at the time, wrote,

> The FAA believes that requiring the use of CRS [child restraint seats], which would require all families traveling with children under 2 years of age to purchase tickets for those children, would significantly raise the net price of travel for those families. As a result, such price increases would divert some family travel from the air transportation system to the highway system. Consequently, entire families would be subject to far higher fatality rates, which would produce a net increase in overall transportation fatalities. . . . I believe the FAA has effectively addressed this recommendation and I consider our actions complete.

CHAPTER
TWENTY-ONE

The harvest in Buena Vista County began on an overcast day in September when the wind made the temperature feel like 38 degrees at eight o'clock in the morning. The sun broke through around noon, but then clouds moved in once again, and the temperature climbed to nearly 60 degrees by late afternoon. At that time of year the sun didn't go down until almost eight o'clock in the evening, so the work could proceed apace, even with the occasional drizzling rain that blew across the fields in shifting layers of spectral mist. And yet by the end of the month, despite losing half an hour of daylight, the temperature soared to almost 83 degrees at midday under a cloudless sky. On those days, the sky was so blue that it reminded many people of the day in July when 1819 Uniform came plunging to earth and changed so many lives.

And indeed, as the harvest proceeded, the office of Chuck Eddy, the sheriff of Buena Vista County, had "taken on the look of an airplane salvage yard," as Bill Zahren put it in the *Sioux City Journal*. Among the parts found since the crash were shredded aluminum scraps of the horizontal stabilizer, a four-foot section of the engine's outer casing, parts of the cowling that had surrounded the missing fan disk, booster blades from the compressor stages of the engine, hydraulic lines—and enticingly, blades that had been installed on 00385, the missing fan disk. One young Iowa farm boy found an intact first-stage fan blade that was probably worth $1,000 in reward money. Instead of turning it in, he brought it to school for show-and-tell. On Tuesday, October 10, at around 3:30 in the afternoon, Janice Sorenson, fifty-eight, was running her combine through a field, harvesting corn near her farmhouse north of Alta, Iowa. Her family had been working that same 440-acre plot of ground since the late 1800s. The day was cool and pleasant, with clear skies and low humidity, and the workday had been slipping by uneventfully. Then she found that her combine wouldn't move forward. "I felt resistance on the right-hand side, and it felt like something was stopping me. I backed up the combine and saw the fan blades sticking out of the ground. After I got out of the combine and got closer, I was really in shock." She had no doubt about what it was. General Electric had stationed an investigator named Jerome Clark (no relation to John C.) in Buena Vista County, and he had aggressively promoted the cash rewards and circulated photographs of the missing pieces. In its fall from thirty-seven thousand feet the fan disk dished out and fell flat side to the earth, as John Clark had predicted it would. It was heavy, and it was going fast. When it hit the mud, it partially buried itself.

Janice Sorenson drove her combine the quarter mile to her home and called the sheriff's office. Sheriff Eddy was in Des Moines. He left as soon as he received word that a piece of the disk had been found. He knew that no state trooper would try to stop him in his sheriff's prowler, so he let it run wide open. When Eddy arrived at the Sorensons' farm, "[The disk] was still there in the ground," he said. "There was just about—I wouldn't even say six inches of it sticking out of the ground. It was kind of spinning as it came down and just buried itself—threw up the dirt, and the dirt come right back down on top of it, and you couldn't hardly see it."

The disk was a dazzling silver as it lay in the cut-corn stubble. The blades were bent and torn and some were missing. Janice's husband Dale helped to dig the disk out with a shovel. He drove his tractor over to the spot. He wrapped rags around the disk to avoid scratching it and put a chain through the bore. Then he lifted it with the bucket of his tractor and drove it to his turkey shed, where running hot water was available. With the disk hanging from the loader, Dale Sorenson sprayed off the mud with a hose. And even in its beat-up condition, it was, indeed, a beautiful object with its gleaming silver blades. In the bucolic farmland scene, it had the look of something that had traveled light years across the universe, a gift from an alien race in another galaxy.

As soon as Jerome Clark phoned General Electric, John Moehring called for a Lear jet to fly him to Iowa. The 406-pound piece of the fan, including disk and blades, was loaded onto that plane and rushed to Cincinnati, where by Wednesday night it was put under black security in Cell 10. Some of the old-timers at GE were able to take a look at it, and they knew what they were seeing. James Wildey, the senior metallurgist at NTSB, was chosen to lead the metallurgy group, including several experts from GE, one from United, along with a representative from the FAA. When he arrived at GE in the morning, Wildey walked into Cell 10 and saw the fan disk sitting on a skid on the floor. He walked up to it and peered at the fractured surface where about a third of the disk was missing. Already he could read any number of tales that the disk had to tell. For example, the number ten fan blade with all its fittings had been found at the Sioux City airport with its dovetail intact. That meant that as the disk cracked, the split had propagated right through the dovetail slot holding that blade. He had already seen the containment ring with seven evenly spaced witness marks showing where the fan blades hit. He guessed that those marks were made by the blades attached to the smaller piece of the fan disk, which was still missing. But most importantly, he read the cracked surface as only a trained metallurgist could.

"You could see that there was a brittle fracture region," said Wildey, "which is typical of a fatigue crack. And that's mainly what was visible on the fracture surface . . . the presence of a large fatigue crack that reached a critical size and broke through the disk. So that part was relatively straightforward. There was a preexisting crack in the disk, and then questions started to pop up: Well, why wasn't this crack found? When did they have to inspect it?"

To get answers to those questions, Wildey and his team would ultimately have to destroy the very evidence that would prove their case. "We could see that there was a chipped-out region, a cavity at the bore surface." The chipped-out region, the pit, was on the inside surface of the hole, or bore, in the center of the disk. The pit, or cavity, was measured by General Electric and found to be "0.86 inch aft from the forward bore face. . . . The dimensions were 0.015 inch radial depth, 0.055 inch axial and at least 0.030 inch in the circumferential direction of the bore," according to GE's own account. Although Wildey could see that the disk had cracked from the pit outward toward the fan blades, "at the time when we were first looking at it we didn't know what exactly that meant."

If the smaller third of the fan disk were found in a cornfield and if it contained more information, Wildey would be grateful. But it might never be found. What they had in hand might be all the information they ever received. Consequently, in testing, "you are very conservative," said Wildey. "You try to get as much information as possible before you start doing destructive testing." Destructive testing would ultimately involve grinding through the metal of that pit to find out what material was in there and why the pit existed where there should have been smooth and unblemished titanium alloy.

The first job was to get the fan disk into the lab and clean it. Even though Dale Sorenson had hosed it off, even though it looked clean to the naked eye, it had been in service for almost two decades, and then it had been sitting out in the mud and the rain for more than two months as helicopters and high-tech spy planes flew overhead and searchers tramped past it. Wildey wanted to look right into the heart of the metal. He did not want to be inadvertently looking at grease and mud or any stray organic material when he should have been looking at titanium or at whatever substance had made that metal fail. The first step was to use a brand new toothbrush designed for cleaning false teeth. Those toothbrushes can be dissolved by acetone, so the technician used soap and water and methanol to clean the crack, blowing the alcohol off with compressed air so that it didn't evaporate and leave stains.

On Thursday, October 12, 1989, while Wildey's team was working on the disk at the Evendale facility, Harold Halverson was disking a field of cut corn in Buena Vista County, running his tractor behind the combine that his son Allen was driving about half a mile east of where Janice Sorenson found the larger piece of 00385. It was about three o'clock in the afternoon, a sunny day with temperatures in the mid-70s. "The disk bounced," said Allen, and his father stopped his tractor and stepped down onto the corn stubble. He slowly walked back to look. Before nightfall, the missing third of the fan disk was in the back of Jerome Clark's station wagon. That same day General Electric delivered a check to Janice Sorenson for $116,000 for the larger piece of 00385 and the many parts and blades attached to it. You could have knocked her over with a feather.

The GE Lear jet flew out again, picked up the second piece of the disk, and flew it back, where it joined its mate in Cell 10. On October 16, it was sealed into a protective plastic bag and set aside untouched. Later that month, when asked under oath if the rewards program reached "a successful conclusion," William Thompson said, "Yes, it did."

But GE was not yet through with the search. By Friday, the company had organized more than a hundred people from metal detector clubs in Iowa, Nebraska, Minnesota, and Missouri. As Sheriff Eddy said, they "searched some fields for us." Mick Erickson from Lincoln, Nebraska, found a bit of a fan blade. A few other bits of 1819 Uniform were found, but for the most part, said Eddy, "they found old harness buckles from back when they were plowing with horses, wrenches, nuts, bolts, and everything for machinery, screwdrivers, and all kinds of stuff out there." On that farmland that had been worked for 150 years, they also found a jack knife, square nails, coins, a corn husking peg, and the bells from a genuine old-fashioned horse-drawn sleigh.

Employees from United Airlines took Susan White and Georgeann del Castillo to a dormitory at Briar Cliff College and sequestered them in a room. "I wanted to be out," White said. "I wanted to be amongst everyone. [But] United supervisors wouldn't allow us to mingle with the passengers. The only interaction we had with them was in the bathroom area." White had intimately bonded with her passengers. She had Cynthia Muncey's tears on her blouse, her sweat on her skin. White wondered where Cindy was now. The pathology report would list no injuries. It would say only, "Smoke inhalation (blood CO saturation 30%)." She had no idea what had become of Cinnamon, whose papers had been in her pocket. White had come all this way, and now she needed to complete her emotional journey with her passengers, whatever their fate, but United would not allow it. A woman from the Red Cross came to sit with the two flight attendants. The three women talked all night. White said that her ears and nose were clogged with Iowa loam, "and it kept coming out for weeks."

The next day White's father flew in. The NTSB interviewed her with representatives of the FAA, United Airlines, and her union attending. White was released, but she was afraid to get on a plane, glad that her father was there. Thursday night she and her father drove out of Sioux City and found a hotel. White could not turn off the lights in her room. "When I'd turn the light out, when I closed my eyes, I'd see just the fire and the bodies, and the crash, and I just—it was too terrifying for me, so I just lay there in the bed with the lights on all night."

White said that she had been "just the happiest person in the world" before the crash. She loved people, and her outlook on the world was tirelessly bright and enthusiastic. Everyone loved her. But after three weeks of not sleeping, she was a wreck. She took a leave from work in order to concentrate on the therapy she received, but United Airlines kept calling her. "I couldn't handle the pressure of them trying to get me to come back." Reluctantly, she returned to work. Each time someone asked her about the crash, she would tell the story, but she would also suffer flashbacks and nightmares in her hotel room at night. Then she'd show up at work the next day exhausted, and the next crew would ask her to tell the story again. "So every time I'm at work I couldn't escape it." After a year of that, she suffered a breakdown in front of all the passengers and flight attendants on a trip. She returned to therapy and gradually put her emotions back together. After that she was just fine until the attack that destroyed the World Trade Center.

One of White's good friends, Jason Dahl, was the captain of United Flight 93 on September 11, 2001, when it was hijacked and crashed near Shanksville, Pennsylvania. White was happily married by then, and she and her husband were supposed to leave for Greece that day. Instead they wound up at the Dahls' house planning a memorial service. "And that's when Two Thirty-Two really hit me. It hit me almost harder, or just as hard, as it did [in 1989]. And I didn't realize that I hadn't dealt with it. I still had issues. I had no idea." After the attack on the World Trade Center, she wound up back in therapy. But she continued to fly, though not without difficulties.

"Anything unsettling on the airplane, severe turbulence, an approach [to] landing that doesn't quite feel right, my palms sweat and I have horrible anxiety. No one would know it, but I feel it so intensely inside. Usually those nights when experiencing those feelings is when I'll have a nightmare about crashing."

In 1979, at the age of twenty-two, Nicholas Edward Cherolis graduated from college as a materials engineer. He was snapped up by General Electric, which had recently formed its first team devoted to nothing but analyzing the way metal parts fail in aircraft and engines. The group that Cherolis joined was a coterie of elite alchemists, sorcerers and their apprentices, who would delve into the heart of the crystalline structures inside of metals. They had an odd way of speaking, a language of their own, and when it came to metallurgy and failure analysis, they formed a closed and clubby society. Cherolis told me he'd "gone off and done a little fracture mechanics and fractography class with my buddy Doug Pridemore [of GE]," when the case of United Flight 232 came along. Ten years into his career, "it was perfect timing. I was totally prepared," he said. The fan disk that Janice Sorenson and Harold Halverson dug out of the Iowa mud was a perfect match for Cherolis, who at thirty-two was reaching the peak of his skills. By then he was passionate about an obscure discipline called failure analysis.

When the fan disk arrived in Evendale, the team in the lab was busy examining the parts of the engine that had already come in. The smear tests, done by Joe Epperson at the NTSB labs in Washington, had already given hard evidence that fragments from the number one fan had cut the number one and number three hydraulic lines. When the electron beam went down into the inner electron shells of those atoms and found titanium, the team knew that metal could have come only from fragments of the fan disk or its blades. Now the team had the disk in hand and had to dig down to the final level and show why the disk broke apart in the first place.

"The most likely thing is that it has split from a fatigue crack," Cherolis said. "The old guy in the group gets out his pictures and says, 'See, here's the history,' and he had a cross section of an engine with little circles showing past failures of the same sort." As a metallurgist in the field of failure analysis at a company that made turbine engines, Cherolis knew that he would eventually be called upon to analyze titanium that had been tainted. It was a matter of letting the wheels spin and being patient. Cherolis also knew that disk 00385 could have been damaged in handling or that the stresses induced in the disk during manufacture might not have been properly accounted for. "But by that time this engine series was well wrung out," he said, "and that possibility was pretty slim. There were still problems in the turbine [of the CF6-6], but the fan hadn't had any stress problems."

Cherolis first looked at the larger piece of the disk on Thursday morning, October 11. He said, "You could see it [the crack] had come from the bore area. You can read a fracture backwards to where it starts. And it doesn't look like a normal fracture that's purely fatigue. There's a depression of missing material at the origin that a layman would call a pit." The crack had begun in that pit, the chipped-out cavity that Wizniak had called the origin. Cherolis expected to see smooth, continuous machined metal on the inside surface of the bore. He saw instead that tiny hole where a piece of material had fallen out. To Cherolis's eye, it was evidence as damning as a bloody thumbprint at a murder scene.

Once the disk was cleaned, Cherolis and his team began taking photographs of that surface and the crack that grew from it, all the way to the rim of the disk. First he mounted a Polaroid camera on a tripod to take overall photos. Then he used a device called a macroscope to take photographs at five to ten times magnification. The team established X and Y coordinates on the fractured metal so that each photograph could be matched with others to orient all the features in space. This also allowed them to determine the direction in which the fracture was propagating and how fast it had been growing.

Wildey, leading the team, could see how the cracked surface changed as it moved out from the bore. The crack clearly began as a fatigue crack, but then it abruptly changed to what Wildey called "single load," something that was ripped apart by brute force, or in the language of metallurgy, "with a single application of load." The fatigue area nearer the bore looked completely different as the result of repeated cracking by small increments each time a load was put on the part. The word *load* means pull or force. The pull comes from centrifugal force, the force that results from spinning. Usually such a fatigue crack would let go on takeoff because that's when the load is greatest. (And this is what the engineers hope for, since the pilot can usually abort the takeoff.)

Above that fatigue crack, along the edge of the single-load cracking, Wildey could see a shear lip, a flap of metal that droops off of one side at about a 45-degree angle when metal is torn apart. He said that when the piece pulled apart on the day of the crash, it was "like Thor smiting it with his hammer. This is a big deal. This is the Big Bang that everybody hears when this thing breaks. This is the clap of thunder" heard by farmers on the ground. "You're at a stress level that's exceedingly high and most often you're just ripping the part apart and it's all done. But because we don't have that shear lip down there in that fracture region, it says that there's some kind of brittle fracture mechanism that's occurring down there. An experienced fractographer would be drawn to that area without a shear lip instantaneously." And he would say, "There is a lack of deformation going on here that indicates for sure that there is a brittle fracture mechanism." Wildey knew. Cherolis knew. Now the team had to prove it.

As the day wore on, Cherolis viewed the small pit inside the bore at higher and higher magnifications, taking photos at each step. "And you compare the surface finish away from it to the surface finish in it," he said. On the healthy metal surrounding the pit, he could see the dimpled appearance that resulted from shot peening. That process gives a texture to the titanium that is almost like skin. It compresses the metal near the surface and thereby introduces stresses that help prevent cracks. But down in the pit, at higher magnifications, he could see two things of great interest. One was evidence of shot peening inside the pit. That meant that before the disk was completely finished, a bit of material had already fallen out to create the pit. Moreover, inside the pit he could see that the shot peening had fractured the metal further, which told him that the material was, indeed, brittle in there. "It looked like little pieces were missing out of that," Cherolis said. "Well, it doesn't do that on nice ductile material." Healthy titanium alloy should not fracture under the force of shot peening. So the material in the pit had not behaved the way titanium should. Titanium should stretch under the load of spinning. The material in the pit, almost ceramic in its consistency, would not stretch. "The GE guys really don't like to admit that there could be micro-cracks within the [pit]," said Cherolis.

United Airlines, for its part, denied that the cavity existed in a detectable form before the first flight. In its official report United said, "At all times prior to the inflight event, the cavity was filled with metal and was not visually detectable." In fact, the major parties to the event wrote their own reports detailing what they wanted the NTSB to conclude. General Electric went so far as to print its report in the exact same format as the official NTSB report, including the same typefaces, so that the GE report could easily be mistaken for a genuine NTSB report.

In terms of whether or not the defect was detectable, Cherolis said that during the machining process, tools would cut metal from every surface to achieve the final shape of the disk, and when a tool hit the brittle material in the pit, "it was like hitting a rock in peanut butter." His conclusion: "In my mind it was probably already micro-cracked" before it was ever installed on an engine. Tellingly, electron micrographs would clearly show cracks in the micro-structure, "and not all in the direction that the stress [of spinning] would make them." There are "extra little cracks in random directions." In a sense, it makes no difference who's wrong and who's right. If the defect hadn't begun to crack during manufacture, it would have cracked the first time the engine was spun up to speed.

In its final report, the NTSB put it this way:

> The Safety Board believes that at the time of manufacture of the disk, the cavity at the fatigue origin point was originally filled, or nearly filled . . . making the defect more difficult to detect. . . . The cavity was most likely created during the final machining and/or shot peening process and . . . the shot peening probably created the microcracking parallel to and just below the cavity surface. Moreover, the shot peening quite likely created the mechanical deformation on portions of the cavity bottom.

After that, every time an engine bearing fan disk 00385 was started, the crack grew a bit more, elongating outward from the bore toward the rim and the dovetail slot where the number 10 blade was attached. When that fatigue crack had grown to about one inch long and half an inch deep, the disk was ready to let go on the next flight. That flight took place July 19, 1989. You can see it in the photographs: the fatigue crack is flat where the metal broke as a crack through a broken plate of glass would be. But when the disk let go, the crack propagated and tore through healthy titanium as if through living flesh, leaving ragged edges. The fracture traveled through the metal at the speed of sound.

"It's trying to fly apart all the time," Cherolis said, "and the whole art of making a jet engine is keeping it all together and figuring out how long your parts will last. And you actually retire them with no cracks in them and throw them away, because statistically one could start cracking some time in the next several hundred cycles. And without a defect, that all works wonderfully. But you put a defect in there, then the crack starts right away, and all your calculations are trying to avoid starting a crack. And here it's already there."

Wildey and Cherolis now had to answer the next question. They knew how the disk broke. It had something brittle in that little pit, something that cracked and fell out, destroying the integrity of the titanium matrix. So what was that something? By the time Cherolis finished his work, it was late at night. Someone at GE telephoned Floyd Brate at about midnight and woke him up, saying he'd better get to the lab now. He was an expert in making detailed replicas of cracks. Other technicians were called in too. It was time to find out what material lay inside the pit.

CHAPTER
TWENTY-TWO

Charles Martz, the ex-Navy fighter pilot, sat in C-Zone next to eighty-year-old Luella Neubacher. She was telling him about her career as a senior Olympic runner. She was headed to Austria for a big race. In 1953 at the age of twenty-two, Martz had begun his career as a fighter pilot. He flew the F9F-8 Cougar off of the aircraft carrier USS *Bennington* in Navy Fighter Squadron 13. "That was the best kind of duty you can ever have," he said. Martz was a real old-fashioned fighter jockey. He had a low, growling voice and a slow, measured way of saying things. When you're in the cockpit of a swept-wing, jet-powered fighter plane, where unsuccessful landings on the pitching deck of a ship are usually fatal, you learn to move with deliberate precision. When he left the Navy, Martz continued to fly private planes. In fact, he should never have been on that DC-10 because he had a leased Cheyenne II, a Piper six-seat plane, in which he flew himself around the country looking at cable television systems for his company to buy. But it was the slow season for his business, and it seemed more economical on that trip to hop a commercial flight.

Martz was quite frank about saying that he was terrified. "I'd been the guy up front, and here I'm sitting in this aluminum tunnel and had no control whatsoever." Neubacher had no idea what was going on and continued chattering away with her travel stories, while

Martz stared at the dead control surfaces out the window and nodded dumbly, barely able to hear what she was saying. He listened to the changes in power, watched the tilting of the wings, and soon realized that the crew was steering the plane with the engines. Charlie Martz may have been the only person outside the cockpit who completely understood the situation. "There was no way to land this airplane without major damage." He began saying his mental good-byes to his wife Janie and family and friends. He was fifty-eight years old and recognized that he'd had a good life. He was overcome by a sense of sorrow because he had left early that morning and had not kissed Janie good-bye. She'd been sound asleep. He hoped that she would know how much he loved her. As the plane descended through a thin layer of scattered clouds, Martz decided that he had better say something to the chatty Luella Neubacher to let her in on what she was about to experience. He turned to her and said, "I hate to tell you this, but I've been flying a long time, and I know this is going to be more than a hard landing. We're going to crash." Neubacher fell silent at last. She studied Martz for a moment and thought about what he'd said. Captain Haynes had already announced that the landing would be just as bad as could be imagined. Jan Brown was now giving her final briefing, instructing people on how to brace. Susan White and Jan Murray and the other flight attendants were cruising the aisles, giving last-minute advice. Rene Le Beau was walking backward through first class, trembling while holding up the seat-pocket card, living out the last moments of her life while bravely doing her duty. Brad Griffin and Peter Allen, Gerald and Joanne Dobson, were all watching her.

Luella Neubacher deliberately unlatched her seat belt, stood up, and took her old gray overcoat from the overhead bin. She said, "You never know when you're going to have to walk home." Georgeann del Castillo scurried over and told her to get back in her seat, and she did so in her own sweet time. Nobody was going to tell Luella Neubacher how to live the last minutes of her life.

"Suddenly I became very, very angry," Martz recalled. "I had been in love with aviation since I was five years old and had always told myself that if I die in an aircraft crash, I want to go down in flames, sitting up front, fighting for my life. But here I was locked in this tin can with three hundred other people, unable to do a damn thing to help myself or anyone else." He called it "outrage," as he battled "the urge to scream." A few days before the flight, he had been sitting on his patio in the sunshine, having breakfast with his daughter Gail and reflecting on why so many bad things had to happen to her mother Janie. She'd had three cesarean sections and three surgeries for cancer, and only the week before had discovered a lump in her left breast. She was scheduled for a biopsy in a few days. He told his daughter that he'd been flying airplanes for thirty-five years and never experienced anything more serious than a small hydraulic leak. As 1819 Uniform slewed back and forth, up and down, he reflected that the chickens had come home to roost "because there was no way to get this plane on the ground safely."

When the announcement came over the loudspeaker that four minutes remained before touchdown, Charles Martz knew far too much for his own good. Then the two-minute warning came and the command to brace, and Martz said, "I was so angry by then with my frustration that I gave the seat belt another tug, held a pillow between my hands against the seat in front of me, turned my head to the right on the pillow, and watched out through the window." If he was going to crash, he was by god going to witness it.

Working in the high-security laboratory at GE, technicians took all the photographs at various magnifications that Wildey and his team thought they needed of fan disk 00385. Then they moved the larger of the two pieces of titanium to a power saw and cut the entire fracture from bore to rim as you might cut a piece out of a doughnut. "You essentially make a cut parallel to the entire fracture," said Cherolis. They now had a long piece that was light enough for one person to carry. It contained the pit where the crack had begun, the progressive fatigue area, as well as the tear created when the disk let go.

Floyd Brate was an expert in a technique called replication. Everyone working on the analysis wanted to extract as much information as possible from the disk before they began the process of destroying that tiny pit, which would be the last step in the analysis. Brate would make exact replicas of the fracture out of several different materials. He first washed the part with deionized water. Then he wet acetate tape with acetone to soften it, and covered the fracture with it so that it would adhere to the surface and mold to all the fine features of the metal. When it had solidified, he pulled the acetate tape off and repeated the process several more times.

"I did pull acetate tapes off," Brate said, "and we lifted fluorescent penetrant off of that, which was analyzed on a scanning electron microscope. So there was a prior crack there where FPI penetrant seeped in the crack." General Electric manufactured disk 00385 from September through December of 1971, and then installed it on an engine, which was sent out to Douglas in Long Beach and hung on a DC-10. Fan disk 00385 was removed from that engine and inspected in September of 1972. It was then installed on various engines over time, and it was removed and inspected again and again: in November of 1973, in January of 1976, in June of 1978, in February of 1982, and in February of 1988. At each of those times, the disk was subjected to fluorescent penetrant inspection. The process is simple and seemingly foolproof in theory. (Practice is another matter.) The inspector submerges the disk in—or sprays the disk with—a yellow-green oily liquid. "It has to sit for half an hour or more," said Cherolis. If there are any cracks in the metal, the dye will seep into them through capillary action. Then the inspector washes off that penetrant fluid, being careful not to wash it so aggressively that he washes it out of the cracks. He then dusts the disk with a powder, called a developer, that acts as a blotter and draws the fluid out of the cracks to make them more readily visible. Under ultraviolet light, any crack would fluoresce yellow-green. The FPI inspection in 1973 was done at the GE Airline Service Department in Ontario, California. The other five inspections were conducted at the United Airlines CF6 Overhaul Shop in San Francisco. In early 1988, someone noticed that the engine carrying fan disk 00385 showed some corrosion in another unrelated part. The engine was disassembled, and while the fan disk was off of the engine, it was subjected to its last fluorescent penetrant inspection.

The inspector coated the disk with the dye, and the dye should have shown the defect, as well as the fatigue crack that had grown from it over the years. By that time, the crack had grown to about half an inch long and a quarter inch deep. By aerospace engineering standards, it was large. It should have attracted the attention of anyone looking at it.

Cherolis summed it up: "During that last fluorescent penetrant inspection of the fan disk at the airline shop, if everything was done right, a bright yellow-green line one half inch long would have appeared on the part under black light. So it would be like a glowing line drawn in the part well within the detectable range. Everyone who has tried to perform that inspection on a real part that is over 300 pounds can see how it might be missed. So the event was a combination of the defect, the lack of detection over many inspections, and the design of that airplane all coming together." However, the uninitiated person, imagining a bright fluorescent line on a piece of metal, cannot so easily see how it might be missed. One would think that it should have been obvious. Yet it was not.

"And I don't know whose fault that was," Brate said. "We lifted the penetrant off on the initial first two replicas." A process called secondary ion mass spectroscopy was used on the acetate tape impressions that he had made. The test detected molecules of the various phosphorous compounds used in the fluorescent dye. Gas chromatograph mass spectroscopy was also used on the wash water from the ultrasonic cleaner. Those phosphorous compounds were detected in that water as well. In the years since the crash, there has been some debate about where those phosphorous compounds came from and whether the NTSB detected dye in the crack or not. In sworn testimony during the NTSB hearings, witnesses said that no phosphorus was found and no shot peening had occurred inside the pit.

In 2013, Robert MacIntosh said, "The Public Hearing testimony was conducted as a fact-gathering exercise and before all the factual evidence was able to be assembled. Later, in the end process of writing the final report, as I recall, Jim Wildey had evidence based on reliable observation on both the FPI fluid and the multiple cracking within the shape of the pit."

Wildey responded, "I personally was never convinced that there was any evidence one way or another about the presence of phosphorous compounds (from the inspection process) on the fatigue region. However, the fatigue region itself did contain surface features that corresponded to the size of the crack at the last inspection. These features were duplicated in tests that GE performed and clearly show that the crack was open during the last United inspection and capable of sucking up the FPI fluid. One of the main arguments presented by United was that the bore surface had residual compression stresses that closed the crack and prevented penetration of the FPI fluid. This is clearly not true, based on the appearance of the fatigue crack region." Wildey's team could mathematically calculate how big the crack was at the last inspection by knowing how fast it was growing over time. And this calculation told them that the crack was large enough to take up the penetrant dye.

This sort of detailed technical argument is of purely academic interest to engineers and metallurgists, since no one disagrees that the crack was there and was not detected. In the end, no one was willing to blame the inspector for missing it. His boss told me that the man had suffered terrible emotional symptoms. In fact, a concerted effort was put into keeping the technician's identity secret. It has never been released. His identity was concealed by a number. Each inspector had a stamp with a unique number used in signing off his work. David Cookson, in charge of researching the records for United Airlines, researched that stamp number and discovered not only the inspector's name but also the fact that he knew the man personally. "I researched the number. I'm sorry I did. To me at the time—just a personal note—it was somewhat upsetting to find out I knew the person who had accomplished the inspection. . . . I can imagine he would have problems. And that's what troubled me. The guy was doing his job. And he did it to the best of his ability. There were defects in the disk prior to his inspection. But I'll never say that he missed it. I never will say that. Because I don't know. I don't know what the circumstances were. . . . Unfortunately, he happened to be the guy that inspected the disk."

After Floyd Brate had made replicas of the crack and had detected the fluorescent dye, technicians used a water-cooled saw with an abrasive blade to cut off the bore end of the long piece they had removed from the fan disk, including the suspect material in and around the pit. The team now had a piece small enough to fit into the scanning electron microscope and could begin looking at the crystalline structure of the metal in fine detail. In preparation for this step, according to Cherolis, a technician named Ivan Miller put the part, which now looked like a piece of abstract jewelry, into an ultrasonic cleaner to remove any oil or dirt that still might be adhering to the fine structure of the metal. Then he put the piece into the electron microscope and turned on the vacuum pumps to evacuate all the air so that the electron beam didn't burn up the filament. In the darkened room, the screen was soon glowing a winter bluish white with the image, as he dove down and down, as if through living tissue, into the structure of the titanium. The day was long, but in the end, Cherolis, and Pridemore were looking at finished photographs from the scanning electron microscope. They also used the scanning electron microscope to perform electron diffusion spectroscopy, to look down into the electron shells and see what sort of atoms were in that pit. But as had happened with the sister disk 00388, the signals from the foreign material were too weak to read.

"Unfortunately," said Wildey, "nitrogen is one of those elements that's very difficult to detect in that process, so we were still a little mystified or a little uncertain as to what was going on there."

As United Flight 232 approached Sioux City and the crew began telling everyone to brace for the worst, Charles Martz sat looking out the window and said to himself, "Well, this is the only crash I'm ever going to be in after about three thousand hours of flying. So I'm going to sit here and look out the window and see it." Martz sat four rows behind Jerry Schemmel, three rows ahead of Schemmel's best friend Jay Ramsdell. Martz was sitting on the boundary that would separate the two friends forever. He was furious, and rightly so. He turned to Luella Neubacher and told her to go ahead and brace, and he'd watch out for her. As the plane descended lower and lower, "I could see the airport off the right wing as we sort of wobbled to the right. We were descending in an erratic fashion. It was easy to see that we were going way too fast and descending too rapidly." In a normal landing, the plane comes down at three hundred feet a minute. This DC-10 was approaching the ground at more than sixteen hundred feet a minute.

Resting his head on the pillow and looking out the window, he could hear "the desperate pounding of my heart in my ears as the adrenaline took over." The green cornfield rushed by, "almost a blur." At that point, Martz heard both engines rev up. "But the right wing tip hit the dirt, and the landing gear departed." He recalled that when he saw that wing tip hit the ground, "finally, I closed my eyes and mentally kissed my ass good-bye." At that point, he thought, "It won't be long now. Something's going to hit me in the head and it will all go black." He said, "I remember being whipped back and forth and banging against the cabin wall on the right, careening down the runway, flailing about, waiting for the final blackout, the last fragile moments of life, wondering, waiting, furious, frightened, and alone. And finally everything did go black."

When the noise and motion stopped, he enjoyed no moment of reprieve, no time to think, as some passengers had in B-Zone. Choking smoke began to fill the aft cabin immediately. "There was an instant of silence and then a surge of moans and screams as the injured and terrified realized what had happened," Martz said. "I was awake the entire time and was truly amazed to find that I was still alive and able to think, move, and breathe." Within seconds, however, the smoke in the aft cabin grew, "deep black, acrid, utterly frightening," he said. "You had to hold your breath for as long as you could."

Martz had an advantage over everyone else in C-Zone. As a Navy fighter pilot, he had been trained to get out of a cockpit while inverted, in the dark, on fire, and even under water. When the screeching of metal stopped and he heard the people around him begin to scream and moan, he looked at Luella Neubacher hanging from her seat belt beside him and decided that he'd release himself, then release her, and they'd get out together. He released himself but retained no recollection of doing so. His Navy training had taken over. He tried to look up to locate his seatmate, but he could see "nothing except the floor lighting running left and right immediately above my head." He saw no people. "I looked to the right and everything was darkness. I looked to the left at about eye level and saw flames outside through a window. I stood up and kicked at the window. There's no way to kick a window out of an airplane. I looked further to the left and saw a fire blazing at the open end of the fuselage, perhaps five feet away." He decided that he would rather suffer severe burns than die of smoke inhalation.

More than two decades later, Martz said, "I did something that I've always regretted, and I carry that with me to this day. It was just a sad, sad thing, because I fumbled around trying to find Mrs. Neubacher, and I couldn't find anybody. I said, well, there's fire to the rear. I figured where there's fire, there's oxygen." He moved toward the opening and ran into a man who stopped him and said, "It's burning out there."

"I know," Martz said. "Let's go."

"No way," the man said.

Martz pushed past him. He never saw the man again. Martz now ran toward the flames, gaining as much momentum as he could on the uneven surface beneath his feet. He leapt into the flames. "It was wide open," he said with a note of astonishment in his voice. He had literally jumped through fire to freedom, while those around him perished. He burned a finger going through but was otherwise untouched.

"Suddenly I was standing in a muddy cornfield outside the airplane in bright sunshine." He walked a few steps and stopped, thinking, "It's not that bad. Maybe I can go back in and get that lady." But, he continued, "At that moment there was an explosion and a burst of fire to the right . . . as more fuel fed the fire." He thought, "Charlie, you're alive and well, there's no use in being a dead hero going back into that inferno. Get the hell out of here."

The oxygen bottles and fire extinguishers began exploding. Martz said he was thinking, "I have survived the crash. The cabin is filled with smoke. Stuff is exploding." He walked farther away from the wreck, torn by indecision.

"And I finally said, Forget it." Of course, he could not forget it, not even when he spoke to me at the age of eighty-one. With her favorite gray coat on, ready to walk out with him, Luella Neubacher died of the smoke.

James Wildey, working at the GE lab, cut a half-inch piece of the defect and mounted it in Bakelite plastic to make it easier to handle. He then held the specimen by hand, pressing it against a rotating circular platform with finer and finer grits of diamond or alumina, "until you get down to stuff that is so fine I can't even describe it to you, to make a mirror surface on this metal." It took about an hour of polishing to achieve that finish. This was the final piece of physical evidence, and he was destroying it little by little to demonstrate the ultimate cause of the crash of 1819 Uniform. The process was called step polishing, and it involved gradually grinding away the defect in the metal and then polishing it and testing it at each step using the electron microscope to determine what atomic elements it contained.

A technician sat at the electron microscope at GE and pinged the inner shells of electrons inside that pit. Only this time he used a more sensitive test than the energy dispersive spectography. With EDS, they had seen the energy of the X-rays dwindle away and not give a clear signal of what was in the pit. The technician switched modes to use X-ray wavelength dispersive spectroscopy (WDS). Cherolis said, "WDS uses a different type of detector to measure the wavelength of the X-rays, and the wavelength tells you the energy."

The X-rays coming off of that area were put through a device called a diffractometer, "a crystalline substance with a known atomic spacing," Wildey explained. "Because of the way that the X-ray inter-acts with a crystal, it will diffract only at specific angles." In WDS, the diffraction angle then told him, even at low energy levels, what atomic element he was looking at. It is so accurate that it also told him the amount of that element. "EDS is used whenever possible because it is simpler and faster, and for many elements it is perfectly okay. For specific elements, EDS cannot distinguish the energy peak from two different elements when they are close together, and is not really good at the low energy X-rays. In these cases, and for more precise measurements, WDS is used."

Once the technician had subjected the sample from disk 00385 to the WDS procedure, the wavelength readings came back loud and clear: the pit was full of nitrogen, and not in trace quantities either. The serviceable metal cast by TIMET in 1971 had contained .008 percent nitrogen, an allowable level. In this defect, the percent by weight of nitrogen went as high as 2.07. Moreover, where the nitro-gen was at its highest, the aluminum and vanadium were at their lowest, destroying the properties that make the alloy useful. It was conclusive: the titanium had been contaminated with nitrogen when it was first melted at TIMET in Henderson, Nevada, in 1971. When titanium is combined with enough nitrogen, it becomes a ceramic material. Even at a concentration of 2 percent, nitrogen makes tita-nium brittle. Those brittle "inclusions," as they're called, can fracture and fall out. Then the little hole or pit that's left can start a crack that begins to grow outward with the centrifugal pull of the spinning fan. Wildey's team performed another test with an indenter to measure hardness. The material in the pit was far harder than titanium alloy should have been. That's why the defect was known as hard alpha. Titanium stretches and bends. Hard alpha breaks. The original spot of hard alpha had fallen out, leaving a pit that was about 1.4 milli-meters (about .06 inch), not quite the width of a grain of rice. The full name the metallurgists use for such a defect is nitrogen-stabilized hard alpha inclusion.

* * *

Charles Martz came out the back of the fuselage, leaping through fire, and set foot on the soft earth beside the runway. In a speeding, almost giddy, daze, rejoicing in his bittersweet survival, he stepped up onto the concrete surface. He could scarcely believe he was alive. He raised his eyes to look out over the sunburned, smoky landscape and saw "the goddamndest mess I've ever encountered, like a small battlefield." He saw at least a dozen people still in their seats. Their clothes were torn or blown or burned from their bodies, "completely naked in front, missing limbs, missing faces, some breathing, some moaning, and others just deader than a door nail." As he walked along the runway, he came upon a United Airlines pilot. "He tried to sit up," Martz said. "I saw a huge triangular hole in his forehead and I told him to just lie still and that help was on the way, but it was too late for him." Martz walked on and encountered a lady whose hair and clothing were burned away, her stockings melted onto her legs. Next a man completely naked in front, black from soot. "Finally, I will never forget stopping near a lovely young girl still strapped to her seat, breathing slightly. Her blouse was white, her slacks were blue. At the end of the trousers were two snow-white ankle bones where her feet used to be. I had never seen the whiteness of bones that are freshly exposed like that. Her beautiful blue eyes were wide open, staring at the sky. I spoke to her. Nothing at all, as the blood drained from her body." At this point in his description, Martz groaned audibly with the pain of dredging up those memories, and said with regret, "She was just a *pretty* gal."

Only a minute or two had passed. He turned back toward the burning fuselage and saw that a fire truck was spraying foam on the wreck. He saw two men come out of the flames. Larry Niehus sprayed them with foam. Two priests dressed in the protective gear of fire fighters entered the burning fuselage to administer the last rights to some of the dead before the heat and melting structure drove them out. As Martz turned away, aware that he could no longer help those people, a pickup truck pulled up beside him. "And here I am, I've got my tie on, I've got on a blue oxford button-down shirt, pen and pencil still in the pocket, and looking like I'm ready to sell insurance."

The driver of the truck looked at him and said sternly, "What are you doing here?"

"Well," Martz said, jerking his thumb over his shoulder, "I just came in on Flight Two-Thirty-Two."

The driver thought Martz was an ambulance-chasing lawyer, but Martz convinced him that he really had been on the plane that lay burning beyond the trail of the dead. As Martz boarded the truck for the ride to the triage area, he realized that he was completely uninjured except for that small burn on one finger. He hiked over to Graham Aviation and called his wife Janie. That night, along with Martha Conant, Rod Vetter, John Transue, and others, Martz boarded the United Boeing 727 to Chicago. He experienced no anxiety about flying. "We're not going to crash again. I was sure of that." As an experienced fighter pilot, he also took comfort in seeing the old pilot who flew them to Chicago that night. "He was a crusty old bird, they were very smart about that. He had the look of a trusted aviator who was going to get you there safely."

In midair, he crossed paths with the Grumman Gulfstream carrying the NTSB Go Team. He didn't reach the Westin Hotel at O'Hare Airport until two in the morning. Once in his room, he tuned the television to CNN. "That was the first time I'd seen the video of the crash," he said. "And that's when I started to shake. I had been relatively calm until I saw that video, and I said, 'Jesus Christ, how could anybody survive that?' I got up, walked over to the bar in my room, and downed two quick shooters of vodka." Then he went to the mirror and looked at the face in the glass. "It was mine. It was alive."

In bed at last, he slept soundly. He rose at six in the morning, caught the shuttle to the airport, and boarded the first flight back to Denver. United had planned a flight for survivors later that morning, but Martz wanted to get out of there. He was going to put the crash behind him and get on with his life. He needed to see Janie.

CHAPTER
TWENTY-THREE

When a fatigue crack grows due to vibration, it may be put under strain millions of times. In the cult of metallurgy, such a phenomenon is known as a high-cycle crack. Fan disk 00385 was put under strain each time it flew, so the total number of times the crack grew was in the thousands. It was therefore known as a low-cycle crack. Wildey described the characteristics of a low-cycle crack: "It's flatter. It's smoother. And it's striated in that it has these clamshell marks or beach marks, as they've been referred to"—metallurgists at General Electric used the term *river marks*—"where the crack, as it progresses, will leave behind these growth rings that are the sign that the crack is propagating under tensile stresses over time." To Wildey's trained and unaided eye, from five feet away, he couldn't see individual striations—they were too small—but he could see the overall way the surface reflected light in an undulating pattern. The striations ranged from more than three hundred thousand per inch near the pit to about two thousand at the far edge of the area of fatigue. The crack, in other words, had started by growing 1/300,000th of an inch on each flight.

"That's hardly anything," said Cherolis. "But it's moving." And it's accelerating. By the end, it was growing by one half of a thousandths of an inch on each flight. "Freaky, isn't it?" he remarked.

Cherolis and Pridemore went through the photos taken in the

electron microscope and counted the striations, as you would with the growth rings in a tree. "We don't count every single one of them," Cherolis said. "Because it would be very hard to keep track of exactly where you were. So we take snapshots at intervals across the fracture and mathematically connect them up." Cherolis and Pridemore each counted the fine lines on the same photographs and then compared their results to make sure that they didn't diverge by too much. Of Pridemore, Cherolis said, "He's a guy who really knows how to do striations."

They then plotted the density (cracks per inch) versus the depth (distance from the pit). They fitted a curve to the data to produce a beautiful power law diagram and then calculated the area under that curve. "I think we used Mathcad at the time of Sioux City," Cherolis recalled. (More recently, they employed a computer program called Excel.) "There is also a graphical method you can use that is quite accurate, breaking the area under the curve into a series of rectangles and triangles. I usually do this to make sure I didn't input anything wrong into the software for integration. You do not just stop at what you need to prove a defect or primary cause," he added. "In a case this important and significant, you go over and above." All of these efforts were aimed not merely at learning what had gone wrong but at preventing accidents in the future.

Cherolis knew well what he was looking at in this hard alpha defect and the crack that grew from it. "The crack accelerates its growth as the crack grows deeper into the metal"—that is, the farther it grows out from the center of the disk, the faster it grows with each flight or cycle. When they had calculated the area under the power law curve, it came out to about fifteen thousand cycles. Once Cherolis and Pridemore had that number, they asked how many times the disk had flown since 1972.

By that time, Young, Moehring, Cookson, and others from the NTSB and GE and United had researched the records deeply, and they all knew: fan disk 00385 had flown 15,503 times. At the time of its last fluorescent penetrant inspection, that disk had flown 14,743 times since its debut in early 1972.

"I was pleased at how close it was to the real number of flights," Cherolis said of his and Pridemore's calculations.

When I asked Cherolis if someone should have seen the crack in 00385, he said, "Ah. That's the tragic thing. Somebody's probably losing sleep over that." If that crack was on a test bar, "no one could miss it," Cherolis said. "It's a piece of metal. It's asked to do a certain job. And you do everything you can to make sure that it's as good as it can be. You just hope the airplane's on the ground or just taking off and they can reject the takeoff." He added, "It's sad. But that's just how things work. And it still is that way. What's less likely is that a hard alpha is going to be in titanium with the newer processes" for making that metal.

The materials used in making fan disks are much better today than they were in the 1970s. The process of making titanium has changed radically. For example, while the billet used to make fan disk 00385 was sixteen inches in diameter, billets in use by the time of the crash were only ten inches, making it easier to detect flaws. In addition, GE changed its specification to call for makers of titanium to use such exotic techniques as electron beam cold hearth melting and plasma torches. As a result, hard alpha defects are less frequent. In fact, by 1990, GE claimed that the electron beam "melting process addresses the residence time limitation of VAR [vacuum arc remelting], permitting assurance of dissolution of any hard alpha inclusions which may be present in the raw material."

I asked Wildey, "Could this accident happen today?"

"Yes," he said.

Dave Randa and I had finished our lunch at Fox Fire, the bar and grill in Geneva, Illinois. He was telling me his impressions from the time immediately after the crash. Since he and his mother Susan had been splashed with blood, a nurse at the hospital called a friend of hers who also had a nine-year-old son. She brought a pair of yellow shorts and a blue T-shirt to the hospital for Dave to wear. The nurse gave Susan a pair of her surgical scrubs. Then Dave and Susan were taken to the dormitory at Briar Cliff College. "But the biggest thing was that I had lost my Cubs hat," Dave said.

The dorm was overrun with reporters, and Dave commented to one of them that he had been on his way to a Cubs game and had lost his favorite Cubs hat. When Jim Randa arrived in Sioux City, he drove his wife and son to the house of Susan's brother in Chicago. The Cubs heard about the lost hat and sent over a package with a new hat, as well as signed photos of Dave's favorite players, Andre Dawson and Mark Grace. They also sent ten box-seat tickets, "second row right behind the batter's box," Dave said. "Unbelievable tickets. Absolutely loved it. Beautiful day. You could reach out and almost touch the players. When you're nine, that's amazing. And at that time, it was so hard to get that type of ticket. Vance Law, I want to say, hit two home runs. Got to meet him. Great person." Dave remembered correctly. Law hit one homer off of Jeff Brantley and the other off of Atlee Hammaker. "They really took care of us. The locker room after—Andre Dawson and Mark Grace were so nice. They were just spectacular." A brilliant Saturday afternoon in the friendly confines of Wrigley Field, and on that glorious day the Cubs beat the San Francisco Giants 5 to 2. Life did not get any better than that, Dave thought.

By the time the Randa family returned to Colorado, however, Dave was having nightmares and flashbacks and couldn't sleep for long. "I'd wake up scared of the plane crash, scared of death, scared of somebody breaking in." He was now afraid of things that had never entered his mind before.

Susan said, "Dave was afraid of everything. He slept on the floor of our room for like six months."

After that his parents put a baby monitor in his room. That way, when he woke from a nightmare, he could talk to them or summon them to his room "to soothe me," he said, and laughed. Baby monitors weren't made for nine-year-olds, he said. It took years to gradually calm the fears and tone down the flashbacks. "I don't think I consistently slept through the night until I was thirteen or fourteen."

The crash left scars in other ways too. One day when he was in the sixth grade, a kid on the basketball court started an argument with Dave. As the argument heated up, the kid said, "I wish you had died." The court fell silent. Everyone knew what the boy meant. Not died in an automobile accident. Not died of cancer. He wished that Dave had died in the crash of United Flight 232. It happened again at a relative's house. Again the dispute was over basketball, only this time it was his own cousin who said, "I wish you'd died." Dave flew into a rage and "we fought it out," right down into the dirt.

Dave's emotional system was permanently changed. His feelings and reactions to the crash grew fainter, more distant, but they were always there. He loves golf, and his favorite course is right next to an airport where business jets take off and land. When the emotion gets too intense, Dave speaks of himself in the second person. "When planes are flying around you at low altitudes, you kind of have to back away from the ball and regroup and focus." As an adult, at moments such as that, he could push the flashbacks down, practice his breathing exercises, and continue with the game. But he was like a veteran of combat. He could not move through life as smoothly as someone who had not had that experience. "It made me grow up fast."

Yet the flashbacks remain, as I learned when I said the word *brace.* "Even now I can see 'em. I can still hear them," Dave said. He looked into the distance. "When you said *brace,* I hadn't remembered *brace* for a long time. And I can hear the flight attendant's voice right behind me saying, 'Brace.'" Susan White's voice was forever imprinted in Dave's emotional system.

Dave lived in the affluent community of Boulder, and when he returned to school at the age of nine, many of his classmates said, "Aw, you're so lucky, I'll bet you're rich now." Nothing could have been further from the truth. "I wouldn't wish this on anybody. It took away a lot of my youth. It's bad. It's awful." As a result, he made an interesting decision, especially for a young man. Dave was given money, a settlement, a remedy as it's called, for the wrong done by the companies that caused the crash. And like other passengers, he agreed not to disclose the amount. "It's not much money," Dave said.

"But I've never touched any of it. It just sits there. It's invested. I don't want to spend it. I don't want to do anything with it." It is almost as if the money is a proxy for the place in Dave's heart that came to be occupied by the crash. It lives in him now. But he wants to keep it separate. By putting the money in its separate place, he is putting the crash in its separate place as well. They both exist and always will. Apart.

Three months after the crash, United Airlines returned Dave's favorite Cubs hat. "It smelled like the crash and I never wore it. But it was good to have back."

On Thursday night, July 20, 1989, after the bodies had been recovered from the field, and the morgue had begun to function, Chaplain Gregory S. Clapper allowed himself to go home to rest. He was "pretty burned out." He said he "got into bed and just hugged my wife and wept. And she wept too." Clapper would find himself at the forefront of a great deal of the healing and coping that was to come. He would be arranging memorial services, giving talks, and generally making himself available for anyone who needed a shoulder to cry on. At one point, another Air National Guard chaplain named Bob Hicks, who had once dealt with the crash of an airliner, advised him, "Remember Paul in Romans said to weep with those who weep and rejoice with those who rejoice." Clapper, being young and inexperienced, had been concerned with his professional image. Hearing that passage, however, helped him to understand that, in the end, "one of the best things you can do is put your arm around somebody and cry with them."

I told Clapper about Martha Conant's experience on the afternoon of the crash, standing in the mess hall when a social worker said, "God still has work for you to do." Conant found the idea insulting, that God caused the crash, killing children while saving her.

"I'm a United Methodist," Clapper said, "which means I'm a Wesleyan, which means I'm an Arminian. That's a school of theology that believes in human freedom. So I'm not a Calvinist." Many people in Siouxland come out of the reformed Calvinist tradition.

"Their basic view is, God controls everything. God wanted this to happen. My view is, I don't believe in the god who would want this to happen. I believe that we are truly free."

And "free, sinful, limited humans often screw up. And in this case, they found a microscopic flaw in the flywheel of the engine. So I said, We're not perfect. We build things that break. So this human invention broke. That's what happened. Where we can use our freedom is in how we deal with this afterwards. Whether you come out injured, or whether you've lost a loved one, or whether you saw terrible things as a helper, the point is not to obsess on the fact that we live in a contingent world where bad things happen, but to say, Well, what do I do with the rest of my freedom? And one of the ways that I talk about that is, I really do believe in mystery. That even as a Christian, there's mystery. So that the people who want to say, 'Well, God is in charge,' in order to remove all mystery, I say, No. I say, Look at some of the things in scripture. I say, Let's take scripture seriously. Even in the Garden of Eden: Why was there a talking snake there to begin with?"

He laughed.

We were talking in a conference room in the new public library in Arlington Heights, Illinois, where his brother had done volunteer work. His brother had died recently, and Clapper had come from his home in Indiana to dispose of the estate and clean out the house. He was grieving again, and it brought up reflections on United Flight 232.

"So," he said, "there's a lot of mysteries that we just have to deal with, and my faith is that we have been given the resources—through the Holy Spirit, through Christ's work—to deal with them. I think the only way you can deal with that mystery is—put it in dialogue with the other mysteries in your life. And I said, I think you're not honest with yourself if you don't acknowledge that there are other mysteries. So for instance, I use the story of Susan talking to her father." He means Susan White, the happy, effervescent homecoming queen from Wadsworth, Ohio. When White entered the Air

National Guard building and tried to call her mother and was so shaken that she could barely dial a phone, "Susan was encountering, was experiencing, the mystery of the giftedness of life," said Clapper. "Did that somehow cancel out all the negative things that just happened? No. But I think you move into the future when you start integrating those two, bringing them together. So it's not one or the other. It's not, Life is crap and its meaningless. And it's not, Everything is powerful and beautiful. It's both."

He had come full circle. "To come back to your initial question," he said, "Why? Am I better than that five-year-old or anything like that? I just have to say—and I think all Christians should say—*I don't know*. I don't know why you were saved. And I don't know why that young child was killed. This is a true mystery. And so I enter into it with you. I cry with you if you allow me into that space. I'll walk with you. And this is something that a lot of chaplains I know that were involved in Iraq and Afghanistan—talking with their soldiers— they'll say, Look, I'm gonna journey with you on this. I'm not here to explain it. I'm gonna journey with you. There's a sense of humility there that I think connects with people, because I think in their heart of hearts we know, Oh, I don't have an answer. So let's walk into that mystery together."

All the while that Clapper and I sat in that small conference room, flushed with sunlight from the great open spaces and the wide windows of the library, a security guard was making his rounds. He came past our windows again and again, and I was moved more than once to wonder what he was doing there. What could possibly happen in the public library in the safe and quiet suburb of Arlington Heights, Illinois? But, of course, I knew: What could possibly happen on a routine flight from Denver to Chicago on an ordinary Wednesday afternoon? What could happen in sleepy Sioux City, Iowa? The guard was the everyday reminder of the presence of incipient calamity in our midst. The forces of chaos are always there and can manifest themselves at any moment, from out of the clouds, unannounced. And indeed, are we not all on that last flight, launching ourselves triumphantly on our determined path, but inescapably finding that we are circling with little control over our own fate? In the midst of that journey, the gift is to celebrate it, as Susan White had when she exclaimed, "*I'm alive!*"

Clapper said that many people had told him, "I wish I could have done more." His answer was, "I think it has to do with human pride. In our heart of hearts, we really think that we can make everything all better. And that goes back to me fantasizing as a child: I'm going to be John Wayne, I'll run up the hill, I'll kill all the enemies, I'll rescue the girl, and do all the good stuff. But in reality, we can't make everything all better. And if you face that truth and accept it, that's really an assault on your pride. And so that gets to this huge spiritual issue, and that is control. It assaults our human pride to realize that we are not in control. And so when people say, 'There must have been something else I could have done,' in reality at some point, I hope they get to the point of saying, 'No, there wasn't. I really did all I could do.' You shouldn't stay up every night saying, 'Well, if only I'd turned this corner and seen this other person, maybe I would have caught 'em before they died . . . No! Get off your high horse. Who the hell do you think you are?"

Dennis Swanstrom asked Clapper to organize the service for the first anniversary of the crash. At the opening reception, Clapper was thinking of Susan White and wondering if she would be there. He didn't know if she would even recognize him. But in the reception line they saw each other, and she leapt into his arms and gave him a big hug and said, "Oh, Chaplain Clapper, you helped me make the most important phone call of my life!" In the year since the crash, White had found the man she wished to marry, a United pilot named Dan Callender. White took Clapper aside and said, "I've been talking to Dan, and we want you to be part of our wedding."

Clapper conducted their premarital counseling and then traveled to Wadsworth, Ohio, and conducted the ceremony with White's Lutheran minister—the same minister she had imagined would announce her death in the church where she grew up. Now at last, she was married in that same church. Happily married. Clapper said, "To me that wedding will always be a symbol of hope, that good things can come out of tragedy. Not to try to make the tragedy less tragic. But God can bring good things out of tragedy." In fact, this motto is etched on a glass panel at the entrance to the NTSB training center: "From Tragedy We Draw Knowledge to Improve the Safety of Us All."

CHAPTER
TWENTY-FOUR

The engineers at General Electric knew enough about failing titanium parts to predict that an accident of this sort had a fair chance of happening. The manager of the Propulsion Branch of the FAA, Robert Follensbee, put it this way: "The requirement on the transport airplanes is that the rotor system [rotating parts] must be assumed to fail, no matter what the engine is. We learned in the 1960s that you can't really prevent that, no matter how hard we've tried. . . . It's something that's going to fail and can destroy the airplane."

David Rapoport, the lawyer who represented Al Haynes and crew, along with Jan Brown, Susan White, Tim Owens, and others, said, "Those who knew most about the engines were doing their best at all phases [of the investigation] to keep outsiders from carefully studying what the management at GEAE knew about the danger and when they knew it. With hard and soft alphas (known insidious problems from the start) why would or should anyone assume [that] changing melt practices would do anything to protect the flying public from dangers that went into the field in the early 1970s? The NTSB was misled."

As early as 1970, rotating titanium parts were giving evidence of their vulnerability to defects. Here are a few examples of uncontained rotor bursts since that time. "Uncontained" means that high-speed shrapnel was released, in some cases damaging the plane and even puncturing the tail and fuselage.

- April 19, 1970: A fan disk burst on a Scandinavian Airlines DC-8. The pilot was able to stop the plane on the runway in Rome, Italy, before taking off. A hard alpha defect caused the failure.
- May 2, 1972: A turbine wheel blew up on a DC-10 in Tucson, Arizona.
- December 28, 1972: A fan disk burst in Atlantic City, New Jersey.
- January 10, 1973: Another fan disk exploded, this one in Grand Junction, Colorado.
- March 16, 1979: In Okinawa, a compressor disk failed due to a hard alpha defect.
- June 25, 1983: In Manila, a compressor disk exploded from a hard alpha defect. Shrapnel penetrated the stabilizer.
- July 5, 1983: A compressor disk on a DC-8 blew up during takeoff from Chicago. Hard Alpha was the cause. The titanium had been triple-melted, so GE knew that melting titanium three times was no guarantee that a part would be free from defects.
- April 10, 1995: A General Electric CF6-50C2 engine on an Egypt Air Airbus A300 blew up due to a disk failure caused by a hard alpha defect. The pilot was able to stop the plane before takeoff. The disk that failed had undergone a fluorescent penetrant inspection that missed the crack.
- June 7, 2000: Compressor wheels blew up on a Varig Brasil Airlines Boeing 767 powered by General Electric CF6-80 engines. The metal was defective.

The philosophy of making rotating parts for jet engines is based on the assumption that new parts contain no defects. GE calculates the life of the part based on that assumption. That assumption clearly cannot be counted on. As an alternative, the NTSB has recommended what it calls a "damage tolerance" philosophy, which assumes that the part has a defect. In proposing this, the Board said, "In addition to the separation of the fan disk involved in the UA

232 accident, there have been many examples of life-limited engine components failing before they reached their life limit. The Safety Board believes that this fact demonstrates the need for a revision of the certification, design, and maintenance philosophies for turbine engines."

The official NTSB report concluded that the cause of the accident was "the inadequate consideration given to human factors limitations in the inspection and quality control procedures used by United." Jim Burnett, the chairman and a staunch advocate of airline safety, dissented from that conclusion. He listed three causes of the accident. The first was "the manufacture by General Electric Aircraft Engines (GEAE) of a metallurgically defective titanium alloy first stage fan disk mounted on the aircraft's No. 2 engine and the failure to detect or correct the condition." The second was United's failure to detect the flaw. The third was the faulty design of the DC-10, which left it open to damage by fragments from exploding engines. Remove any one of those three causes, and the accident would not have happened.

The inspector cannot be faulted for missing the crack when he performed the last fluorescent penetrant inspection of disk 00385 in 1988. The NTSB said that FPI is "inadequate" and "deficient." Although that test was standard practice in 1988, today the aerospace industry is leaning more heavily on ultrasound and eddy current inspections, a much more effective technology in which a magnetic field is used to detect cracks.

The question of General Electric's culpability in the crash of 1819 Uniform still hangs in the balance. In the minds of many people involved in this event, including Jim Burnett, GE was primarily to blame. It is indisputable, however, that GE also built the finest contemporary jet engine in existence—as fine as it can be, given the limitations of the physical materials in our world. The model CF6-80C2 is a beautiful engine. The world of aviation has embraced it, giving GE the highest market share in the business. In 2007, you could buy a GE engine for about $6,250,000. And if anyone wonders why an airline wouldn't inspect those spinning wheels more frequently, the first shop visit for a CF6 engine might have cost up to two million dollars that year.

In the end, General Electric achieved something stirring and powerful and remarkable. It took aviation technology to its highest level in the history of powered flight. And yet in doing so, it embraced a technology that was inherently flawed, inherently bound to fail, however infrequently. United Airlines, which bought the engine, understood that bargain. Even though GE failed to produce a perfect engine, and even though United failed to execute its maintenance perfectly, it was the failure of McDonnell Douglas to shield the hydraulic lines—or to separate them more effectively—that brought 1819 Uniform down.

On the afternoon of the crash, Margo Crain was sitting on the floor, leaning against the wall in the Air National Guard mess hall, when Garry Priest approached and asked how she was doing. Crain looked into his eyes, and "I felt like he was almost like an old friend already." She recognized him as the handsome young man she had admired in the boarding lounge. Now sitting and talking seemed almost a miracle, when so many of her fellow passengers would never sit and talk to anyone again. Crain and Priest had been granted a strange gift: the knowledge of how precious and fragile life is.

They may have talked for an hour, cementing their bond that evening. When Priest's boss, Bruce Benham, told him that they had been offered a bed at the local TV weatherman's house, Priest bade Crain good night and promised to see her again. He left, even as Crain was shepherded with so many others to the hospital and then on to Briar Cliff College and its steamy dorm swarming with dazed people who smelled of fuel and smoke.

Crain and Priest saw each other a few more times in the months that followed the crash. They both lived in Denver and attended meetings of the support group that formed there. Each time they saw each other, a bit more of the tinder representing the intensely shared moment of their survival was ignited. When Crain's divorce came through at last, Priest helped her to move out of her house. Priest, the

big strong guy with the S on his chest, was lifting her furniture, toss-
ing her life around. The day was giddy and emotional, his Superman
to her Lois Lane.

Then they found each other at Sioux City again for the first anniversary of the crash. Crain and her father drove there from Denver.
They stopped at a liquor store to pick up something for a drink at the
hotel. As they were waiting at the cash register, a television played
the news. Crain looked up and saw her own face.

"Dad! That's me!" They lifted their gaze to watch. A news channel had interviewed her a few weeks earlier for the anniversary, and
now in a liquor store in Sioux City, Iowa, she was watching herself
talk about the crash.

That evening the survivors gathered at a restaurant that was a
bit overdesigned, with flocked wallpaper and faux stained-glass windows, padded captain's chairs, and candles in colored glass vases
with plastic wicker sleeves.

The next day came up overcast for the prayer service. The sky-
blue program was printed with the twenty-third psalm and a hymn
called "Immortal, Invisible, God Only Wise." A podium had been
set up on the airfield so that the crowd could face the crash site. The
prayer service was scheduled to take place at 4:00 p.m. on July 19,
1990. As the people assembled, said Gary Brown, "we had almost
no time. There was a black cloud that came out of the west. It started
raining five minutes or ten minutes before the first anniversary service." And everyone made a mad dash for the hangar, where another
podium was hastily set up.

Jammed inside the Iowa Public Service Company hangar, with
the rain and thunder lashing the ramp outside, soaking the blowing corn, the crowd milled about and talked. It rained so hard that
manhole covers all over the city were blown off by the force of the
water coming down the storm drains, and Perry Creek rose ten feet.
Two children were swept away near Thirty-Third and Jackson and
pinned under a parked car, as Chaplain Clapper asked everyone to be
seated. The crowd, however, was so big that fully half of the people
had nowhere to sit. Clapper stood before the congregation and said,

"We cannot rewrite history, though our hearts ache to do so. But we can open ourselves up to the God of the present, the God whose future is not limited by the past, the God who makes all things new." Then an a capella quartet from the Grace United Methodist Church sang. The fighter pilots from the 185th chose that moment to take off for the presentation of the missing man formation. This is a tribute to the dead in which one aircraft pulls out of the normal formation, leaving a hole as the planes pass in review. It is ordinarily performed at altitude, but the clouds were too low.

As the A-7s thundered past on the way to form up, the noise of those turbines rattled every piece of metal in the hangar, and the hundreds of startled people jammed in that white-painted room jerked around to see. Then Clapper called for a minute of silence, during which many people wept, even as glum-looking children fidgeted and looked around. The silence was ended by the howling passage of the missing man formation.

"And when you looked out of the hangar, said Gary Brown, "they were eye level. I'm telling you, they should have had their landing gear down they were so close to the ground. That was a very moving service."

A Catholic priest read from Ecclesiastes. Then Clapper read the twenty-third Psalm and introduced a rabbi, who read excerpts from a sermon that Rabbi Kenneth Berger had delivered to his congregation on Yom Kippur Day in 1986. It was entitled "Five Minutes to Live" and was inspired by the astronauts who were killed when the space shuttle *Challenger* exploded. It was a meditation on how much richer life is when you behave as if we have only five minutes to live.

As Captain Haynes left his chair on the podium and approached the microphone to say a few words, the crowd rose to its feet for a deafening round of applause. His words were brief and succinct, and he seemed on the point of tears throughout as he expressed "sympathy and our respect to the memory of the hundred and twelve."

As the presentations drew to a close, Gary Brown was still upset, watching the sheets of rain outside. He had helped to organize the memorial service, "and you know, I'm pissed. I'm like, All that planning to have that thing outside, we had a news media staging area, and I'm just beside myself. And we were going live nationally." Clapper made his way through the crowd. Brown began ranting at him about the rain. "Gary," Clapper said calmly, "if we had done that outside like we originally planned we'd have all been—" and here Clapper stretched his arms wide—"this far apart. As it is, you couldn't be in this hangar without physically touching someone. And it's made it so much more personal. So you've got to look at it this way: it's just God crying with us."

Not everyone saw that day in the same way. Margo Crain described it as "long" and "somber." Afterward, a number of survivors hatched the idea to have pizza and beer, to revel in this bonus of life that had been granted them. Someone volunteered a hotel room, and the group gathered there and began drinking in earnest. They were, she said, "celebrating life and being there after a year and a long day. We actually pretty much partied, I can tell you that. I don't remember drinking that much beer in my life at one time." At the end of the night, Garry Priest drove her back to her hotel in his truck. The party was not at the hotel where Crain was staying. When they pulled up, Crain pointedly stayed in her seat. And then without warning, she was in his arms, and they were kissing. "We were actually necking in the truck," she said. As their passion rose, they heard a knock on the window—so loud, like an explosion—and the two jerked apart to find a police officer standing in the parking lot. Crain laughed and rolled down the window. "Yeah, I'm staying here," she said. The police officer went away, "and we just kind of called it quits for the evening." But she knew that the spark they had ignited a year before would not soon die out. "At the time I just really felt, wow, okay, maybe something like this could happen."

She said, "I was up pretty much all night that night." She and her father began the trip home the next morning. Crain was so tired and emotionally spent that her father drove the whole way.

Once they had settled back into life in Colorado, Priest seduced a willing Margo Crain with serenades of the songs he had written, which he sang as he played guitar. The crash had jolted Priest out of his eager ascent of the corporate ladder, and he quit his job with Bruce Benham to pursue his ambition as a musician and a DJ.

"We did share a very special bond, a mutual attraction," Crain said. "And I realized that he'd always be someone in my life because of the bond we had with the crash in the beginning." Although she married someone else three years after her divorce, she said she can now pick up the phone to call Priest, "and the years just kind of melt away."

She said, "I keep thinking back to that very day we stepped on that plane. I remember boarding after Garry. He was tall and very good looking and I was like—Ooo! Just like a normal person would. But to just think back then and that now, twenty-three years later, he's still in my life and still a very, very dear person, and it's just amazing how sometimes the timing and the threads of your life just work together and around each other and bring you back full circle. It's just amazing. I always have held a certain special place in my heart for him. My daughter had the biggest crush on him when she was little. My sister did too. And you know that that understanding and that bond with an old friend will always be there."

Crain and Rod Vetter have also remained friends, and she and her husband have visited him and stayed at his house. "It's another very special friendship and bond."

Denny Fitch died of cancer in May of 2012, having helped to fly so many to safety all those years before. When Priest heard the news, he sent an e-mail to Crain with copies going to many of the other passengers he still knew. In his e-mail, Priest talked about "the 232 Family," and Crain realized that she had married into that family in a blood wedding on that terrible day and would forever be a part of it.

On the day of the first anniversary, deep thunder rolled around the area all day long, but most of the rain had fallen just before the ceremony. Once it let up, Crain with many others rode out in a van and stood in the muddy field where she had run through the corn the year before. It was planted in beans that year, 1990. She could see the RTR site with its four towers in the distance and the Grassy Knoll where she had stood and looked back at the wreckage and smelled the awful smells and where Jerry Schemmel had handed Sabrina Lee Michaelson to her. Now she let it wash over her, the recognition that this thing, this worst of things, had happened to her, to all of them, and that they were standing here now in the middle of a summer that might never have come, and she with her bare tan legs and her white sneakers and her short white dress with the white bow at the base of its V-neck, a pink flower pinned to her lapel and her brown hair all curly and tumbling around her shoulders and the air warm and muggy on her face and arms, all sensations made so much sweeter by the fact that they might never have been.

She bent over and reached down and pulled on something sticking out of the ground. She had found a part of 1819 Uniform. And as she moved about in the field with Bruce Benham and Garry Priest and the others, she bent and plucked and bent and pulled, like a little girl in a field of daisies, only she was pulling lengths of wire that had been buried as if by an unimaginable force, and each length of wire that she pulled free unearthed more and more parts, tiny electronic components, devices, shards of plastic and scraps of aluminum melted into odd shapes. Some of the fragments had identifying numbers on them and some were still painted with yellow-green inhibitor. She saw rivets and bolts, nuts and doublers, and a few hefty remnants as big as a man's hand. And it dawned on her that this was not merely a scarred patch of earth. It was a virtual warehouse of scrap metal, avionics, knobs, switches, dials, parts, evidence. . . . And as many of the others had done, Margo Crain wondered what else had been left behind in that mud.

EPILOGUE

Will Wernick, who was not quite seven years old at the time of the crash, shared a thought that many other people on the plane, most of them children, had after the engine exploded: "One of the things I was most excited about was getting to see the emergency slides come out of the plane. I flew a lot, and I always wanted to see that." As the bluegrass banjo picker, Pete Wernick, led his son out of the burning plane, Will was still expecting to see the emergency slides deploy. "And it didn't happen, and I remember being somewhat disappointed that we didn't get to see the slides."

Will and Pete and Joan would each receive $200,000 in compensation for the crash. (About $360,000 in 2013 dollars, more than a million dollars in total.) With it they would pay off all their debts, pay off their house, and pay Will's college tuition.

Ellen Badis said her nightmares continue to this day. "I hardly ever have a good dream. Very seldom. I don't dream in color. My dreams are always someone or something getting me. Going to get me. And then I wake myself up screaming." She said that she and her husband Adrienne are now drawn magnetically to disasters of any kind. She said that if a plane crashed nearby, she would open their house to survivors. Despite the old feelings it brings up, she has always loved telling her family's story.

I asked Ellen if she thought that, on balance, going through the experience had been a positive or negative influence in her life. She answered with long pauses, saying several times, "That's a tough one." But she concluded, "It's really mixed. Of course, it's positive that we're here, and we're just so blessed to have made it out and walking. We have our limbs and our mental abilities. But at other times, it's just been tough too." She heaved an exhausted sigh and said, "I just can't, I just can't—it's hard."

Bruce Benham didn't know it at the time, but when he appeared on the TV show *Nightline* with Jerry Schemmel and Garry Priest on the night of the crash, Ellen Badis was across town at Briar Cliff College, watching with Margo Crain, Susan Randa, Aki Muto, and others. As the program began, Ellen leapt up and pointed at the screen, saying, "That's who saved Aaron!" She had been in such a state of shock when Benham handed her the two-year-old boy that she hadn't even thought to ask who he was. She later tracked him down and wrote him a letter of thanks.

Amy Mobley, who had married Doug Reynolds nineteen days before the crash, said that as a result of the accident, "my children have really not gotten to see anything. We don't go on vacation anywhere. Disney World, Disneyland. It would just be more practical to fly, but we just don't do it. We don't do carnivals. They've missed out on a lot."

Rusty Mobley, Amy's younger brother, didn't feel that way. He said, "Nothing's going to ever happen to me flying again. There's just no logical way."

Terri Hardman came away from the experience without deep psychological scars. Indeed, she felt that it might have been good for her children in a way. "I think it probably affected my children more than

me, and in some ways I didn't think it was all bad. I think they realized they were vulnerable, and I think we slowed down driving quite
a bit." She said the people at school, their friends, their neighbors,
were "amazing." She had a large social support network. "It taught
me something about reaching out to people."

"I like to take the good parts," she said. "We became closer as a
family. I think we all realized how lucky we are to be here. My kids
have graduated from college, have children. I have seven grandkids.
And every so often it's brought up that—you know—there was a
possibility we'd have none of this."

Ron Sheldon boosted Terri Hardman, Aki Muto, and all those others
up to Clif Marshall on top of the fuselage. Sheldon had been on his
way from Denver to his home in Granville, Ohio, outside of Columbus. He was traveling with his business partner, Tom Postle, who
was seated two rows behind him. Postle had a Bible in his lap and had
been praying with Ruth Anne and Bruce and Dina Osenberg. On the
night of the crash, Sheldon wound up at Briar Cliff College, his hand
swollen "like a softball" from resting his head on it during the crash.
He had been looking everywhere for Postle, but ominously, his partner was on none of the lists that were being hastily assembled.

Sheldon wandered the hot and crowded, narrow pastel-tiled pas-
sageways of the dorm and came full circle to his room with an apple
and a bottle of water that he had found in the cafeteria. Scarcely had
he closed the door when he heard a knock. "I opened the door and
there was Tom Postle. He had a big bandage across his head and over
his ears, and it had a bloody spot on it, and we had a great reunion
right there, just jumping up and down and hugging and happy to see
each other." Together they went back to the cafeteria and ate soup
and sandwiches and traded stories into the early hours.

The next day, they caught a flight to Chicago together, and
United employees quietly hustled them off the plane to avoid the
press. They changed planes for Columbus, and Postle's wife met
them and whisked them away. Sheldon had some nightmares over

the years but no ill effects to speak of, either from his combat experience in Vietnam or from United Flight 232. He went to a counselor who told him he didn't need therapy.

Ruth Anne Osenberg and her family suffered ongoing physical and emotional effects from the crash, and yet she remained tirelessly cheerful throughout the ordeal. In one message, she wrote to me, "Tucson grandsons, Hayden and Logan were here for the day a couple of weeks ago. While here they watched the movie, *Madagascar*, something or other. I think it was the second in the series, and I was watching with them. In it there was a part where the characters were in an airplane and the plane developed problems. As it came closer to the ground it began to hit trees etc. and was breaking apart. That's when Grandma got up and left the room. Couldn't believe that a children's movie with a plane crash had me shaking inside and out. PTSD via animation."

Dina Osenberg had finished her sophomore year of college when the crash happened. Back at school for her junior year, she discovered that she couldn't stand being in classrooms when they were too crowded. "Two months into the school year, I dropped out." She could not focus enough to get her homework done. "I wanted to be with my parents. There were days I didn't want to get out of bed. There was definite depression."

She returned to college in the new year. "It was hard," she said, but she had always wanted to be a teacher and to work with children, so "I had to do this." It took her five years to finish college, but she finished. As a result of the crash, she became "a control freak," especially when it came to driving. When her sons were in the first and second grades, she wouldn't let them take a school bus. She didn't feel comfortable when they rode with another parent either.

About flying she said, "There's a lot of places in this world that I want to go to, and the only way to get there is flying." She still had a residual emotional reaction after more than two decades. "I don't like turbulence." Her boys loved turbulence, so she put on a happy face for them and tried to look on the bright side. And when her sons were little and she had to fly with them, she said, "From day one, I told my husband, we are buying them a seat. It's another three or four hundred bucks. And he wasn't always willing to spend that." Then Dina explained to him how Jan Brown had told people to hold their babies on the floor on that appalling day. And Dina's husband realized how really mad it was to try to take a baby on an airliner without a proper seat.

Brad Griffin had been on his way to play in a golf tournament with his brother when he was ejected from his first class seat and thrown into the corn, where Clapper found him. Griffin was treated at St. Luke's for the second-degree burns on his feet and left arm, but the doctors failed to notice that he had eight broken ribs, three compacted vertebrae, and a collapsed lung. Brad's family arranged to have him air-lifted to University Hospital in Denver, where he was put in a body cast. When the doctors realized that he couldn't breathe, they cut the cast and "took a liter-and-a-half of fluid out of me." In addition, he had suffered brain damage, two torn rotator cuffs, and a cracked wrist. He had one giant bruise from the back of his head to his buttocks. When he arrived at the hospital in Colorado, the doctors observed a big cut on one hand that looked almost like an old scar. It was completely sealed as if it had been cauterized, but it was obviously pink and new. The doctors concluded that as he flew out of the plane, his hand encountered white hot metal, which passed through the flesh and simultaneously injured him and sealed the injury.

Griffin was in a full body cast for nearly two months. Once he arrived home, a walk to the end of his driveway would leave him exhausted and sweating. "But I'd just try to do that every day." His company was building a house down the block, and he'd try to walk outside and check on its progress. It took him two years of rehab to recover from his wounds. He did not have nightmares or flashbacks. His attitude was, It's beautiful to be alive. Brad Griffin thought he was the luckiest guy in the world.

After his long rehabilitation, he continued his career for more than two decades. He died of pancreatic cancer on October 4, 2013.

In 2012, I asked Aki Muto how she was doing, and she surprised me by saying that she was a flight attendant for Finnair, working a route between Helsinki and Tokyo. "My life after the accident is OK, I would say. It is difficult to say because there is no other life to compare!"

Muto began flying with Lufthansa in 1991, less than two years after the crash. She now says, "It has been many years, and flying is getting very natural to me. I do not feel scared any more." At the end of her note, she wrote, "Oh, my son is crying. I have to go."

Nine years after the accident, Muto married at the age of twenty-eight. She gave birth to a baby boy in 2010. Now, she said, "I enjoy every single day with my son." Without a hand from Clif Marshall and Ron Sheldon, there would have been no son and no future generations from Aki Muto.

Captain Al Haynes, who saved the aircraft in the initial minute or so after the explosion, quietly returned to his regular piloting duties on Wednesday, November 1, 1989, the forty-fourth day after the complete destruction of his ship.

Haynes was forced by law to retire at age sixty.* He flew his last flight on August 27, 1991. The night before, a crowd of people turned up for the retirement party in Denver, including the cabin crew from United Flight 232, except for Rene Le Beau. Many people from Sioux City attended too, among them Gary Brown and Dave Kaplan. James Hathaway, the Air National Guard fire chief, attended, along with George Lindblade. Dr. Banjo, Pete Wernick, hid in a hallway outside the ballroom at the hotel. When the party was under way, he

---

* Haynes was probably at the peak of his abilities as a pilot and could have flown safely for many more years. The rule was widely recognized as a bad one, and in 2007, the age for mandatory retirement was raised to 65. It could still be raised further. All pilots will tell you that they like those "crusty old birds" like the pilot who flew survivors to Chicago from Sioux City on the night of July 19, 1989.

began playing his banjo, slowly moving toward the ballroom so that the bluegrass tune rose in a gradual crescendo. Lindblade said it was "a real tear jerker."

The next morning United Flight 455 took off under the command of Captain Alfred Clair Haynes, bound for Seattle. William Roy Records flew as first officer. Peter Allen, who had sat in first class next to Dennis Edward Fitch, flew Dvorak's position—Dudley Joseph Dvorak had not yet returned to work. Al Haynes put the air traffic control communications on the entertainment system—as it had been on United Flight 232—so that people could listen in on headphones as controllers all across the country congratulated him. The flight attendants cut a cake and served pieces to all the passengers as if they were at a wedding. The fire department at Seattle-Tacoma Airport was prepared to spray an arc of water over the plane in a traditional salute to a retiring captain. Late in the flight, however, Jan Murray alerted Lindblade that an emergency had developed in the aircraft. Lindblade tapped Gary Brown and Hathaway, who were seated ahead of him.

Gary Brown had been lifting a cocktail to his lips. He put it down.

The Sioux City rescue professionals made their way aft, wondering if history were about to hideously repeat itself—this time with them on board instead of waiting on the ground. In fact, a passenger was having a diabetic seizure. Gary Brown and his crew cleared passengers out of the way and had them reseated. They then propped up the ill man in a center seat. The plane was on short final. Gary Brown and Kaplan sat on either side of the man to hold him up. After touchdown and rollout, Jan Brown called the cockpit and Peter Allen answered. She announced the medical emergency and said they needed to be met by an ambulance. Then she asked the passengers to remain seated until the man was off the plane.

A moment later, Allen called back, saying, "You were kidding, right?"

Jan Brown confirmed that the emergency was real, and then watched as Gary Brown and Dave Kaplan carried the victim out of the plane.

"The terminal building was completely full of newsmen," Gary Brown later recounted, "so there was lots of security. Dave Kaplan and I were both in uniforms, which look a lot like law enforcement uniforms," because emergency services used to be under the sheriff's office. "And here we are carrying this guy, and nobody bothered to tell the cops." The man was still thrashing about because of his seizure. "They thought we had a prisoner who was fighting with us. So it was like an almost instantaneous wrestling match. Big dog pile in the Jetway."

Gary hollered at the police, "Put down your clubs and get an IV started before we lose this guy! Give us a little room here, we need an ambulance." The situation gradually resolved itself, and the patient later recovered.

Someone commented that Gary Brown didn't feel comfortable when a plane arrived unless it was met by emergency vehicles. And Jerry Schemmel said the same thing to Captain Haynes.

Jan Brown was heard to say, "The boys from Sioux City saved us again."

The investigators from the NTSB and other agencies, as well as from General Electric and United Airlines, went on to contribute to the improvements in aviation safety in the twenty-first century. As Robert Benzon put it, "Each of us was affected by the accident, but went on with our work over the years since Sioux City on many similar events. It was a tough, tiring, family-affecting job that few appreciate." Benzon was the investigator in charge for the crash of American Airlines Flight 587, an Airbus A300 that went down in Belle Harbor, New York, in 2001. The second-worst aircraft accident in U.S. history, it killed all 260 people on the plane and five on the ground. Benzon was also the investigator in charge on US Airways Flight 1549, the Airbus A320 that ditched in the Hudson River in 2009. All on board survived, thanks to the remarkable skill of Captain Chesley "Sully" Sullenberger.

* * *

Within months of the crash, the FAA had formed the Titanium Rotating Components Review Team to improve the manufacturing and inspection of all of the spinning parts on turbines. In 1990, the Jet Engine Titanium Quality Committee was founded to track defects in batches of titanium or components made from it. Participation became mandatory for all companies producing titanium or jet engines. Many hard alpha inclusions were found after 1989, but most were discovered before a disk or wheel had time to fracture.

There are many ways to think about the last flight of 1819 Uniform. James Wildey, the metallurgist for the NTSB, chose this point of view: "In a way it shows how safe aviation is. It took a whole series of really unlikely events to make this accident happen. That the defect got into the metal at all was unlikely. That it was located in the disk at the point that was going to be under the most stress was also unlikely. If the defect had been a little bit bigger, it might have been detected. If it had been a little bit smaller, the disk would have been retired from service before it broke apart. This disk was almost at its life limit. If the defect had been located pretty much anywhere else in the fan disk, the stresses would have been low enough [that] it wouldn't have failed." If it had been located a little farther inboard, it would have been machined off. If it had been located farther from the centerline, it would have been detected. He said that if the flaw had been closer to the surface, a chemical test would have revealed it, but the workers at GE machined the final shape *after* that test, not before it. They could not perform the chemical test on the final shape because that test used nitric hydrofluoric acid to etch the surface and reveal the grain of the metal. It was a destructive test that would ruin the final shape. Then (at least according to one theory) the tools that cut the final shape happened to reach and expose the defect. It was a chance occurrence that the tool reached the level where the defect lay. The defect was then on the surface of the metal. If it had not been chipped out already, it was ready to be chipped out during the finishing process.

"These small events happen all the time and don't cause a crash." But, said Wildey, "in this case, they all ganged up on the one spot there and caused the accident. . . . It illustrates how many different types of things have to go wrong in the aviation industry to have a catastrophic failure like this."

Flying on commercial airliners in First World countries is the safest means of travel that exists today.

The dead from United Airlines Flight 232 are still among us. Photographs of them and their belongings are on file, in perpetuity, in the archives of the Iowa Department of Criminal Investigation.

Joan Wernick said she took two lessons from the crash. "You're going to die when you're supposed to die. And then you get," she said, using the concept she learned from her mother, "'the grace of the present moment.'" She explained: "You are going to get the grace to deal with whatever tragedy comes up. My mother used to tell me, 'You don't get it beforehand. You won't get it afterward. You just get it at that time.'" Joan said, "You can anticipate this grace. Why [else] would I have been calm when this plane was crashing? If I think about it, I should have been really upset. I wasn't. I was very peaceful." Jan Brown, Martha Conant, and many others said the same thing: facing death was the most peaceful moment of their lives.

One day when Sabrina Lee Michaelson was in the seventh grade, she logged onto a message board on the Internet. It's not clear which one, perhaps a forum on AOL about United Flight 232. On it, she wrote,

> Hello, my name is Sabrina Lee Michaelson. I was the little baby girl on flight number 232. I went to your website hoping to find information about the plane crash I was in. Surprisingly I found out that my brother had written bout it and I never knew. I do not remember anything of it but feel very lucky to have survived it. And that my whole family survived it makes me feel very very lucky. To think that if it wasn't for

Jerry [Schemmel] I wouldn't be alive today. My family and I
still do stay in touch with Jerry and his family to this day but
once again I would like to thank him for saving my life. Thank
you. Now i am 12 years old in the 7th grade . . . .
. . . Sabrina Michaelson

By 2008, Sabrina was a beautiful young woman with a large
Doberman pinscher she doted on and a wide circle of friends. She
had had her left eyebrow pierced, and she liked to wear sparkly rings
and dangling earrings. Sometimes she used turquoise eyeliner. In
early July that year, as the sun had just begun its lowering arc toward
the south and toward summer's long waning, she abruptly put an end
to the story by taking her own life, twenty days short of her twentieth
birthday. Schemmel told me, "I have tried hard over the last couple
[of years] to find out more about what led to her death, but her family has never responded to any of my inquiries." And that was after
nearly two decades of sending him cards every year and photos of the
girl he saved. I wrote to Sabrina's friends and family on many occasions, but received no response.

So we don't know why, and perhaps we will never know why.
She killed herself in Arizona, where vital records are not public. The
cause of her suicide may have been clinical depression. Death may
have been foreshadowed in the entire arc of Sabrina Lee's life, beginning with the crash, which would have embedded itself permanently
in the landscape of her unconscious emotional memories, even if
she remembered none of it consciously. And then she lived with the
never-ending repetition of the crash through the yearly reminders
of the man who saved her. Even at the age of twelve, she identified
herself to the world as the baby girl who was saved by the stranger.
Sabrina is buried at Queen of Heaven Cemetery in Mesa, Arizona.
The inscription reads, "Those we have held in our arms for a little
while we hold in our hearts forever." The plaque displays photographs of Sabrina on ski slopes, in a bathing suit at perhaps the age
of twelve, and with her Doberman near the end of her life.

* * *

Rene Le Beau was thrown from the plane. She was found dead, out of her seat, lying on her side, stretched out, with her long red hair flowing all around her. She was twenty-three years old and had been flying for seven months.

Mark Fageol, chief photographer for the *Sioux City Journal*, left the newspaper business and became a railroad engineer. He drove a train on a regular run from North Platte, Nebraska, to Marysville, Kansas.

The last scheduled airline flight of a DC-10 in the United States occurred on January 7, 2007, when Northwest Airlines Flight 98 arrived in Minneapolis from Hawaii. When this book went to press in late 2013, Biman Airlines of Bangladesh had the last two DC-10s that were still being used for scheduled flights carrying passengers. The airline sold one for scrap after its last flight and was attempting to donate the other to a museum somewhere in the United States.

On June 18, 1990, a healthy baby boy, Emil, was born to Sylvia and Jeffrey Tsao.

NOTES ON SOURCES

I conducted all interviews in 2012, except where noted. Citing each instance of material from those interviews would make the "Notes" impractically long. Instead, I provide a list of all the interviews in alphabetical order. All actions by and quotations from people on the list come from those interviews unless otherwise attributed.

In cases where a source is not obvious, I cite it in a note, with the corresponding page number from this book and an identifying phrase.

Where I cite interviews, I do so by giving the person's last name only; when there may be confusion between two names (for example, Jan Brown and Gary Brown), I use whole names. A last name can sometimes refer to more than one source. For example, "Cherolis; Cherolis 2008," refers to my interview with Nicholas Cherolis and a published paper by him (previously cited) in 2008.

Dennis Fitch died in 2012 before I was able to interview him. Personal material and quotes from him come from Rosa Fitch, his widow, and from an interview by Errol Morris.

In cases where a person was not available to verify the spelling of his or her name, I have compared documents from the NTSB and United Airlines with published sources (*New York Times, Los Angeles Times,* and *Sioux City Journal,* for example). Where I could determine it, I have used people's names in accordance with their preference, such as Frank (not Francis) Hilldrup and Jim (not James) Walker. Where a given name appears in shortened form in official documents, I have used that form (Joe Epperson, for example).

I have left conversational quotes as transcribed from the interviews and verified them with the individuals involved.

I exchanged hundreds of follow-up personal communications with those I had interviewed. These took the form of e-mails, letters, and phone calls or conversations in person. They are cited as "pers. comm." In some cases, I had personal communications with someone I did not formally interview.

Unless otherwise cited, all references to documentation from the National Transportation Safety Board (NTSB) come from the investigation identified by the number DCA89MA063, Docket 437. The NTSB distributes this collection of scanned pages in TIFF format (a digital file with a name ending in .tif, such as A39915-ADD6.tif). Much of Docket 437 is arranged as exhibits, so any citation using the word *Exhibit* comes from this NTSB docket. If the exhibit has an author listed, I cite the author's name and the date where available. If an exhibit has no author named, I cite exhibit numbers. If a document is not part of an exhibit, I cite the TIFF file name and page numbers. When I cite an exhibit without page numbers, I am citing the entire exhibit.

Where I have used the published report of the investigation, known as "Aircraft Accident Report" AAR-90/06, I cite that as "AAR-90/06" followed by page numbers.

The NTSB began a four-day public hearing on October 31, 1989, in Sioux City, Iowa. A court reporter recorded everything that was said. The NTSB published this as the "Official Transcript of Proceedings." I cite this document (in file A39915-ADD2.tif) as "NTSB Transcript," followed by page numbers.

General Electric prepared an accident report of its own. It was directed to Robert M. MacIntosh Jr., investigator in charge at the NTSB, and dated March 23, 1990. The document (in file A39915-ADD5.tif) is titled "Aircraft Accident Report United Airlines, Inc.

Landing Accident July 19, 1989, Sioux City, Iowa, Comments Submittal to the National Transportation Safety Board." I cite this document as "GE Comments," followed by page numbers.

Erasable white boards in an office adjacent to the temporary morgue were used to list information about each victim of the crash. Information from those boards is taken from photographs of the boards and cited as "White boards."

The 185th Tactical Fighter Group, Iowa Air National Guard, is abbreviated as 185th.

I have struggled with how to acknowledge everyone who helped to make this book possible and there are truly too many to name. The people of Flight 232 opened their hearts to this project in ways that I could not have imagined. They included passengers, flight attendants, flight crew, air traffic controllers, fire fighters, law enforcement officers, journalists, emergency responders, doctors, nurses, pathologists, forensic dentists, families of those who lost their lives, volunteers from the Air National Guard and elsewhere, the Iowa Department of Public Safety, investigators from the NTSB and other agencies, and many others. They are the true creators of this book.

I would also like to thank the many early readers who made valuable contributions to this book. I could not have written *Flight 232* without tireless support from my wife Debbie. She and I would like to thank the people of Siouxland for their generous assistance and warm hospitality. They made us feel that we had found a second home there.

Special thanks to Carolyn Lorence.

LIST OF INTERVIEWS

Ayers, Ellen, respiratory therapist, St. Luke's Hospital. Telephone, August 3.

Badis, Ellen, passenger, seat 17-F. Telephone, May 2.

Barrett, Arthur, ultrasound inspector, United Airlines. Telephone, February 12, 2013.

Bates, John, air traffic controller. Telephone, June 6, and pers. comm.

Bayless, Brad, passenger, seat 17-H. Telephone, April 11.

Bendixen, Romaine "Ben," flight surgeon, 185th. Telephone, August 2 and 5, and pers. comm.

Benham, Bruce, passenger, seat 16-H. Telephone, March 22.

Benzon, Robert, investigator, NTSB. Telephone, July 10, and pers. comm.

Boxum, Bob, cameraman, KTIV. Telephone, March 9, 2013.

Brate, Floyd, electron microscopist at General Electric. Telephone, November 28.

Brown, Gary, director of Woodbury County Disaster and Emergency Services. Telephone, July 9; personal, July 17, 18, and 19; January 14, 2013; and pers. comm.

Brown, Jan, chief flight attendant. Personal, September 7 and 28, and December 10; February 27, 2013; and pers. comm.

Brownstein, Yisroel, passenger, seat 38-J (assigned 38-H). Personal, May 17.

Cherolis, Nicholas Edward, metallurgist at General Electric (now at Rolls-Royce). Telephone, October 2; November 2 and 28; January 19, 2013; May 24 and 25, 2013; and pers. comm.

Clapper, Gregory S., chaplain, 185th. Personal, July 28, and pers. comm.

Clark, John C., investigator, NTSB. Telephone, October 17, and pers. comm.

Collins, Patricia, volunteer at the morgue. Telephone, July 30.

Conant, Martha, passenger, seat 38-D. Telephone, March 14 and June 2, and pers. comm.

Cookson, David, maintenance records at United Airlines. Telephone, March 5, 2013.

Crain, Margo (remarried as Baker), passenger, seat 19-C. Telephone, March 17 and May 20, and pers. comm.

DeJong, Marliss, volunteer in the morgue. Telephone, September 15.

Dieber, Sheryl, nurse, St. Luke's Hospital. Telephone, June 20, 2013.

Domina, Don, alarm room operator, 185th. Telephone, December 18.

Doughty, Rob, public relations, United Airlines. Telephone, February 15, 2013.

Dvorak, Dudley, second officer. Telephone, October 16, and pers. comm.

Eck, Mary Sue, editor, *Medjugorje Magazine*. Telephone, June 6.

Eddy, Chuck, sheriff of Buena Vista County, Iowa. Telephone, February 2, 2013.

Fageol, Mark, chief photographer, *Sioux City Journal*. Telephone, October 20.

Feeney, Tony, passenger, seat 32-G. Telephone, April 14, and pers. comm.

Feyh, Jason, passenger, seat 31-F. Telephone, December 20.

Filippi, John, forensic dentist. Telephone, September 26 and 29, and pers. comm. (Filippi did not wish to be quoted, but he graciously provided information.)

Fitch, Rosa, widow of Dennis Fitch. Personal, February 27, 2013, and pers. comm.

Ford, Liz, Siouxland Paramedics. Personal, January 14, 2013.

Gochenour, Sam, FAA technician. Personal, July 16, and pers. comm.

Griffin, Brad, passenger, seat 2-E. Telephone, April 12 and July 13, and pers. comm.

Hardman, Terri, passenger, seat 18-G. Telephone, July 3.

Harrington, Lawrence, lieutenant colonel, 185th (now colonel, retired). Telephone, June 18; personal, July 18; and pers. comm.

Hartter, Lynn, volunteer rescuer, 185th. Telephone, February 22, 2013.

Hatch, John, passenger, seat 38-C. Telephone, August 3.

Haynes, Alfred Clair, captain. Telephone, October 3; January 29, 2013; and pers. comm.

Henry, Jason, volunteer in the morgue. Telephone, August 2, and pers. comm.

Herbek, Gene, Acting Woodbury County medical examiner. Telephone, February 6, 2013.

Hilldrup, Frank, chairman, Structures Group, NTSB. Telephone, October 5.

Hjermstad, Julie (remarried as McCallister), mother of Eric, eleven, and Alissa, eight, passengers in row 18. Telephone, September 4.

Hutton, David, assistant fire chief, 185th. Telephone, December 18.

Kraemer, John C., director of Forensic Operations, Iowa Department of Public Safety. Telephone, November 5, and pers. comm.

Lindblade, George, videographer. Personal, July 17; January 14–15, 2013; telephone, December 14; and pers. comm.

Logemann, Jerry, fire fighter, 185th. Telephone, December 5.

Lopatkiewicz, Ted, public affairs officer, NTSB. Telephone, June 28, and pers. comm.

MacIntosh, Robert M., Jr., investigator in charge, NTSB. Telephone, July 12, and pers. comm.

Marshall, Clifton, passenger, seat 19-G. Telephone, March 16, and pers. comm.

Martz, Charles R., passenger, seat 27-J. Telephone, March 20, and pers. comm.

McCann, Pat, Lieutenant, Sioux City Police Department. Personal, January 15, 2013.

McDowell, Pamela, sister of Cynthia Muncey, passenger, seat 29-A. Telephone, September 27 and December 13, and pers. comm.

McGrady, Donna, flight attendant. Telephone, September 20.

McKelvey, Debbie, passenger, seat 11-H. Telephone, April 1, 2013.

Melhaff, Arthur, foreman of Nondestructive Testing, United Airlines. Telephone, February 13, 2013.

Milford, David, passenger, seat 37-A. Telephone, September 21.

Milford, Kari, passenger, seat 37-D. Telephone, September 21.

Mleynek, Dale, air traffic controller. Telephone, August 3, and pers. comm.

Mobley, Amy (married as Reynolds), passenger, seat 13-J. Telephone, May 7.

Mobley, Rusty, passenger, seat 13-H. Telephone, March 23.

Murray, Virginia Jane "Jan," flight attendant. Telephone, September 6.

Muto, Aki, passenger, seat 20-D. E-mail, May 6, and pers. comm.

Niehus, Larry, fire fighter, 185th. Telephone, March 12, 2013.

Nielsen, Dennis, supervisor of flying, 185th. Telephone, February 19, 2013.

Norton, Tim, FAA technician. Telephone, June 21, July 3; personal, July 16; and pers. comm.

Olivier, Paul, passenger, seat 33-B. Telephone, February 12, 2013.

Osenberg, Bruce, passenger, seat 21-C. Telephone, March 9.

Osenberg, Dina (married as Corrado), passenger, seat 21-D. Telephone, March 20.

Osenberg, Ruth Anne, passenger, seat 21-E. Telephone, March 9, and pers. comm.

Owens, Tim, flight attendant. Telephone, November 14, and pers. comm.

Palmer, Ward, triage officer, Siouxland Health Services. Telephone, February 22, 2013.

Poole, Marcia, reporter, *Sioux City Journal*. Telephone, June 20; personal, July 16; and pers. comm.

Porter, Ed, photographer, *Sioux City Journal*. Telephone, October 19.

Priest, Garry, passenger, seat 15-G. Telephone, May 17 and June 23, and pers. comm.

Quinlan, John, reporter, *Sioux City Journal*. Telephone, July 7.

Randa, Dave, passenger, seat 38-A. Personal, April 3, and pers. comm.

Randa, Jim, father of Dave. Telephone, September 5.

Randa, Susan, passenger, seat 38-B. Personal, August 23 and pers. comm.

Randall, Brad, director of morgue operations. Telephone, January 9, 2013, and pers. comm.

Rapoport, David, lawyer. Telephone, February 18, 2013; personal, March 1, 2013; and pers. comm.

Records, William Roy, first officer. Telephone, March 28 and November 16, and pers. comm.

Rehnberg, Upton, passenger, seat 9-A. Personal, March 12.

Reinders, Mark, reporter, *Sioux City Journal*. Telephone, July 11.

Schaden, Richard F., lawyer. Telephone, May 15.

Sheldon, Ron, passenger, seat 19-E. Telephone, August 22.

Shen, Kathy (married as Tam), flight attendant. Telephone, August 30.

Socie, Darrell F., professor of mechanical engineering, University of Illinois. Telephone, November 19.

Sorenson, Janice, farmer. Telephone, October 22.

Stevens, Mary, director of the St. Joseph Center-Museum at Queen of Peace, Inc. Personal, July 17.

Swanstrom, Dennis, commander of 185th. Telephone, June 13; personal, July 18; and pers. comm.

Swetnam, Richard, air traffic controller. Telephone, June 12, and pers. comm.

Transue, John, passenger, seat 9-C. Telephone, March 31.

Trombello, Joseph, passenger, seat 18-B. Telephone, June 5, and pers. comm.

Vetter, Rod, passenger, seat 19-D. Personal, March 7, and pers. comm.

Walker, Jim, volunteer rescuer, 185th. Personal, July 18, and telephone, November 11.

Wernick, Joan, passenger, 17-C. Telephone, January 13, 2013.

Wernick, Peter, passenger, seat 17-E. Telephone, May 8.

Wernick, Will, seat 17-D. Telephone, June 27.

White, Susan, flight attendant. Telephone, August 6; personal, February 27, 2013; and pers. comm.

Wildey, James, senior metallurgist, NTSB. Telephone, July 11 and September 23; February 4, 2013; and pers. comm.

Wizniak, Edward, chairman, Engine Investigation Group, NTSB. Telephone, October 23.

Zahren, Bill, reporter, *Sioux City Journal*. Telephone, October 22.

Zielezinski, Mark, control tower supervisor. Telephone, May 15 and June 19; personal, July 17; and pers. comm.

NOTES

PROLOGUE

1 Gregory S. Clapper drove into the hills: Clapper; Clapper, Gregory S., 1999, *When the World Breaks Your Heart: Spiritual Ways of Living with Tragedy* (Nashville, TN: Upper Room Books).

1 Sioux Gateway Airport: In 2002, the name of the airport was changed to the Sioux Gateway Airport Colonel Bud Day Field.

CHAPTER ONE

4 "picnic" lunch: Fitch.

7 Far ahead of Martha Conant and . . . Dave Randa: All scenes in the cockpit reconstructed using Jan Brown; Dvorak; Haynes; Murray; Records; Corrie, Stephan J., 1989, *Cockpit Voice Recorder Group Chairman's Factual Report of Investigation*, September 1, Exhibit 12-A; *Transcript of ATC Communications Involving UAL232 H/DC10, July 19, 1989, Sioux City Approach Control*, 1989, August 4, Exhibit 3-B; *Transcript of the Aeronautical Radio, Inc. (ARINC) Communication Recording Pertaining to United Airlines Flight 232 on July 19, 1989* (undated), Exhibit 2-E. Also, Morris, Errol, 2001, "Leaving the Earth," from his television series *First Person*, at http://www.youtube.com/watch?v=OPu0chBQe UK (accessed September 18, 2013). Additional material comes from Haynes, Al, 1991, "The Crash of United Flight 232," talk given at NASA Ames Research Center, Dryden Flight Research Facility, Edwards, CA, May 24, at http://www.clear-prop.org/aviation/haynes .html (accessed August 10, 2012).

8 Walter Sperks, eighty-one: "Services for Air Crash Victims," 1989, *Chicago Tribune*, July 26, at http://articles.chicagotribune.com/1989-07 -26/news/8902200585_1_kimberly-brothers-mr-cheng (accessed June 10, 2013).

10 DC-10 manual does briefly mention: Exhibit 2-G, p. 64; *DC-10 Flight Manual Handbook*, p. 357, published in "Excerpt from United Airlines *DC-10 Flight Manual Handbook*, "Irregular Procedures Section" (undated, unsigned), Exhibit 2-G.

12 acutely aware that a United Airlines 747: Jan Brown; NTSB Aircraft Accident Report AAR90-01, "United Airlines Flight 811, Boeing 747-122, N4713U, Honolulu, Hawaii, February 24, 1989." Available from www.ntsb.gov.

13 Jerry Schemmel: Schemmel, Jerry, 1996, *Chosen to Live: The Inspiring Story of Flight 232 Survivor Jerry Schemmel* (Littleton, CO: Victory Publishing); Schemmel, pers. comm., May 25, 27, and 31, and June 7, 2013.

14 As she passed into B-Zone: Seating arrangement reconstructed using Diegel, Raymond P. (undated), *Survival Factors Group Chairman's Factual Report of Investigation*, Exhibit 6-A, pp. 49–50; Diegel, Raymond P. (undated), *Occupant Injury Chart and Seating Diagram,* Exhibit 6-Z. In addition, I compared this information with seating charts published by the *Rocky Mountain News*, July 21, 1989; and *New York Times*, July 25, 1989, at http://www.nytimes.com/1989/07/25/us/passengers-and -crew-in-dc-10-crash-in-iowa.html (accessed February 2, 2012). Those charts contained errors, and where possible, I have corrected those errors by verifying seating with the passengers themselves or relying on Diegel (undated).

15 Sundstrand model AV557B: Corrie 1989, pp. 2–3.

16 At around the time Dudley Dvorak declared: All scenes in the control tower reconstructed using Bates; Mleynek; Swetnam; Zielezinski; Corrie, 1989; Exhibit 2-E; Exhibit 3-B; Haynes 1991; Morris 2001.

19 airplane is a submarine of the air: Description of DC-10 flight controls from *Hydraulic Power and Flight Controls Systems Descriptions*, Exhibit 9-C.

21 crew was then completely disconnected: GE Comments, p. 98.

23 "There is no one out there": NTSB Transcript, p. 135.

23 At about 3:40 the emergency dispatcher: Greco, David, 1989, *The Today Show*, NBC, July 20.

24 Dale Mleynek called Al Smith: Mleynek; FAA tape of control tower transmissions. In response to Freedom of Information Act Request

number 2013-002768, Teresa A. Bruner, regional administrator, South-west region, of the FAA, wrote a letter to me dated April 1, 2013, stating that all FAA records pertaining to the crash of United Flight 232 had "been discarded in accordance with our records retention directive, FAA Order 7210.3, Section 4." However, Mleynek provided a copy of those transmissions, while Lindblade provided copies of other transmissions.

24 Smith and his wingman Romaine "Ben" Bendixen: Bendixen; Bendixen, Romaine, undated, untitled, unpublished memoir.

CHAPTER TWO

27 Fitch had first noticed: Murray; Morris 2001.

28 "A flight attendant is not a pilot": Morris 2001.

29 He clearly saw that the motor pumps: Exhibit 2-D, p. 3.

30 Or it might enter into an uncontrollable flutter: MacIntosh.

31 Fitch passed Paul Burnham: White boards.

31 Allen would eventually escape: Haynes; Rehnberg; Allen, Peter, pers. comm., December 23, 2013.

31 "Unlock that fuckin' door!": The NTSB does not print swear words. It inserts the symbol #, which stands for "expletive deleted." Haynes told me, "I got very infuriated with the constant knocking on the door." I tried to give him an easy out by suggesting that he'd said "that goddamned door." He told me, "No, I said the F-word."

33 pilots who later attempted landings: Clark; NTSB Transcript, pp. 186–187.

37 "maintenance experts": Haynes 1991.

37 "They know this airplane cold": Morris 2001.

38 later that evening, the chief training officer for the DC-10: Williams, Mary Alice (Anchor), 1989, *NBC News Special Report*, July 19.

CHAPTER THREE

40 Couleur . . . had a titanium shoulder: White boards.

41 "Hey, we're in this thing together": Schemmel 1996, p. 28.

41 Charles Kenneth Bosscher: DeJong; Schemmel 1996, p. 49.

41 "I never would forget that face": Schemmel 1996, p. 50.

42 Two rows behind Ramsdell: Feeney; Poole; Poole, Marcia, 1989, "Survival Amazes Teen Who Jumped," *Sioux City Journal*, July 27, p. A:1:5.

43 past Karin Elizabeth Sass, thirty-two, who was pregnant: White boards.

44 He was so keyed up with adrenaline: The term *adrenaline* is colloquial

shorthand. A description of the chemicals involved in stress can be found in Laurence Gonzales, 2004, *Deep Survival: Who Lives, Who Dies, and Why* (New York: W. W. Norton), p. 36.

45 Brown spun on her heel and rushed back: Jan Brown; Dvorak; Haynes; Records; Corrie 1989. Jan Brown did not remember leaving the cockpit and returning to tell Dvorak about the tail. She remembers her conversation with Haynes taking place within the first ten minutes of the flight. But the knocks on the door and the conversation were picked up on the cockpit voice recorder. At 3:40 and 45 seconds in the afternoon, almost twenty-five minutes after the explosion, Haynes began by saying, "We almost have no control of the airplane." She did remember saying "that rear wing" instead of "the horizontal stabilizer," which confused the pilots at first.

46 "a good bit larger": NTSB Transcript, p. 814.

48 Jasumati J. Patel, whose jewelry: White boards; photographs.

50 At about nineteen minutes to four in the afternoon: Dvorak; Haynes; Records; Morris 2001; Grossi, Dennis, 1989, *Flight Data Recorder Group Chairman's Factual Report of Investigation*, September 5, Exhibit 10-A.

51 "getting in tune": Morris 2001.

51 "It just became like the airplane": Morris 2001.

51 "My husband was a hero": Fitch, Rosa, pers. comm., July 8, 2013.

51 "The first time Dave mentioned": Randa, Tammy, pers. comm., February 23, 2013.

54 She was feeding her red rosary beads: Eck; Stevens; Eck, Larry, and Mary Sue Eck (undated), "Mary Was Their Co-Pilot," *Medjugorje Magazine*, pp. 20–29. See also Heise, Kenan, 1996, "Survived Iowa Plane Crash," *Chicago Tribune*, November 14, at http://articles.chicago tribune.com/1996-11-14/news/9611140077_1_plane-convent-crash (accessed September 19, 2013).

54 Her tattoo of a bunny: White boards.

54 "had to hold onto the seats": NTSB Transcript, p. 30.

CHAPTER FOUR

55 General Electric made the engines: General Electric Aircraft Engines is now called GE Aviation. I use *GE* or *General Electric* throughout.

55 CF6 engines that powered November 1819 Uniform: Technical information about jet engines from Gunston, Bill, 2006, *The Development of Jet and Turbine Aero Engines* (Sparkford, England: Patrick Stephens);

Hünecke, Klaus, 1997, *Jet Engines: Fundamentals of Theory, Design and Operation* (Osceola, WI: Motorbooks International); General Electric website at http://www.geaviation.com/engines/commercial/ (accessed June 16, 2012). Confirmation and additional technical information from Benzon; Cherolis; Clark; MacIntosh; Wildey; Wizniak.

55 thirty-nine thousand pounds of thrust: NTSB Transcript, p. 205.

56 Spinning at about thirty-five hundred: Besuner, Philip M., et al., 1990, "Stress and Fatigue Crack Growth Analyses of the CF-6 Fan Disk Failure during United Airlines Flight 232" (Sunnyvale, CA: Aptech Engineering Services), February, pp. 1–4; NTSB Transcript, p. 401.

57 air goes through four low-pressure stages: Lironi, Paolo, 2007, "CF6-80C2 Engine History and Evolution," *Engine Yearbook* (London: Simon Barker), p. 80.

59 Most people never fully realize: Newhouse, John, 1982, *The Sporty Game: The High-Risk Competitive Business of Making and Selling Commercial Airliners* (New York: Alfred A. Knopf), reprinted in Fielder, John H., and Douglas Birsch, 1992, *The DC-10 Case: A Study in Applied Ethics, Technology, and Society* (Albany, NY: State University of New York Press), pp. 55–57.

59 When Boeing was about to introduce the 707: Johnston, A. M., 1991, *Tex Johnston: Jet-Age Test Pilot* (Washington, DC: Smithsonian Institution Press), pp. 202–204. See also http://www.youtube.com/watch?v=rILk6-4SMJQ (accessed January 10, 2013).

60 By the time United Flight 232 crashed: Fielder and Birsch 1992, pp. 56–57.

60 It began powering commercial flights in 1971: General Electric website at http://www.geaviation.com/aboutgeae/history.html (accessed April 25, 2012).

61 engine has put in more hours of service: General Electric website at http://www.geaviation.com/engines/commercial/ (accessed April 9, 2012).

61 The mechanics swapped engines freely: Young, John G., 1989, *Maintenance Records Group Chairman's Factual Report of Investigation*, October 23, Exhibit 11-A; *Aircraft Engine Historical Data*, Exhibit 11-B; *Maintenance Release Documents* (undated), Exhibit 11-C.

63 Debbie and Ruth were tennis partners: McKelvey.

69 Cinnamon was traveling alone: White.

70 press later reported: Zahren, Bill, and John Quinlan, 1989, "Pilot Could Be Seen Struggling," *Sioux City Journal*, July 21, p. A:12:1.

CHAPTER FIVE

72 It had rained a bit earlier in Washington, D.C.: All weather reconstructed using *Historical Weather* at www.wunderground.com/history (accessed September 18, 2013).

72 At about 4:30 in the afternoon, the director: MacIntosh.

73 in 1985 a Japan Airlines 747: Aviation Safety Network at http://aviation-safety.net/database/record.php?id=19850812-1 (accessed July 15, 2013).

73 "Bob, this is a big one": Benzon; MacIntosh.

75 She had sent a postcard: Scene reconstructed using Jan Brown; Conant; Griffin; Hatch; McDowell; McGrady; Owens; Dave and Susan Randa; White.

80 Fitch understood that they had 369,000 pounds: AAR-90/06, p. 11.

80 nearly 250 miles an hour: The speed varied widely as the plane went through its phugoid oscillations. In the last few minutes, the flight data recorder showed speeds ranging from 179.50 knots (206.6 miles an hour) to 215.00 knots (247.1 miles an hour). Grossi, 1989, pp. 57–61.

80 "But," he later said: Morris 2001.

80 Sioux City airport leased about a thousand acres: NTSB Transcript, p. 61.

81 left engine spooled up: As the right wing began dipping, the right (number three) engine went from 38.91 to 81.01 percent power at impact, but its power lagged behind that of the left (number one) engine. Grossi, 1989, p. 60.

81 relationship between the position of the throttle: NTSB Transcript, p. 169.

82 Some of the banks of seats were thrown high: Owens. Also, this was reported by numerous eyewitnesses and can be seen on the video of the crash, available at laurencegonzales.com.

CHAPTER SIX

85 seven-foot fan on the front of the CF6-6: Information about titanium and other metals from Donachie, Matthew J., Jr. (ed.), 1988, *Titanium: A Technical Guide* (Metals Park, OH: ASM International); Lütjering, Gerd, and James C. Williams, 2003, *Titanium* (New York: Springer-Verlag); International Titanium Association, 2011, *Titanium the Metal*, video provided by Jennifer Simpson, executive director (see www

.titanium.org for more information). Confirmation and additional technical information from Benzon; Brate; Cherolis; Clark; MacIntosh; Socie; Wizniak; Wildey.

87 varying the thickness: Lütjering and Williams, 2003, p. 356.

87 It is so tough that about half a million square feet: Lütjering and Williams, 2003, p. 354.

87 Christopher Glynn: NTSB Transcript, p. 409.

91 most likely Roland Stig Larson: Diegel (undated), Exhibit 6-Z, p. 27 and seating charts.

93 He may have been seeing Larry Niehus: Dvorak; Niehus; Records.

96 As the A-7 pilots watched, the tail came to a stop: Dickens, Bobby L. (undated), *Witness Group Chairman Report of Factual Investigation,* Exhibit 4-A, p. 17. Major Harry E. Greer III, who had just landed an A-7, wrote in this report, "The large tail section spun off and slid to a stop on the taxiway in front of us about 1,000 feet."

96 "We hit so hard": Morris 2001.

97 suffered minor injuries: Diegel (undated), Exhibit 6-Z, pp. 16–30 and seating charts.

97 "Like a pinwheel": Morris 2001.

98 Bachman turned away: Quinlan, John, 1989, "Flight 232 Tower Crew Works as Team," *Sioux City Journal,* August 26, p. A:1:2.

98 went unsteadily down the tower stairs: Associated Press, 1989, "Traffic Controller Honored," *Sioux City Journal,* August 19, A:1:1.

99 "MAC, I, we have the airplane down one half mile from the airport": Undated, unsigned transcript of emergency services radio transmissions, titled "Transcripts Siouxland Health Services United Flight 232," p. 10.

CHAPTER SEVEN

100 Brad Griffin had his hands on the first class seat: Clapper; Griffin.

103 When the command to brace came: Dave and Susan Randa; White.

108 Kari and Thomas were able to let themselves down: Kari and David Milford.

108 For mysteriously, money had begun to appear: Gary Brown; Kaplan, Dave, pers. comm., December 22, 2013; Walker; Zortman, R. Doc, pers. comm., October 25, 2013.

110 "Ladies and Gentlemen, this is your first flight attendant": *United Airlines Land Evacuation Checklist,* Exhibit 6-E.

CHAPTER EIGHT

114 before 1819 Uniform was within sight: Gary Brown; Lindblade 1989.

114 The radio chatter, however, betrayed: Lindblade, George, 1989, *Alert 3: The Crash of UA 232 Sioux City, Iowa, July 19, 1989* (Sioux City, IA: G. R. Lindblade).

115 Gary Brown had lobbied: Gary Brown; Lindblade.

117 "We have a DC-nine, er, ten": Lindblade 1989.

117 "We encountered dense smoke": Lindblade 1989. Also unpublished 1989 interviews by Lindblade.

118 "It was very hot": Lindblade 1989.

119 food service staff began carrying out: Gary Brown.

119 Eighty-eight people arrived at Marian for treatment: Lindblade 1989.

119 "I'll tell you a secret": Dieber.

119 acting Woodbury County medical examiner, Dr. Gene Herbek: Herbek; Lindblade 1989.

120 Some time that afternoon, a forensic pathologist: Herbek; Randall.

121 DeJong worked there: DeJong; Herbek; Randall.

CHAPTER NINE

125 great fan at the front of the CF6-6 engine: Information on jet engines from Gunston 2006; Hünecke 1997; General Electric website at http://www.geaviation.com/engines/commercial/ (accessed June 16, 2012). Confirmation and additional technical information from Benzon; Cherolis; Clark; MacIntosh; Wildey; Wizniak.

126 "It is usual to design each fuel burner": Gunston 2006, p. 29.

127 "We elected to design": NTSB Transcript, pp. 439, 447.

129 Ward Palmer, Johnson's paramedic supervisor: Palmer; Lindblade 1989.

130 Among those volunteers, Jim Walker: Gary Brown; and Walker.

131 "there were a lot of people": NTSB Transcript, p. 86.

131 As Bendixen approached, Chaplain Clapper: Bendixen; Clapper; Dvorak; Records.

132 Upton Rehnberg worked for Sundstrand: Scene reconstructed using Jan Brown; Rehnberg; Transue; Rehnberg, Upton (undated), *Brace, Brace, Brace* (unpublished memoir).

134 wall of flame had passed through the coach cabin: Crash sequence in this and other chapters reconstructed using interviews with passengers, crew members from the flight deck and cabin, and videos taken by Scott Plambeck of the 185th and Bob Buxom from the television

station KTIV. I checked those sources against eyewitnesses on the ground and in the control tower. Additional information from Benzon; MacIntosh; Walker; Wizniak; Zahren; and Diegel (undated), Exhibit 6-A.

135 clear that she would not be able to escape: Jan Brown; Transue.

136 From the time of the crash: NTSB Transcript, p. 128.

137 most urgent job Harrington had before him: Operations in morgue reconstructed using Collins; DeJong; Filippi; Henry; Herbek; Randall; photographs; white boards; Diegel (undated), Exhibit 6-Z.

137 Harrington now recalled that a C-130: Harrington; Gonsolley, Bob, 1989, "Area Helicopter Service Enables Hospitals to Respond Quickly to Crash," *Sioux City Journal*, August 6, p. unknown; photographs.

137 Moments later the phone rang: Filippi.

CHAPTER TEN

139 In 1989, the *Sioux City Journal*: Scenes of reporting reconstructed using Fageol; Poole; Porter; Quinlan; Reinders; Zahren. Also, Olson, Cal, 1989, "When United Flight 232 Crash-Landed," *Editor and Publisher*, August 12, pp. 14–25; Poole, Marcia, 1997, "Close Enough to Feel," master's thesis, University of Nebraska, August.

144 "There was so much out there": Poole 1997, p. 15.

144 woman named Lynn Hartter: Hartter; Nielsen. Also, Dickens (undated), pp. 10–12.

146 "It is doubtful, however": Poole 1997, p. 30.

147 Zenor, however, was in shock: Poole 1997; Zenor, Shari J., 1989, "Typical Day Becomes Day of Disaster," *Sioux City Journal*, July 20, p. A:12:1.

150 Just before the crash, a volunteer: Kaplan, Dave, pers. comm., December 13–18, 2013.

150 Jim Allen, a lieutenant with Engine 5: Rescue of the pilots reconstructed using Bendixen; Clapper; Dvorak; Haynes; Records; White; Lindblade 1989; Morris 2001. Also, Schossow, Rebecca, and Bobbi Peters, 1989, "How Did Individual Units React? Here Are Two Stories," *Sioux City Journal*, August 6, p. A:8:5.

150 "trapped in this wreckage": Lindblade 1989.

153 "a large amount of cash blowing around": Gary Brown; Walker.

154 Dave Kaplan, one of Gary Brown's volunteers: Kaplan, Dave, pers. comm., December 22, 2013.

154 United Airlines issued a denial: "United Denies Money Rumor," 1989, *Sioux City Journal*, July 25, A:4:5.

CHAPTER ELEVEN

155 Margo Crain, thirty-one, was on her way to Chicago: Crain; Crain, Margo, undated, untitled, unpublished memoir.

156 Ruth wore a ring: White boards.

157 To make a useful engineering material: Description of making titanium compiled using Wildey; Young 1989; *United Airlines Fan Disk and Fan Rotor Inspection Records* (undated), Exhibit 11-G; *Fan Disk Serial Number MPO00385 Manufacturing Records* (undated), Exhibit 11-K; *Titanium Billet and Disk Forging Manufacturing Records* (undated), International Titanium Association 2011; Exhibit 11-L; Donachie 1988, pp. 37–44; GE Comments, pp. 73–74; NTSB Transcript, pp. 463, 468–469.

159 "There is a significant 'art' content": Lütjering and Williams, 2003, p. 61.

159 In early 1971, TIMET had to blend: GE Comments, pp. 73–74.

159 They then chemically cleaned the chunks: GE comments, pp. 73–74.

159 "an arc, of specified amperage": GE Comments, p. 74.

160 They were searching for places: NTSB Transcript, pp. 463–464.

160 "There's basically two levels of quality": NTSB Transcript, pp. 468–469.

161 technicians then impressed the identifying label: NTSB Transcript, pp. 500–507.

161 It left on a Glen Cartage truck: Titanium Metals Corporation of America, sales order 59-55796, March 26, 1971, *Certificate of Test, Notice of Shipment*, found in *Titanium Billet and Disk Forging Manufacturing Records* (undated), Exhibit 11-L, p. 7.

167 Muto and Skaanes sat on the ground: Photograph provided by Bendixen.

168 Boese's neck was broken: Diegel (undated), Exhibit 6-Z, p. 19 and seating charts.

170 As the clock struck midnight: Skaanes, Gitte, pers. comm., February 25, 2013.

CHAPTER TWELVE

171 Robert MacIntosh left his office at NTSB: Benzon; Lopatkiewicz; MacIntosh.

172 Theirs was not the only Go Team: NTSB Transcript, pp. 196–197.

175 Ten minutes before 1819 Uniform crashed: Scene reconstructed using

Badis; Bayless; Benham; Martz; Amy Mobley; Rusty Mobley; Priest; Joan Wernick; Pete Wernick; Will Wernick. Also, Schemmel 1996; Martz, Charles R., 1989, *Recollections of the Crash of UAL Flight 232 July 19, 1989, Dictated by Charles R. Martz* (unpublished memoir), November 6.

177 man sitting behind him, Walter Williams: White boards; Diegel (undated), Exhibit 6-Z, p. 13 and seating charts.

177 In some places the ceiling had been crushed: AAR-90/06, p. 39. Also, photographs of the burned victims trapped in the wreckage and video taken July 20, 1989, by Dan Potts, a paramedic.

178 "I knew at that moment": Schemmel 1996, p. 57.

178 "I remember being in the brace position": Diegel 1989 (undated), Exhibit 6-Z, pp. 49–50; NTSB Transcript, p. 918.

179 "I know I couldn't see anything": Schemmel, 1996, p. 60.

182 When the engine blew up, Sister Mary later said: Eck; Eck and Eck (undated).

183 When he reached them: Schemmel 1996, pp. 66–67.

CHAPTER THIRTEEN

184 When the billet of titanium: NTSB Transcript, pp. 500–501.

184 "All of the preforming work": NTSB Transcript, pp. 500–501.

185 ring of metal was cut from around the bore: NTSB Transcript, p. 503.

185 As James W. Tucker: NTSB Transcript, p. 557.

186 Douglas installed the engine on a brand new DC-10: AAR-90/06, p. 15.

187 Tony Feeney, the skinny fourteen-year-old boy: Feeney; Diegel (undated), Exhibit 6-Z, p. 54.

187 Feeney made the sign of the cross: Briggs-Bunting, Jane, David Diamond and Jack Hayes, 1989, "Here I Was Sitting at the Edge of Eternity," *Life*, September, pp. 28–39.

188 "The teenager clearly remembers": Poole 1989.

188 "After impact, I made my way": Hayes 1989, pp. 28–39.

188 startling number of people who were thrown out of the plane: Bendixen; Gary Brown; Clapper; Nielsen; Olivier; Owens; Palmer; Walker. Also, Zahren, Bill, 1989, "Fax Helps Father's Injuries Heal," *Sioux City Journal*, July 30, p. A:16:3.

190 In the moments immediately after the crash, the control tower was quiet: Bates; Gochenour; Mleynek; Norton; Zielezinski; FAA tower tapes provided by Mleynek and Lindblade.

192 "Sam says he's got survivors out there": Mleynek, Zielezinski.

195 Air National Guard nurse named Pam Christianson: Dee, Emily, 1990, *Souls on Board* (Freeman, SD: Loess Hills Press; Sioux City, IA, Pine Hill Press), p. 89.

CHAPTER FOURTEEN

198 Wandering around inside the McDonnell Douglas plant: Personal visit to McDonnell Douglas, December 1979.

199 It had taken twenty million hours: NTSB Transcript, p. 815.

200 Charles Burgess was the last member of *Titanic*'s crew: Lord, Walter (1955), 1987, *A Night to Remember* (Holt, Reinhart & Winston; reprint, Mattituck, NY: Amereon House), p. 169 (citation from American edition).

201 270,000 parts: Hornburg, Robert, senior engineer, DC-10, McDonnell Douglas, pers. comm., December 1979.

202 "I had to put her on the floor": Michaelson, Lori, interviewed by KTIV, Channel 4, Sioux City, July 19, 1990.

208 Gerald Harlon "Gerry" Dobson, forty-six: Ayers and Associated Press, 1989, "Crash of Flight 232 Claims 112th Victim," *Sioux City Journal*, August 21, p. A:1:1.

208 His wife Joann and their companions: Diegel (undated), Exhibit 6-Z, p. 2 and seating charts.

208 Dobson couldn't talk but was able to communicate: Quinn, Laura, 1989, "Harlon 'Gerry' Dobson, 46; United Plane Crash Victim," *Philadelphia Inquirer*, August 21, at http://articles.philly.com/1989-08-21/news/26146807_1_plane-crash-victim-state-trooper-bob-dobson (accessed September 25, 2013).

209 Shen would likely have been killed: Jan Brown; Shen.

209 Nurses and specialists who happened to be visiting: Quinlan, John, 1989, "Scores of Siouxland Nurses Show Up to Care for Injured," *Sioux City Journal*, July 25, p. A:22:1.

210 She returned to St. Luke's to find a young man: Ayers and Diegel (undated), Exhibit 6-Z, p. 21 and seating charts.

212 Jan Brown wound up: Jan Brown; Murray.

213 Joan Wernick, Dr. Banjo's wife: Joan Wernick.

CHAPTER FIFTEEN

215 At one or two o'clock on the morning: Scene reconstructed using Benzon; Gary Brown; Hilldrup; Lopatkiewicz; MacIntosh; Swetnam.

219 stately edifice on a bluff: Personal visit to Briar Cliff University (formerly College), July 16, 2012.

223 Mark Zielezinski, still in the control tower: Zielezinski.

224 Leo Miller, the Sheriff of Woodbury County: Lindblade 1989.

224 In the hours after the crash, Chaplain Clapper: Clapper; Clapper 1999.

CHAPTER SIXTEEN

227 moon was still up: Scene reconstructed using Benzon; MacIntosh. Also, NTSB Transcript, pp. 198–201.

227 Daniel Murphy, the postmaster: Gunsolley, Bob, 1989, "Flight 232's Mail Survives Nearly Unscathed," *Sioux City Journal*, August 2, p. A:1:1.

228 Wizniak, who was seventy-eight years old: Scene reconstructed using Benzon; MacIntosh; Wizniak. Also, NTSB Transcript, pp. 198–209, 265; Wizniak, Ed, 1989, *Powerplants Group Chairman's Factual Report of Investigation*, October 10, Exhibit 8-A.

231 Even as late as the Saturday after the crash: "United Experts Unable to Answer Pilot Pleas," 1989, *Omaha World-Herald*, July 22, p. 1.

232 John Moehring took charge: NTSB Transcript, pp. 258–260.

232 Christopher Glynn: NTSB Transcript, pp. 365–366.

233 searchers found three of the twenty nuts: Wildey, James F., 1989, *Metallurgist's Factual Report 89-117*, October 13, Exhibit 15-C, p. 2; GE Comments, p. 108.

234 At about six o'clock on the evening of the crash: DeJong; Filippi; Herbek; Randall; Lindblade 1989.

236 "Conventional wisdom suggested": Randall, Brad, 1991, "Body Retrieval and Morgue Operations at the Crash of United Flight 232," *Journal of Forensic Sciences*, March, pp. 403–409.

236 "First there was a reference point": Randall.

237 the guardsmen, squatting on the painted concrete floor: Herbek; photographs.

239 Gary Brown began to realize: Gary Brown and Lindblade 1989.

239 Randall explained that if an accident such as this: Information about the National Disaster Medical System from Filippi; Herbek; Randall; U.S. Government website at http://www.phe.gov/Preparedness/responders/ndms/teams/Pages/dmort.aspx (accessed December 15, 2012).

240 Once a body was ready to be moved: DeJong; Filippi; Herbek; Randall.

240 first person, given the number 1: White boards; "Cause of Death for MEN, by age, from crash of United Flight 232, on 7-19-89" (undated,

unpaginated draft autopsy report), provided by Bendixen. Also, Diegel (undated), Exhibit 6-Z, p. 27.

240 "Two cranes were connected to the remaining landing gear": Monserrate, Robert, and Dennis Chapman, 1990, "The Crash of United Flight 232: The Use of Forensic Personnel in the Collection and Identification of the Victims, the Psychological Aftermath, and Recommendations," presented at International Symposium on the Forensic Aspects of Mass Disasters and Crime Scene Reconstruction, FBI Academy, Quantico, VA, June 23–29.

CHAPTER SEVENTEEN

243 On February 24, 1989, United Airlines had enjoyed: Doughty; NTSB Aircraft Accident Report AAR-92/02, "Explosive Decompression, Loss of Cargo Door in Flight, United Airlines Flight 811, Boeing 747-122, N4713U, Honolulu, Hawaii, February 24, 1989," adopted March 18, 1992, available at www.ntsb.gov. Also, Reinhold, Robert, 1989, "Aboard Flight 811: Passengers' Routine Dissolves into Terror," *New York Times*, February 26, at http://www.nytimes.com/1989/02/26/us/aboard-flight-811-passengers-routine-dissolves-into-terror.html?pagewanted=all&src=pm (accessed May 11, 2013).

243 United Flight 173: NTSB Aircraft Accident Report AAR-79-7, "United Airlines, Inc., McDonnell-Douglas DC-8-61, N8082U, Portland, Oregon, December 28, 1978," June 7, 1979, p. 9, available at www.ntsb.gov.

244 obscure the logos on the wrecked aircraft: As with most law and custom in aviation, this practice was borrowed from maritime conventions. When the Cunard cruise liner *Carpathia* arrived in New York carrying the survivors of the *Titanic,* along with a number of the sunken ship's lifeboats, crews from the White Star Line immediately set about sanding out the name *Titanic* from the bows of those boats. Lord (1955), 1987, p. 163.

244 Some airlines still do this: "Thai Airways Tries Logo Cover-up after A330-300 Skids Off Runway," 2013, *The Australian*, September 10, at http://www.theaustralian.com.au/news/world/thai-airways-tries-logo-cover-up-after-a330-300-skids-off-runway/story-e6frg6so-1226715235550 (accessed September 19, 2013).

250 Jason Henry, a lifeguard: Scene reconstructed using DeJong; Henry; Herbek; photographs; white boards; Monseratte, Robert, Iowa Department of Public Safety, pers. comm., June–September 2013. Also, Diegel (undated), Exhibit 6-Z.

252 "We found them together": Monseratte, Robert, pers. comm., August 5, 2013.

253 Kingsbury died of: Diegel (undated), Exhibit 6-Z, p. 26.

CHAPTER EIGHTEEN

256 MacIntosh and Benzon and Wizniak: Scene reconstructed using Benzon; Hilldrup; MacIntosh; Wizniak; Hilldrup, Frank, 1989, *Structures Group Chairman's Factual Report*, October 10, Exhibit 7-A; Levy, Laura, 1989, *Laser Transit Group Chairman's Factual Report of Investigation*, September 14, Exhibit 7-B; Phillips, Greg, 1989, *Systems Group Chairman's Factual Report of Investigation*, September 15, Exhibit 9-A.

256 In November of 1973: File no. 1-0043, NTSB Aircraft Accident Report AAR-75-2, 1975, "Aircraft Accident Report, National Airlines, Inc. DC-10-10, N60NA near Albuquerque, New Mexico, November 3, 1973," January 15, p. 12, available at www.ntsb.gov (accessed September 14, 2013).

257 When the DC-10 was being designed: AAR-90/06, p. 62; FAA Advisory Circular 25.1309-1, September 7, 1982, at http://www.faa.gov/regulations_policies/advisory_circulars/index.cfm/go/document.information/documentID/788801 (accessed September 19, 2013).

257 "a failure condition": NTSB Transcript, p. 764.

257 one in a billion: NTSB Transcript, p. 764; FAA Advisory Circular 25.1309-1, p. 5.

257 was already known at that time: AAR-90/06, p. 68.

257 "Probable malfunctions must have only": Starlof, William C., 1970, "Special Conditions for McDonnell Douglas Corporation Model DC-10 Airplane," memorandum issued in Washington, D.C., January 15, p. 5, A39915-ADD6.tif, p. 16.

257 Captain D. B. Robinson of the Air Line Pilots Association: Letter from Robinson to James L. Kolstad, chairman of the NTSB, October 11, 1990, appended to an undated, unsigned, document entitled "Air Line Pilots Association Analysis and Recommendations Regarding United Flight 232 July 19, 1989, Sioux City, Iowa," A39915-ADD5.tif, pp. 1441–1444.

257 In addition, the FAA had recommended shielding hydraulic lines: GE Comments, p. 70.

258 Now some two hundred people from various agencies: Quinlan, John, 1989, "Aerial Search to Resume Today," *Sioux City Journal*, July 28, p. A:1:1.

262 "At NTSB hearings": Rapoport, David E., and Michael L. Teich, 2011, "The Erosion of Secrecy in Air Disaster Litigation," *Issues in Aviation Law and Policy*, vol. 10 (no. 2), pp. 231–249.

263 "The National Transportation Safety Board determines": AAR-90/06, p. 102.

265 Jason Henry, the young lifeguard: Scene reconstructed using DeJong; Henry; Herbek; photographs; white boards; Monserrate, Robert, pers. comm., June–September 2013; Diegel (undated), Exhibit 6-Z.

266 "Iowa Examiner Slow but Sure": "Iowa Examiner Slow but Sure in Identification of Jet Victims," *Omaha World-Herald*, 1989, July 22, p. 8.

269 Robert Monserrate of the DCI: Monserrate, Robert, pers. comm., July 11, 2013.

270 J. Kenneth Berkemier: Lindblade 1989.

271 "I know that he was very happy to learn": Monserrate, Robert, pers. comm., August 6, 2013.

271 Ellen and Adrienne Badis were on their way home: Badis; Joan Wernick; Pete Wernick.

272 "Sure," said Schemmel: Schemmel 1996, p. 32.

CHAPTER NINETEEN

275 John C. Clark, the senior performance engineer: Scene reconstructed using Benzon; Clark; Hilldrup; MacIntosh; Walker; Wizniak; Clark, John, 1989, *Specialist's Factual Report on Search for Fan Disk*, September 18, Exhibit 16-A; Clark, John, and Jeremy Akel, 1989, *Specialist's Factual Report on Recorded Radar Data*, September 18, Exhibit 16-B.

275 "And within ten minutes": NTSB Transcript, p. 218.

281 they had killed 112: The NTSB rules state that a person must die within a month to be counted as a fatality from a crash. Dobson was killed by the crash but did not die within that month, so the official death toll was 111.

282 John Young, an investigator from the NTSB: Clark; Cookson. Also, Young 1989, Exhibit 11-A.

282 "their dead letter file": NTSB Transcript, p. 635; Associated Press, 1989, "Plane Engine's Records Examined," *Sioux City Journal*, July 27, p. A:4:1.

282 records from that period of time at both ALCOA and GE: AAR-90/06, pp. 80–83.

283 seven others passed the tests: NTSB Transcript, pp. 516–521; AAR-90/06, pp. 51–55.

283 "Within the very first few days after this event": The newspapers reported that the NTSB "recalled" the disks, but that wasn't the case. See Associated Press, 1989, "NTSB Recalls DC-10 Fan Disc," *Sioux City Journal*, July 30, p. A:1:5. The disks were returned to GE, per Wildey, James F., 1989. *Metallurgist's Factual Report 89-115*, October 13, Exhibit 15-A; NTSB Transcript, pp. 260–261.

283 In the evenings, after MacIntosh had led the daily meeting: MacIntosh; NTSB Transcript, p. 261.

283 Bruce Benham, thirty-seven, and his young colleague Garry Priest: Scene reconstructed using Badis; Benham; Priest; Sheldon; Vetter; Joan Wernick; Pete Wernick; Will Wernick; also, interview of Vetter on *The Today Show*, July 20, 1989.

285 crash happened on Wednesday, July 19: Young 1989, Exhibit 11-A; *General Electric Fan Disk Ultrasonic Inspection Records* (undated), Exhibit 11-M; *Ultrasonic Inspection Records. Second Disk Serial Number 00385* (undated), Exhibit 11-N; PB90-910406; AAR-90/06, pp. 41–61.

287 titanium can change its nature entirely: Donachie, 1988, pp. 40, 44–46.

287 Wildey traveled to Evendale to examine the disk: Rest of this section based on Cherolis; Wildey.

288 Ellen Badis, with Aaron freshly delivered into her arms: Scene reconstructed using Badis; Benham; Clapper; Gochenour; Schemmel 1996.

CHAPTER TWENTY

292 By the first week in August: Clark; Wizniak; Sanford, Harvey M., 1989, "GE Offers Farmers Rewards for Parts of United Engine," *Sioux City Journal*, August 8, p. A:10:1; Schossow, Rebecca, 1989, "Reward Doesn't Encourage Parts Search," *Sioux City Journal*, August 30, p. A:5:2.

292 Steve Lullman, who worked at Mellowdent Hybrids: Green, Larry, 1989, "Reward Offer Fails to Spark Gold Rush of Engine-Part Searchers on Iowa Farms," *Los Angeles Times* August 19, at http://articles .latimes.com/1989-08-19/news/mn-523_1_engine-failure (accessed July 14, 2013).

293 John Moehring from GE coordinated: Gary Brown; Harrington; and MacIntosh.

293 driver of the semi left on Wednesday: Associated Press, 1989, "NTSB Inspecting Engine," *Sioux City Journal*, August 4, p. A:1:4.

294 "There are guards at the door": NTSB Transcript, p. 274.

294 "We asked those people," Glynn said: NTSB Transcript, p. 367.

294 latest high-tech spy planes: Gary Brown; Clark; Harrington; Swanstrom; Walker. Also, Clark 1989, Exhibit 16-A.

296 "We had a significant penetration": NTSB Transcript, pp. 367–368.

296 To back that up, electron microscopy revealed traces: NTSB Transcript,
pp. 371–382.

297 entire event took five to six milliseconds: NTSB Transcript, p. 399; GE
Comments, p. 102.

297 harvest began: Clark, 1989, Exhibit 16-A, p. 6.

297 When Martha Conant first came out of the broken tail: Conant; Hatch;-
Dave and Susan Randa; Vetter.

301 Within two weeks after the crash: Scene reconstructed using Jan
Brown; Clapper; Harrington; Swanstrom; Walker; along with photographs provided by Bendixen, Harrington, and the Iowa Department
of Public Safety and video provided by Lindblade.

303 While Swanstrom and his people were cleaning: Hilldrup; MacIntosh;
Phillips 1989, Exhibit 9-A.

303 They built a wooden disk: NTSB Transcript, p. 279.

303 In the meantime, the parts gathered by Gregory Phillips's on-site team:
Cherolis; Wildey. Also, Phillips 1989, Exhibit 9-A.

304 "The duct work for that engine shows scars": Porter, Ed, 1989, "NTSB
Tour Brings Culprit No. 2 Engine into Focus," *Sioux City Journal*, July
22, p. A:9:1.

304 "FAA officials said": "FAA: Jet Lost All Hydraulics," 1989, *Omaha
World-Herald*, July 20, p. 1.

305 metallurgist in his group, Joe Epperson: Epperson, Joe (undated), *Metallurgist's Factual Report 90-1*, Exhibit No. 91, pp. 1–2.

305 "This accident was never supposed to": Letter from Robinson to Kolstad, 1990.

310 "The FAA believes that requiring the use of CRS [child restraint
seats]": FAA response to NTSB Recommendation A-10-123, October
14, 2010.

CHAPTER TWENTY-ONE

311 as the harvest proceeded: Zahren, Bill, 1989, "Farmers Harvesting
Engine Parts," *Sioux City Journal*, October 6, p. A:1:3.

312 Janice Sorenson, fifty-eight, was running her combine: Clark; Sorenson; Clark, John, 1989, *Specialist's Factual Report on Search for Fan
Disk*, October 19, Exhibit 16-A, Supplement 1; Zahren, Bill, 1989, "Alta

Woman Discovers Part of 232 Fan Disk," *Sioux City Journal*, October 11, p. A:1:6; Zahren, Bill, 1989, "Disk Harvester's First Thoughts Go to Investigators," *Sioux City Journal*, October 12, p. A:14:1; Schossow, Rebecca, 1989, "Search for DC-10 Parts to Intensify," *Sioux City Journal*, October 14, p. A:1:2; "Searchers Make New Discoveries," 1989, *Sioux City Journal*, October 23, p. A:1:1.

313 As soon as Jerome Clark phoned General Electric: Engine number one and three were placed in an adjacent secure room called Cell 9. Moehring said, "In essence, the cell ten and cell nine area, and for that matter, the laboratories, were, for all practical purposes, an out-post of . . . the NTSB officers, as were myself and all of the team." NTSB Transcript, pp. 274–276.

314 pit, or cavity, was measured: GE Comments, p. 62.

314 first step was to use a brand new toothbrush: Cherolis; Cherolis, Nicholas E., 2008, "Fatigue in the Aerospace Industry: Striations," *Journal of Failure Analysis and Prevention*, vol. 8, pp. 255–258, DOI 10.1007/s11668-008-9146-5.

315 On Thursday, October 12, 1989: Clark; Zahren, Bill, and John Quinlan, 1989, "Investigators Find Crack in Fan Disc," *Sioux City Journal*, October 13, p. A:1:1; Zahren, Bill, and John Quinlan, 1989, "Alta Farmer Receives Check for $116,000," *Sioux City Journal*, October 13, p. A:1:1; Schossow, Rebecca, 1989, "Piece of Fan Blade Found in Metal Detectors Search," *Sioux City Journal*, October 15, p. A:1:3.

315 Later that month, when asked under oath: NTSB Transcript, p. 242.

315 By Friday, the company had organized: Eddy; Schossow, 1989.

315 Employees from United Airlines took Susan White and Georgeann del Castillo: White; del Castillo, Georgeann, pers. comm., August 7, 2013.

316 "Smoke inhalation": Diegel (undated), Exhibit 6-Z, p. 16.

317 Nicholas Edward Cherolis graduated: Brate; Cherolis; MacIntosh; Wildey. Also, Wildey, James F., 1989, *Metallurgist's Factual Report 90-2*, October 24, Exhibit 15-D.

320 It compresses the metal near the surface: Lütjering and Williams 2003, p. 114.

320 "At all times prior to the inflight event": United Airlines, 1990, *United Airlines, Inc. Flight 232, McDonnell Douglas DC-10, N1819U, Sioux City, Iowa, July 19, 1989*, p. 18, in file A39915-ADD5, p. 22.

321 "The Safety Board believes that at the time of manufacture": AAR-90/06, p. 79.

CHAPTER TWENTY-TWO

323 Charles Martz, the ex-Navy fighter pilot: Martz; Martz 1989.

325 Working in the high-security laboratory at GE: This section reconstructed using Brate; Cherolis; MacIntosh; Wildey. Also, NTSB Transcript, pp. 295–326.

326 General Electric manufactured disk 00385: Young 1989, Exhibits 11-A, -B, and -C.

326 It was then installed on various engines over time: AAR-90/06, p. 15.

327 "The Public Hearing testimony": MacIntosh, Robert M., pers. comm., January 26, 2013.

328 concerted effort was put into keeping the technician's identity secret: Barrett; Cookson; Melhaff. Arthur Melhaff was the Foreman of Nondestructive Testing at United Airlines and as such, he was the boss of the man who performed the last fluorescent penetrant inspection of disk 00385. Melhaff told me the inspector's name and Cookson confirmed it. Although I searched for him extensively, I was unable to find the inspector and saw no reason to publish his name unless he could speak for himself. Both Melhaff and Cookson believed that he had died.

329 In preparation for this step, . . . a technician . . . put the part: Cherolis, Nicholas E., pers. comm., July 20, 2013: "Last weekend I visited with Doug Pridemore who was my best buddy and who also re-read all of the fractographs I took to check my data and help us get an accurate number of striations. He also remembers that Ivan Miller was the operator of the SEM when we examined the fracture from flight 232. Today I called Ivan Miller who has been retired for a while and he is pretty sure it was him also."

333 serviceable metal cast by TIMET in 1971: TIMET, "Certificate of Test, Chemical Analysis," April 1, 1971, in Young 1989, Exhibit 11-L, p. 9.

334 Two priests dressed in the protective gear: Gunsolley, Bob, 1989, "Airport Crash Plan Far Exceeds Requirements," *Sioux City Journal*, August 11, p. A:10:1.

CHAPTER TWENTY-THREE

336 When a fatigue crack grows due to vibration: Cherolis; MacIntosh; Wildey; GE Comments, pp. 62, 78; Cherolis 2008.

338 by 1990, GE claimed that the electron beam: GE Comments, p. 78.

CHAPTER TWENTY-FOUR

346 "The requirement on the transport airplanes": NTSB Transcript, p. 749.

346 few examples of uncontained rotor bursts: AAR-90/06, pp. 69–70.

347 April 10, 1995: NTSB Safety Recommendation A-95-84 and -85, August 25, 1995, at: www.ntsb.gov/doclib/recletters/1995/A95_84_85.pdf (accessed February 2, 2013).

347 June 7, 2000: NTSB Safety Recommendation A-00-104, August 9, 2000, at www.ntsb.gov/doclib/recletters/2000/A00_104.pdf (accessed February 2, 2013).

347 "In addition to the separation of the fan disk": AAR-90/06, p. 99.

348 Jim Burnett, the chairman and a staunch advocate: AAR-90/06, p. 108.

348 NTSB said that FPI is "inadequate": NTSB Safety Recommendation A-00-104, 2000.

348 In 2007, you could buy a GE engine: Lironi, 2007, p. 85.

349 On the afternoon of the crash: Crain; Priest.

350 next day came up overcast for the prayer service: Prayer service reconstructed using Gary Brown; Jan Brown; Clapper; Crain; Lindblade; Priest; White; photographs provided by Crain and by Iowa Department of Public Safety. Additional detail and quotes are from *Flight 232 One Year Later*, a series of television programs presented by KTIV, Channel 4 News, July 1990.

350 It rained so hard that manhole covers: Sanford, Harvey M., 1990, "Gully-Washer Drenches City," *Sioux City Journal*, July 20, p. A:1:1; Sanford, Harvey M., "Two Children Hurt When Water Sweeps Them under Parked Car," *Sioux City Journal*, July 20, p. A:10:1.

353 Denny Fitch died of cancer in May of 2012: Fitch.

EPILOGUE

355 Will Wernick, who was not quite seven years old: Except where noted, the people involved told me their stories for the epilogue.

360 Al Haynes, who saved the aircraft: Haynes; Associated Press, 1989. "Flight 232 Pilot to Resume Duties without Any Fanfare," *Sioux City Journal*, October 29, p. A:16:1.

362 The investigators from the NTSB: Benzon.

363 Within months of the crash: Cherolis; Wildey.

364 The dead from United Airlines Flight 232: Kraemer; Monserrate, Robert, pers. comm., September 18, 2013.

364 One day when Sabrina Lee Michaelson: Both Jerry Schemmel and I tried to contact the Michaelson family on numerous occasions without success. The material about Sabrina came from a Facebook page in memory of her that appeared here: https://www.facebook.com/groups/24325251317/?ref=ts&fref=ts (accessed June 1, 2013). Her posting at age twelve appeared here: http://mydeathspace.com/vb/show thread.php?10429-Sabrina-L-Michaelson (accessed June 1, 2013). Photographs of her grave appear here: http://billiongraves.com/pages/record/SabrinaLeeMichaelson/1935223 (accessed June 1, 2013).

366 Rene Le Beau was thrown from the plane: Jan Brown; photograph.

366 last scheduled airline flight of a DC-10: Thornton, Paul, 2007, "A Final Flight into the History Books," *Los Angeles Times*, January 7, at http://articles.latimes.com/2007/jan/07/opinion/op-thornton7 (accessed September 20, 2013). See also Biman Bangladesh Airlines press release dated November 13, 2013, here: http://www.biman-airlines.com/about/news?id=46e17663-312b-46ba-93d6-3d7e508f36b8 (accessed December 18, 2013).

366 On June 18, 1990, a healthy baby boy: Tsao, Jeffrey Y., 1991, "A Tragedy in Sioux City," *Parents Magazine*, September, pp. 102–106.

INDEX

Page numbers in italics refer to illustrations.